Labour, British radicalism and the First World War

Manchester University Press

Labour, British radicalism and the First World War

Edited by Lucy Bland and Richard Carr

Manchester University Press

Copyright © Manchester University Press 2018

While copyright in the volume as a whole is vested in Manchester University Press, copyright in individual chapters belongs to their respective authors, and no chapter may be reproduced wholly or in part without the express permission in writing of both author and publisher.

Published by Manchester University Press
Altrincham Street, Manchester M1 7JA
www.manchesteruniversitypress.co.uk

British Library Cataloguing-in-Publication Data is available

ISBN 978 1526 10929 3 hardback
ISBN 978 1 5261 0930 9 paperback

First published by Manchester University Press in hardback 2018

This edition first published 2020

The publisher has no responsibility for the persistence or accuracy of URLs for any external or third-party internet websites referred to in this book, and does not guarantee that any content on such websites is, or will remain, accurate or appropriate.

Typeset by Toppan Best-set Premedia Limited

Contents

List of figures and tables vii

Notes on contributors viii

List of abbreviations xii

Introduction – Lucy Bland and Richard Carr 1

1 Peace, but not at any price: British socialists' calls for peace on the eve of the First World War – Marcus Morris 17

2 At the crossroads: the Labour Party, the trade unions and the choices of direction for the democratic left – Chris Wrigley 35

3 'One of the most revolutionary proposals that has ever been put before the House': the passage of the Parliament (Qualification of Women) Act 1918 – Mari Takayanagi 56

4 Labour and socialism during the First World War in Bristol and Northampton – Matthew Kidd 73

5 A stronghold of liberalism? The north-east Lancashire cotton weaving districts and the First World War – Jack Southern 91

6 Living through war, waging peace: comparing Mary Macarthur and Sylvia Pankhurst – Deborah Thom 108

7 'Industrial unionism for women': Ellen Wilkinson and the unionisation of shop workers, 1915–18 – Matt Perry 126

8	The unsung heroines of radical wartime activism: gender, militarism and collective action in the British Women's Corps – Krisztina Robert	145
9	Charlie Chaplin's war: a British radical in tumultuous times – Richard Carr	166
10	Irish Labour and the 'Co-operative Commonwealth' in the era of the First World War – Marc Mulholland	182
11	Russia's war and revolutions as seen by Morgan Philips Price and Arthur Henderson – Jonathan Davis	201
12	The Stanford connection: David Starr Jordan, eugenics and the Anglo-American anti-war movement – Gavin Baird and Bradley W. Hart	220
13	The problem of war aims and the Treaty of Versailles – John Callaghan	240

Index	257

List of figures and tables

Figures

6.1	Mary Macarthur addressing strikers and supporters in Cradley Heath, 1910	118
6.2	Sylvia Pankhurst outside the headquarters of the ELFS in Old Ford Road, Bow	118
8.1	'Tempora Mutantur!', *The Bystander*, 17 February 1915	146
8.2	'The W.A.A.C. at the Front: A Woman Chauffeur in a "Tin Hat"'	153
8.3	*The Wrens: Being the Story of their Beginnings & Doings in Various Parts* (London, 1919)	155
8.4	Staff photograph of a British army unit on the Western Front, outside an Army Service Corps garage, *c.* 1919	158

Table

5.1	World trade in cotton textiles	92

Notes on contributors

Gavin Baird currently serves as a legal analyst on the Competition Team at Google Inc. He is a graduate of California State University, Fresno and the London School of Economics, where he was a Marshall Scholar. He has conducted academic research on an array of topics ranging from fiscal policy following the Great Depression to modern global antitrust law.

Lucy Bland is Professor of Social and Cultural History at Anglia Ruskin University, Cambridge. She has written widely on the history of feminism, gender and sexuality. Publications include *Banishing the Beast: English Feminism and Sexual Morality, 1885–1914* (1995, 2nd edition, 2002), two books with Laura Doan: *Sexology in Culture: Labelling Bodies and Desires* and S*exology Uncensored: The Documents of Sexual Science* (both 1998) and *Modern Women on Trial: Sexual Transgression in the Age of the Flapper* (2013). She is currently writing a book provisionally entitled *Britain's 'Brown Babies': Children of Black GIs and British Women Born in World War II*.

John Callaghan is Professor of Politics and Contemporary History at the University of Salford. He is the author of *Socialism in Britain Since 1884* (1990), *The Retreat of Social Democracy* (2000) and *Labour and Foreign Policy: A History* (2007).

Richard Carr is Senior Lecturer in History and Politics at Anglia Ruskin University. He has published widely on twentieth-century history. Publications include a political biography of *Charlie Chaplin* (2016), and the monograph *Veteran MPs and Conservative Politics in the Aftermath of the Great War* (2013).

Jonathan Davis is Senior Lecturer in Russian History and Co-director of the Labour History Research Unit at Anglia Ruskin University. He was co-editor, with Paul Corthorn, of *The Labour Party and the Wider World* (2008), *Britain's Second Labour Government, 1929–1931: A Reappraisal* (2011) with John Shepherd and Chris Wrigley, and *Labour and the Left in the 1980s* (2017) with Rohan McWilliam. He is the author of *Stalin: From Grey Blur to Great Terror* (2008), and has published articles on delegates' visits to the Soviet Union in the 1920s in *Revolutionary Russia*, on the influence the Russian Revolutions had on Labour's ideology in *Scottish Labour History*, and on Labour's contemporary political thought in *Renewal*. He is currently writing a global history of the 1980s.

Bradley W. Hart is an assistant professor in the College of Arts and Humanities at California State University, Fresno. His previous works include *George Pitt-Rivers and the Nazis*, a biography examining the life of a prominent Nazi sympathiser, and *The Global 1920s* (with Richard Carr). His forthcoming book, *Hitler's American Friends*, explores the relationship between the American far right and the German government before Pearl Harbor. Hart's research interests include right-wing extremism, Anglo-American relations, British imperial history and the history of international journalism.

Matthew Kidd received his doctorate from the University of Nottingham in early 2016. His research focuses on the relationship between socio-political identities and progressive ideologies in nineteenth- and early twentieth-century Britain. His doctoral thesis examined the political, cultural and ideological transition between working-class radicalism and labour politics in two urban constituencies, Bristol and Northampton, during the period 1867–1918. He has published several articles on topics ranging from pro-war socialism during the First World War to the conceptual framework of radical and labourist ideology. He is currently preparing a book on progressive politics in urban southern England between 1867 and 1924. Matthew is a project researcher at the University of Gloucestershire, where he is working on a project entitled 'Cheltenham's Lower High Street: Past, Present and Future'.

Marcus Morris is a senior lecturer in Modern European History at Manchester Metropolitan University. His research and publications have focused on the European, and in particular British, labour and socialist movements in the late nineteenth and early twentieth centuries, placing them within the broader popular and political cultures. His current research is centred on the idea of internationalism in rhetoric and reality within these groups and the movement's response to the threat of war in the years before 1914. He has an article forthcoming on the general strike as a means to avoid war in *Labour History Review*. He is also the co-editor of *The Legacy of Thomas Paine in the Transatlantic World*, which is forthcoming with Routledge and has a chapter on film and class in *Histories on Screen:*

The Past and Present in Anglo-American Cinema and Television, which is forthcoming with Bloomsbury Academic.

Marc Mulholland is a lecturer with the History Faculty and Fellow of St Catherine's College, Oxford University. He works on modern Irish history and the international left. His publications include *Bourgeois Liberty and the Politics of Fear: from Absolutism to Neoconservatism* (2012) and *Terence O'Neill* (2014). His biography of Emmanuel Barthélemy, a mid-nineteenth-century French revolutionary and criminal, is to be published by Hutchinson in 2018.

Matt Perry is a reader in Labour History at the University of Newcastle. He has published widely on British and French twentieth-century labour history. He has written on the protests of the unemployed. Publications include *The Jarrow Crusade Protest and Legend* (2005) and *Prisoners of Want: The Experience and Protests of the Unemployed in France, 1919–45* (2007). His *Memory of War: César Fauxbras and the Voice of the Lowly* (2011) explored the memory of the First World War generation in France through the perspective of novelist César Fauxbras. His latest book is *Red Ellen Wilkinson: Her Ideas, Movements and World* (2014). He is currently working on a book scrutinising the subjectivity of French mutineers in the wave of unrest of 1919.

Krisztina Robert is Senior Lecturer in History at the University of Roehampton in London. Her main research area is the social and cultural history of First World War Britain, focusing on women's wartime work and war experience. Her research interests in this respect include constructions of femininity, particularly visual, material and performative representations; definitions of militarism, martial symbolism and iconography, especially regarding uniforms; discourses of modernity in representations of the war; and new wartime conceptualisations of space, such as the Home Front. A related interest of hers is developing new theoretical and methodological frameworks to enable the simultaneous examination of discursive constructions and lived experience. She has delivered conference papers and published articles and chapters on these subjects.

Jack Southern is Lecturer in Public History at the University of Central Lancashire. His research focuses on culture and identity, particularly in relation to the North of England. He has published articles and curated museum displays based on different aspects of the British cotton industry. He is currently working on a monograph examining interwar Lancashire, based on his doctoral thesis.

Mari Takayanagi is Senior Archivist in the Parliamentary Archives, where she has worked since 2000 in various roles including public services, outreach, preservation and access. She was awarded her doctoral thesis,

'Parliament and Women, c. 1900–1945', by King's College London in 2012. Subjects of her research include legislation affecting women's lives and gender equality, women and parliamentary committees to 1945, and women staff in the House of Commons and House of Lords. She is joint project manager and co-curator for Parliament's 'Vote 100' exhibition project, celebrating the centenary of votes for all men and some women in 2018. Her article, 'Women and the Vote: the Parliamentary Path to Equal Franchise 1918–1928', will be published in *Parliamentary History* in 2018, and she has been commissioned to write on suffrage centenaries for the forthcoming *Routledge Companion to Women's Suffrage*.

Deborah Thom is technically retired but still teaches history and sociology to students and has been a fellow and tutor at Robinson College, Cambridge since 1987. She was one of the five academic advisers to the Imperial War Museum on their First World War galleries that opened in 2014. Recently she has written on women and war in Ireland, corporal punishment and British feminism.

Chris Wrigley is Emeritus Professor of Modern British History at Nottingham University. His books include *David Lloyd George and the British Labour Movement* (1976), *Arthur Henderson* (1990), *Lloyd George and the Challenge of Labour: 1918–22* (1990), *Lloyd George* (1992), *British Trade Unions since 1933* (2002), *AJP Taylor: Radical Historian of Europe* (2006), *Churchill* (2006) and the edited volumes *A History of British Industrial Relations 1875–1979, 3 volumes (1982–97)*, *Challenges of Labour: Central and Western Europe, 1917–20* (1993), *The First World War and the International Economy* (2000), *The Blackwell Companion to Twentieth Century British History* (2003) and *Britain's Second Labour Government, 1929–31* (2012).

List of abbreviations

ADM	annual delegate meeting
AUCE	Amalgamated Union of Co-operative Employees
AWA	Amalgamated Weavers Association
BSP	British Socialist Party
BWA	Burnley Weavers Association
BWL	British Workers' League
CSMA	Cotton Spinners and Manufacturers Association
CWS	Co-operative Wholesale Society
DORA	The Defence of the Realm Act
ELFS	East London Federation of Suffragettes
IAOS	Irish Agricultural Organisation Society
ILP	Independent Labour Party
IRA	Irish Republican Army
ISB	International Socialist Bureau
ITGWU	Irish Transport and General Workers Union
LCC	London County Council
NAEE	National Alliance of Employers and Employed
NFWW	National Federation of Women Workers
NLRC	Northampton Labour Representation Council
NUBSO	National Union of Boot and Shoe Operatives
NUDAW	National Union of Distributive and Allied Workers
NUWSS	National Union of Women's Suffrage Societies
SDP	Social Democratic Party
SFL	substituted female labour
SPD	Sozialdemokratische Partei Deutschlands
TUC	Trades Union Congress
UDC	Union of Democratic Control
USDAW	Union of Shop, Distributive and Allied Workers

WAAC	Women's Army Auxiliary Corp
WFL	Women's Freedom League
WILPF	Women's International League for Peace and Freedom
WL	Women's Legion
WLL	Women's Labour League
WPC	Women's Peace Crusade
WRAF	Women's Royal Air Force
WRNS	Women's Royal Naval Service
WSPU	Women's Social and Political Union
WVR	Women's Volunteer Reserve (or Women's Corps)

Introduction

Lucy Bland and Richard Carr

As politicians and the general public alike debate the meaning of the First World War in the context of recent centennial anniversaries, this volume contributes to the discussion over what the conflict meant for various facets of British radicalism, broadly interpreted. The book emerges from a public conference held at Anglia Ruskin University in Cambridge on 3 May 2014, which saw papers from academics and archivists, and was attended by a divergent range of people from local Labour activists to doctoral students. The discussions seen at this event explored various social, economic and political themes related to Britain's path between 1914 and 1918 – and thus this book crosses over a number of historiographical debates too. The aim with the following introduction is not to provide a sweeping discussion of all facets of this work, but to draw out the relevant key themes and discussion points.

A significant part of this volume, though by no means all, concerns the evolution of the Labour Party itself. With the Labour Representation Committee only formed in 1900 (and assuming the label of the Labour 'Party' in February 1906), the war arrived at a time when Labour was still rather embryonic – and in a large part then a client of the majority non-Conservative force in British politics, the Liberal Party. Formed as a coalition of middle-class reformers from groups such as the Fabian Society and the working-class representatives from the major trade unions, the Labour Party spent much of the 1900s wrestling to keep together disparate elements, all the while being a long way from actually forming a government in its own right. This was a challenging time. For some lower middle-class voters, the achievements of the 'New Liberalism' under Herbert Asquith and David Lloyd George rendered Labour's political relevance questionable – and their impact was always limited at this time by the property (and gender) requirements inherent in the pre-1918 franchise. The legacy of co-operation with the Liberals through the late nineteenth century also posed something of a quandary for Labour: were decent Liberals worthy of opposition at all?[1] In 1906, twenty-four of the twenty-nine Labour MPs returned to Parliament were elected in seats the Liberals had agreed not to contest – in line with the Lib–Lab Pact of 1903.

After the Liberal government passed legislation to ease the legal standing of trade unions, facilitate the delivery of free school meals for local authorities opting to introduce such schemes, and provide an old age pension for those over the age of seventy, Labour was initially able to applaud and vote for such measures, but not assume much of the credit for them. In the following years constitutional struggles over the House of Lords and Ireland produced hung parliaments in the two elections of 1910, thereby giving Labour's forty-two MPs greater influence than they otherwise may have enjoyed in a 670 seat House of Commons. Yet this was again only relative. Before the First World War Labour issued manifestos to exert pressure on others, principally reforming middle-class liberals, not with the prospect or even intention of forming a government on their own. Certainly without the conflict, and its puncturing of the generally optimistic liberal faith, along with the realignment of the Liberals as coalition partners with the Conservatives, it is difficult to envisage Labour taking office, as they indeed did, by 1924.

This narrative is broadly understood by today's Labour politicians. Speaking in 2014, the ex-serviceman and then shadow minister Dan Jarvis MP noted that 'the forces that led to [Labour's breakthrough] were already well underway before 1914, not least the fracturing of the Liberal Party. But there can be no doubt that the First World War accelerated these trends, and changed the balance of British politics forever. And its echoes would influence Labour politics for many years to come.'[2] In this regard, of course, every party has sought to 'own' the First World War, with the justification that victory was eventually achieved on the backs of working-class men and women under a Liberal prime minister supported by Andrew Bonar Law's Conservatives. Interest in the latter political force has also seen something of a renaissance through the work of younger scholars such as David Thackeray and Nigel Keohane.[3] But the fact that the war ended with Labour introducing its famous Clause IV, which – for all the symbolism over practical politics it embodied – promised to nationalise (or socialise) the means of production, distribution and exchange, renders it a key moment even within this generally reformatory context. If Eugenio F. Biagini and Alistair J. Reid were keen to stress 'the predominantly radical liberal nature' of what the Labour Party historically proposed, the First World War certainly marks a point at which socialism moved to the forefront of the agenda in various ways.[4]

The war clearly created particular procedural and policy dilemmas for Labour. As Rhiannon Vickers notes, for Labour the war 'revealed the problems of forming a party out of an alliance of left-wing groups.'[5] While the parliamentary left would splinter in the wake of election defeats in 1931, 1951, 1979 and 2015 over how the theory of socialism should be applied in practice, the First World War provided a point at which Labour split, quite literally, over matters of life and death. In part, the issue was arguably that Labour did not yet have a coherent foreign policy with which to oppose the other parties. Here we should certainly acknowledge the recent revisions of Edward McNeilly – and the idea that Labour tried to exploit radical concerns over the repressive political climate in Russia, particularly with an eye to assuming the post-Gladstone moral leadership regarding horrors committed abroad.[6] However, for many the party remained concerned with the British rather than the international diplomatic sphere. And thus for Lucian M. Ashworth, whereas 'before the First World War, Labour regarded itself as a party primarily concerned with the problems of domestic policy ... the First World War was to change all this'.[7] The war made Labour a national party not only in that it began to stand candidates across the country, but that it took serious stances on diplomatic policy that managed to achieve meaningful political impact.

Foreign policy aside, and partly because of the parliamentary arithmetic, Labour was usually a chronicler rather than shaper of major trends at this stage. And things were certainly changing. Indeed, for W. G. Runciman the First World War was a moment that produced a new type of capitalism which marked a shift away from late Victorian values and the domination of the aristocracy, and which survived into the latter part of the twentieth century.[8] Lloyd George's dynamic leadership at the Treasury, the Ministry of Munitions and subsequently Number 10 Downing Street catapulted the machine of government into a whole new order. And for Runciman, as 'the roles of [government] ministers and officials – in the regulation of the economy and the provision of welfare' changed, so too did British capitalism.[9] After 1918 these trends stuck, and 'governments continued to be involved in industrial and labour policy to an altogether greater degree than they had been before 1914' – a state of affairs that lasted even through the Thatcher era.[10] As Larry Gerber somewhat corroborates, the First World War did not begat a return to laissez-faire, but the emergence of a corporatist system in both Britain and America. As such, the war is best understood not only as an eruption that shook the world before another global conflict did similarly twenty years later, but the start of a corporatist ethos that would last for decades.[11] The reforms brought in by the Liberal coalition during the First World War – greater regulation of the private sector, higher taxation of luxury goods and income, and the ultimate use of state force: conscription – created a new political climate in which all parties would have to adjust.

Beyond the British context, for Thomas Piketty the two world wars formed a powerful (yet temporary) disjuncture in capitalism's general trend towards inequality. The death of future elites on the battlefield, the loss of imperial possessions after 1918 (and particularly 1945) and the extraordinary high rates of taxation levied by most western democracies augured the start of a golden age of equality lasting from roughly the 1920s to the 1970s.[12] While there are limits to the First World War as harbinger of the big state approach, just as historians have revised preconceptions of, say, Gladstonian liberalism being totally opposed to state intervention, the broad patterns hold up.[13] The Conservative-implemented Geddes Axe of the early 1920s could trim back the thickets of government, but they would only grow back thicker and faster. Thus W. H. Greenleaf's *Rise of Collectivism* owed much to the impact of the First World War. For Greenleaf, 'a belligerent nation in the circumstances of modern war turns over to a system of control in which a major proportion of its productive capacity and economy, indeed its life as a whole, comes in one way or another under public supervision; and the role of government is thus greatly augmented'.[14] This was, he lamented, true of Britain between 1914 and 1918.

Labour would accommodate themselves within this new order, rather than seek to fundamentally challenge it. While the Conservative Party would go on to portray Labour (often successfully, as seen in the Zinoviev letter of 1924) as in the pay of Soviet Communism, this was never close to true. Thus, through his examination of the sociological literature, Chris Chamberlain has observed that 'what is clear is that the Labour Party does not connote "socialist revolution" or "socialism in one country" or, indeed, even "socialism" in the minds of the great majority of its supporters'.[15] This would be true in the 1920s and 1930s, and in many ways aided the party's ability to claim former Liberal supporters. Although it was hastened by syndicalist influence before 1914, *The Strange Death of Liberal England* would be confirmed in the 1920s by moderate rather than revolutionary Labour.[16] And thus, even with the epoch-defining moment of the 1917 Russian Revolution, the later valedictory accounts of Soviet Russia put forward in the 1930s by the Webbs and the future Barbara Castle were the exception and not the rule here. Indeed, as Martin Pugh has noted, the period after 1918 in fact saw several *Tory* defections to Labour – not least former ex-servicemen, such as Oswald Mosley and Stanley Baldwin's son, Oliver.[17]

Changes were afoot for women too. As Caroline Rowan has shown through her analysis of the Women's Labour League (WLL), 'Labour Party feminism played an important role during and after the War in asserting the political importance of working-class women's domestic experience, and laid the foundations for further campaigns in the twenties and thirties on housing, women's health and maternity, which might not otherwise have been considered "political" at all.'[18] Recent biographies of future Labour ministers as children (Alice Bacon, Barbara Castle) or industrial militants (Ellen Wilkinson, discussed in this volume) further cite the war in the personal development of later national politicians.[19] Some of this has clearly helped broaden commemoration of the war away from a concentration on simply men's experiences on the battlefield. Indeed, during the initial round of 2014 commemorations, Labour MPs, including then leader Ed Miliband, were eager to acknowledge 'those who served their country in other ways – from the nurses who risked their lives on the Western Front to those who played their part on the Home Front'. Dan Jarvis likewise urged people to 'remember the heroes and heroines of the home front as well as the frontline'.[20] In this regard, studies of Labour and the war have tended to mirror the general shift away from 'high politics' and the views of Maurice Cowling's 'fifty or sixty politicians who really mattered', towards greater consideration of gender.[21]

Many women did indeed serve in the war, but a significant number were stanch pacifists, or at least anti-militarists. However, the leaders of the two main suffrage organisations, the Women's Social and Political Union (WSPU) and (after 1915) the National Union of Women's Suffrage Societies (NUWSS), officially supported the war, the WSPU moving from militancy to militarism and patriotism, and symbolically changing its newspaper's name from *Suffragette* to *Britannia*. When, at the NUWSS council meeting in February 1915, Millicent Fawcett declared that until Germany was out of France and Belgium 'I believe it is treason to talk of peace', all the NUWSS officers (except the treasurer) and one-half of the national executive resigned. One hundred and eighty British women requested to attend the Women's Peace Congress at The Hague in April that year (the Netherlands being neutral) but Winston Churchill at the Admiralty 'closed' the North Sea. After The Hague Congress, rupture between pacifists and patriots became irreparable. The former concentrated on problems of post-war reconstruction. And they set up the Women's International League for Peace and Freedom (WILPF) in autumn 1915, which by 1917 had grown in membership to 3,500. Some feminists worked with Belgian refugees, assisted enemy alien women and their families, as well as supporting the families of conscientious objectors. In addition to WILPF, the Women's Peace Crusade (WPC) was founded in 1916 to provide socialist opposition to the war – first in Glasgow, but spreading to other cities. It worked with the Independent Labour Party (ILP) (the only political party to oppose the war). By 1917 there were forty-five local WPCs through Scotland, Wales, Northern England and Midlands.[22] Other women worked alongside socialists and trade unionists in organisations such as the Women's International League, and Sylvia Pankhurst's East London Federation of Suffragettes also actively campaigned against the war.[23] In this regard women's peace activism dovetailed, as Marcus Morris' chapter in this book notes, with many British socialists' call for peace.

When people mention 'women and the First World War' one question that is often posed is 'did women's war work earn women the vote?' The Representation of the People Act 1918 (also known as the Fourth Reform Act) extended the franchise to include virtually all men over the age of twenty-one by abolishing the former property qualifications (and including men under twenty-one who had served in the war). Women over thirty who were either independent householders or married to householders were also granted the vote. The female franchise was therefore very limited and it was not until 1928, a decade later, that politicians finally granted the suffrage to women on equal terms as men. Some historians believe that the limited vote was a 'reward' for the efforts made by women to support the war effort, although of course the fact that the vast majority of women munitions workers were too young to receive the franchise undermines this argument. The War Cabinet was concerned to extend the suffrage to all men who had contributed to the war effort, requiring not simply a change in the property qualification but also in that of residency (which at the time required twelve months residence – impossible for men in the armed forces). Given that the groundwork for granting women's franchise had been prepared before the onset of the war (and in fact women had been close to gaining the vote on a number of occasions) a small majority of the Cabinet were prepared to consider extending the suffrage to women too.[24] Nonetheless, many politicians were anxious that if women were to be included in the new franchise bill, they would outnumber men, and it was agreed that the least objectionable way to keep the numbers of women down was by raising their voting age. Suffragist Millicent Fawcett, who was consulted on the bill, was prepared to go along with this, believing that married women and mothers (the majority of whom were over thirty) in having given their sons and husbands to the war, deserved the vote even more than (the generally younger) industrial workers.[25] Politicians viewed women over thirty as much more likely to be married, have children and have less interest in pursuing employment, in other words, they were less likely to upset the pre-war status quo.[26]

Sandra Stanley Holton argues that gaining the suffrage was not so much a top-down process led by Cabinet ministers, but a response to pressure from women suffragists, which continued on through the war.[27] Nicoletta Gullace convincingly points to the more indirect way that certain feminists contributed to women's winning of the vote. She suggests that patriotic feminists, especially Emmeline and Christabel Pankhurst and Millicent Fawcett, all involved in urging women into war work, developed a right-wing wartime nationalist feminism that renegotiated citizenship – away from gender, property and legal majority, towards patriotism (women were patriotically 'sacrificing their sons'), duty and service, and British blood. 'Patriotism replaced manhood as the fundamental qualification for the parliamentary vote.' Individuals – regardless of gender – who put their lives at risk in the service of the nation were deemed worthy of partaking in citizenship, while pacifists, 'shirkers' and conscientious objectors were not. This new language of service to the state – a language of citizenship – uncoupled manhood from citizenship, and was crucial to women winning the vote in 1918.[28]

So, given such extensive previous analysis, why this book? The answer lies in the fact that while studies of the First World War and its meaning clearly abound, there lacks a major and comprehensive volume on the Labour Party, the British labour movement and the radicalism generated by the First World War. To date, historians have considered such questions at the intersection of others – perhaps naturally – but there has been no volume to date that tackles all the issues explored in the following. For all its clear utility, John Horne's monograph on *Labour at War: France and Britain 1914–1918* is a transnational study now over one-quarter of a century old.[29] Likewise, Adrian Gregory and Senia Paseta's excellent 2002 edited volume on *Ireland and the Great War* considers the Labour Party in passing, but is naturally centred on events across the Irish Sea.[30] Elsewhere, Gregory's own *The Last Great War: British Society and the First World War* and Martin Pugh's recent *New History of the Labour Party* denote one chapter each to the theme of labour/Labour and 1914–18.[31] Content related to individual chapters of this work have received monographs – such as Janet Watson's *Fighting Different Wars* and Susan Grayzel's *Women and the First World War* – but the point is there is no unifying monograph which ties many of these divergent strands together.[32] That is the aim here.

This volume begins with three chapters looking at the Labour Party at a national level, and Westminster politics per se. First, Marcus Morris teases out the different attitudes to the conflict the British left could take up before and during 1914. Moving beyond simplistic assumptions of a pro-cuts to defence spending ILP (and their allies) and a jingoistic, verging on pro-war Labour right, Morris invites us to reconsider how the common goal of peace could be pursued through seemingly divergent means. On the one side stood those who viewed military spending as inevitably leading to war – why improve one's military, after all, not to use it – but on the other side emerged a 'patriotic Labour' who urged Britain not to remain defenceless in the face of German aggression. In this regard, spending on arms was a way to prevent rather than increase the likelihood of conflict. As Robert Blatchford put it, 'there is no "war party" in England: only a party of defence'. As such, and as Morris highlights here, it was tactics rather than principles that often divided figures of Labour right and left. Together with works such as Matthew Johnson's recent *Militarism and the British Left*, this chapter therefore helps us reconfigure our attitudes towards pacifism and political progressivism.[33]

Chris Wrigley then provides a vital sweeping overview of the path the British Labour Party took during the war in Chapter 2. Utilising comparative data highlighting the labour movement across Europe, Wrigley shows how the trade union movement played a key role in the growth of the Labour Party in a much-needed transnational context. Here we see Labour moving from the status of a client of the Liberals in the summer of 1914 to one where it could meaningfully compete to form a government of its own in under a decade. This remains an important debate. For all the war did the personality of Ramsay MacDonald some damage with ex-servicemen England after 1918, the conflict did not interrupt the almost continual rise the party experienced between the nine general elections that took place between 1900 and 1929. Across that period, Labour stood more candidates, gained more votes, increased their percentage of the vote and gained more seats at every single general election, which the exception of seats in 1924. In this light it is instructive to consider how Labour successfully navigated the war through Wrigley's prism.

This changing polity would be reflected in the gender of parliamentarians too. Mari Takayanagi, Chapter 3, examines the Parliament (Qualification of Women) Act of November 1918 whose significance has been largely overlooked, all attention centring on the Act earlier that year which gave women over thirty (with a small property qualification) the right to vote. The November 1918 Act, which was enacted ten days after the Armistice, for the first time permitted women to become Members of Parliament. It contained a surprising anomaly: there was no age (or property) qualification, which meant in theory that women too young to vote could nevertheless become MPs. (This was to occur when Jennie Lee, aged twenty-four, became a Labour MP just before the 1928 extension of the suffrage to women over twenty-one had come into effect.) The Act was introduced by Liberal MP Herbert Samuel, a senior backbencher who had held office in the past, and it was supported by the government with very little opposition.

It is possible that many believed there was no danger of the Act leading to an influx of women into the House, which indeed proved to be the case. While seventeen women stood for Parliament in the December 1918 election, only one was elected, Constance Markievicz, but as member of Sein Féin opposed to the British Parliament, she refused to take up her seat. The first woman to become an MP was Nancy Astor, who won a by-election the following year when her husband moved to the Lords. Despite feminist groups campaigning in the interwar years for women's access to the House of Lords, it was not until 1958 that this was granted. Women still remain grossly under-represented in Parliament today (following the June 2017 election there are 208 women MPs out of a total of 650) but the Act helped pave the way for women to enter other professions, such as the law. Takayanagi convincingly argues that its radicalism and contribution to gender equality needs greater recognition.

Our volume then moves away from Westminster to two local case studies. In Chapter 4 on the broad labour movements in Bristol and Northampton, Matthew Kidd invites us to re-think our assumptions about the First World War changing everything concerning British capitalism. Piloting wider discussions surrounding the concordats between labour and capital, and indeed between men and women, through the prism of these two local case studies, Kidd provides a valuable discussion of British political culture during the conflict. Refining the work of Patrick Joyce among others, Kidd explores questions of class and the degree to which the war changed the way workers conceptualised the world around them. Those seeking to understand the Labour Party's path to collectivism as the solution to capitalism's ills and its path to superseding the Liberals as the predominant force of anti-Conservatism in British politics will also find much of value from this chapter, which relies heavily on archival material mined from some underutilised sources.

Moving further north, Jack Southern, in Chapter 5, then explores the impact of the outbreak of war on the weaving districts of north-east Lancashire, with particular reference to Burnley, the 'world's weaving centre', where 40 per cent of male labour and 76 per cent of female labour worked in the cotton industry. Indeed on the outbreak of war all the weaving districts of north-east Lancashire employed three times more women than the national average. Weaving was dominated by small manufacturers, many of who had worked their way up from the 'shop floor', promoting a view of north-east Lancashire as a 'stronghold of Liberalism'. But it was not individualist liberalism so much as an industry built on kinship and community networks, giving loyalty to the employers and security to the employees through a family wage (although some women weavers received [nearly] equal pay and had a strong sense of economic and political entitlement).

On the outbreak of war, however, the familial system started to break down, as men signed up to fight and the mills began to close. While some of the machines could theoretically be switched to weaving cotton khaki, woollen khaki entailed expensive modification of the looms and thus was not pursued. Many women became their family's sole breadwinner, but they faced a spiralling cost of living and many families sort welfare relief. It was female campaigners who spearheaded local welfare issues, including those focusing on women's maternity and infant health. Women were also active in trade unions, especially the Amalgamated Weavers Association (AWA) and they made up the majority of its membership, although the top positions continued to be held by men. While there was a brief post-war revival in the Northern cotton industry, the 1920s and 1930s saw wage reductions and a plummeting trade union membership in the area. By the 1930s such membership was being replaced in Burnley by the National Unemployed Workers Committee Movement. The war had seen the beginning of a slow decline in the cotton industry, which was never to recover; the pre-war community networks that had contributed to north-east Lancashire's relative radicalism and greater gender equality also never re-materialised.

The First World War witnessed a radical transformation in the level of the formal economic activity of women, most notably bringing women in large numbers into the munitions factories. Trade unions were strengthened by wartime labour shortage and women's union membership rose by 160 per cent during the war. Deborah Thom compares two central figures who were organisers of women during the war: Mary Macarthur and Sylvia Pankhurst. Macarthur was a leading light of women's trade unionism before the war, best known for her involvement in the Cradley Heath chain-makers' strike of 1910 and her role as general secretary of the National Federation of Women Workers (NFWW). She was instrumental in aiding the expansion of the war economy through the recruitment of women workers. Sylvia Pankhurst likewise worked with women during the war, but her organisation, the East London Federation of Suffragettes, campaigned overtly against the war, campaigning for peace and opposing the introduction of conscription. She had broken ties with her mother and sister, Emmeline and Christabel Pankhurst and their WSPU, to form her own group, which aimed to place class at the heart of feminist struggle. The East London Federation gave practical help to women in surviving wartime hardships, working with and for East End women around issues of rent, food prices, child care, community restaurants and clinics. Both Macarthur and Sylvia Pankhurst were socialists but Pankhurst was an internationalist and a supporter of the Russian Revolution, changing the name of her organisation's paper in 1917 from *Women's Dreadnought* to *Workers' Dreadnought* accordingly. In 1920, Pankhurst was one of the founders of the British Communist Party.

While Pankhurst moved towards greater internationalism and away from Parliament as the favoured model of socialism and class politics, in May 1918 Macarthur was the first woman selected by the Labour Party (or indeed by any political party) to stand as a parliamentary candidate. As Mari Takayanagi points out in Chapter 3 in this volume, the selection occurred before the Act permitting women to stand had even been enacted. The distinctive political careers of these two impressive women reflect wider questions about what kinds of socialist politics appealed to, and were open to, women during and after the war. While Pankhurst and Macarthur followed very different paths, what united them during the war was their joint commitment to bettering the position of women, whether through fighting for equal pay or providing welfare for soldiers' wives and children.

In Chapter 7, Matt Perry focuses on another important woman organiser, Ellen Wilkinson. Best known as a leading figure in the 1936 Jarrow March and as Education Secretary under Attlee's government, her First World War organising has largely been forgotten. In 1915, the Amalgamated Union of Co-operative Employees (AUCE) (which later became the National Union of Distributive and Allied Workers [NUDAW] and later still the Union of Shop, Distributive and Allied Workers [USDAW]) appointed Wilkinson as their first woman in the post of national organiser. In the department stores and in retail more generally, women were replacing men who were signing up to fight. As a national organiser for AUCE, Wilkinson had particular responsibility for recruiting the new female entrants into the workforce. She fought for 'substituted' female labour (replacement on grounds of equivalent skills and hence justifying equal pay for equal work) as opposed to 'dilution' (replacing skilled labour with less skilled, and hence less pay).

Wilkinson was involved in AUCE's first strike over substituted female labour, which took place in Carlyle in late 1915/early 1916, lasted only a week and was a resounding victory, resulting in equal pay. There was further success in Lanarkshire the following month, and other Scottish victories followed. Wilkinson believed in women's ability to lead union struggles, but was well aware of the attitudes of many in the labour movement towards female activists. Nevertheless, the AUCE admired her organising powers, and in October 1917 it founded a woman's department with her at its head. Having a woman's department was seen as one way of avoiding separatism while ensuring that a union addressed women's specific concerns. The AUCE opposed craft unionism, adopted industrial unionism and emphasised militant grass roots activity. Wilkinson's involvement affected her subsequent politics, and she, like Sylvia Pankhurst, welcomed the Russian Revolution and was likewise a founding member of the British Communist Party. Unlike Pankhurst, and despite her commitment to extra-parliamentary politics, Wilkinson became a Labour MP in 1924, but always remained distinctly on the left.

Krisztina Robert, in Chapter 8, looks at a rather different group of women, those who joined the Women's Volunteer Reserve (WVR) or Women's Corps. Feminist historians have tended to view the 'true' radical heroines of the First World War as munitions workers, women trade unionists and feminists – women who demanded equal pay or protested against the war; these are precisely the women discussed in the chapters by Thom and Perry. Robert however argues that the WVR can themselves be seen as radical in their challenge to the established social order. They did not accept a second-class status but pushed for wider recognition as militarised female subjects. Established in 1914, the WVR saw their role initially as participating in home defence, but once invasion seemed unlikely, the WVR leaders arranged vocational training, including in previous 'male' occupations, such as truck driving. From

1917, with military manpower shortages, women were replacing men in auxiliary military roles as members of the newly formed WAAC (the Women's Army Auxiliary Corp) and the other women's services (Women's Land Army, Women's Royal Naval Service [WRNS] and Women's Royal Air Force [WRAF]).

Drawing on wartime press articles and photographs, post-war memoirs and oral history interviews, Krisztina Robert identifies two main strategies, both actual and discursive, through which the women constructed the meaning of their work. The first one, militarisation, entailed working under martial discipline at military sites, wearing service uniforms of khaki (controversial for some) and performing duties previously done by soldiers, sailors and airmen. The second strategy included a strong emphasis on occupational training and/or previous experience as an entry condition into the WVR, with emphasis on the mental and physical difficulty of the jobs and the use of modern technology in the work processes. The WVR's egalitarian entry criteria lessened class distinctions to some degree, giving a cross-class membership. The chapter concludes that through these strategies WVR members created a new gender role, namely auxiliary soldiering, which combined the previously incompatible concepts of military service and 'women's work'. The WVR thus carved out a radical martial form of war participation for women along with new martial female identities.

The book then takes a different direction to look at British trends and how they fit into the shifting global sands. In Chapter 9, Richard Carr builds on his recent biography of the filmmaker Charlie Chaplin, who rose to become the most famous man in cinema, and one of the famous in the world, all told. British-born Chaplin would view the war from the comfortable surroundings of Los Angeles, California, but he would be profoundly shaped by its developments. This chapter teases out his reaction to the conflict, and the controversy his reluctance to serve at the front generated. It then moves on to discuss how the conflict affected Chaplin's own left-wing politics, which were always of a radical nature but did not universally subscribe to the increasing consensus that the big state was a force for good. Chaplin was not a Labour member or, given his residency, somebody who would ever vote in a British general election. But he was a radical, and someone whose politics has been underexplored to date. Looking beyond wartime films such as *Shoulder Arms* and *The Bond*, this chapter focuses on Chaplin the living, breathing radical propagandist.

Rather closer to home, Marc Mulholland, in Chapter 10, also includes much discussion on the notion of collectivism and the big state. Exploring such questions through Ireland (part of the UK until 1921), Mulholland walks us through the divergent beliefs and tactics of collectivised unskilled urbanised labour, and the craft-based co-operative tradition. His analysis then turns to the question of a 'Co-operate Commonwealth', its potential organisation, and the role of labour during the struggle for independence. Throughout we see the distinctly Irish dimension to the debate over collectivism versus the co-operative: the rural and undeveloped nature of much of Ireland's countryside leading the Irish Labour Party to argue for the 'organisation of the people into trade unions and co-operative societies' by the early 1920s. In looking back to the clan system that had pre-dated British rule, Mulholland interestingly notes, Sinn Féin MPs could argue for much the same thing. Through this chapter, we also gain interesting insights into the manner in which the Irish left perceived the epoch-defining events of the revolution in Russia.

Speaking of Russia, Jonathan Davis then recounts how 1917 served as a formative moment in the development of two influential left-leaning voices, and by extension, the Labour Party itself in Chapter 11. By analysing the then liberal journalist Morgan Phillips Price – later to join Labour and, from 1929, serve as an MP – and Arthur Henderson, then Labour leader and a member of the Lloyd George Cabinet, we gain a new perspective on Labour's shifting sands. Charting the shift such men made from being uncomfortable opposing the Liberals to, by 1918, being willing to back Clause IV and all the nationalising elements there within, Davis reconfigures the Russian Revolution as a significant influence in the development of the British Labour Party.

Such international influences continue, in Chapter 12, with Gavin Baird and Bradley W. Hart's consideration of David Starr Jordan, a largely forgotten figure in Britain, but someone with significant academic and political clout in the USA. Although Starr Jordan's fame largely rested on his role as the first president of Stanford University, his interventions into diplomacy lent heavily on his belief in eugenics. As Baird and Hart illustrate, during the lead-up to the war and in the period before America entered the Allied side, Starr Jordan used his academic prominence to stress the dysgenic impact of the conflict on both sides of the Atlantic. Tracing his story from California to the corridors of Westminster, this chapter chronicles the interactions of an American pacifist with the Snowdens, Ramsay MacDonald and Fabian thinkers, such as Graham Wallas.

We end, logically enough, with the issue of war aims and the peace treaties. In Chapter 13, John Callaghan walks the reader through the various debates and contradictions seen in the Labour movement prior to the end of hostilities, as well as the dilemmas soon posed by the march of events thereafter. Along the way, he discusses Labour's reactions to the diplomatic path pursued by Edward Grey in the summer of 1914, the subsequent impact of the Union of Democratic Control, and then Labour's relationship with the Lloyd George government and Wilsonianism abroad. Callaghan also, like Davis and Wrigley before him, includes vital discussion of the continuation of hostilities beyond 11 November 1918. Here his chapter may be of particular use to those considering Labour's later attitudes to colonialism and the League of Nations too.

All in all, this volume is intended to cover both Labour and labour, but also other forms of radicalism. Indeed, since the very term 'radicalism' has proven so malleable for historians, this broad approach seems a necessary precondition for any analysis. In perhaps the quintessential consideration of its various *Currents*, Biagini and Reid stressed the continuities of 'popular radicalism through the nineteenth and into the twentieth century'.[34] But understanding radicalism requires not merely chronological considerations but thematic ones too, for the reformist axis of British liberals, socialists and others unhappy at the various inequalities of capitalism ranged across causes, such as 'open government and the rule of law, … freedom from intervention both at home and abroad, and for individual liberty and community-centred democracy'.[35] Since the instruments and patterns of conformity – the state or the church on the one hand, marriage and the domestic sphere on the other – were so all encompassing, their opponents could scarcely be any less varied. Recent edited volumes have served to only widen the analytical scope into issues of divorce and the popular press as a statement on non-conformity, and begun to look at the Anglo-American and generally transnational dimension to such questions.[36] Likewise, Emily Robinson has been at the forefront of a greater consideration of language – where terms such as 'radical' and 'progressive' carry heavy 'historical baggage', but also allow politicians and social actors 'to gesture towards a supposedly self-evident (though, in practice, undefined and open) set of political principles'.[37] In short, there is much to debate here.

All that said, by covering everything from actions in Parliament to the challenging of patriarchy we hope to have made a contribution to the ongoing way in which we understand and interpret a tragic but transformative moment in modern British history. Existing assumptions regarding high politics, gender relations, industrial militancy and transnational narratives are all explored in the pages that follow. The transnational turn is built upon through looking at America, Ireland and Russia, and social, political and cultural historians will all hopefully find much of value in what follows. Certainly this collection makes a contribution to the tripartite developments raised by the innovative Modern British Studies group at the University of Birmingham: the 'uneven and often hesitant development of new forms of mass democracy', the effects of 'globalisation [on] Britain's place in the world' and the 'shifting patterns of rule' experienced in Britain in the nineteenth and twentieth centuries.[38] There is doubtless more to do, but this volume can at least help push several of the debates contained here on somewhat. Refinements to the arguments expressed remain, of course, more than welcome – and in this time of commemoration where we consider the meaning of 1914–18, perhaps only appropriate.

Notes

1. See, for example, Jon Lawrence, 'Popular Politics and the Limitations of Party: Wolverhampton, 1867–1900', in Eugenio F. Biagini and Alastair J. Reid (eds), *Currents of Radicalism: Popular Radicalism, Organised Labour and Party Politics in Britain, 1850–1914* (Cambridge, 1991), pp. 65–83.
2. Dan Jarvis, 'Labour and the First World War', *Labour List*, 18 June 2014 at http://labourlist.org/2014/06/full-text-dan-jarvis-labour-and-the-first-world-war-speech/ (accessed 11 October 2017).
3. See David Thackeray, *Conservatism for the Democratic Age: Conservative Cultures and the Challenge of Mass Politics in Early Twentieth Century England* (Manchester, 2013); Nigel Keohane, *The Party of Patriotism: The Conservative Party and the First World War* (Farnham, 2010). For the aftermath see also, Richard Carr, *Veteran MPs and Conservative Politics in the Aftermath of the Great War* (Farnham, 2013).
4. Eugenio F. Biagini and Alastair J. Reid (eds), 'Introduction', in Biagini and Reid, *Currents of Radicalism*, p. 19.
5. Rhiannon Vickers, *The Labour Party and the World, Volume 1* (Manchester, 2003), p. 56.
6. Edward McNeilly, 'Labour and the Politics of Internationalism, 1906–1914', *Twentieth Century British History*, 20:4 (2009), 431–53.
7. Lucian M. Ashworth, 'Rethinking a Socialist Foreign Policy: The British Labour Party and International Relations Experts, 1918 to 1931', *International Labor and Working-Class History*, No. 75, Rethinking the Left in Victory and Defeat (Spring, 2009), pp. 30–48, 30.
8. W. G. Runciman, 'Has British Capitalism Changed Since the First World War?', *The British Journal of Sociology*, 44:1 (1993), pp. 53–67.
9. Runciman, 'Has British Capitalism Changed', p. 56.
10. Runciman, 'Has British Capitalism Changed', p. 57.
11. Larry G. Gerber, 'Corporatism in Comparative Perspective: The Impact of the First World War on American and British Labor Relations', *The Business History Review*, 62:1 (1988), pp. 93–127.
12. Thomas Piketty, *Capital in the Twenty-First Century* (London, 2014), passim.
13. Biagini and Reid, 'Introduction', p. 19.
14. W. H. Greenleaf, *The British Political Tradition, Vol 1: The Rise of Collectivism* (London, 1983), pp. 50–1.
15. Chris Chamberlain, 'The Growth of Support for the Labour Party in Britain', *The British Journal of Sociology*, 24:4 (1973), pp. 474–89, 480.
16. George Dangerfield, *The Strange Death of Liberal England* (London, 1935).
17. Martin Pugh, '"Class Traitors": Conservative Recruits to Labour, 1900–30', *The English Historical Review*, 113:450 (1998), pp. 38–64.
18. Caroline Rowan, 'Women in the Labour Party, 1906–1920', *Feminist Review*, 12 (1982), pp. 74–91, 90.
19. Rachel Reeves and Richard Carr, *Alice in Westminster: The Political Life of Alice Bacon* (London, 2017); Lisa Martineau, *Politics & Power: Barbara Castle* (London, 2011); Paula Bartley, *Ellen Wilkinson: from Red Suffragist to Government Minister* (London, 2014); Matt Perry, *'Red Ellen' Wilkinson* (Manchester,

2014); Laura Beers, *Red Ellen: The Life of Ellen Wilkinson, Socialist, Feminist, Internationalist* (Cambridge, MA, 2016).
20 Labour Party press release, 4 August 2014, at http://press.labour.org.uk/post/93762440584/one-hundred-years-ago-britain-entered-into-the (accessed 11 October 2017).
21 See the introduction of Maurice Cowling, *The Impact of Labour 1920–1924: The Beginning of Modern British Politics* (Cambridge, 1971).
22 Jill Liddington, *The Long Road to Freedom: Feminism and Anti-militarism in Britain Since 1820* (London, 1989), chs 5 and 6; Anne Wiltsher, *Most Dangerous Women: Feminist Peace Campaigners of the Great War* (London, 1985), chs 4 and 5; Jo Vellcott, *Pacifists, Patriots and the Vote: the Erosion of Democratic Suffragism in Britain During the First World War* (New York, 2007).
23 Barbara Winslow, *Sylvia Pankhurst: Sexual Politics and Political Activism* (London, 1996), ch. 4; Mary Davis, *Sylvia Pankhurst: a Life in Radical Politics* (London, 1999), ch. 3; Shirley Harrison, *Sylvia Pankhurst: a Maverick Life* (London, 2004), chs 15–19.
24 Martin Pugh, *Women and the Women's Movement in Britain, 1914–1959* (London, 1992), ch 2.
25 Harold L. Smith, *The British Women's Suffrage Campaign, 1866–1928* (London, 1998, 2nd edn 2007), pp. 132, 83.
26 Pugh, *Women and the Women's Movement in Britain*, p. 42.
27 Sandra Stanley Holton, *Feminism and Democracy* (Cambridge, 1987) pp. 134–50.
28 Nicoletta Gullace, *"The Blood of Our Sons": Men, Women and the Renegotiation of British Citizenship During the Great War* (New York, 2002).
29 John Horne, *Labour at War: France and Britain 1914–1918* (Oxford, 1991).
30 Adrian Gregory and Senia Paseta, *Ireland and the Great War: 'A War to Unite Us All'?* (Manchester, 2002).
31 Adrian Gregory, *The Last Great War: British Society and the First World War* (Oxford, 2008); Martin Pugh *Speak for Britain! A New History of the Labour Party* (London, 2009).
32 Janet Watson, *Fighting Different Wars* (Cambridge, 2004); Susan Grayzel, *Women and the First World War* (Longman, 2002). And see also Angela Woollacott, *On Her their Lives Depend* (London, 1994); Deborah Thom, *Nice Girls and Rude Girls: Women Workers in World War 1* (London, 1998); Cathy Hunt, *The National Federation of Women Workers, 1906–1921* (Oxford, 2014).
33 Matthew Johnson, *Militarism and the British Left, 1902–1914* (Basingstoke, 2013), passim.
34 Biagini and Reid, 'Introduction', p. 1.
35 Biagini and Reid, 'Introduction', p. 3.
36 See e.g. Anne Humphreys, 'Divorce and the New Woman', in Joseph Bristow and Josephine McDonagh (eds), *Nineteenth Century Radical Traditions* (London, 2016) pp. 137–56; and the essays by Jon Mee and Adam I. P. Smith in Ella Dzelainis and Ruth Livesey (eds), *The American Experiment and the Idea of Democracy in British Culture, 1776–1914* (Farnham, 2013).
37 Emily Robinson, *The Language of Progressive Politics in Modern Britain* (London, 2017), p. 3.
38 Modern British Studies at Birmingham, Working Paper No. 1, February 2014.

1

Peace, but not at any price: British socialists' calls for peace on the eve of the First World War

Marcus Morris

The Edwardian period was one of growing militarism, international rivalry and an ensuing arms race, while the threat of war loomed ever larger. With this heightened and widespread tension, British socialists and those in the labour movement more generally had no option but to respond. Though primarily concerned with domestic matters, they did respond consistently from early in the century and with increasing force, starting invariably from an internationalist and anti-war standpoint, while also looking to the Second International for guidance. Like the International, they rarely spoke with one voice on the subject and offered multiple responses.[1] Broadly speaking, despite those multiple voices, two particular strands of thought have traditionally been seen to have dominated within the socialist and labour movement. A majority response, centred on Labour and especially the ILP and judged favourably, is seen to be anti-war and closely aligned with pacifist traditions in Britain, characterised by persistent calls for peace and a reduction in arms expenditure.[2] The second, and seen as very much the minority and somewhat heretical response, is centred on H. M. Hyndman, Robert Blatchford and elements of the Social Democratic Party (SDP) and the *Clarion* movement.[3] They are portrayed as being pro-war, or at least war-mongering, pro-armaments, constantly highlighting the so-called 'German menace'. As a result, the movement is often portrayed as having offered two distinct responses and has been praised or condemned accordingly.

In the standard historiography, Hyndman and Blatchford have come in for somewhat of a mauling with a simplistic interpretation of their views dominating. In contrast to the 'committed internationalists', Keir Hardie and Ramsay MacDonald, they are seen as 'rabid nationalists'.[4] Walter Kendall thus suggested that they were 'allied with some of the most reactionary elements in the country'.[5] They have also been consistently presented as 'notorious chauvinists', while Geoffrey Foote has concluded that 'Hyndman's Marxist terminology concealed a crude national chauvinism'.[6] They were patriots first, socialists second (with these seen as mutually exclusive). Indeed, it has been claimed that 'Blatchford became contemptuous of internationalism', as evidenced in his popular slogan, 'Britain for the British'.[7] In a similar vein, Rhiannon Vickers argues that Hyndman tended 'to support an independent nationalism rather than any creed of international working-class solidarity', and Ruth Kinna that he 'demonstrated the ease with which socialists could lose sight of internationalist goals'.[8] Hyndman is also presented as being anti-German and a 'Germanophobe'.[9] Raymond Challinor has even declared that 'proud to be British, Hyndman looked with disdain at all aliens' – something that was seen as applicable to Blatchford too.[10] As war approached, then, they became 'the most rabid war-mongers of them all' and with their supporters 'found stronger ties to nation than to class'.[11]

Such views of Hyndman, Blatchford and their supporters contrast with those traditionally presented of Labour, the ILP especially, and their leadership. Though a much more positive interpretation, it is equally simplistic. They are a party of pacifism, or at least peace, which consistently preached an anti-war message and did all it could to prevent war breaking out.[12] Much is made, in particular, of leading figures from within the movement, especially Hardie and MacDonald, who are seen as the most internationalist and committed to peace (at almost any price) of British socialists.[13] In many ways, historians have taken their cue from the party itself. The chairman of the 1913 Labour Party annual conference, for instance, argued that 'the Labour Party is here to denounce war and war-mongering in any disguise, to warn and to arm our fellow workers of all nations against the common foe'.[14] Traditional assessments of the responses are thus based on such contemporary views, but this can be problematic, especially when the ideological and political bases that informed them are taken into consideration.

There clearly were differences in the movement's responses to the growing tension, with clear division along the lines highlighted. We should thus neither deny those differences nor contemporaries' hostility to the varied responses. However, these contemporary reactions, and especially the mutual criticism, have clouded much of the historical interpretation and the context that framed them has been overlooked. Both sides of the debate were keen to distance themselves from the other. Hyndman would write, for example, that the ILP were 'ignorant, blind, emotional' pacifists (indeed, these were terms of abuse for their brand of socialism more generally), while MacDonald sought to distance himself from Hyndman and Blatchford who he said had 'never abandoned their anti-German chauvinism'.[15] The *Labour Leader*, the ILP's newspaper, also censured them for their 'disgraceful, dangerous, emotional junketing'.[16] Yet, as will be shown, their differences were not as marked as these comments might suggest, while they were exaggerated for political purpose. Throughout the Edwardian period domestic socialist rivalry was played out in international forums and through foreign policy. Clearly, the tensions of the period were a genuine source of consternation, but they were also too good a political opportunity to resist and perfect for the socialist game of one-upmanship. Thus T. D. Benson, treasurer of the ILP, wrote to Hardie in 1906 concerned that the party was 'publishing and doing nothing'. He therefore questioned if 'there is no question for us to take up. What about militarism? Is there any danger of that becoming a burning question? We ought to strike a definite note on it.'[17] They were consciously looking for political capital out of potential crises. Such observations, then, are not something we should be solely basing historical interpretation on.

More recently there has been some excellent work that has sought to challenge some aspects of these standard views. There have been over the last decade or so some significant reinterpretations of Labour's foreign policy from the likes of Paul Bridgen, John Callaghan, Edward McNeilly and Rhiannon Vickers.[18] They have demonstrated how Labour's response to foreign affairs was more complex than previously suggested and how it was 'a party in which a variety of foreign policy ideologies existed.'[19] They have also illustrated how Labour's response to war in 1914 was not as straightforward as traditionally suggested and in part this chapter builds on these studies. Despite these reassessments of Labour, there have been few of Hyndman and not one of Blatchford. My own work has questioned the charges of national chauvinism levelled at Hyndman, while Graham Johnson's important study has challenged the assumptions surrounding the ideology of the SDP stopping in 1911.[20] This chapter consciously adds to this existing work, extending the period of study to 1914. Yet, there remains very little that has considered the responses of the socialist movement collectively, focusing on similarities rather than differences.[21] Groups and individuals are primarily looked at in isolation, which means that important and connected aspects of the responses to the growing tension have been missed.

In taking a broader and comparative look, this chapter will add complexity to the story of British socialism and war, and especially calls for peace. Furthermore, it argues that it is too simplistic to suggest there were two distinctly different strands and in doing so historians have missed the clear similarities in the vast majority of British socialists' responses. Too often, the separate groups and individuals of the movement are considered in isolation. Labour and the ILP were not 'peace-at-any-pricers', while Hyndman and Blatchford certainly did not think they were warmongering or chauvinistic. Moreover, they all saw themselves as peace campaigners, albeit in quite different fashions. This chapter will consider these groups' differing responses together and show that beyond peace (which is often ignored) there were a number of key shared assumptions that bound British socialists and those in the labour movement together and underpinned their responses. War was something to be avoided and there was a shared desire for peace, but this was not to be prized over all other safeguards and liberties, while 'national defence' was paramount. The chapter will ultimately conclude that we should see British socialists' responses to the growing tensions as not divergent, rather that these groups had the same goals but different tactics for achieving them.

Hyndman, Blatchford and the 'German menace'

From 1904, with Russia's defeat to Japan, Hyndman and Blatchford believed that Germany had overtaken her as the greatest threat to peace in Europe. Hyndman warned that 'an attack by Germany on France is quite conceivable' at the behest of a 'ramping self-idolater like the Kaiser'.[22] Such fears were only heightened by the Moroccan crisis in 1905, in which they favoured France's claim (as the lesser of two evils), with Hyndman declaring that 'the Germany of the Kaiser and his friends has taken the place of Russia as the most reactionary and perturbing power in the world'.[23] From this moment, then, they became focused on the perceived threat posed by the 'German menace'. It was a theme that they would return to regularly in the years before the outbreak of war in both labour and socialist forums and, controversially, in Conservative newspapers like the *Daily Mail* and the *Morning Post*. Their views centred on the perceived threat that they believed Germany posed due to her armament plans, her militaristic tendencies (which they believed German socialists could not restrain) and her desire, as they saw it, to attack Britain. Thus, Blatchford suggested in a letter to the *Manchester Guardian* that generally 'an armed autocrat is a danger to the peace of the world'.[24] Hyndman, meanwhile, noted that 'I regard the menace of militarist Germany as a great and growing danger not only to the people of this island, but to democracy and Socialism generally'.[25] By no means did they stand alone within or without the movement in setting out such views and certainly reflected popular sentiment. Blatchford was undoubtedly the most frenetic of those advocates from within the movement, while he and Hyndman were heavily criticised by many of their fellow socialists. Little attention, though, has been paid to how they justified their actions, how they understood their actions and what their intentions were in highlighting the 'menace' in this context.

Key to their understanding was their belief that a threat genuinely existed and to ignore that threat would only act as a catalyst to it becoming a reality. As Hyndman wrote to the leading German socialist Karl Kautsky: 'I am quite satisfied that nothing whatever is to be gained by pretending we are living in days of peace and international concord.'[26] They saw it as their duty to call attention to a genuine problem and admit the realities of the international situation, rather than sticking their heads in the sand. They were particularly critical of European statesmen and leading British politicians in this regard. After spending time on the Continent, Hyndman thus wrote to Sir Frederic Macmillan that 'things, in my opinion, are in a much more dangerous position in Europe than is at all understood here. It seems to be assumed by our statesmen that, so far as we are concerned, huge armaments abroad are kept up merely for amusement and that Germany has abandoned her intentions to dominate Europe.' He concluded that 'it is strange to read Grey's speeches when outside England.'[27] They were also critical of their fellow socialists for continually falling back on platitudes of internationalism, as were their supporters. As an article in *Justice*, the SDP's newspaper, noted: 'we are internationalists in our point of view, but we are also realists in our methods.'[28] This was expanded upon by Harry Quelch, one of their leading supporters in the SDP, who said that socialism 'deals with actualities' and that it was 'based upon the social reality of hard fact.'[29]

Hyndman thus summed up their feelings by commenting in *Justice* that 'the danger of war does exist to-day, and it is foolish to try to disguise it.'[30] Indeed, another article argued that 'peace demonstrations, and pacific utterances by monarchs and statesmen notwithstanding, it is impossible to ignore the increasing danger of war between this country and Germany'. As such, 'it is idle to pretend that there is not such danger except what is cause by the irresponsible utterances of the jingoes on both sides.'[31] Thus, in calling attention to the danger of war their aim was twofold: first, was to make this a topic for discussion among the working class of Britain, especially those within the labour and socialist movement. Hyndman noted this in a letter of 1908: 'I have already done what Blatchford and I set out to do. We have brought the whole discussion down into the street.'[32] It was for this reason why newspapers like the *Daily Mail* was their chosen medium, for it boasted a daily readership of one and a half million. Accordingly, when the paper offered to pay Blatchford for his articles he replied: 'I said I did not want paying ... I wanted to get the public ear.'[33] Their second aim was, by admitting realities, to bring about more effective discussion between Britain and Germany; Hyndman writing that we should 'endeavour to bring together [Britons and Germans] in friendly intercourse, always keeping our attention on the actual facts.'[34]

Hyndman and Blatchford also wanted to bring British and German socialists together for more meaningful discussions. They believed that German actions represented a roadblock on the road to international socialism, Hyndman noting that 'German domination on the Continent might easily check for a time the growth of Socialism.'[35] In part, this was also a response to the perceived inaction of German socialists and their unwillingness to face up to reality from the Moroccan crisis onwards. Hyndman argued that the German Social Democrats could not form a viable alternative to Prussian militarism and were unwilling to do so.[36] In many ways this reflected a wider gulf and mistrust between British and German socialists. Their relationship was, perhaps, best described by a leading figure in the ILP, Bruce Glasier: 'If only our Social Democratic German friends were a little more social and little more democratic!'[37] At the heart of the mistrust was a belief that German socialists were coming to regard the international movement as their movement. An article in the *Labour Leader*, for example, noted how the ILP 'oppose the German socialists in their attempt to swallow up the movement'.[38] By 1911, at the SDP's annual conference in Coventry, Hyndman would even accuse the Germans of deliberately sabotaging the International's anti-war campaign. He thus concluded that 'I venture to think that the real supporters of peace among the Socialists are those who, like Blatchford and myself, recognise the growing antagonism, admit that war is quite probable, and do our very utmost to awaken not only our own countrymen but the rest of the world to truth.'[39]

Though consistently critical of Germany's militaristic tendencies and wider militarism, the most controversial aspect of their responses to the growing threat was their calls for increased armaments spending, especially a 'big navy', and their fears surrounding the perceived inadequacy of the nation's defence. It is here where they are and were perceived to be clearly warmongering. A. J. A. Morris, for instance, has argued that 'Hyndman and Blatchford demanded not only more battleships but also conscription for home defence, pitching their claims as loudly, frequently and consistently as Lord Roberts, Rudyard Kipling and other assorted extremists of the bellicose political right.'[40] Yet again, though, this was not how they understood it. In defending their position, Hyndman wrote in 1910 that 'I am in favour of a powerful navy … not in order to maintain the ruinous system of today', as most did, 'but to safeguard the glorious system [socialism] of tomorrow.'[41] Blatchford, moreover, would suggest that 'I do not believe there are "war-mongers" in England' and 'I have never seen nor heard of a single Englishman mad and bad enough to wish our nation to make war upon Germany. There is no "war party" in England: only a party of defence.'[42] Moreover, they made it clear that this was neither an attack on Germany but on its leaders and their actions, nor was it a case of Germanophobia. Hyndman thus argued that 'to speak … of antagonism to the German Government, on my part, as involving hatred to Germany … is as absurd as to say that I hate England because I detest and denounce Lord Morley's rule in India.'[43] He could not 'hate' Germany, for 'it is quite ludicrous to imagine for a moment that an active Social-Democrat, and therefore a man pledged up to the hilt against war, can hate any nation.

We are of necessity Internationalists.' Indeed, he added somewhat disingenuously that if 'German Social-Democracy could and would help to overthrow our upper classes in this island ... I for one should welcome their coming and would give them all the assistance in my power.'[44]

Hyndman and Blatchford's calls for increased spending on armaments centred on two beliefs. First, was the imperative for national defence, partly predicated on the belief that Britain's were currently inadequate, partly on the belief that this was agreed socialist policy and also on the belief that Britain deserved defending because of the liberty she allowed – assumptions, as we will see, shared with many in Labour too. Blatchford argued that 'there is no nation where the subject has an equal liberty of free speech and action'.[45] An article in *Justice* from 1910, meanwhile, called on fellow socialists to take a 'definite and reasoned attitude in relation to national defence' arguing that 'British independence is worth defending'. In doing so, the article outlined their position:

> There are two imaginable positions for us with regard to the national defence. Either we hold that it is a matter of indifference to the working class whether the governing class that oppresses it is native or foreign, and consequently Socialists have no interest in national defence; or we hold that we have an interest in sustaining the independence of the nation. The former attitude is not, I fancy, openly taken by any considerable body of English Socialists. The Social-Democrats of Germany repudiate it. So do most Socialists in France.[46]

Thus, Harry Quelch concluded that 'it might be agreed to as a general rule, that it is the duty of Socialists in the national defence if national liberty and independence and popular rights are in danger.'[47] Those socialists who called for increased armaments, then, consistently justified their position as being in line with that of the international socialist movement.[48] At the 1913 British Socialist Party (BSP) annual conference Hyndman therefore declared that 'he was opposed to militarism as much as the International; but the International Socialist Party had declared by its resolutions that every nation had the right to defend itself by the force of arms'.[49] In the British case, the navy was the principal force of arms, taking the place of a continental citizen army, and so had to be strong enough to defend Britain from invasion and from blockade. Hyndman feared that as Britain was 'dependent for six-sevenths of our food on foreign countries, we could be starved out even by chance superiority at sea'.[50]

Many British socialists formulated their socialism within a construct of the British nation, which enjoyed political liberties denied to others and was the safeguard of such liberties. Indeed, in this vein Harry Quelch argued at the SDP annual conference in 1911 that 'there must be ... an adequate defence', in the form of 'a strong navy for England', 'for the hope of these countries [he listed Holland, Denmark and Belgium] to preserve their national autonomy rested upon the British navy'.[51] Socialism may have been international moreover, but that did not preclude nationalism. Many British socialists thus built their constructions of socialism on national identity and internationalism, advocating a form of radical patriotism.[52] This was not unique to Britain, with Kevin Callahan demonstrating how French and German socialists deeply 'valued their own national identities' and that 'the discourse surrounding the issue of anti-militarism was couched in terms of defending one's own national traditions'.[53] Hyndman succinctly outlined this position in a letter to Leo Maxse: 'we are *inter*-nationalists not *anti*-nationalists'.[54] Thus, he insisted that 'national defence need not mean nationalist jingoism' and that 'international co-operation for the general emancipation of the proletariat ought not to mean that Social-Democrats are wholly indifferent to national aspirations'.[55] Such conceptions, then, were central to why Hyndman, Blatchford and others would advocate the strengthening of Britain's defences against a foe that did not grant such liberties.

The second justification offered for increasing armaments was the argument that countering the threat Germany posed was the best way to avoid war. Blatchford summed this up in an article in the *Daily Mail*, stating that 'if we do not want war with Germany we must be strong enough to cause Germany to want peace'. He went further, claiming that 'Germany puts her destiny into the hands of soldiers; we leave ours in the hands of politicians. Germany acts; we talk. Words count for nothing in the game of blood and iron. Arm or surrender.' He concluded saying that 'we can choose our alternative; no middle course is open to us'.[56] In a subsequent pamphlet published on the subject he called on fellow socialists to 'face the facts' for 'Socialism is not yet nearly strong enough to abolish war' and thus 'the only way to prevent war is to make ourselves so strong that no other nation will care to attack us'.[57] Hyndman also argued something similar, declaring that 'a sham defence is worse than no defence at all'.[58]

At the heart of all their warnings, though, in their minds at least, was the desire for peace – something invariably missed by historians. Hyndman wrote in *Justice* that 'we tell the truth [about the German menace] because we wish our country to keep clear of war with Germany'.[59] He regularly repeated the claim that peace was their primary aim and that 'the first Socialist interest must be peace'.[60] For Blatchford it was equally simple: 'I want peace, because I want socialism, and because I hate war'.[61] He believed, therefore, that 'Mr Hyndman and I have taken the very unpopular course of warning the Labour Party' and wider public. This was 'not because we want war; but because we are anxious to prevent it'.[62] In many ways then, they saw themselves as martyrs for the call of peace and the socialist cause, willing to risk the wrath of their fellow socialists to ensure the preservation of both. As *Justice* concluded:

We are assuredly no patriots in the sense of desiring the workers here to concern themselves in the least degree in defending their masters' land or their masters' property. But we do desire to retain our national autonomy and such political rights as we already possess, and we cannot but regard a war between England and Germany as a disaster, and the ascendency of Prussia as a menace to international democracy and Socialism.[63]

Thus peace and socialist interests were at the heart of Hyndman and Blatchford's responses to the international threats of the Edwardian age, and they were responding in the way that they thought best to preserve them. This angered some in the movement, but they shared a number of key assumptions with many of their critics.

Opposition, labour and national defence

Within the SDP there were some strong voices of protest raised to Hyndman and Blatchford, their focus on the supposed 'German menace' and their calls for armaments. The two most vocal were Theodore Rothstein and Zelda Kahan. Rothstein argued from as early as 1907 that Hyndman's continued warnings about the 'German menace' were 'playing into the hands of the jingoes by fanning still more the embers of prejudice and enmity which exist in this country against Germany and thus preparing the ground for a popular war with Germany'.[64] Kahan took things a stage further, proposing a resolution urging the SDP executive to disassociate the party from Hyndman's statements in 1909. Then, in 1911, she proposed a resolution at the party's annual conference that outright condemned him.[65] Indeed, some other prominent members left the SDP at the same moment in protest at 'Mr Hyndman's pro-armaments propaganda'.[66] In the main, though, Hyndman withstood these assaults on his position, with one correspondent to *Justice* concluding that 'to the impartial mind, H. M. Hyndman's recent "eye opener", with others' views, calls for serious thinking rather than mere abuse'.[67] The *Social-Democrat* also defended Hyndman, believing that he was 'most unfairly ... attacked by the leaders and organs of the British Labour Party', for 'it is not because he wants war, but because he wishes to overt war, that his warning has been sounded'.[68] From outside of the SDP and *Clarion* supporters, and especially within the ILP, though, there was very public and vociferous criticism of the two, as socialist opponents sought to gain political capital from the incident.

In an article pointedly titled 'Heralds of War', the *Labour Leader* responded to Hyndman and Blatchford's warnings by concluding that 'no more humiliating incident has disfigured the history of our movement. It is as if madness has suddenly afflicted some of our friends'.[69] Another article argued that one of the most regrettable results of the 'warlike outbursts of Mr Blatchford and Mr Hyndman has been the discredit into which they have brought the name of Socialism'.[70] Indeed, Keir Hardie went further claiming that Hyndman 'has ransacked the columns of the gutter press for innuendo and insults levelled against the representatives of the German Empire', while he accused Blatchford of suffering from a 'bad attack of nerves'.[71] Hardie did not just make his attacks in public, privately chastising Hyndman in a series of letters: 'you have chosen for the moment to cast in your lot with those enemies of progress who recognise in war and militarism one of their strongest allies, and having done so, you must abide by the consequences'.[72]

Most of the criticisms that came from Labour and the ILP, though, remained very deliberately in the public sphere. Simply put, there was great political capital to be made from the situation. This does not mean that differences did not exist, and criticisms of Hyndman's and Blatchford's tactics were genuine, but central to their condemnation was the desire to score political points over domestic opponents. The growing tension was clearly seen as something that they could gain political capital from, especially if their response was distinctive to others in the movement. The ILP also sought to manipulate the situation to their advantage in the international sphere within the Second International. For instance, when Hyndman was again put forward to be the British section's representative to the International Socialist Bureau (effectively the International's executive) they blocked it, Bruce Glasier declaring that 'the reelection [sic] of Hyndman after his jingo utterance [on calls for a "big navy"] would be an outrage upon international Socialist sentiment'.[73] Of course, it was a member of the ILP that was elected in his place and they gained overall control of the section.

Labour and the ILP, then, even if their goals were shared, set out to present a different message to Hyndman and Blatchford. They believed, in the words of Ramsay MacDonald, that 'the Labour Party must make itself the organ of the tendency in the nation which made for peace and internationalism'.[74] Therefore, an article in the *Labour Leader* suggested that 'our duty is to speak up for peace, and our friendship with the German people. Our duty is to organise resistance to the panic, the falsehood, and the gluttonous greed of capitalism that is clamouring voraciously for armaments.'[75] In the years leading up to the outbreak of war this is something that Labour consistently did, directing public calls for peace and campaigning for what they believed was the best way to achieve this. In this age of militarism, Labour consistently presented an anti-militarism opposition and regularly condemned the increased spending on armaments both in the press and from the platform. Such calls were at the heart of their tactics to avoid war. However, in Parliament their calls were not always so consistent, with the Labour MPs for areas like Barrow-in-Furness and Greenwich where armaments firms were the largest employers regularly voting with the government for increased expenditure – though it was not simply just a case of ensuring jobs, as is discussed below. Nevertheless, the majority argued that increased armaments would not decrease the threat of war; they would only serve to escalate the tension. Many leading Labour figures, Keir Hardie especially, were also of the belief that the only way to secure peace was through collective working-class direct action. It is for this reason that they advocated the general strike if war should break out.[76] Despite the different tactics outlined for achieving peace, though, many in Labour and the ILP also shared a number of assumptions in response to the tension of the period with Hyndman, Blatchford and their supporters.

Leading ILP figure Bruce Glasier had written in 1906 that 'patriotism ... has been an essential element in civilisation' and thus was an essential element in socialism.[77] He elaborated on this in 1910: 'internationalism does not involve the extinction of nations, but the brotherhood of nations'.[78] In that sense, nationalism was the necessary condition and prerequisite for the true internationalism that could bring about the social revolution. One earlier contributor to the *Labour Leader* put this in rather different terms: 'my people, of dear, dear England. We Socialists have the right to love England, because we do not love England narrowly and alone ... the capitalist has no Fatherland'.[79] Like Hyndman and Blatchford, the anti-war socialists of Labour and the ILP also laid claim to be patriots. Indeed, they claimed that only socialists could be true patriots, insisting that capitalism had no country. It was a natural step, therefore, to a shared assumption in the importance and legitimacy of national defence.

In 1910, the *Labour Leader* declared that 'no sane politician would dream of opposing expenditure necessary for national defence', while Ramsay MacDonald told Parliament in 1911 that Labour 'stood for adequate national security'.[80] In the face of attacks from Hyndman, who alleged that the ILP advocated 'national surrender', Hardie responded by claiming that 'I know no-one who suggests national surrender' and so accepted the 'imperative necessity for National Defence'.[81] Their reasoning behind this was also shared with Hyndman and Blatchford. Britain enjoyed greater political liberty, and a freer and more effective democracy (however illusory this actually was), which was worth defending. Labour's opposition to armaments and their calls for peace were conditional, while they drew a distinction between opposing increased armaments spending and the defence of the nation. They may have maintained that the nation's defences were currently adequate, unlike Hyndman and Blatchford, but this was not peace at any price. If British liberty was threatened then she must be defended. Many, then, were willing to adopt a variety of measures to ensure national defence. Thus in 1904, before tensions were heightened, an article on conscription in the *Labour Leader* concluded that 'were conscription necessary for the safety of home defence there would be no objection to its adoption.'[82] The Labour MP, G. H. Roberts, who opposed increased spending (but later served in Lloyd George's coalition government during the war), explained to his fellow MPs in 1910 that Labour not was opposed to an efficient navy and were actually agreed that the navy must be strong enough to defend Britain: 'we look upon the Navy as a force of national insurance, and the real difference between us is that we on these benches say that every pound spent ... beyond what is actually necessary is a waste of national resources.'[83]

In part, it was this adherence to the necessity of national defence that prompted a number of Labour MPs to vote for increased armaments expenditure. Douglas Newton has shown how regularly they did this: in 1906 seven voted with the government; in 1907 three refused to support a reduction motion; in March 1909 two supported the government; in July 1909 this increased to five; in March 1910 eight voted with the government; and in March 1911 six voted against a motion to reduce the size of the navy.[84] Thus by 1913 Philip Snowden noted that the party had ceased to offer 'determined and united opposition to naval expenditure.'[85] One Labour MP, J. A. Seddon, explained his decision to support further spending in the *Labour Leader* in 1910, which also illustrates the feelings of many Labour supporters and their apparent lack of enthusiasm for the reduction of arms: 'our difficulty is patent to every labour candidate. Declaim against war and the crowd will cheer. Place reduction of armaments in your election address, the same crowd will reject you. Give them a rude shock ... estimates that will stagger humanity. If this fails, I see nothing but a bloody Armageddon.'[86]

As tensions continued to grow and war looked ever more probable, the threat posed to Britain's defence seemed more real and many of the most ardent anti-militarists from Labour modified their tone, sounding increasingly like Hyndman and Blatchford in the process. Philip Snowden, who had most forcefully put forward the argument that war only served the interests of armaments firms and their shareholders, perhaps illustrated this best.[87] Though insisting that in socialism 'you have a stronger safeguard of peace than in all your battleships and all your armed camps', he conceded that 'much as we who sit on these benches oppose war, I am sure we would not hesitate for a moment to vote any sum, however large, if we were convinced that it was absolutely necessary for the defence of our own shore'. In response to such statements Blatchford observed that 'the Labour Party seem to have fallen between two schools. They object to expenditure on the Navy and the Army; but they have never spoken out boldly for the abolition of the Navy and the Army.'[88]

Labour's response, especially the majority who believed in the necessity of national defence, showed that, in the words of Paul Bridgen, 'at a time of perceived national strife, it was becoming clear that many believed

Labour's place should be at the side of the government.'[89] Or, at least, it should be at the side of the *British* working class. Thus Keir Hardie, though despondent at the seemingly widespread war enthusiasm, wrote just after war had broken out that 'a nation at war must be united especially when its existence is at stake. With the boom of the enemy's guns within earshot, the lads who have gone forth to fight their country's battles must not be disheartened by any discordant notes at home.'[90] Such considerations conditioned Labour's response once war had broken out and, most importantly, Britain's interests and perceived freedoms were directly threatened. A party that more or less supported military action for national defence was going to support the war effort with only limited dissension. Indeed, across Europe socialists supported their nations' war efforts, citing self-defence – France had been invaded, Germany and Austria-Hungary stressed the Russian threat – and justifying their response in light of the Second International's repeated affirmation of the right of nations to self-defence. As John Horne has concluded in his study of the French and British labour movements during the war, 'nation and labour, nation and working class, were perceived in the light of the international crisis to be intimately connected', with labour leaders 'rallying in an emergency to what they accepted as the national cause'.[91]

Same ends, different means

Not only does the support for the war in 1914 indicate that Labour, and to a lesser extent the ILP, were not anti-war, but so does their acceptance of the need for national defence and military means sufficient to ensure that. Moreover, their reasoning for this was clearly similar to those they perceived to be, or at least publicly condemned as, warmongers. They also shared the assumption that the growing tension needed to be brought to the public's attention and needed further discussion in socialist circles. In their calls for peace, fewer armaments and reduced spending, and in denouncing militarism they were not pointing to a German threat like Hyndman and Blatchford – they did not believe one existed – but were hoping to bring these issues to the forefront of people's minds. They fervently believed that it was through the workers and direct action that war could be avoided, rather than military capability or statesmen's negotiations. A marker of this shared goal, at least with Hyndman and Hardie, can be seen in their co-operation in making repeated calls for meetings of the International Socialist Bureau to consider a joint socialist response to the growing tension. No meetings were held due to German opposition, who saw no cause for concern. August Bebel commenting that 'it is our impression that people in England are rather nervous and see the situation as more serious than it is'.[92] Of course, such a response only heightened Hyndman's anxieties. Nevertheless, Hyndman chaired a meeting organised by the ILP to welcome an official delegation of German socialists, stating that though he may 'appear to the audience to be a kind of Nemesis. He desired … to assert … that he stood to-day, as he had always stood, for peace and fraternity among the workers of all nations.'[93]

In the context of domestic rivalry, competing ideas and individual competition it is unsurprising that British socialists made much of the different responses to the growing tension that emanated from the various elements of the domestic (and international) movement. Yet, there were a couple of key differences in their responses. First, there was clear division over how great a threat Germany posed or whether she posed a threat at all. As such, this was not a debate about whether Britain's shores should be defended, but whether they needed defending at this particular juncture. The second major difference centred on tactics and what was seen as the best way to maintain peace. For Hyndman and Blatchford, calling attention to the tensions and preparing for their escalation was the best course of action. For many in Labour and the ILP this would only hasten war and thus they preached peace, while campaigning for direct action in the form of a general strike in the event of war. Nevertheless, co-operation and joint campaigns were undertaken, especially as the threat of war loomed ever greater. Thus on 21 July 1914, just under two weeks before war broke out, 'at a meeting of the British Committee of the International Bureau, representatives of all sections of the British movement, a manifesto was adopted (drafted by Mr Hyndman) declaring resolutely for peace, urging the British government to remain neutral in the event of war.'[94] Famously, on 2 August, most sections of the movement would come together in one last demonstration against war in Trafalgar Square, with the likes of Hyndman and Hardie speaking from the same platform and newspapers publishing their message across the country.[95] Such co-operation indicated that the shared assumptions discussed were recognised as well as their differences.

Historians have invariably taken the differences as their starting point, while the similarities have been played down or missed. Yet, their shared assumptions were at the heart of their responses to the growing tension and conditioned their contrasting views of the situation. Ultimately, the vast majority of British socialists, including Hyndman and Blatchford, were calling for peace. Indeed, they saw peace as a prerequisite of socialism and was the only circumstances in which it could be truly achieved. They shared a number of further assumptions in their calls for peace: that internationalism did not preclude their nationalism, radical patriotism and positive appraisal of the British system; that national defence and the safeguarding of British liberties was necessary in the face of outside threat; and that it was necessary for socialists to warn their fellow countrymen of the present and real dangers. To be sure, real differences existed, and domestic groups often responded negatively to one another. Yet too much has been made of these differences, while Hyndman and Blatchford had too readily been presented in overly simplistic and misrepresentative ways. The shared assumptions of these different groups are illustrative not only of their wider beliefs, but also helps us explain the so-called collapse of European socialism in 1914, when socialists across Europe declared this a war of national defence or in support of other nations' defence. We should view the response of British socialists to the threat of war, then, as a case of shared goals, but differing tactics to achieve them. Ultimately, for virtually all in the movement peace was the primary aim, but they were not willing to see its preservation at any costs, especially at the expense of national defence.

Notes

1 The Second International was a supra-national collective of disparate national socialist groups and parties formed around the end of the 1880s and beginning of the 1890s. Reflecting the different national traditions, theoretical backgrounds and challenging personalities they often struggled to reach agreement on key issues. For recent examinations of the International's response see Kevin J. Callahan, 'The International Socialist Peace Movement on the Eve of World War 1 Revisited: the Campaign of "War Against War!" and the Basle International Socialist Congress in 1912', *Peace & Change*, 29:2 (2004), pp. 147–76; Marc Mulholland, '"Marxists of strict observance"? The Second International, National Defence, and the Question of War', *The Historical Journal*, 58:2 (2015), 615–40.
2 For that pacifist tradition see Martin Ceadel, *Pacifism in Britain, 1914–1945: The Defining of a Faith* (Oxford, 1980).
3 The SDP was the latest iteration of the Social Democratic Federation formed in the 1880s, changing to the SDP in 1906. It would join with other socialist groups in 1911 to form the British Socialist Party (BSP). For this history, see Martin Crick, *The History of the Social Democratic Federation* (Keele, 1994). Throughout this chapter I will use SDP, except when referring directly to the BSP, for consistency. The *Clarion* newspaper was founded in 1891 by Blatchford and A.M. Thompson, from which a number of associated clubs and societies would grow.
4 Stefan Berger, *The British Labour Party and the German Social Democrats, 1900–1931* (Oxford, 1994), p. 20.
5 Walter Kendall, *The Revolutionary Movement in Britain 1900–21* (London, 1969), p. 51.
6 John Callaghan, *Socialism in Britain* (Oxford, 1990), p. 73; Geoffrey Foote, *The Labour Party's Political Thought* (Basingstoke, 3rd edn, 1997), p. 23.
7 Paul Ward, *Red Flag and Union Jack: Englishness, Patriotism and the British Left, 1881–1924* (Woodbridge, 1998), p. 53.
8 R. Vickers, *The Labour Party and the World, I: the Evolution of Labour's Foreign Policy, 1900–51* (Manchester, 2003), 40; Ruth Kinna, 'William Morris and

the Problem of Englishness', *European Journal of Political Theory*, 5:1 (2006), 85–99, 97.
9 For example, see Berger, *Labour*, p. 213; A. J. Davies, *To Build a New Jerusalem: The British Labour Party from Keir Hardie to Tony Blair* (London, 1996), p. 63; Paul Ward, 'Socialists and "True" Patriotism in Britain in the late 19th and early 20th centuries', *National Identities*, 1:2 (1999), 179–94, 188.
10 Raymond Challinor, *The Origins of British Bolshevism* (London, 1977), p. 14.
11 Davies, *Build a New Jerusalem*, p. 63; Neil Redfern, *Class or Nation: Communists, Imperialism and Two World Wars* (London, 2005), p. 17.
12 For example, see Robert Dowse, *Left in the Centre: The Independent Labour Party 1893–1940* (London, 1966); Alastair J. Reid and Henry Pelling, *A Short History of the Labour Party* (Basingstoke, 11th edn, 1997), pp. 26–7.
13 For example see Kenneth Morgan, *Keir Hardie: Radical and Socialist* (London, 1975); David Marquand, *Ramsay MacDonald* (London, 1977).
14 Vickers, *Labour*, p. 57.
15 A. J. A. Morris, 'Labour and Foreign Affairs: a Search for Identity and Policy', in K. D. Brown (ed.), *The First Labour Party 1906–14* (London, 1985), pp. 268–91, 270–1; Berger, *Labour*, p. 213.
16 Morris, 'Labour', pp. 270–1.
17 London School of Economics Archives (hereafter LSE), ILP/4/1906/135, T. D. Benson to Keir Hardie, 12 March 1906.
18 Paul Bridgen, *The Labour Party and the Politics of War and Peace 1900–1924* (Woodbridge, 2009); John Callaghan, *The Labour Party and Foreign Policy* (Abingdon, 2007); Edward McNeilly, 'Labour and the Politics of Internationalism, 1906–1914', *Twentieth Century British History*, 20:4 (2009), 431–53; Vickers, *Labour*.
19 Bridgen, *Labour*, pp. 15–16.
20 Marcus Morris, 'From Anti-colonialism to Anti-imperialism: The Evolution of H. M. Hyndman's Critique of Empire, c.1875–1905', *Historical Research*, 87:236 (2014), 293–314; Graham Johnson, *Social Democratic Politics in Britain, 1881–1911* (Lampeter, 2002).
21 The most important examples that do are Ward, *Red* and Douglas Newton, *British Labour, European Socialism and the Struggle for Peace 1889–1914* (Oxford, 1985), which takes the traditional view.
22 *Justice*, 12 November 1904.
23 *Justice*, 3 March 1906.
24 *Manchester Guardian*, 26 August 1908.
25 *Scotsman*, 8 January 1913.
26 Letter from Hyndman to Kautsky, 11 May 1991 reprinted in Rosalind Travers Hyndman, *Last Years of H. M. Hyndman* (London, 1923), pp. 297–8.
27 British Library, Additional MS 55242 f.226. Hyndman to Sir Frederic Macmillan, 3 November 1912.
28 *Justice*, 22 January 1910.
29 Johnson, *Social*, p. 134.
30 *Justice*, 22 August 1908.
31 *Justice*, 8 August 1908.
32 West Sussex Archive (hereafter WSE), MS 458 f.748, Maxse Papers, Hyndman to Leo Maxse, 7 September 1908.

33 Newton, *British*, p. 209.
34 *Justice*, 22 August 1908.
35 H. M. Hyndman, *Further Reminiscences* (London, 1912), p. 401.
36 *Justice*, 2 and 9 February 1907.
37 *Labour Leader*, 21 June 1907.
38 *Labour Leader*, 22 July 1904.
39 *Daily Mail*, 31 August 1908.
40 Morris, 'Labour', pp. 270–1.
41 H. M. Hyndman, *Tariff Reform and Imperialism* (London, 1910), p. 19.
42 *Daily Mail*, 19 August 1908.
43 Hyndman to Kautsky, 11 May 1911 reprinted in R. T. Hyndman, *Last Years*, pp. 297–8.
44 Hyndman, *Further*, pp. 393, 394–5.
45 *Clarion*, 16 April 1909.
46 *Justice*, 22 January 1910.
47 *Social-Democrat*, June 1905.
48 Of course, there was much debate at the International too, see Mulholland, 'Marxists'.
49 *Justice*, 17 May 1913. This was not a propaganda message, but a sincerely held view, which he repeated to his second wife in their correspondence. For example, see LSE, COLL MISC 1192, File 1, Hyndman to Rosalind Travers, 24 January 1914. It can also be seen in their calls for a 'citizen army', see Harry Quelch, *Socialism and the Armed Nation* (London, 1900).
50 Hyndman, *Further*, p. 395.
51 *Manchester Guardian*, 17 April 1911.
52 For a fuller discussion of this see Ward, *Red*.
53 Kevin J. Callahan, '"Preforming Inter-nationalism" in Stuttgart in 1907: French and German Socialist Nationalism and the Political Culture of an International Socialist Congress', *International Review of Social History*, 45:1 (2000), 51–87, 54, 72.
54 WSE, Maxse Papers, MS 483 f.642 Hyndman to Maxse, 1 February 1908.
55 *Justice*, 16 February 1907.
56 *Daily Mail*, 16 December 1909.
57 Robert Blatchford, *The Grim Logic of Facts: An Answer to Upton Sinclair* (London, ?1913), p. 13.
58 *Morning Post*, 6 July 1910.
59 *Justice*, 14 March 1908.
60 *Daily Mail*, 31 August 1908.
61 *Manchester Guardian*, 26 August 1908.
62 *Daily Mail*, 19 August 1908.
63 *Justice*, 8 August 1908.
64 *Justice*, 14 September 1907.
65 *Justice*, 22 April 1911.
66 *Manchester Guardian*, 28 April 1911.
67 *Justice*, 13 August 1910.
68 *Social-Democrat*, November 1908.
69 *Labour Leader*, 14 August 1908.
70 *Labour Leader*, 21 August 1908.

71 *Labour Leader*, 14 August 1908.
72 LSE, ILP/4/1910/476. Hardie to Hyndman, 30 September 1910.
73 Sydney Jones Library, Liverpool University, Glasier Papers, GP/1/1/1134, Bruce Glasier to Katharine Glasier, 30 August 1910.
74 *Labour Leader*, 3 February 1910.
75 *Labour Leader*, 2 April 1909.
76 For more on those calls Marcus Morris, 'The General Strike as a Weapon of Peace: British Socialists, the Labour Movement and Debating the Means to Avoid War Before 1914', *Labour History Review*, forthcoming.
77 *Labour Leader*, 26 October 1906.
78 *Labour Leader*, 10 October 1910.
79 *Labour Leader*, 20 February 1897.
80 Ward, *Red*, pp. 104–5.
81 LSE, ILP/4/1910/476Hardie to Hyndman, 30 September 1910; LSE, ILP/4/1910/477, Hyndman to Hardie, 1 October 1910.
82 *Labour Leader*, 3 June 1904.
83 Newton, *British*, p. 238.
84 Newton, *British*.
85 Howard Weinroth, 'Left-wing opposition to naval armaments in Britain before 1914', *Journal of Contemporary History*, 6:4 (1971), 93–116, 116.
86 Newton, *British*, p. 238.
87 Philip Snowden put this argument forward in many forums, most forcefully in *Dreadnoughts and Dividends: Exposure of the Armaments Ring* (Boston, 1914).
88 Ward, *Red*, pp. 107–8.
89 Bridgen, *Labour*, p. 61.
90 Foote, *Labour*, p. 66.
91 John Horne, *Labour at War: France and Britain 1914–1918* (Oxford, 1991), pp. 42–3.
92 Georges Haupt, *Socialism and the Great War: The Collapse of the Second International* (Oxford, 1972). For more on these calls see Johnson, *Social*, p. 124.
93 *Labour Leader*, 23 October 1908.
94 *Socialist Review*, October–December 1914. They met several times before war broke out on 4 August.
95 *Manchester Guardian*, 3 August 1914.

2

At the crossroads: the Labour Party, the trade unions and the choices of direction for the democratic left

Chris Wrigley

Before the First World War, the British Labour Party was distinctive among European labour movements for its lack of socialist objectives and for its closeness to a party often in office, the Liberal Party. It was also unusual because of the very powerful position within the party of trade unionists. In 1912 trade unionists comprised 98.0 per cent of its affiliated members compared to the 1.6 per cent of the socialist societies.[1] Trade unionism had long been established in Britain before the late nineteenth-century moves which led to the Labour Representation Committee being formed in 1900. In contrast, in Germany the socialists were for a long time the bigger group in the powerful Sozialdemokratische Partei Deutschlands (SPD) until trade union membership caught up at the turn of the twentieth century. In the Second International, formed in 1889, the most moderate delegates were those from the USA, followed by the British, and the most revolutionary were the Bolsheviks. In 1914, it was possible that the British labour movement might move in the same, non-socialist direction as the Americans. By late 1918 it was very clear that British Labour had moved in a democratic socialist direction, more in line with other western European democratic socialists, and was hostile to revolutionary socialism.

This essay reconsiders the role of the trade unions in the major decisions made by the British Labour Party during the war, placing the decisions in the wider contexts of developments in continental labour and socialist politics. In Britain, the Parliamentary Labour Party made the crucial decision to support the war at its outbreak. After that political decision, much, but not all, of the Labour Party's increased political importance and the nature of its politics was due to the great increase in strength of the trade unions. The Labour Party was aided also by the divisions in the Liberal Party and the weakening of that party's organisation.

Supporting the war

The trade union majority of the British Parliamentary Labour Party supported the war on 5 August 1914. This was in spite of Labour holding a demonstration against entering the European war in Trafalgar Square on 2 August. In deeming the situation to have changed, as Britain was at war from 23:00 hours on 4 August, British Labour responded similarly to the Labour movements in other belligerent countries. In Germany, all SPD Reichstag members voted for war credits in the face of probable Tsarist Russian forces invading eastern Prussia, though in its closed group meeting fourteen of ninety-two had opposed this (but had followed party discipline in voting as a bloc). In France, in spite of the assassination of their leader, Jean Juares, on 31 July, French socialists voted war credits, being mindful of the likelihood of a further German invasion (after Prussia's in 1870–71). In Belgium socialists also voted financial support for the government. In Britain opposition to voting war credits in the Parliamentary Labour Party amounted to four MPs, James Ramsay MacDonald, James Keir Hardie, Fred Jowett and Tom Richardson, with a fifth, Philip Snowden, abroad, all of whom were non-trade union ILP members. They believed that the German invasion of Belgium was being used as an excuse for Britain to support France and they maintained the radical tradition of hostility to Tsarist Russia. MacDonald had written a few days earlier, 'Russia in arms with us to free Europe from an autocracy, whether political or military, is a grim joke!'[2] The anti-war proportion of British Labour MPs was similar to the Reichstag's anti-war SPD members (15.2 to 13.5 per cent). The Labour Party joined the other parties in a parliamentary truce for the duration of the war, and it also put its organisation behind the recruiting campaign.

Keir Hardie had been deeply committed to international socialist action against war, championing a general strike against war at Second International conferences in 1910, 1912 and 1914. Earlier he had been a prominent opponent of the Boer War, along with John Morley, John Burns and David Lloyd George. At the outbreak of war in 1914, Morley and Burns resigned from the government but Lloyd George took the violation of Belgian neutrality as sufficient cause to support involvement in this war. The ILP opponents of British entry in to the war predicted great suffering if Britain joined the conflict. Fred Jowett, chairman of the ILP, warned on 3 August, 'It will be the greatest war the world has ever seen, a crime against civilisation, a disaster compared with which the Napoleonic wars were a mere skirmish ... the people, the common men and women of all lands who have no cause to quarrel, they will have pay in millions of lives and in anguish and sorrow.'[3] In similar vein, on the previous day MacDonald observed in private conversation with the newspaper owner, Sir George Riddell, 'In three months there will be bread riots and we [the Labour

Party] shall come in.'[4] However, the great majority of the population supported the war. Although the anti-war ILP MPs took a principled stand, their principles in this situation were out of touch with public opinion, much as the Scottish Labour Party was in 2014–15, with similar results. In the by-election in Merthyr in late 1915, after Keir Hardie's death, a vehemently pro-war independent Labour candidate won. In the 1918 general election, MacDonald, Snowden, Jowett and Richardson all lost, as did the anti-war Liberals.

Arthur Henderson and the trade unionist MPs were more in touch with dominant working-class attitudes to the war. After the Labour Party's first wartime conference in January 1916, one local newspaper noted, 'The patriotic attitude which the Labour leaders in Parliament have adopted reflects a patriotism shared by the vast majority of trade union members. The delegates adopted resolutions which show that those they represent want their country to win.'[5] At the conference James Sexton of the Dock Labourers' Union moved a resolution similar to one that had been successfully moved four months earlier at the Trades Union Congress (TUC), which stated that the conference 'considers the present action of Great Britain and its Government fully justified in the present war, expresses its horror at the atrocities committed by Germany and her ally by the callous and brutal murder of non-combatants, including women and children, and hereby pledges the conference to assist the Government as far as possible in the successful prosecution of the war'. The motion was carried by 1,502,000 to 602,000 votes.[6]

In July and August 1914, the pro-war Labour MPs readily made common cause with French socialists and trade unionists in their war effort. Lloyd George used public funds to foster support for the war among suffragettes and trade unionists, funding groups of munitions workers to go to see conditions British soldiers suffered on the Western Front.[7] John Hodge, who was chairman of the strongly pro-war Socialist National Defence Committee, went to France in August 1915 to speak about British trade unionists' support of the war effort. He spoke at a meeting of invited socialists and trade unionists at the Elysee Palace with Raymond Poincare, the French President, as well as addressing 104 Socialist deputies at the Chamber of Deputies and then speaking at several provincial centres. According to Hodge, he declined to be funded by the government (but asked it to pay for an interpreter), saying that 'to go to France as an emissary of the government would be fatal'. He went three times.[8]

Henderson had been an opponent of the Boer War but he supported this war. His three sons all volunteered for the army in the autumn of 1914, and the eldest, David, was killed in action on the Somme in September 1916. John Hodge was among other Labour MPs to suffer such a loss. Indeed, when Lloyd George spoke to the Labour Party representatives to get support for his government, he rebutted Snowden's question as to whether he was in favour of the slaughter in the war, with the observation, 'Mr Snowden must know that there are men in this room who have sons fighting in the war.'[9]

However, James Winstone, Vice-President of the South Wales Miners' Federation and a Baptist lay preacher who was the Labour candidate who unsuccessfully tried to succeed Keir Hardie in the Merthyr Tydfil constituency in the November 1915 by-election, also had a son at the Western Front. This did not outweigh, in the eyes of Conservatives, Liberals and 'patriotic Labour' people, that he was associated with Ramsay MacDonald and the ILP. Sir Arthur Steel-Maitland, Chairman of the Conservative Party, unsuccessfully pressed Henderson to agree that the electoral truce 'pre-supposed a condition of unanimity in wishing to prosecute the War to a conclusion' but Henderson refuted this and asserted that Labour 'had the right to run anyone they pleased, as had the Liberals and Unionists'.[10] The outcome was that C. B. Stanton, also an ILP member but pro-war, resigned as the local miners' agent and stood successfully as an independent Labour candidate, with the support of Conservatives and Liberals, regardless of the electoral truce.

The Labour Party was also effective in representing working-class concerns on the home front, not least through the War Workers' Emergency Committee. The Labour Party's Executive Committee set up the committee after it had called a meeting on 5 August 1914 of labour, socialist co-operative and women's organisations. Labour's Executive Committee also agreed that day to call on the government 'to maintain the aggregate volume of employment (including the possibility of additional public enterprises), to control the price and distribution of food, and to ensure supplies of milk for those most in need'.[11] As a result of these decisions the bulk of the Labour Party was well positioned to represent much of the working class and many others during and after the war.

The size and extent of trade unionism

During the war 5,670,000 men served in the Armed Forces, a high proportion (perhaps 38 per cent) of the pre-war British male labour force. The remaining labour was put in a powerful position in a wartime labour market that needed all the labour it could get. In these conditions trade unionism flourished, organising fresh occupational and geographic areas. Germany had a higher proportion (55.5 per cent) of its men enlisted, 11.1 million of some 20 million by the end of the war. In Austria-Hungary 7.8 million men joined the armed forces, in France 8.3 million, in Italy 5 million and in Russia (by the time of the October Revolution) 15.3 million.[12] Hence the pressures on the British labour market were common to all the European belligerents.

British trade union membership rose from 4,145,000 in 1914 to 6,533,000 in 1918. In the post-war boom of 1919–20 trade union growth rose further to a pre-1946 peak of 8,348,000 in 1920. The war and the post-war boom carried on the unusually favourable conditions for trade union growth of the pre-war upturn in trade. The considerable growth in trade union membership in a reduced civilian labour force was reflected in the higher trade union density (proportion of union membership among all those legally able to join a trade union). The density rose from 14.6 per cent in 1910 to 23.0 per cent in 1914 and 48.2 per cent in 1920 (a density not surpassed until 1970). While trade union membership and trade union density fell with the severe economic recessions of 1921–22 and 1931–33, trade union membership did not fall to the pre-war high of 1914 even in 1933.

The extended boom of most of 1910–20 saw trade unionism increase among women. The numbers of women employed in war work and other work such as teachers and accountants, rose from 3,277,000 to 4,940,000 between 1914 and 1918, rising from 24 to 37 per cent of the workforce. By April 1915, 63 per cent of women workers in engineering and 55 per cent in leather and leather goods were already working overtime.[13] It was claimed in the Ministry of Munitions that regulations issued regarding women's pay (Circulars L2 and L3) were 'the first examples in British history of the prescription by the government of national standards of wages and conditions of employment for women'. They prescribed the minima below which no employer could go. Apparently, women described the regulations as 'Magna Charta of women's labour'.[14] UK female trade union membership rose from 437,000 (a density of 8.0 per cent) in 1914 to 1,209,000 in 1918 (a density of 21.7 per cent) and to a pre-1940 high of 1,342,000 in 1920 (a density of 23.9 per cent).[15]

Trade unionism in these years grew in hitherto lightly unionised areas. Between 1911 and 1921, trade union density in the electricity industry rose from 2.2 to 33.4 per cent. In agriculture, horticulture and forestry the rise was from 0.7 to 23.5 per cent. There were substantial rises in union density in other previously relatively poorly unionised sectors: paper and board (5.8 to 50.2 per cent); insurance, banking and finance (6.7 to 22.4 per cent); chemicals (9.6 to 23.6 per cent); entertainment (12.2 to 50.2 per cent); timber and furniture (13.2 to 28.2 per cent); bricks and building materials (14.7 to 47.0 per cent); pottery (14.7 to 50.1 per cent) and gas (20.2 to 56.4 per cent).[16]

French trade unionism, which was much smaller than British, followed a similar pattern. In France the estimated total of 283,000 trade union members of 1913 rose to 499,000 in 1918 and a peak of 1,264,000 in 1921. The post-war growth in trade union membership was greatly assisted by groups, notably government employees, who had hitherto been excluded from trade unions under the law of 21 March 1884.[17] In France some

35–40 per cent of the paid labour force was female before the war, a greater proportion than in Britain (about 24 per cent). The French proportion of women workers increased by up to 25 per cent by early 1918, but after the war the proportion of women fell back, partly due to trade union hostility.[18] In the Netherlands, which was neutral but was greatly affected by the war, trade union density rose from 17.5 per cent at the outset to 20.1 per cent in 1915, to 26.3 per cent in 1917 and to a peak of 40.6 per cent in 1919, similar to the British and French patterns.

In Germany, in contrast to Britain and France, trade union membership dropped heavily in the war, falling from 2,436,300 in 1914 to 1,198,800 in 1916, but it recovered rapidly in the politically more favourable conditions at the end of the war, reaching 9,192,900 in 1920 (a density at 45.2 per cent). There was rapid expansion in previously lightly unionised areas. As well as the public sector areas in which trade union membership had been illegal before the war, such as the railways, there was rapid trade union growth after the war in sectors where employer hostility was less effective than hitherto, notably in coal mining in the Ruhr and elsewhere, agriculture and white-collar work. In the case of agriculture the Deutscher Landarbeiterverband grew from 16,349 members in late 1918 to 624,935 members a year later.[19] In 1913, women comprised 8.8 per cent of German trade unionists. The Auxiliary Service Law of December 1916 required men to undertake war work. Women took large numbers of jobs in previously male spheres, such as engineering, metalworking, the electrical and chemical industries. The numbers of women joining trade unions, especially textile workers, rose rapidly at the end of the war. However, as in Britain the removal of women who were substitute labour from factory employment was quick in 1919, demobilisation decrees speeding them out.

Austrian trade unionism broadly followed the German pattern. Membership fell from 263,400 in 1914 to 180,700 in 1916, but rose to 329,700 in 1917 and peaked at 1,198,700 (a remarkable density of 59.0 per cent) in 1921. In Vienna in the final two years of the war, many women joined trade unions. In metalworking, the female percentage of the labour force rose from 18.5 per cent in 1913 to 26.6 per cent in 1915 and to 36.2 per cent in 1917. In Austria about 1 million women entered the paid labour force during the war, up some 40 per cent.[20]

The trials of war enhanced the role of trade unions in the economy and society of Britain and other belligerents, with trade unionism embracing groups hitherto rarely touched by trade unionism. Labour movements in Western Europe and North America emerged from the war and the post-war boom much stronger for a while, before economic recession undercut their positions. The eagerness of trade unions, especially of the skilled, to hasten women out of their wartime work did little to encourage feelings of solidarity among women.

Trade unionists, politics and the state

With the wartime labour shortages and the vital need for munitions, coal, food and much else the British government took pains to consult the trade union leaders over industrial changes, manpower and other policies. This was notably so from the Shell Conference, 21 December 1914.[21] When Lloyd George stated British war aims on 5 January 1918 he did so to a conference of trade unionists (not to the TUC, as is often claimed). Parliament was not in session then, but the prime minister was eager to appeal to labour at a time of growing war weariness and a need for tougher manpower measures.[22]

With the state taking control of increasingly large sectors of the economy, the government sought national bargaining on wages and conditions rather than have to make very time-consuming factory-level or local agreements. There were national wage agreements not only for industries, such as engineering and coal, but also for the first time, in 1917, in gas supply and, in 1918, in flour milling, chemicals, soap and tramways.[23] State recognition of unions for national collective bargaining was often followed by the successful negotiation of war bonuses, further boosting trade unionism in industries, such as hosiery in the Midlands and jute in Dundee. Many weakly organised industries set up joint councils to discuss all kinds of workplace problems as well as for bargaining. A few were private initiatives, as in pottery, but many stemmed from government initiatives.[24] Increased union power and national pay awards caused employers to be more willing to be represented in a national body, with the Federation of British Industries being formed in 1916.[25] The government was very happy to deal with employers organised in such a body as a balance to the more powerful trade unions. The state governing in association with the trade unions and employers has given rise to views of there being 'corporate bias'.[26] Such views have some credibility for the war and for the post-war boom, but do not fit the situation after 1921 as trade unionism weakened and various joint councils of employers and unions collapsed.

During the post-war boom employers and the state in Western European and North American countries were able to meet some of the expectations of higher wages, shorter working hours, and better housing and welfare. However, the state disengaged as quickly as it could from industrial relations, other than when strikes were believed to being used for political ends, as over the campaign for the nationalisation of the coal mines in Britain in 1918–20. In France the authorities were concerned about radical trade unionism and radical politics in the Saint-Denis area of Paris, which was notable for its large number of metalworkers. Mayor Philippe, when calling for the setting up of a workers' council, spoke of a 'new Commune'.[27] The war and post-war boom years often united disparate groups of workers: skilled, unskilled, women and white collar. When the war emergency had ended, popular wrath against war profiteers had abated and economic hard times had returned, such unity weakened and the groups divided. Governments in Britain and continental Europe assisted such divisions, often by playing consumers against producers. Trade unions also played a part in such divisions, by prioritising skilled against the unskilled, the older against the younger (notably when redundancies were occurring) and male workers against female workers.

In Britain trade unionists' enhanced status in the economy was accompanied by greater recognition in politics. After the resignation of Ramsay MacDonald as chairman of the Parliamentary Labour Party soon after the outbreak of war, the post went to Arthur Henderson, a leading trade unionist who had held the post in 1908–10. He became the Labour Party's first Cabinet Minister in 1915 in H. H. Asquith's wartime coalition government. Henderson's Lib–Lab background, their shared admiration for Gladstone and Asquith's role in bringing forward labour measures when home secretary in 1892–95, made it easy for Henderson and represented a continuation of pre-1914 Labour Party politics.[28] However, Asquith's empathy with trade unionists was limited. In the early part of the war Asquith continued to be more concerned about John Redmond and the Irish Nationalists, who declined to join his coalition government, than about Labour. Asquith's relations with Henderson were good, but there remained an element of upper middle-class patronising attitudes in his relations with the Labour members of his administration. Such attitudes were not exclusive to Asquith. Christopher Addison, then a junior minister, wrote that Edwin Montagu, the Minister of Munitions, 'had heard yesterday that Henderson was putting up his demands still further and demanding to be a fully fledged labour Minister. Henderson is a good fellow in many ways; but he is not clear-headed and not very courageous sometimes in difficult positions. I am afraid he is not at all conscious of his limitations …'[29] A similarly patronising outlook was displayed in his diary by Maurice Hankey, Secretary of the War Cabinet, when Lloyd George included Henderson in that body: 'Henderson is an untried man, and it is scarcely possible that his education can have fitted him for the job.'[30] Lloyd George, when discussing the miners' pay claim of 1912, told his friend Riddell that Asquith 'regarded the working-classes as a separate race from the intellectuals.'[31]

Although Henderson held the post of President of the Board of Education, then Paymaster-General, under Asquith – and was a member of the War Cabinet under Lloyd George, 1916–17 – his role in government was very much to facilitate good industrial relations as the government pressed ahead with major changes in working practices and with widening enlistment to the armed forces. Henderson specified such a role of overseeing labour matters if he joined the Asquith's coalition government. Steel-Maitland advised Bonar Law, the Conservative leader, in advance of Bonar

Law meeting Henderson that Henderson 'says unless Labour is mobilised properly, an adequate supply of munitions cannot be made … His further attitude is that it is no use his joining the government (and it might create more trouble than advantage) unless he were in a position to help directly in this mobilisation.'[32] Henderson pressed hard in early August 1916 to be relieved of departmental responsibilities and to act on labour matters as minister without portfolio.[33] Henderson also pressed as a member of the small War Cabinet to be given his particular areas of interest, pointing out that Lord Curzon had been accommodated with India and the Foreign Office. He listed:

1. Man Power in the wide sense, i.e. including National Service, the Ministry of Labour and the Labour Departments of the Ministry of Munitions and Admiralty.
2. Reconstruction, so far as Labour is concerned, i.e. Demobilisation, Redemption of Pledges and Industrial Reorganisation.
3. Miscellaneous problems of Civil Administration as they arise, e.g. Liquor Control and Pensions, which specially affect the working classes.[34]

Henderson did oversee some of these areas, notably those involved in labour disputes. However, twenty-three years later, Ernest Bevin took on a wider range of such tasks under Churchill.

Henderson's support for the war effort led to him visiting Russia to encourage Kerensky to keep that country fighting. Although smeared by parts of the British press as 'hob-nobbing with the Bolsheviks', he publicly denounced them months before the Bolshevik revolution of October 1917. The Bolsheviks dubbed him an arch 'social traitor' and the 'British Kerensky'.[35] The Labour Party's leaders, most trade union leaders and a large majority of the Labour Party's members had not been attracted to revolutionary socialism in the past and were not to be when the Communist Party of Great Britain was formed in 1920. So the war years confirmed the commitment to democratic socialism and were not marked by a turning point in attitudes to revolutionary socialism. After the war, Henderson and MacDonald became leading figures of the revived Second International and were committed anti-Bolsheviks. At the French Socialist Congress held in Strasbourg at Easter 1919, Henderson said, 'A revolution that does not increase the sum of human freedom and strengthen its foundations is not a socialist revolution, whatever it may be called.'[36]

Lloyd George, for all his experience in handling organised labour, made the mistake of thinking Henderson could easily be substituted with another trade union Labour MP. After Henderson was forced out in August 1917 over his support for British representation at a proposed socialist conference in Stockholm, Lloyd George secured George Barnes, who was both another trade unionist and a former chairman of the Labour Party (1910–11), to take Henderson's place. Lloyd George may have been over confident of Labour Party support, especially after the Merthyr Tydfil by-election. According to Sidney Webb, at a meeting on 13 August 1917 several trade union leaders and MPs were furious at Henderson's treatment and spoke of 'anyone taking Henderson's place would be a blackleg'.[37] The Labour Party did continue to support Lloyd George's coalition government, but the ousting of Henderson proved to be a further stage in Labour's development as a truly independent party.

Henderson out of the government devoted his considerable organisational abilities to reorganising the Labour Party so that it would be independent and could not be treated in such a way again. Fred Jowett recalled seeing Henderson immediately after his ousting from the government: 'His arm lay along the table, his head hung dispiritedly, he seemed broken by the blow.'[38] Henderson soon recovered. W. Ormsby-Gore, a Conservative MP, wrote to Lord Milner about the House of Commons in the autumn of 1917:

> Arthur Henderson has not put in an appearance in the House and he and J. H. Thomas etc. seem very busy in laying the foundations of a new Labour Party organisation in the country, and leave Parliament alone. Sooner or later they will have to reckon with Ramsay MacDonald, but at present there seems no sign of either conflict or absorption.[39]

By not breaking with Ramsay MacDonald and his fellow anti-war ILP colleagues in August 1914 or later, Henderson and the majority helped avoid a substantial division on the left of the Labour Party such as occurred in Germany between the SPD and Independent Social Democratic Party and, at the end of 1918 with the Communist Party of Germany.

The trade unions' growing political strength was partly due also to their enhanced financial strength. With greatly increased membership, and with very few, if any, unemployed members and no official strikes from 1915 (as they were illegal under the Munitions Acts), union funds grew. Extra wealth strengthened trade unions' organisation generally, and in many constituencies Labour Party organisation depended on the presence of trade unions. Their political funds rose from £37,000 in 1913 to £43,000 in 1917, £133,000 in 1918 and £185,000 in 1920. In some areas a major trade union dominated the parliamentary constituencies. In the case of the Durham Miners' Association, it provided major assistance in Barnard Castle, Blaydon, Durham, Houghton-le-Spring, Sedgefield and Spennymoor in the form of 76 sub-agents, 107 polling agents and 162 clerks. Overall, the trade unions directly sponsored 163 of Labour's 363 candidates in the 1918 general election.[40]

The needs of war also strengthened the Labour movement at the local level. Trades councils found that municipal and other bodies sought trade union representation on committees assisting the war effort, ranging from relieving distress to hearing appeals made by conscientious objectors. After the war, many local councils continued to seek trade union representatives on committees such as those running allotments and also sought the opinions of trades councils on various social and industrial questions. Trades councils and local Labour parties were involved in issues of housing and food.[41] Lloyd George's concern for the big private traders and steady neglect of co-operators during the war accelerated the Co-op Movement changing from being predominantly Liberal (but with some notable exceptions) to Labour, and the formation of the Co-operative Party in 1917.[42]

Internal friction

State intervention, the pressures of long working hours, wartime inflation and food shortages, the presence of substitute labour, concerns about war profiteering, all contributed to tensions at work, and not only between the workforce and management. There was substantial tension between workers in war work such as engineering and their trade union leaders who were helping the government to implement changes under the Treasury Agreement of March 1915 and the statutory version, the Munitions of War Act 1915. Skilled male workers felt their craft privileges were being undermined by the relaxation of working practices and by the influx of female and unskilled male labour.

However, while there was serious unrest in engineering centres in 1915, 1917 and 1918 and there were revolts by shop stewards against trade union leaders, this can be overstated. Willie Gallagher's 1936 reminiscences, *Revolt on the Clyde,* gave a lively account of unrest there, making the militants' activities almost a precursor of the Communist Party's minority movement campaign of the 1920s. His account was later reinforced by scholarly work by Branco Pribicevic and James Hinton. However, Alastair Reid, writing on shipbuilding, has argued that 'the importance of dilution and independent shop floor organisation has been exaggerated, even in the case of engineering'.[43] Yet, across Europe, the engineering and metalworking trades in wartime were centres of worker militancy, be it in Petrograd, Berlin, Milan, Turin or the industrial suburbs of Paris. In Britain, militant engineers were prominent in the leadership of the British Communist Party in 1920, but that party did not attract sufficient support to represent a major break from the democratic socialism of the post-war Labour Party and the great majority of the TUC.

Many of the social causes of social unrest in Britain were identified by the Commissions on Industrial Unrest set up after widespread engineering strikes in May 1917. George Barnes, when summarising the reports issued in July 1917, observed, 'Revolutionary feelings ... are not entertained by the bulk of the men, the majority of whom ... are sensible of the national difficulties.' The reports identified food prices and food distribution, bad housing and sanitation in many industrial areas, industrial fatigue, broken government promises, loss of confidence in trade union officials and the incidence of conscription as being among the causes of discontent. The proposed remedies included that Labour 'should take part in the affairs of the community as partners, rather than as servants.[44] E. S. Cartwright, a leading figure in the tutorial classes movement, an Anglican off-shoot of the Workers' Education Association, attempted to calm alarmist fears in Oxford. He commented to the Master of Baliol:

> It is true that there is a very small body of doctrinaire revolutionaries – many of them middle class people – but they are not characteristic of the English Labour Movement as a whole, and, generally speaking only find a field for their activities in those districts where special circumstances offer it – for example, in South Wales in particular: and anyone who wants to understand why revolutionary doctrines find a more ready hearing there than elsewhere has only got to read the Report of the Industrial Commission on that District to see that social conditions – housing, sanitation and such-like – have much to do with it. The annual Trade Union Congress is the truly representative English Labour body, and for anyone to call this very practical common-sense body revolutionary is to distort the facts.[45]

By 1917 there was growing disillusionment in Britain with the war, as there was in the other belligerent European countries. Shortages of food and fuel, queues and rationing became widespread across Europe. Groups calling for a compromise peace gained support.[46] The 1917 Russian October Revolution in particular gave great encouragement to the minority in Britain who favoured substantial political change.

While the divisions in British trade unionism on the left were marked but did not become as serious in continental Europe, there were also divisions on the right, which for the duration of the war threatened to be more serious. 'Patriotic Labour' in the form of the British Workers' League (BWL) was sponsored by the Conservatives as a stick with which to beat the ILP and any other Labour figures deemed anti-war or inadequately patriotic. The BWL secured more Labour MPs than the anti-war ILP group of Labour MPs. The 'Patriotic Labour' MPs who were members of the BWL, or very closely associated with it, included Abraham, Barnes, Crooks, Duncan, Hancock, Hodge, O'Grady, Roberts, Toothill, Walsh, Wadsworth, Wilkie and Wardle as well as the independent Labour MP, Stanton, while Tillett had spoken on behalf of its predecessor, the Socialist National Defence League, and Havelock Wilson was closely associated with the League. However, as John Stubbs has commented, this group of

Labour MPs were 'well to the right of the main stream of political thought in the labour world'.[47]

The problem for these right-wing Labour MPs came when the BWL began to seek parliamentary seats. The Miners' Federation of Great Britain complained to the Labour Party's National Executive Committee in December 1917. Henderson responded by writing to all involved asking for their 'observations on their [BWL] election policy as stated in their public announcements'. The matter was debated at the January 1918 party conference. Herbert Smith said, 'In Yorkshire the miners had selected a Labour candidate, and then the BWL had the audacity to put down in opposition one of the Miners' own men.' Robert Smillie commented that 'three of the Vice-Presidents of the League were Miners' Members of Parliament, and the League was using the influence of those three names in mining districts to throw discredit among the rank and file.' He went on to say that the conference should make it clear that 'men could not be ... in the Labour Party and run under its auspices and at the same time be members of a blackleg organisation'.[48]

A further problem for the Labour MPs linked to the BWL was that it became ever more apparent that the League was a creature of the Conservative Party. Neville Chamberlain, faced with pressure to have BWL candidates put forward in his West Midlands area, urged that a leading Conservative leader should publicly approve the BWL programme, adding that otherwise 'how are we to persuade the rank and file of our party to accept their candidates?'[49] Victor Fisher, a former BSP activist and the main organiser of the BWL, responded by saying after consulting J. A. Seddon and J. F. Green, the chairmen of his executive committee, they did not wish at present for such an endorsement by the Conservative leader as it would undercut the Labour MPs. Fisher commented, 'If such an announcement is made the inference will immediately be drawn both by "Abingdon Street" and "Victoria Street" that we have simply gone over – lock, stock and barrel – to your party, and that would, in our judgement, rob us of half our value in the work of National Reconstruction. *Furthermore, we feel that it would close many doors that are open to us in the ranks of organised labour*.'[50] Nevertheless, doors were closing fast. Henderson and the Labour Party were successful in getting John Hodge and most of the 'Patriotic Labour' MPs to leave the BWL (which was renamed the National Democratic and Labour Party ahead of the general election).

Yet in the 1918 general election nine National Democratic and Labour candidates won seats (plus George Barnes who became their leader in the Commons). Twenty-eight had stood, with twenty securing endorsement ('the coupon') from the coalition. Three of these were miners: Matthew Simm, Wallsend, James Walton, Don Valley as well as Stanton for the new Aberdare constituency. Two of these defeated leading ILP figures,

Joseph F. Green beating Ramsay MacDonald in Leicester West and Charles Loseby beating Fred Jowett in Bradford East. A third, Clement Edwards, a former Welsh Liberal MP, beat Arthur Henderson in East Ham South. The others were James Seddon in Hanley, Charles Jesson, an organiser for the Amalgamated Society of Musicians and a London County Council (LCC) councillor, in Walthamstow West and Eldred Hallas, a leading figure in general unions in Birmingham, in Birmingham Duddeston. Hallas quickly became disillusioned with Lloyd George's post-war government and joined the Labour Party in October 1919. He did not stand again in 1922. All the others lost as National Liberals in 1922.[51]

There was another threat to the Labour Party from 'patriotic' trade unionists. This was the attempt in early 1918 to set up a purely Trade Union Party, which it was intended to be under TUC control. The leading figure in this move was J. B. Williams, General Secretary of the Amalgamated Musicians' Union. Williams's union was affiliated to the TUC but not to the Labour Party. His son, Joe, had been killed in action during the war.[52] On the 26 June 1918 at the Labour Party conference, Henderson called the move to set up a new party 'a very sinister design to paralyse the whole Labour Movement by those who had done nothing to assist in building up its political side'. J. H. Thomas said in the same debate, 'The pamphlet that had been issued was signed by fourteen or fifteen trade union leaders, and there were not three of them who were speaking in the name of the union attached to their names. These men and those associated with them were not only doing harm to Labour Movement as a whole, but they were disrupting their own particular organisations.' He added, 'They were the people the press were so anxious to hail as the genuine trade unionists, the backbone of the working classes of the country.'[53] Three days later those pressing for a Trade Union Labour Party held a conference in the Caxton Hall, London, which was attended by some 400 delegates, and passed a motion calling on the TUC to set up a Trade Union Labour Party. At the TUC on 6 September 1918, the motion to set up such a party was defeated by 3,815,000 to 567,000 votes (87 per cent to 13 per cent). The TUC vote ended serious talk of a Trade Union Labour Party.[54]

Henderson was skilful in keeping most of the Labour Party together. He resisted calls to disown MacDonald and the other ILP anti-war MPs throughout the war. Less commented on, he also safeguarded the 'Patriotic Labour' MPs, such as Charles Duncan and John Hodge from being deselected at Barrow-in-Furness and Manchester, Gorton.[55] However, some ministers in the Lloyd George Coalition government declined to leave office when a special Labour Party conference held on 14 November confirmed the Executive Committee's decision to leave the government. Others, notably J. R. Clynes, the Food Controller and to be chair of the

Parliamentary Party in 1921–22, were reluctant to leave. Two months earlier he had sent a ringing endorsement of Lloyd George to be used when Lloyd George received the freedom of Manchester on 12 September.[56] Clynes did resign, as did John Hodge, who was even more reluctant to go and waited for his union to order him out. George Barnes, George Roberts, George Wardle and James Parker stayed in office as Coalition Labour, so breaking with the Labour Party.

Trade union membership shrank after 1914–20, but trade unionism remained a presence in some hitherto weak areas. In the case of female workers, they accounted for 16.1 per cent of UK trade unionists in 1920 and in the adverse conditions of 1933 they accounted for 16.4 per cent, so did not fall back to the 10.5 per cent of 1913. Similarly, white-collar trade unionism did not regress to pre-war levels and by 1979 40 per cent of all trade unionists were white-collar workers.[57] Trade unionism remained the solid base of the democratic socialism of the British Labour Party after the First World War.

The patriotic restraint of many trade unionists during the war, when their bargaining position was very strong, ended with the armistice. In the post-war boom of 1919–20, wage increases overtook the rising cost of living for the first time since the outbreak of war. Strikes and lockouts, which had seen a low of 2,466,000 days lost in 1916 rose to 34,969,000 in 1919. Yet, while 1919–21 has been deemed 'red years', in line with similar developments elsewhere in Europe and North America, the unrest was never revolutionary in Britain. Turbulent industrial struggles were over increasing real wages, improving conditions of work (including hours) and attempting to stop the return of 'controlled' industries to full private ownership, not over political power.[58]

Indeed, while the British Labour Party adopted a socialist constitution in 1918 and also drew up a manifesto intended to differentiate it from other parties, there remained a commitment to moderation among many leading trade unionists and this represented a strong continuity with the pre-war years. While trade union militancy after the First World War has attracted much attention, the continuing strength of co-operation between trade unions and employers receives less discussion. The post-war period saw several forms of joint committees of employers and trade unionists ranging from Whitley committees to national bodies. Whitley committees were usually in areas of weaker trade union organisation such as in public utilities, local government, paper-making and cement. In the case of wool, after a major strike in 1925, Ben Turner, the leading trade unionist in the industry, observed that 'when the settlement came the relationships were not as evil as could have expected in days gone by and showed that the movement for joint action was a good one.'[59] This inclination towards industries resolving their own problems through joint committees without recourse to the state was reinforced by the experience of wartime co-operation and by some moderate trade unionists' distaste for the militancy of 1919–21.

Several prominent trade unionists were involved in one of the post-war promoters of industrial co-operation, the National Alliance of Employers and Employed (NAEE), founded in 1916 and continuing up to the Second World War as the National Industrial Alliance. These trade unionists included Arthur Pugh, Secretary of the Iron and Steel Trades Confederation and President of the TUC at the time of the General Strike, James O'Grady, Secretary of the National Federation of General Workers, and Ernest Bevin, who early on served on its General Council in a personal capacity. There were also other bodies, such as the Industrial League and the Industrial Reconstruction Council, which campaigned for industrial co-operation during the post-war years of strife. The NAEE was also blessed by the Labour Party's moderate trade unionist leaders, Arthur Henderson and J. R. Clynes.[60] Such moderation in industrial relations built on a Liberal past, which included the endeavours of A. J. Mundella, a moderate employer and President of the Board of Trade, 1892–95. The outlooks of Henderson, Clynes and Bevin were a long way from the class war rhetoric of the minority French Socialists or the USPD in Germany. As the Liberal Party crumbled, the Labour Party was a natural home for disillusioned Liberal nonconformists, trade unionists, co-operators and working people. The war and its aftermath led to the first Labour government of 1924. Ten years earlier, it had not been realistic to expect a Labour government within a decade.

However, in 1919–20 the cause of industrial co-operation was secondary to the trade unions bargaining through strength and, in 1921–22, their attempts to resist or to mitigate cuts in wages and conditions.

Conclusion

The British trade unions and the Labour Movement generally slowly moved away from being linked to the established political parties in the early twentieth century. Earlier, the bulk of the British trade union movement had supported the Liberals while a lesser number had supported the Conservatives, especially in Lancashire. This had changed in stages. A major stage had been the Taff Vale Judgment of 1901, according to which trade union funds were liable to punitive damages if the unions engaged in strikes. This was contrary to what the unions understood to be the legal position under the 1871 and 1875 trade union legislation, and so the Taff Vale Judgement was seen as taking away their established rights. As a result, there was a rush by trade unions to affiliate to the Labour Representation Committee, which in 1906 changed its name to the Labour Party.

A further and greater stage in Labour moving away from the Liberals came with the First World War. From at least 1917, people in politics started to talk of the possibility of a Labour government before long. The war encouraged the Labour Party to recast its policies for the post-war world as well as adopting a socialist constitution and overhauling its electoral organisation.[61] Rowland Kenny, a socialist journalist who disliked Henderson, later commented that the realities of the politics of wartime had a big impact: 'Henderson and his type progressed at lightning speed, and became Socialist leaders – not merely Labour leaders! – overnight almost.'[62] The wartime trade union leaders did move to a democratic socialism that was a development of the long traditions of British radicalism yet after the war played a central role in the revived Second International, with much of the pre-war left having departed to the revolutionary politics of the Third International and the remaining German socialists playing less of a role than before the war.

By the end of the war the Labour Party had gone from being an auxiliary of the Liberal Party to a challenger for power. It fitted more the continental European pattern of trade unions being linked with independent socialist politics, rather than the US model of them backing existing political parties. Moreover, British trade unionism emerged mostly united behind the Labour Party, with only a relatively few (compared to continental Europe) separate supporters of revolutionary socialism or of right-wing groups of 'patriotic Labour'. The British minority favouring revolutionary politics was smaller than in Germany or in France, where at the 1919 Socialist Congress those voting against the proposed electoral policy amounted to 28 per cent. While there were divisions on the left, the far left for the most part remained strong in only a few areas such as South Wales and Clydeside, and the Communist Party of Great Britain did not divide Labour in a similar way to the experiences of Germany, France and other continental European countries. Also, Britain did not have the 'confessional unions' of Germany, Belgium and elsewhere, nor unions of national minorities, such as those of Polish workers in Germany.

The First World War strengthened British trade unionism and reinforced its support for the Labour Party. Arthur Henderson, a former Liberal councillor and Liberal Party agent, became the major trade union face of the Labour Party between 1908 and 1932, while Ernest Bevin of the huge TGWU, a notable opponent of communism at home and abroad, was the major trade union face of the Labour Party in the 1930s and 1940s. The First World War, like the Second World War, was highly important in the development of British trade unionism and the further binding of it to the Labour Party. The First World War also ensured that the British Labour Party would be a truly independent party bidding for power and that its political platform would be moderate and democratic socialist.

Notes

1. The remainder were trades councils and local Labour parties, 1,073 co-operators and 3,500 members of the Women's Labour League. Labour Party, 'Report of the Executive 1913', *Report of the Special and Annual Conferences, 1914*, p. 3.
2. Ramsay MacDonald, *Labour Leader*, 27 August 1914; quoted in Merle Fainsod, *International Socialism and the World War* (Cambridge, MA, 1935), p. 34.
3. Fenner Brockway, *Socialism over Sixty Years: The Life of Jowett of Bradford* (London, 1946), p. 129.
4. Lord Riddell, *Lord Riddell's War Diary* (London, 1933), p. 6.
5. *Gloucester Journal*, 29 January 1916.
6. Labour Party, *Report of the Annual Conference of the Labour Party, 1916* (London, 1916), pp. 100–1, 105.
7. David Lloyd George, *War Memoirs, Volume 1* (London, 1933), pp. 291–2.
8. John Hodge, *Workman's Cottage to Windsor Castle* (London, 1931), pp. 269–75.
9. Diary, 10 December, 1916. Riddell, *War Diary*, p. 230.
10. Steel-Maitland to Bonar Law, 4 November 1915. House of Lords Record Office, Bonar Law Papers, 31/5/5. Henderson also blocked a Conservative MP's attempt to change payment of MPs on the grounds 'it would be a breach of the political truce just as much as the abandonment of Home Rule or Welsh Disestablishment'. Henderson to Asquith, 6 March 1916. Copy in Bonar Law Papers, 53/6/71. Bonar Law agreed to support the rejection of the proposal. Bonar Law to Henderson, 5 April 1916. Bonar Law Papers, 53/6/71.
11. Labour Party Executive Committee minutes, 5 August 1914, 10.30 a.m. and 2.00p.m. For the importance of the committee see Royden Harrison, 'The War Emergency Workers' National Committee, 1914–1920', in Asa Briggs and John Saville (eds), *Essays in Labour History, 1886–1923* (Basingstoke, 1971), pp. 211–59 and J. M. Winter, *Socialism and the Challenge of War* (Basingstoke, 1974), pp. 184–223.
12. Chris Wrigley, 'Introduction', in Chris Wrigley (ed.), *Challenges of Labour; Central and Western Europe, 1917–20* (London, Routledge, 1993), p. 2. Max-Stephan Schulze, 'Austria-Hungary's economy in World War 1', in S. Broadberry and M. Harrison (eds), *The Economics of World War 1* (Cambridge, 2005), pp. 77–111, 79.
13. A. W. Kirkaldy, *British Labour: Replacement and Conciliation 1914–1921* (London, 1921). House of Lords Record Office; Lloyd George Papers, D/11/4/1.
14. Note in a folder of September 1915; Addison Papers, Box 2. For Circulars 2 and 3 and the arguments surrounding their implementation, see Humbert Wolfe, *Labour Supply and Regulation* (Oxford, 1923), pp. 275–96, 384–5, 394–404. Minimum wages had been fixed for 140,000 women under the Trades Boards Act 1909.
15. G. Bain and R. Price, *Profiles of Union Growth* (Oxford, 1980), p. 37.
16. Bain and Price, *Profiles of Union Growth*, pp. 43–75.
17. Marjorie R. Clark, *A History of the French Labor Movement, 1910–1928* (Berkeley, CA, 1930), pp. 61–5.
18. The post First World War figures depend much on the work on the CGT of Antoine Prost, *La CGT a l'epoche du Front Populaire, 1934–1939: essai de Description Numerique* (Paris, 1964); M. Labi, *La grande division des*

travailleurs. Premier division de CGT, 1914–1921 (Paris, 1964); and Annie Kriegel, *La Croissance de la CGT,1918–21: essai statistique* (Paris, 1966). For the consolidated figures and a discussion of issues concerning French trade union statistics, see Jelle Visser, *European Trade Unionism in Figures* (Deventer, Netherlands, 1989), pp. 53–61, 67.

19 Richard Bessel, *Germany after the First World War* (Oxford, 1993), pp. 136–9, 205. J. Ronald Shearer, 'The Social Consequences of Modernisation: Rationalisation and the Politics of the Labor Market in the Ruhr Coal Mines, 1918–1929', in Klaus Tenfelde (ed.), *Sozialgeschie des Bergbaus im 19 und 20 Jahrhundert* (Munchen, 1992), pp. 421–31. Simon Constantine, *Social Relations in the Estate Villages of Mecklenberg, c. 1880–1924* (Farnham, 2007).

20 Bain and Price, *Profiles of Union Growth*, p. 133. Visser, *European Trade Unions in Figures*, pp. 19, 70 and 151. Susan Grayzel, *Women and the First World War* (Harlow, 2002). Sieder Reinhard, 'Behind the Lines: Working Class Family Life in Vienna', Jean-Louis Robert, 'Women in France during the First World War' and Ute Daniel, 'Women's Work in Industry and Family: Germany, 1912–18', in Richard Wall and Jay Winter (eds), *The Upheaval of War: Family, Work and Welfare in Europe 1914–1918* (Cambridge, 1988), pp. 109–38, 251–67, 267–96. Geoff Eley, *Forging Democracy: The History of the Left in Europe, 1850–2000* (Oxford, 2002), pp. 100–1. Richard Bessell, *Germany after the First World War* (Oxford, 1993), pp. 136–7, 140–1.

21 For an overview see Chris Wrigley, 'The First World War and State Intervention in Industrial Relations 1914–18', in his *A History of British Industrial Relations, 1914–1939* Volume 2 (Brighton, 1987), pp. 23–70.

22 Chris Wrigley, *David Lloyd George and the British Labour Movement* (Hassocks, 1976), pp. 222–4.

23 R. Charles, *The Development of Industrial Relations in Britain* (London, 1973), pp. 132–4.

24 On pottery, see W. H. Warburton, *The History of Trade Union Organisation in the North Staffordshire Potteries* (London, 1931), pp. 225–6.

25 Stephen Blank, *Industry and Government in Britain* (Aldershot, 1973), p. 14. Labour Research Department, *The Federation of British Industries* (London, 1923).

26 Keith Middlemas, *Politics in Industrial Society* (London, 1979).

27 Roger Magraw, 'Paris 1917–20: Labour Protest and Popular Politics', in Wrigley, *Challenges of Labour*, pp. 125–48, 138.

28 J. P. Alderson, *Mr. Asquith* (Methuen, 1905), pp. 88–100, 263–5.

29 Addison's diary, 4 August 1916; Bodleian Library, Addison Papers, Box 99. Not surprisingly, Addison omitted his unflattering appraisals of Henderson when he published his diaries, *Four and a Half Years*, 2 Volumes (London, 1934) after he had joined the Labour Party.

30 Diary, 3 December 1916. Stephen Roskill, *Hankey: Man of Secrets, 1877–1918* (London, 1970), p. 325.

31 Diary, 26 May 1917. Riddell, *War Diary*, p. 253. It may be indicative that Asquith misremembered an author as the daughter of 'a porter at some wayside station in the North of Ireland' when she had been married to the station-master at Larne. *H.H.A. Letters of the Earl of Oxford and Asquith to a Friend*, First Series, 1915–22 (London 1933), p. 5.

32 Steel-Maitland to Bonar Law, 21 May 1915; Bonar Law Papers, 50/5/25.
33 Diary, 4 August 1916. Addison, *Four and a Half Years*, p. 236.
34 Henderson to Lloyd George, 13 January 1917. Lloyd George Papers; F27/3/6.
35 Wrigley, *Henderson*, pp. 114–16.
36 'Report of the Executive Committee, June 1918-June 1919' in Labour Party, *Report of the Nineteenth Annual Conference, 1919* (1919), p. 20.
37 Sidney to Beatrice Webb, 13 August 1917. Norman Mackenzie (ed.), *The Letters of Sidney and Beatrice Webb*, Volume 3 (Cambridge, 1978), p. 92.
38 Brockway, *Socialism Over Sixty Years*, p. 158.
39 W. Ormsby-Gore to Milner, Parliamentary Report, 1 November 1917. Bodleian Library, Milner Papers, Volume 117, ff. 106–9. Ormsby-Gore was later Secretary of State for the Colonies (1936–38) and the fourth Baron Harlech.
40 Duncan Tanner, *Political Change and the Labour Party 1900–1918* (Cambridge, 1990), p. 485. G. D. H. Cole, *A History of the Labour Party from 1914* (London, 1948), p. 87.
41 Chris Wrigley, 'Trade Unions and Politics in the First World War', in Ben Pimlott and Chris Cook (eds), *Trade Unions in British Politics* (London, 1982), pp. 78–97.
42 T. F. Carberry, *Consumers in British Politics* (Manchester, 1969), pp. 16–18. Sidney Pollard, 'The Foundation of the Co-operative Party', in Briggs and Saville, *Essays in Labour History 1886–1923*, pp. 185–210. Tony Adams, 'The Formation of the Co-operative Party Reconsidered', *International Review of Social History*, 1 (1987), 48–68. Peter Gurney, *Co-operative Culture and the Politics of Consumption in England, 1870–1930* (Manchester, 1996), pp. 208–16. Nicole Robertson, *The Co-operative Movement and Communities in Britain, 1914–1960* (London, 2010), pp. 155–69.
43 Branco Pribicevic, *The Shop Stewards' Movement and Workers' Control 1910–1922* (Oxford, 1959). James Hinton, *The First Shop Stewards' Movement* (London, 1972). Alastair Reid, 'Dilution, Trade Unionism and the State During the First World War', in Steven Tolliday and Jonathan Zeitlin (eds), *Shop Floor Bargaining and the State* (Cambridge, 1985), pp. 46–74, and *The Tide of Democracy: Shipyard Workers and Social Relations in Britain, 1870–1950* (Manchester, 2010).
44 *Yorkshire Post and Leeds Intelligence*, 23 July 1917.
45 E. S. Cartwright to A. L. Smith, 12 October 1917. Milner Papers, 117, f.50.
46 See, for example, Cyril Pearce's study of anti-war sentiment in Huddersfield, *Comrades in Conscience* (London, 2001).
47 J. O. Stubbs, 'Lord Milner and Patriotic Labour, 1914–1918', *English Historical Review*, 345 (1972), 717–54, 729.
48 Labour Party, *Report of the Annual Conference of the Labour Party, January and February 1918* (1918), pp. 109–12 (23 and 24 January 1918).
49 Neville Chamberlain to Arthur Steel-Maitland, 10 November 1917. His comments were echoed by Steel-Maitland, who forwarded Chamberlain's letter to Bonar Law on the same day. Scottish Record Office, Steel-Maitland Papers, GD 193/99/2/119 and 147. Abingdon Street and Victoria Street were the locations of the Conservative Party and Labour Party headquarters.
50 Victor Fisher to Steel-Maitland, 16 November 1917. Steel-Maitland Papers, GD193/99/2/111. Seddon had been a Labour MP, 1906- December 1910, and

was to be a MP for the BWL, under its new name, National Democratic Party, 1918–22. Emphasis added.
51 The best account is Roy Douglas, 'The National Democratic Party and British Workers' League', *Historical Journal*, 15:3 (1972), 533–52.
52 He was to chair the TUC in 1923. Glasgow University, 'The Musicians' Union: A Social History', at http://gtr.rcuk.ac.uk/projects?ref=AH%2FI027215%2F1 (accessed 20 June 2015).
53 Labour Party, *Report of the Eighteenth Annual Conference of the Labour Party, June 1918*, pp. 11–12 and 40–1.
54 *The Times*, 7 September 1918.
55 Labour Party, *Report of the Eighteenth Annual Conference*, p. 5. John Hodge, *Workman's Cottage to Windsor Castle* (London, n.d.), pp. 261–3.
56 Clynes to Sir Alexander Porter for Lloyd George, 11 September 1918. House of Lords Record Office, Lloyd George Papers, F/10/5/5. *The Times*, 12 September 1918.
57 Clegg, *History of British Trade Unions*, p. 534. Chris Wrigley, 'The Trade Unions between the Wars', in Wrigley, *History of British Industrial Relations*, Volume 2, pp. 108–9.
58 This is argued at length in Chris Wrigley, *Lloyd George and the Challenge of Labour* (London, 1990), especially pp. 289–314.
59 Chris Wrigley, *Cosy Co-operation under Strain: Industrial Relations in the Yorkshire Woollen Industry 1919–1930* (York, 1987). J. A. Jowett and K. Laybourn, 'The Wool Textile Dispute of 1925', *Journal of Local Studies*, 2:1 (1982), 10–27.
60 Chris Wrigley, 'Trade Unionists, Employers and the Cause of Industrial Unity and Peace, 1916–1921', in Chris Wrigley and John Shepherd (eds), *On The Move: Essays in Labour and Transport History Presented to Philip Bagwell* (London, 1991), pp. 155–84.
61 J. M. Winter, *Socialism and the Challenge of War* (London, 1974). Ross McKibbin, *The Evolution of the Labour Party, 1910–1924* (London, 1975).
62 Rowland Kenney, *Westering: An Autobiography* (London, 1939), p. 119.

3

'One of the most revolutionary proposals that has ever been put before the House': the passage of the Parliament (Qualification of Women) Act 1918

Mari Takayanagi

On 21 November 1918, ten days after Armistice Day and just a few weeks before the general election of 14 December 1918, an Act of Parliament was passed which enabled women to become Members of the House of Commons. The Parliament (Qualification of Women) Act was very short, stating in full:

> A woman shall not be disqualified by sex or marriage from being elected to or sitting or voting as a Member of the Commons House of Parliament.[1]

With no age or property qualifications, this Act was a milestone for gender equality, almost the first piece of legislation to allow women to enter a new area of public life with no caveats at all. The Representation of the People Act 1918, which gave women over the age of thirty who met minimum property qualification the vote for the first time, had passed nine months before, in February 1918. This had been preceded by decades of peaceful and militant campaigning for votes for women, many questions and debates in Parliament, and a Speaker's Conference on Electoral Reform. By contrast, there was no long parliamentary history associated with the battle for female MPs, and little lobbying by women's campaign groups on this issue before 1918. The level of controversy over the vote had been so high that the idea of female MPs was viewed as truly outlandish on the few occasions it was raised during the long campaign for votes for women. The spectre of female MPs had occasionally been raised by anti-suffragists as part of a 'thin end of the wedge' argument; for example, by Edward Bouverie who mused in 1873 what would happen if a 'lovely spinster' in Parliament had a proposal of marriage on the eve of a great division; 'Why the fate of a Government might depend on the occurrence.'² An anti-suffrage pamphlet tellingly titled 'The woman MP: a peril to women and the country' was published in 1909.³ As a result of such arguments, suffragists anxious not to endanger their primary cause did not promote the prospect of women MPs, indeed they sometimes made a point of saying that granting the vote would not include eligibility to sit in Parliament. The veteran suffrage campaigner Emily Davies wrote to *The Times* in 1907: 'Many of the advocates of women's suffrage are decidedly opposed [to women MPs] ... the question of women in Parliament is not practical politics.'⁴ The possibility of future women MPs therefore did not play a major part in the debates on the Representation of the People Bill. It was mentioned occasionally, for example: 'There is probably not much doubt about this, that when women get the vote they will come into this House. I should certainly like to have the young ones here as well as the old. (Laughter).'⁵ But generally parliamentarians and women lobbyists alike treated it as a separate issue that could be determined only after the vote was settled.

Unlike the Representation of the People Act, the Parliament (Qualification of Women) Act barely gets more than a passing mention by historians. It seems to fall between stools; historians analysing the passage of the Representation of the People Bill may not regard it as within scope,⁶ but because it was passed during the 1910–18 Parliament and before the end of the war, it is easily overlooked or covered only briefly in analyses of the post-1918 feminist movement.⁷ Those who do refer to it usually remark on it briefly as an appendix to getting the vote, for example Martin Pugh: 'After [the vote] ... came a greater surprise; ... MPs conceded, almost without debate, the right of women to sit in the House of Commons, preferring to settle the issue rather than leaving it to Returning Officers to decide whether to accept women's nominations as valid.'⁸ The fullest account of the passage of the Act appears in Pamela Brookes' *Women at Westminster*, but this is descriptive rather than analytical.⁹ It is also occasionally assumed that with the vote came the right to stand, or that it came it a year later with the Sex Disqualification (Removal) Act 1919.¹⁰ Overall, despite the symbolic and actual significance of allowing women to become members of the House of Commons it is rarely asked – if it was so surprising an event, so little lobbied for, why did it happen at all, why so soon after women got the vote, and why were there no age qualifications?

Resolution in the House

The Act originated from a resolution in the House of Commons introduced by Herbert Samuel on 23 October 1918: 'That in the opinion of this House, it is desirable that a Bill be passed forthwith making women eligible as Members of Parliament.'[11] The parliamentary session was to end less than 1 month later, on 21 November 1918; a very tight timescale for a bill to pass. Herbert Samuel (later Viscount Samuel) was Liberal MP for Cleveland and, in 1918, he was a backbencher, having been a government minister in various positions between 1906 and 1916. Earlier in 1918, he had made a speech to the London School of Economics in favour of women in Parliament.[12] In his *Memoirs* Samuel explained how although he had always been generally in favour of women's emancipation, he had been alienated by the actions of suffragettes, despite having a wife who was an enthusiastic suffragist. Looking back, Samuel regretted not having actively supported women's suffrage earlier and remarked 'Perhaps it was a feeling that I ought to make some amends that led me to take the initiative in Parliament in promoting legislation to make women eligible to the House of Commons.'[13] He had previously doubted the degree of women's public interest, but the war had 'made women familiar with many aspects of public life'.[14] Such arguments had been made frequently during the suffrage debates of 1917–18 and were often repeated by those discussing whether women should become MPs.[15]

Samuel's resolution was neither supported nor opposed by the government. The government at this time was a coalition led by the Liberal Prime Minister David Lloyd George. The Chancellor of the Exchequer, Andrew Bonar Law, had previously told Parliament that the opinion of the law officers was that women were not entitled to sit in Parliament. He added, 'I have seen their decision, and, as usual, they were wise enough not to give their reasons.'[16] The War Cabinet's discussions on 14 October 1918 included the eligibility of women to sit in the House of Commons as the last item on its agenda for the day, but they decided 'to leave the question to the decision of the House of Commons'.[17] It was Samuel who took the question to the House. As a senior MP outside of the Government, he was well placed to do so.

Samuel's resolution was called 'One of the most revolutionary proposals that has ever been put before the House', by an opposing Conservative MP during the debate.[18] Samuel's first point was that this was a logical consequence of the earlier passage of the Representation of the People Act. 'You cannot say that 6,000,000 women shall be voters but that not one shall ever be a legislator … we have given up the old narrow doctrine that woman's sphere was the home.'[19] His opponents countered with 'wait and see'; Sir Frederick Banbury, notorious opponent of all women's causes, warned that 'No one knows … what the result of this great change [the Representation of the People Act] may be … I venture to say that we should not proceed further.'[20] Basil Peto argued if they had realised that extending the franchise would lead to women MPs, 'I think the right to vote would never have been granted to women during the present

Parliament.' With the general election fast approaching, it was argued that the House of Commons was now a moribund House which had no business passing such an important piece of legislation.[21] Lord Robert Cecil argued against this, saying that Parliament could not neglect its constitutional duty by refusing to give an opinion; 'If we think it is a good thing, then the sooner it is done the better; and if we think it is a bad thing, then it ought not to be done at all.'[22]

The responsibility of returning officers

The most immediate practical argument put forward was that if there were no bill, the decision about women candidates would be the personal responsibility of individual returning officers at the forthcoming general election. The exclusion of women was a matter of common law, not statute law. 'It will be made a test question in every constituency' so should be dealt with first.[23] Despite the argument of some MPs that probably 90 per cent of women 'have not the slightest desire to enter this House or to be ruled and guided by members of their sex in this House'[24] a number of women were already lining up to stand. The first woman candidate was Nina Boyle from the Women's Freedom League (WFL), who put herself forward for the constituency of Keighley by-election in April 1918 as a test case. If her nomination was refused she was prepared to contest the decision in the courts.[25] Nina Boyle was one of the founders of the Women Police Volunteers during the war: '... she did not think it right that lack of precedent should be allowed to debar women.'[26] It was claimed that this was the first time in Great Britain that the name of a woman appeared on a nomination paper;[27] the example of Helen Taylor, who had tried to stand back in 1885, had been long forgotten.[28] Boyle made it clear that she was doing this as a test and that the result of the election was not important as the successful candidate would have to stand again shortly in the general election.[29] Her concern was to stop discrimination, rather than attain personal power.

The candidacy of Nina Boyle is also significant in that it demonstrates that at least one of the major feminist organisations had recognised the importance of establishing the legitimacy of women parliamentary candidates very soon after the limited franchise had been won. The WFL took great interest in both civil and criminal legal matters,[30] and had discussed the issue of running or supporting women parliamentary candidates in detail as early as their conference on 23–24 February 1918, just a few weeks after the passage of the Representation of the People Act on 6 February. Although the issue of whether to support only independent women candidates or also party political women was contentious, and lack of money a major barrier, the WFL conference was in agreement that women should stand for Parliament. Several delegates suggested Parliament might choose to bar even successful women candidates; Boyle recalled Charles Bradlaugh, repeatedly returned by constituents but not allowed to take his seat in the House of Commons.[31] The suffrage campaigner Ray Strachey wrote in 1928 regarding the Parliament (Qualification of Women) Act, 'The passing of this Act came as a surprise to the suffragists, who had expected a long struggle on the subject',[32] yet for the WFL activists it cannot have been such a surprise. Edith How-Martyn wrote that having obtained the vote, 'the forward spirits among suffragists at once began to talk of the possibility of getting women MPs'.[33] The NUWSS was altogether more cautious, their Executive Committee minutes for 11 April 1918 stating that 'Mrs [Ray] Strachey had advised the secretary of the Keighley society to take no action until it was clear whether Miss Boyle would be allowed to stand'.[34] Subsequently the NUWSS, now the National Union of Societies for Equal Citizenship, also threw itself into campaigning for women MPs.[35]

The Times recorded that 'Miss Boyle claimed a moral triumph' after her nomination was refused only on a technicality; she presented two nomination papers, but one was signed by someone who was not an elector and the other by someone outside the constituency. The deputy returning officer would have accepted her nomination otherwise.[36] Having succeeded in establishing a principle and setting a precedent, Nina Boyle did not try to stand again.[37] In May the ILP announced they had added Margaret Bondfield and Mrs Snowden to their list of parliamentary candidates, and Labour adopted Mary Macarthur at Stourbridge, making her the first woman to be officially selected by a political party.[38] These early candidatures are sometimes overlooked by historians keen to point out that women candidates only had twenty-three days to prepare for election after the passage of this Act,[39] possibly not realising that at least some of them had been preparing beforehand. Even women who were only formally selected by political parties after the Act was passed may have been approached many months before; Violet Markham was asked by Liberals to stand in Mansfield as early as 28 February.[40] By the time of Samuel's resolution in the House of Commons a further three women were intending to stand as Independents.[41] Perhaps aware of this situation, the Liberal MP Major Chapple predicted that parties would not select women and they would stand as additional candidates, which would lead to 'evils which arise from minority representation.'[42] Chapple was correct in that a large number of women would stand as Independents in the 1918 general election, although incorrect that they would succeed and this would lead to minority representation. Seventeen women stood at the general election in 1918, of whom one was Conservative, four Labour, four Liberal, two Sinn Fein and six Independents.[43]

Arguments in favour

Apart from the practical point about returning officers, Samuel made a number of arguments about the value of having women MPs. He argued that the House of Commons needed to be more representative, drawing a parallel with the Labour MPs: 'this House gains greatly by the presence here of direct representatives of labour ... it is the same with respect to the distinctive standpoint of women'.[44] Indeed the Labour Party were supportive of Samuel's resolution, although they had previously refused to put forward a bill on women MPs back in August, on the grounds that it was not possible to pass a private members' bill during wartime conditions.[45] Labour leader William Adamson spoke of women's role in industry, as well as the need to have them in the House to bring 'the human touch which has hitherto been absent'.[46] Samuel pointed out that in the past others had been excluded by qualifications of property, as had groups such as Catholics, Jews, Quakers and atheists.[47] Samuel may have empathised with these minority groups; he was the first nominally practising Jew to become a Cabinet minister, while holding personally atheist beliefs.

Several MPs argued that women would have a valuable contribution to make to select committee work. During second reading Willoughby Dickinson said 'At this very moment there is a Committee sitting upstairs which I believe would be strengthened by the admission of women'.[48] He was referring to the Joint Select Committee on the Criminal Law Amendment Bill and Sexual Offences Bill, which was examining proposals for changes in the law on venereal disease and the age of consent. MPs generally argued that there was a need for the point of view of women in issues such as housing, health, education and child welfare. Another argument made in Parliament was that women had proved their worth on local government bodies. There was a long tradition of women serving in local government; as well as those who served in a voluntary capacity, some 3,000 women had been elected representatives in local government bodies in Britain for decades before 1918.[49] Samuel mentioned he had been a member of an association formed to promote the election of women to these bodies, and as president of the Board of Trade had secured the passage of a bill allowing women to be elected to town councils.[50] Indeed, a woman was currently occupying the important office of deputy chairman of the London County Council.[51]

The experience of other countries

Examples from various other countries were cited in parliamentary debate, including that of New Zealand by Basil Peto. He declared 'for twenty-five years women had ... been eligible to sit as Members there, and that so far not a single one had been elected',[52] implying that there was therefore no urgency to legislate on this matter so soon after giving women the vote. Nobody corrected him, but this was factually wrong: women were not entitled to become MPs at this time in New Zealand. New Zealand was the first country in the world to allow women to vote in 1893, but this did not allow them to sit as MPs.[53] In a similar argument Frederick Banbury quoted the example of Australia, saying a 'Miss Eva Goldstein' had failed to get into every single parliament in Australia.[54] (He meant Vida Goldstein, who had unsuccessfully stood for the Australian Commonwealth House of Representatives and Senate.)[55] However Banbury had grossly simplified the situation in Australia, where although white women were allowed to vote at an early date (between 1894 and 1908 depending on state), they were not eligible to stand in most states before 1918.[56]

Although premature, the points made by Peto and Banbury were prophetic in that both New Zealand and Australia had a low proportion of women MPs for many years to come. Reasons included political parties refusing to select women; women not having a municipal vote until the First World War, which deprived them of a route to parliamentary experience (this incidentally suggests the importance of women's long participation in local government in the UK); women wealthy enough to run formed only a small class in an immigrant country where they were a minority of the population; and women outside capital cities had almost insuperable problems of travel. Eventually Australian women were caught in a circle of illogic: they so rarely won seats that this was used as justification for not selecting them.

In contrast to New Zealand and Australia, J. D. Rees spoke of Finland and how women had been MPs and 'filled the most important offices, and I am bound to say they acquitted themselves right well – a fact which I have hitherto concealed, until I knew that women got the vote in this country'.[57] Finland was not only the first country in Europe to give women the vote and allow them to be MPs in 1906, but also had no fewer than nineteen women MPs elected to the Eduskunta in 1907, out of a total of 200. The UK would not reach the dizzy heights of nineteen women MPs simultaneously until 1945. Many of the first women MPs in Finland were frontline labour activists, holding positions in workers' associations and unions.[58] Unfortunately the subsequent re-imposition of 'russification' in Finland after 1907 'had the effect of rendering the enfranchisement of women meaningless in practical political terms' until the Russian revolutions of 1917.[59] Nevertheless, in 1918 there were twenty-four women in the Finnish Parliament, comprising 12 per cent of members.

'Packed on the bench like herrings': the culture of the House of Commons

Further arguments against the resolution and at the second reading included various along the lines that the House of Commons was not a suitable place for a woman. Women should not be brought into the dirty business of politics.[60] Some MPs feared that women MPs would be the beginning of the end. 'Once admitted to the House there is no possible reason why a woman should not be the Speaker or the Speakeress of the House as well as occupying any other position.'[61] A real die-hard Conservative MP, Admiral of the Fleet Hedworth Meux, declared, 'Suppose you have a female Prime Minister, and suppose she is in a state which every woman who loves her husband ought to be, what is going to happen?'[62] Meux also argued strongly that women were physically not fit for late sittings. 'We go on till eleven or twelve o'clock at night. Is that a thing for any woman to do? ... I say that no woman is fit by her physical organisation to stand the strain of Parliament.' Meux said that at big debates MPs sat 'packed on the benches like herrings and I have seen right Hon Gentlemen so crowded on the Front Benches that they have had their arms round one another's waists.' He also expressed concern for the birth rate; 'the ambition of every right minded woman when she is married is to produce a beautiful child, a boy more beautiful than her husband or a girl more beautiful than herself.'[63] Meux got short shrift from his fellow MPs: Samuel said in strong words that Meux's speech 'was of a kind which was distasteful to very many Members of the House.'[64]

'You ought not to strain at the gnat': conversions

Interestingly a number of MPs, who had previously vehemently opposed women's suffrage, were now in favour. Though some continued to say they thought it had been the wrong decision, they nevertheless saw women MPs as a necessary next step. These included Conservative MP Arnold Ward, who had led the anti-suffrage forces in the Commons to the bitter end.[65] Former Prime Minister Herbert Asquith said, 'You have the camel; you ought not to strain at the gnat.'[66] Sir Charles Hobhouse declared, 'I think I was almost the last person on this bench to offer opposition of the extension of the franchise to women' but now they had it they must also become MPs.[67] Hobhouse was indeed a notorious opponent of women's suffrage, and known for a speech in Bristol on 16 February 1912 in which he had said, 'the absorption of women in politics would prejudice the number, character and vigour of our future race, would lead to the limitation of their capacity and inclination for maternity, and to their unwillingness and incapacity to manage the home.'[68]

Decisive division

Overall the case for change made during debates on the resolution was 'overwhelming ... the whole attitude of society has changed and has done so progressively. No doubt there were times when some ecclesiastical opinion doubted whether women had souls.' The resolution was passed on a division with 274 votes to just twenty-five.[69] 'The only sound ... heard in the Chamber when the figures were announced was an involuntary burst of laughter from the Ladies Gallery.'[70] Observers in the Ladies' Gallery included Edith How-Martyn, who was to stand as a candidate in the 1918 election.[71] Major Terrell subsequently declared that MPs only voted for the resolution 'in the hope thereby of saving their seats', and invoked the curious argument, 'That sort of thing is contrary to true democratic principles.'[72] Banbury argued that had the resolution vote been by secret ballot rather than open voting 'we should have won'.[73] These intriguing arguments demonstrate just how important and powerful the future female electorate was perceived, or feared, to be.

Samuel's resolution swiftly led to a bill, backed by the government. Lord Robert Cecil, Assistant-Secretary for Foreign Affairs, introduced it.[74] At second reading on 4 November 1918 Sir Charles Henry asked why the bill was under the auspices of the Foreign Office, to which Cecil answered light heartedly, 'Because it is the most enlightened office in the state.' He added that perhaps he had been asked to take charge because he had an interest in the subject. Samuel declared Cecil 'is undoubtedly one of the most enlightened Members of the House',[75] Lord Robert Cecil was indeed known for his independent views including his sympathy towards women's suffrage.

The age question: a curious anomaly

Perhaps the most curious aspect of the bill, and Act as it was passed, was that women were allowed to become MPs at the age of twenty-one, the same as men. The Representation of the People Act 1918 had allowed women who met certain property qualifications to vote at age thirty; this restriction was adopted to avoid women becoming the majority of the electorate because of the demographic imbalance caused by the loss of men during the war.[76] But as the Parliament (Qualification of Women) Act 1918 had no such age restriction, women could stand as MPs before they would be able to vote. This would eventually lead to a number of underage women candidates over the years, and even the anomaly of an MP elected despite not being able to vote for herself. Jennie Lee was just twenty-three when selected as Labour candidate for North Lanark and twenty-four when elected in a by-election on 21 March 1929. This was not too earth-shattering as it happened only a couple of months before women were first allowed to vote at twenty-one in the general election on 30 May 1929, and Lee remarked in her autobiography, 'The Tories could not attack me on account of my youth for all the political parties were angling for the flapper vote.'[77] Nevertheless the *Manchester Guardian* remarked 'It is amusing to reflect that no girl of her own age had a chance of voting for the youngest woman MP.'[78]

Samuel argued that the thirty-year rule for women voters was an arbitrary distinction so women voters would not outnumber men, and this simply did not apply to candidates. He even explained, 'I was myself a candidate for Parliament some years before I was a voter.'[79] Samuel was an unsuccessful Liberal candidate for South Oxfordshire in 1895 and 1900; he was asked to stand in 1893 while still an undergraduate at Oxford.[80] The fact that a man did not have to be able to vote to be a candidate is perhaps surprising; yet the assumption that by 1885 almost all adult males were enfranchised has been shown to be false by historians who have pointed out the difficulties for many men (especially young men) in fulfilling the registration requirements for the occupation, household, lodger and service franchises.[81] Examples of very young historical MPs cited during parliamentary debate included Fox and Russell ('Neither of whom were wholly undistinguished Members of this House') and Pitt.[82] Whig statesmen Charles James Fox was elected at the age of just nineteen; Lord John Russell and William Pitt the Younger were both elected at age twenty-one.

At committee stage Sir Charles Henry moved an amendment to restrict women candidates to those above the age of thirty. 'You are giving them legislative functions when they have not the franchise ... A flapper might present herself for election.' He argued that a girl or a woman legally 'never reaches her majority' and a girl even younger than twenty-one could therefore stand. (Cecil refuted this, arguing that no man under twenty-one could be elected).[83] Henry cited examples of age restrictions in other countries, including France and Italy where a deputy had to be twenty-five, and in France a senator had to be age forty. Since women did not even get the vote in France and Italy until 1945,[84] this was not a terribly obvious or useful argument to make. Banbury argued that when women were able to be MPs at twenty-one they would demand the vote at twenty-one too. 'What really has happened is this: whenever a woman takes a little she generally says "that is all I want ..." but as soon as she gets that she wants something more.' Cecil flatly rejected all these arguments, and William Hume-Williams urged Henry not to press his 'somewhat ungallant self-denying Amendment', and he did not; there was no division.[85]

The bill in the House of Lords

Lord Islington, Under-Secretary of State for India, introduced the bill in the Lords on 12 November 1918. Arguments were generally very similar to those in the House of Commons. Additionally there was a constitutional issue: 'We should not have a quarrel with the House of Commons on a matter affecting the constitution of that House, a contest in which this House would ultimately be beaten.' Islington hoped they would support it 'even though in some cases it may be a support strongly tinged with reluctance and in a spirit of resignation'[86] and this duly happened.

Extending the bill to allow women to sit in the House of Lords was considered. As was pointed out, the title of the Bill was 'quite deliberately drawn to cover both Houses of Parliament'.[87] In the Commons, even Admiral Meux opined, 'The House of Lords is a totally different proposition. They have very reasonable and leisurely hours, and I believe they nearly always go home to dinner. I can see no reason why the women should not go there.'[88] In the Lords, Viscount Haldane tried to amend the bill at committee stage to allow peeresses in their own right to sit in the Lords. 'In what an extraordinary position we should be. A woman may sit on the Throne; a woman may sit in the House of Commons; but the one place where she is not to sit is in the House of Lords.' Lord Islington for the government was unable to accept the amendment 'due to no hostility whatever to the actual proposal' but because it went beyond the scope and spirit of the bill before them, and the lord chancellor backed this up with a great many technical issues.[89] Haldane's amendment was lost on a division, fourteen to thirty-three. This failed attempt was a scene-setter for almost annual debates on the issue during the 1920s; once women were allowed into the Commons, the debate on allowing them into the Lords really began.[90]

Conclusion

The Parliament (Qualification of Women) Act was passed with Royal Assent on the last day of the Parliamentary session, 21 November 1918 – just a few weeks before the general election on 14 December 1918. This swift passage was made possible as the principle of the vote had been already conceded through the Representation of the People Act, the arguments for and against women MPs had been fully aired during the debate on Samuel's resolution, and because of the practical political necessity of settling the issue in time for the upcoming general election.

However, progress in electing women MPs was not nearly as swift as the passage of the Act through Parliament. Seventeen women stood in the 1918 general election, of whom one was elected but did not take her seat (Constance Markievicz, as a Sinn Féin MP). The following year saw Nancy Astor (Conservative) become the first woman MP to take her seat following a by-election. There is no doubt this was an important milestone. Frances Stevenson recorded in her diary the day Astor took her seat, 'It really was a thrilling moment ... after all these hundreds of years, this was the first time that a woman had set foot upon that floor to represent the people.'[91] Mary Stocks declared later in life that, 'Only feminists who lived through the early twenties will be able fully to recapture the successive sensations of horror, stunned surprise, and dawning adulation, provoked by the advent of the first woman at Westminster.'[92]

Despite this initial shock and excitement, the number of woman MPs rose only very slowly during the interwar years, reaching a high of fifteen for a short period in 1931. The number of women candidates in general elections also rose only very slowly, reaching a high of sixty-nine in 1929, with none of the major political parties selecting women in more than a very few winnable seats.[93] Women remain underrepresented to this day, not only in Parliament but in large areas of public life, professions and the corporate world.[94] The Parliament (Qualification of Women) Act was a necessary step, but not in itself sufficient to radically change the composition of the House of Commons. There has been much debate ever since about why so few women have become MPs. Explanations for the interwar period include general attitudes to and discrimination against women, self-perceptions, practical difficulties of a political career, problems of being adopted by selection panels in winnable seats and the first past the post system.[95] Such factors continued well into the twentieth century and beyond; studies of the large number of women Labour MPs elected in 1997 show similar themes including reluctance among women to put themselves forward, a fear of the 'bear pit' atmosphere of the Commons, and problems juggling a political career with a family.[96] It can be argued that it should not matter if an MP is male or female, so long as they represent their constituents, and indeed interwar women MPs generally chose to represent their party and constituents first, and women as a secondary consideration. They mostly fought shy of being pigeonholed into 'women's issues' and generally did not work together as a group, except on rare occasions such as the Woman Power Committee during the Second World War.

Yet it was of intrinsic value for the women's movement once the vote was won that women should become MPs. The Representation of the People Act ensured Parliament would *represent* the female section of society; the Parliament (Qualification of Women) Act meant that Parliament would also be able to *reflect* it, in its composition. Edith How-Martyn argued in a pamphlet 'The Need for Women Members of Parliament' issued shortly after Nancy Astor's election, 'As powerful as the possession of the vote may be, the actual representation within the House by women is immeasurably more so and the chief aim of feminists for the next few years should be to increase the number of women MPs.'[97] Brian Harrison's study of the first women MPs concludes 'The most important of all the women MPs' contributions is the fact that they entered a men's house and succeeded there.'[98] Had the Parliament (Qualification of Women) Act not been passed, it would have cast doubt over the legitimacy of candidates in the 1918 general election, possibly been the subject of court cases and become a running sore throughout the following Parliament. As it was, the issue was stopped in its tracks, and ensured women's organisations could move on to tackle other issues. It helped pave the way for women to enter other professions, for example as magistrates, jurors, solicitors and barristers through the Sex Disqualification (Removal) Act 1919.

The radical nature of the Parliament (Qualification of Women) Act should not be obscured by its relatively quick and uncontroversial parliamentary passage. An area of discrimination had been eliminated at a stroke, without qualification. The principle was established that women could be MPs, at the same age as men, with no special rules around property, marriage or any other constraint. By contrast, there were considerable age and property restrictions placed on women voting in the Representation of the People Act, and negligible progress in areas of parliamentary reform over the following decades, over issues such as plural voting and the composition of the House of Lords. The Parliament (Qualification of Women) Act was a decisive early piece of gender equality legislation and deserves greater recognition as a significant achievement in the area of constitutional reform.

Notes

1 Parliament (Qualification of Women) Act 1918, c. 47. This paper grew out of research for: Mari Takayanagi, 'Parliament and Women c1900–1945' (PhD thesis, King's College London, 2012), available online via the King's Research Portal at https://kclpure.kcl.ac.uk/portal/ (accessed 26 September 2017).
2 House of Commons Parliamentary Debates (thereafter HC Deb), 30 Apr 1873 vol 215 c1219, E. P. Bouverie (Conservative).
3 LSE Library collections (thereafter LSE) pamphlet. A. C. Gronno, 'The woman MP: a peril to women and the country' (Manchester, For the Manchester Branch of the Women's National Anti-Suffrage League, 1909), pp. 33–5.
4 *The Times*, 4 February 1907.
5 HC Deb 20 June 1917 vol 94 c1832, Rowland Hunt (National Party).
6 Nicoletta F. Gullace, *The Blood of Our Sons: Men, Women and the Renegotiation of British Citizenship during the Great War* (Basingstoke, 2002).
7 Claire Eustance, '"Daring to Be Free": the Evolution of Women's Political Identities in the Women's Freedom League 1907–1930 (PhD thesis, University of York, 1993); Cheryl Law, *Suffrage and Power: the Women's Movement, 1918–1928* (London, 1997), p. 110; Johanna Alberti, 'A Symbol and a Key: the Suffrage

Movement in Britain, 1918–1928', in June Purvis and Sandra Stanley Holton (eds), *Votes for Women* (New York, 1999), pp. 267–90.
8. Martin Pugh, *Women and the Women's Movement in Britain, 1914–1999* (Basingstoke, 2nd edn, 2000), p. 43.
9. Pamela Brookes, *Women at Westminster: an Account of Women in the British Parliament, 1918–1966* (London, 1967), pp. 3–6.
10. 'The 1919 Sex Disqualification (Removal) Act allowed women to take up any civil or judicial post that was open to men – like MPs, barristers or magistrates.' Jill Liddington and Jill Norris, *One Hand Tied Behind Us: the Rise of the Women's Suffrage Movement* (London, 2000), p. 272.
11. HC Deb 23 Oct 1918 vol 110 c813, Herbert Samuel (Liberal).
12. *The Vote*, 5 April 1918.
13. Herbert Louis Samuel, *Memoirs* (London, 1945), pp. 129–30.
14. HC Deb 23 Oct 1918 vol 110 c814, Herbert Samuel.
15. HC Deb 23 Oct 1918 vol 110 c844, Newton Moore (Conservative).
16. HC Deb 8 Aug 1918 vol 109 cc1534–5, Andrew Bonar Law (Conservative).
17. The National Archives (thereafter TNA), CAB 23/8, p. 30.
18. HC Deb 23 Oct 1918 vol 110, c833, Basil Peto (Conservative).
19. HC Deb 23 Oct 1918 vol 110, c814, Herbert Samuel.
20. HC Deb 23 Oct 1918 vol 110, c823, Frederick Banbury (Conservative).
21. HC Deb 23 Oct 1918 vol 110, cc830–2, Peto; c823, Banbury.
22. HC Deb 23 Oct 1918 vol 110, cc825–6, Lord Robert Cecil (Conservative)
23. HC Deb 23 Oct 1918 vol 110, c819, Herbert Samuel.
24. HC Deb 23 Oct 1918 vol 110, c829, Peto; c1870, Major Henry Terrell (Conservative).
25. *The Times*, 4 April 1918.
26. *Daily Express*, 2 April 1918, quoted in Joyce Marlow, *Votes for Women: the Virago Book of Suffragettes* (London, 2001), p. 251.
27. Cicely Hamilton, *Nina Boyle* (London, 1944).
28. Helen Taylor was selected by the Camberwell Radical Club as Independent Radical Democrat candidate for Camberwell North in 1885, but her nomination was not accepted by the returning officer because she was a woman. Thanks to Janet Smith from the Women's Legal Landmarks project for this information.
29. *The Vote*, 5 April 1918.
30. The WFL outlived the suffrage struggle and remained in existence until 1961. It took a special interest in criminal justice, including monitoring women in courts and police work. Eustance, 'Daring to be Free'; Anne Logan, *Feminism and Criminal Justice: A Historical Perspective* (Basingstoke, 2008), pp. 20–1.
31. Charles Bradlaugh, MP for Northampton, was an atheist who refused to take the Oath of Allegiance required of MPs in 1880. He was re-elected four times before being allowed to take his seat in 1886. Edward Royle, 'Bradlaugh, Charles (1833–1891)', *Oxford Dictionary of National Biography* (Oxford, 2004).
32. Ray Strachey, *"The Cause": a Short History of the Women's Movement in Great Britain* (London, 1928 [reprinted 1978]), p. 368.
33. LSE Pamphlet, Edith How-Martyn, 'The Need for Women Members of Parliament' (London, 1920), p. 1.

34 LSE, 2NWS/A/1/10.
35 For example on 10 October 1918 a letter on the need for women MPs was issued to the general press. LSE, 2/NWS/A/7/1. Literary and Press sub-committee, press report.
36 *The Times*, 20 April 1918.
37 Nina had undertaken her candidacy with 'very little money' for expenses, and had funds been available she probably would have tried again. Hamilton, *Nina Boyle*.
38 *The Times*, 13 May 1918.
39 E.g. Law, *Suffrage and Power*, p. 116.
40 Violet Markham, *Duty and Citizenship: the Correspondence and Political Papers of Violet Markham 1896–1953*, ed. Helen Jones (London, 1994), p. 94. Markham to J. A. Spender, 28 February 1918. She agreed to stand in November (p. 100, Markham to Cyril Newton Thompson, 14 November 1918).
41 *The Times*, 19 October 1919. Margaret Milne Farquharson (who did not in the end stand), Eunice Murray and Edith How-Martyn.
42 HC Deb 4 Nov 1918 vol 110 c1884, Major William Chapple (Liberal).
43 Brookes, *Women at Westminster*, p. 6. To date there has only ever been one Independent woman MP elected, Eleanor Rathbone between 1929 and 1946 (other women, such as Clare Short, have become Independents after being elected).
44 HC Deb 23 Oct 1918 vol 110 c815, Herbert Samuel.
45 *The Vote*, 2 August 1918.
46 HC Deb 23 Oct 1918 vol 110 c850, William Adamson (1863–1936) (Labour).
47 HC Deb 23 Oct 1918 vol 110 c850, Herbert Samuel. Nonconformists were allowed to become MPs from 1828, Catholics from 1829, Jews from 1858 and atheists from 1886.
48 HC Deb 4 Nov 1918 vol 110, c1872, Sir Willoughby Dickinson (Liberal). Dickinson was a long-standing supporter of women's suffrage.
49 Patricia Hollis, *Ladies Elect: Women in English Local Government, 1865–1914* (Oxford, 1987).
50 HC Deb 23 Oct 1918 vol 110, c817, Herbert Samuel. Samuel referred to the Women's Local Government Society and the Qualification of Women (County and Borough Councils) Act, 1907 c. 33.
51 HC Deb 23 Oct 1918 vol 110, c817, Herbert Samuel. Katharine Talbot Wallas served in this and many roles on the London County Council. Jane Martin, 'Wallas, Katharine Talbot (1864–1944)', *Oxford Dictionary of National Biography* (Oxford, 2004).
52 HC Deb 23 Oct 1918 vol 110 c831, Peto.
53 Patricia Grimshaw, *Women's Suffrage in New Zealand* (Auckland, 1987). Sandra Wallace, *Out of the Home and into the House: New Zealand Women's Fight to Enter Parliament* (Wellington, 1993). Women were eligible to stand for the House of Representatives from 1919 and the first was elected in 1933.
54 HC Deb 23 Oct 1918 vol 110 c823, Banbury.
55 *The Times*, 23 October 1918.
56 Audrey Oldfield, *Woman Suffrage in Australia: a Gift or a Struggle?* (Cambridge, 1992). The first Australian woman MP at state level was elected in 1921.

Indigenous women, and men, did not achieve full equality in voting until 1967.
57 HC Deb 23 Oct 1918 vol 110 c848, J. D. Rees (Conservative).
58 Irma Sulkunen, 'Suffrage, Nation and Political Mobilisation – the Finnish Case in an International Context', in Irma Sulkunen, Seija-Leena Navala-Nurmi and Pirjo Markkola (eds), *Suffrage Gender and Citizenship: International Perspectives on Parliamentary Reforms* (Cambridge, 2009), pp. 83–105.
59 Richard J. Evans, *The Feminists: Women's Emancipation Movements in Europe, America and Australasia, 1840–1920* (London, 1977).
60 HC Deb 23 Oct 1918 vol 110 c835, Craik (Conservative).
61 HC Deb 23 Oct 1918 vol 110 c832, Peto. Betty Harvie Anderson (Conservative) became the first female deputy speaker in 1970, and Betty Boothroyd (Labour) became the first female speaker in 1992.
62 HC Deb 4 Nov 1918 vol 110, c1877, Sir Hedworth Meux (Conservative).
63 HC Deb 4 Nov 1918 vol 110, c1876–7, Meux. Meux was married but had no children. Meux was known as Hedworth Lambton until 1911, when he changed his surname in order to gain an inheritance from an older unrelated woman, Lady Valerie Meux.
64 HC Deb 4 Nov 1918 vol 110, c1880, Herbert Samuel.
65 HC Deb 23 Oct 1918 vol 110 c833–4, Arnold Ward (Conservative). Ward was the son of anti-suffragist leader Mrs Humphrey Ward.
66 HC Deb 23 Oct 1918 vol 110 c839, Herbert Asquith (Liberal).
67 HC Deb 4 Nov 1918 vol 110, c1872, Charles Hobhouse (Liberal).
68 Charles Hobhouse, *Inside Asquith's Cabinet: from the Diaries of Charles Hobhouse*, ed. Edward David (London, 1977), p. 8. Hobhouse's speech was blamed for inciting violence by suffragettes.
69 HC Deb 23 Oct 1918 vol 110 c827, Cecil; c856, division result.
70 *The Times*, 24 October 1918.
71 Brookes, *Women at Westminster*, p. 6.
72 HC Deb 4 Nov 1918 vol 110, c1870, Terrell.
73 HC Deb 4 Nov 1918 vol 110, c1883, Banbury. Also c1877, Meux.
74 Gordon Hewart (Liberal) and Sir Laming Worthington Evans (Conservative).
75 HC Deb 4 Nov 1918 vol 110, c1867, Charles Henry (Liberal); c1879, Cecil; c1882, Herbert Samuel. Cecil was married to Lady Eleanor Lambton, sister of Hedworth Meux who opposed the bill so bitterly.
76 On equal franchise, see Mari Takayanagi, 'Parliament and Women', chapter 4; Mari Takayanagi, 'Women and the Vote: the Parliamentary path to Equal Franchise', *Parliamentary History*, 37:1 (forthcoming, 2018).
77 Jennie Lee, *My life with Nye* (London, 1980), p. 66.
78 Brookes, *Women at Westminster*, p. 66.
79 HC Deb 23 Oct 1918 vol 110 c821, Herbert Samuel.
80 Samuel, *Memoirs*.
81 Neal Blewitt, 'The Franchise in the United Kingdom, 1885–1918', *Past and Present* 32, (1965), pp. 27–56. Duncan Tanner, *Political change and the Labour Party 1900–1918* (Cambridge, 1990). Tanner estimates in 1915 there were 4 million men excluded from the franchise, including 2.5 million younger single men who were less likely to be householders; they may have lived with

parents, or worked as indoor servants, or moved frequently (e.g. soldiers), or rented at a low rate.

82 HC Deb 6 Nov 1918 vol 110 c2192, Cecil; HL Deb 12 Nov 1918 vol 31 c1242, Viscount Haldane (Liberal).
83 HC Deb 6 Nov 1918 vol 110 c2186–7, Henry; c2192, Cecil. Cecil conveniently forgot the example of Charles James Fox. 'Flappers' generally referred to young women under 30 years old.
84 Elizabeth Vallance, *Women in the House* (London, 1979), p. 189.
85 HC Deb 6 Nov 1918 vol 110 c2189, Banbury; c2190, Cecil; c2193, W. E. Hume-Williams (Conservative).
86 House of Lords Parliamentary Debates (thereafter HL Deb) 12 Nov 1918 vol 31, c1236, Under-Secretary of State for India (Lord Islington) (Conservative); c1245, Lord Chancellor (Lord Finlay, Liberal); cc1236–7, Under-Secretary of State for India (Lord Islington).
87 HL Deb 15 Nov 1918 vol 32 c147, Earl of Selborne (Liberal).
88 HC Deb 4 Nov 1918 vol 110 c1877, Meux.
89 HL Deb 15 Nov 1918 vol 32 c140, Viscount Haldane; c148, Earl of Selborne; c143, Under-Secretary of State for India; cc150–4, Lord Chancellor (Lord Finlay).
90 Duncan Sutherland, 'Peeresses, Parliament and Prejudice; the Admission of Women to the House of Lords, 1918–1963', *Parliaments, Estates and Representation*, 20:1 (2000), pp. 215–31. Women were admitted to the House of Lords as life peers by the Life Peerages Act 1958, and as hereditary peers by the Peerage Act 1963.
91 Frances Stevenson, *Lloyd George a Diary: by Frances Stevenson*, ed. A. J. P. Taylor (London, 1971), p. 190.
92 Brookes, *Women at Westminster*, p. xi.
93 David Butler and Gareth Butler, *British Political Facts, 1900–1985* (Basingstoke, 1986), p. 249.
94 'Women in Public life, the Professions and the Boardroom', House of Commons Library SN5170, 2014, at http://researchbriefings.parliament.uk/ResearchBriefing/Summary/SN05170 (accessed 6 July 2016).
95 Vallance, *Women in the House*; Beverley P. Stobaugh, *Women and Parliament 1918–1970* (New York, 1978).
96 Linda McDougall, *Westminster Women* (London, 1998). Sarah Childs, Joni Lovenduski and Rosie Campbell, *Women at the Top 2005: Changing Numbers, Changing Politics?* (Hansard Society, 2005).
97 How-Martyn, 'The Need for Women Members of Parliament', foreword.
98 Brian Harrison, 'Women in a Men's House: the Women MPs, 1919–1945', *Historical Journal*, 29:3 (1986), pp. 623–54.

4

Labour and socialism during the First World War in Bristol and Northampton

Matthew Kidd

Over the last thirty years, formerly dominant interpretations of British political, cultural and social history have come under sustained attack from a diverse range of 'revisionist' scholars. This historiographical vanguard has, to varying extents, drawn attention to the enduring prevalence of populist political attitudes and trans-class social identities in early twentieth-century Britain. While this revisionist challenge has provided a valuable corrective to stage-based accounts of Britain's political development, its leading proponents have not seriously questioned the traditional view that the First World War and its political, industrial and ideological consequences are crucial for explaining the post-war realignment of British politics.[1] This chapter offers a fresh perspective on the war and its consequences by examining the experiences of Labour activists in two industrial centres, Bristol and Northampton, during the war years. Its central aim is to demonstrate that, at the constituency level, there were important attitudinal and ideological continuities between pre-war and wartime Labour politics. Throughout the war, Labour activists in Bristol and Northampton experienced a number of changes at the workplace and in their local communities. By the end of the war, they also faced a changed political landscape in which the historic dominance of the Liberal Party over local political affairs appeared to be nearing its end.[2] Despite the socio-economic and political developments of the war years, Labour activists in both places continued to demonstrate a strong sense of loyalty to many of the principles, outlooks and ideas that had shaped Labour politics in these constituencies since the mid-to-late nineteenth century.

There are three ways in which the case studies of Bristol and Northampton demonstrate wartime continuities within local Labour politics. First, continuities were evident in the way Labour activists articulated their understanding of class, class relations and the social order. As in other urban centres throughout Britain, there were important industrial changes in Bristol and Northampton during the war. Furthermore, as Patrick Joyce has noted, the war also appeared to represent an important historical moment during which adversarial conceptions of class relations became more prevalent among British workers.[3] Yet in Bristol and Northampton, the majority of Labour activists refused to abandon their pre-war conception of class relations. Before the war, these activists had articulated a vision of British society that emphasised the distinctions between different sections of the community. Pre-war Labour activists considered themselves to be spokespersons for the numerically dominant working-class section of this community, which, they argued, lacked the socio-economic privileges, educational opportunities and political representation afforded to others. This emphasis on class distinctions, though, was not synonymous with an emphasis on class conflict. Labour activists distanced themselves from theories that promoted a class war and, instead, argued that their commitment to class politics simply emanated from a desire to make political institutions more representative of society as a whole. While the war years may have helped to transform political and social attitudes among the British population at large, they did little to convince Labour activists in Bristol and Northampton to abandon their historically deep-rooted conceptions of class and society.

Second, this chapter suggests that, in Bristol and Northampton, wartime economic developments did not significantly transform Labour activists' perception of who was, and who was not, part of the authentic 'working class'. This is not to minimise the social significance of these wartime developments. Owing to the shortage of male labour, women and girls throughout Britain began to enter industry in unprecedented numbers.[4] Nevertheless, while this development altered the composition of the workforce, male Labour activists in Bristol and Northampton continued to articulate a highly restrictive and gendered class identity. Similarly, the war provided activists with an opportunity to express their long-held assumptions about nationality and, at times, race. While a small minority of anti-war activists struggled in vain to preserve the supposed internationalist ethos of the pre-war Labour movement, the majority of Labour activists in Bristol and Northampton continued to express patriotic, nationalistic and, at times, xenophobic sentiments throughout the war. Far from transforming male Labour activists' attitudes towards women and non-British workers, the war merely served to draw out many of the assumptions upon which they were based.[5]

Finally, by using Michael Freeden's conceptual approach to ideologies as a guide, this chapter demonstrates that there were substantial continuities between pre-war and wartime 'labourism', the dominant ideology among Labour activists in Bristol and Northampton since the late nineteenth century.[6] Freeden's approach suggests that ideologies are best understood as conglomerates of 'core', 'adjacent' and 'periphery' concepts that obtain their precise meanings by engaging in a 'mutually influential relationship' with one another.[7] Using this model as a basis, this chapter argues that while wartime developments served to modify the programmatic demands of Labour activists, they did not significantly alter the underlying conceptual framework of labourist ideology. Indeed, it was their strong commitment to the concepts at the heart of pre-war labourism, namely democracy, constitutionalism, rights, liberty and collectivism, which shaped Labour activists' responses to the problems generated by the conflict. Their demand for labour representation on local wartime committees emanated from their class-based understanding of democracy. Their disavowal of extra-parliamentary strategies in the aftermath of the 1917 Bolshevik revolution was based upon their long-held reverence for, and democratic reading of, the English constitution. Their hostility and opposition to wartime legislation, such as the Defence of the Realm Act (DORA) and conscription derived from their belief that the English constitution granted certain political and industrial rights to all (male) members of the community. Moreover, while their demands became more collectivist during the war years, this merely represented a continuation of labourism's ideological evolution that had begun in the 1880s. While the programmatic expression of labourism evolved during the war years, its underlying conceptual architecture did not.

Labour politics in wartime Bristol

In the decade before the war, leading trade union and socialist activists in Bristol helped to form the Bristol Labour Representation Committee, a loose political federation that initially made only modest progress in its effort to challenge the political dominance of the Bristol Liberal Party. By the end of 1918, this federation had been reorganised as the Bristol Borough Labour Party, which put forward candidates in four out of five of Bristol's parliamentary seats at that year's 'coupon election'. This newfound sense of confidence in challenging the two major parties was partly the result of the Bristol Labour Party's impressive wartime growth.[8] A considerable increase in trade union membership between 1914 and 1918, most notably in the local Dockers' Union, strengthened the party's finances and helped to broaden its membership base.[9] The co-option of leading party members onto various wartime committees, and the elevation of one of its leaders, Frank Sheppard, to the position of lord mayor in 1917, gave the party an influence in Bristol that it had failed to achieve in peacetime.[10] Labour activists also took heart from internal disagreements in the Bristol Liberal Party. In contrast to the divided Liberals, Labour was able to present itself as the only unified progressive force in Bristol, especially in the predominantly working-class and historically Liberal stronghold of Bristol East. While all of the Labour candidates were unsuccessful in 1918, arguments among Bristol Liberals over their party's role in the Coalition government almost certainly contributed to the increased share of the Labour vote in Bristol.[11]

The wartime growth of the Labour Party and its affiliated organisations, coupled with the apparent ease with which the Liberals now worked alongside their old political foes, convinced local Labour activists that their pre-war strategy was still appropriate in the post-war era. To some extent, the vitality of the Bristol Labour movement during this period obscured some of the divisions that had emerged within it over the question of the war. Despite notable exceptions, leaders of Bristol's ILP branch vehemently opposed the conflict.[12] Under the leadership of Walter Ayles, a devoutly religious city councillor, ILP members distributed pacifist literature and held open-air meetings that often met with apathy or, on some occasions, physical violence.[13] As a result of their opposition to the war, the ILP's branch membership decreased, its financial contributions declined and a number of its leaders served time in prison.[14] However, it is important to note that while the ILP obtained a strong presence on the leadership body of the Bristol Labour Party, its stance on the war was not representative of the party as a whole. Most of Bristol's prominent trade union leaders fervently supported the war effort, as did the leaders of the Bristol Socialist Society.[15] Even A. A. Senington, a leading member of the ILP, broke ranks with his party and claimed that he would be a coward if he sided with Ayles and his colleagues.[16] By sidelining Ayles and other pacifist figures during the 1918 election campaign, the dominant pro-war faction in the Labour Party was able to present the party as the only united and independent progressive force in Bristol.

Class identity in wartime Bristol

Throughout the war, the overwhelming majority of Labour activists in Bristol continued to adhere to their pre-war vision of society, which had depicted classes as distinct, but not necessarily mutually antagonistic, sections of the community. They largely accepted the view that the war effort was a national concern that required the co-operation of employers, workers and all political parties, but still emphasised the distinctive traits, experiences and sufferings of the working class. This is particularly true of delegates to the Bristol Trades' Council, which acted as a local parliament for trade unionists and whose members frequently stressed the class basis of the war effort.[17] The perception that the working class had sacrificed most during the war became a central feature of the Bristol Labour Party's campaign in the 1918 election, during which all of the party's candidates used an unambiguous language of class when appealing to voters.[18] Ernest Bevin, who stood for Labour in Bristol Central, promised voters that he would strive to give his class access to what 'the other class' had, while Luke Bateman, who contested the Bristol East seat, proudly claimed that he had been trained in the 'greatest university – the world, the workshop, in grime, and poverty'.[19] In Bristol at least, the national Labour Party's decision in mid-1918 to open its doors to members of all classes had little impact on changing activists' class-centred approach to politics.

As before the war, however, this exclusivist emphasis on working-class concerns was not synonymous with an antagonistic conception of class relations. Bateman, for instance, denied that he stood solely for 'class legislation'.[20] In the middle of the war, Walter Ayles of the ILP also rejected claims that his party wished to be 'unjust to the wealthy'. The ILP, he explained, sought 'industrial peace' and the reconciliation of 'conflicting interests'.[21] This is not to suggest that antagonistic language was entirely absent from Labour activists' rhetoric. Some, including Bevin, began to speak of 'the capitalists' on a class basis rather than as a heterogeneous group of both 'fair' and 'unjust' employers.[22] But it is important to stress that these views, while undoubtedly growing in prevalence during the war, did not entirely replace Labour activists' pre-war conceptions of society. In Bristol, antagonistic images of society were simply not widespread enough to suggest there had been a fundamental and decisive change in the worldview of Labour activists.

There were also continuities in the way Labour activists understood and spoke of the 'working class'. Before the war, those in the predominantly male Bristol Labour movement had tended to exclude 'other' categories of worker, including women, from their definition of this class. Industrial developments during the war years forced these activists to consider the lives and concerns of these 'other' workers to a greater extent than ever before. In Bristol, as in other towns and cities throughout Britain, the wartime demand for labour increased the possibilities of paid work for women, many of whom subsequently joined the city's existing trade unions.[23] While male Labour activists largely accepted the temporary employment of women in formerly male-dominated industries, they continued to articulate a highly gendered notion of class. In their speeches and written literature, it was still more common for them to use terms such as 'working men' and 'workmen' rather than more inclusive terms such as 'working men and women'.[24] Furthermore, even when male Labour activists did speak directly to women, they tended to appeal to them as wives and homemakers rather than as fellow workers.[25]

The restrictive nature of Bristol Labour activists' class identity was also evident in their statements on the themes of nationality and race. Perhaps unsurprisingly, the war drew out many of the nationalistic assumptions that underpinned this identity. The minority in Bristol who opposed the war fought strenuously against the tide of public opinion by emphasising the internationalist character of the working class.[26] However, statements of this kind were confined to a small group of Labour activists, particularly in the early stages of the war. Instead, most of the city's Labour leaders supported the war effort and couched their pro-war appeals in highly nationalistic terms. In their speeches and literature, they argued that national unity between all classes was of paramount importance because the British (or, sometimes, English) nation was under threat. Frank Sheppard, a leading figure in the National Union of Boot and Shoe Operatives (NUBSO) at this time, was a particularly strong advocate of this stance. If Britain had refused to enter the war, then, for Sheppard, 'everlasting shame and an early decay of our nationality would have followed.'[27] A. A. Senington of the ILP held similar views.[28] Though he agreed with his pacifist colleagues in the ILP on 'questions concerning capital and labour', he believed that industrial issues had, since the outbreak of the war, diminished in importance. In the current conflict, 'they stood as a nation first'.[29]

Labourism in wartime Bristol

In Bristol, there was nothing particularly novel about statements of this kind. Labour activists in the city had been assigning distinctive British and masculine qualities to the working class for many years prior to 1914, and developments during the war years, far from encouraging them to change their views, merely gave activists new opportunities through which to express their long-held assumptions about gender and nationality. For most Labour activists in Bristol, the war years also served to validate their commitment to the central concepts that underpinned labourist ideology. For example, while overt political activity largely diminished during the war years, activists continued to stress the democratic and constitutional basis of their demands, particularly when they demanded labour representation on the wartime committees.[30] For these activists, increased labour representation on these bodies was both necessary and justified owing to the numerical dominance of the city's working-class community.[31] Moreover, the decision to maintain the wartime coalition after the cessation of hostilities, as well as the perceived undemocratic nature of the 'coupon election', gave Labour activists a chance to present themselves as the true heirs of nineteenth-century democratic traditions.[32] Labour candidates in Bristol made much of this fact during the election campaign and claimed that it was only the Labour Party that now stood for a 'free and unfettered Parliament'.[33]

The central place afforded to a 'free Parliament' in Labour's campaign demonstrates Labour activists' commitment to a positive and democratic reading of the constitution. The Russian Revolutions of 1917, while sympathised with, did not convince activists in Bristol to abandon this interpretation.[34] If anything, the perceived threat of Bolshevism encouraged activists to reaffirm their commitment to parliamentary methods of reform. During his campaign in 1918, Bevin assured voters that a strong Labour Party in the House of Commons would act as a 'bulwark against Revolution'. 'Evolution', he argued, 'was the only possible method of securing emancipation for the working people'.[35] Others promoted the programme of the Labour Party in similar terms. At one election meeting, a party activist condemned all action of a 'violent and unjustifiable' nature, while another claimed that Labour only favoured 'constitutional methods and moral persuasion'. Even supporters who interpreted the party's programme in more extreme terms spoke only of a *'constitutional* revolution'.[36] Wartime events did little to break activists' commitment to extending, rather than subverting, the existing constitutional order.

Labour activists also continued to place a strong emphasis on the concepts of rights and liberty. As before the war, they still tended to interpret these concepts through the lens of class and spoke frequently of, for example, the rights of workers and the liberties of the trade unions.[37] In particular, they used a language of rights when discussing regulations under the DORA 1914 and the Military Service Act 1916, which all Labour candidates condemned during the 'coupon election'.[38] Still, while they criticised government restrictions on civil and trade union liberties, Labour activists also advocated a greater role for the state in certain areas of economic activity. Almost immediately after the declaration of war, members of the Bristol Trades' Council demanded the government regulation of food prices and government control of all foodstuffs.[39] During the 1918 election campaign, T. C. Lewis proposed, among other things, a 'just and generous provision' for discharged soldiers and sailors, the retention by the state of all raw materials in its possession and the socialisation of the banks, railways, mines, minerals and all forms of monopoly. James Kaylor, who stood in Bristol North, favoured the nationalisation of 'everything ... necessary for human life'. Ernest Bevin, in a statement used against him by his opponents, stated that he 'could not see the necessity for capital being privately owned'.[40] As the *Western Daily Press* argued, these collectivist sentiments were based upon a 'measureless belief in the capacity of Government departments to control gigantic business enterprises'.[41]

These policies were consistent with the national Labour Party's newly adopted and thoroughly collectivist constitution and programme. While some historians have seen the adoption of *Labour and the New Social Order* as representing an ideological shift within the Labour Party, there was nothing particularly new, in Bristol at least, about the collectivist accent of Labour's message.[42] The majority of local Labour activists had been advocating collectivist proposals since at least the 1880s and had campaigned for greater state control and ownership in numerous parliamentary and municipal campaigns since that time. The collectivist tone of labourism had undoubtedly become stronger since the 1880s. This did not, however, represent a significant ideological departure, but rather an ongoing evolution within labourist ideology. The concepts that shaped Labour activists' wartime demands had been at the centre of labourism's ideological 'morphology' since the late nineteenth century. In Bristol, the war may have changed the programmatic expression of labourism, but it did not change its underlying conceptual framework.

Labour politics in wartime Northampton

The First World War proved to be a turning point in Northampton's political history. Before the war, the Northampton Labour Representation Council (NLRC) was composed of a small but vocal socialist section that strongly favoured political independence, and a larger Lib–Lab current that expressed conciliatory sentiments towards the Liberal Party. By the end of 1918, the experiences of the war years had transformed this fragile alliance into a unified, independent and ambitious electoral machine. This transformation was a direct consequence of three wartime developments. First, the relative absence of anti-war sentiment within the Northampton Labour and socialist movement helped to give the NLRC an internal unity that it did not have before the war. With the outbreak of war, any lingering political differences between its different sections were quickly set aside. The majority of delegates on the Northampton Trades' Council, which represented the town's trade union movement, interpreted the war as a defence of the 'rights of small nations' and supported the government's efforts to defeat 'Prussian militarism'.[43] The local branch of the BSP was also fiercely pro-war.[44] While anti-war opinion did exist within the local ILP branch, this was by no means universal among its members.[45] As in Bristol, unity on the question of the war allowed the NLRC, renamed the Northampton Labour Party in mid-1918, to present a united front when it contested the first post-war general election in November 1918.

Second, the presence of Labour representatives on local wartime committees helped to strengthen a sense of the unity within the Northampton Labour Party. Throughout the war, members from all sections of the party joined a range of local bodies, including the Committee for the Prevention of Distress, the War Pensions Committee, the Food Control Committee and the local Military Tribunal.[46] These experiences were particularly significant in Northampton because delegates sat as representatives of the Labour Party for the first time, not as members of the BSP,

ILP or other constituent sections. Furthermore, the involvement of the party's leaders in various cross-party committees enhanced the party's prestige within local political circles. This was especially true in the case of the Allied War Fund Committee, a charitable scheme that channelled funds to various war-related causes. Devised by James Gribble, a founding member of the local Labour Party, the scheme had raised a total of £27,778 by the war's end.[47] This example of public service was commended by a wide range of eminent individuals and organisations in the town, an expression of gratitude that Gribble, an erstwhile militant socialist, was not used to. He had, after all, been '[P]reaching simple things to Northampton for twenty-five years, but this was the first time he had been able to induce people to take any notice of them!'[48]

Finally, Labour activists' decision to break with their old political strategy emerged out of the contrasting wartime fortunes of the Labour and Liberal parties. Throughout the war, a pacifist element emerged within the Northampton Liberal Party that opposed its leaders' attitude to the war and the political truce.[49] As a result, a number of activists left the Liberal Party altogether during the war years and made the transition into the reorganised Labour Party.[50] Divisions among the local Liberals were particularly apparent in the divergent attitudes and actions of the town's two Liberal MPs. Whereas Charles McCurdy remained a loyal supporter of David Lloyd George throughout the war, Hastings Lees-Smith exhibited scepticism towards the coalition, its policies and, increasingly, towards the Liberal Party itself.[51] The perceived weakness of the Liberal Party, especially when compared to the impressive growth of Labour Party-affiliated trade unions, convinced Labour activists of the desirability and feasibility of independent political action.[52] By the time the armistice was signed in November 1918, the Northampton Labour Party was stronger and more united than ever before, and it put forward Walter Halls of the National Union of Railwaymen as its candidate for the 'coupon election'. While Halls was ultimately unsuccessful in his attempt to unseat the Coalition candidate, the party's adoption of a firmly independent political strategy represented a significant turning point in local progressive politics. The historic and pragmatic Lib–Lab alliance in Northampton, which had dominated progressive politics in the town since at least the late 1860s, finally passed out of existence under the strain of war.

Class identity in wartime Northampton

The war did not have such a transformative impact on local activists' conception of class and the social order. Before the war, Labour activists in Northampton had, like their counterparts in Bristol, portrayed British society as one in which class distinctions, but not class antagonisms, were paramount. Throughout the war, this non-conflicting sense of class remained the most frequently articulated view of class relations in local Labour circles. Indeed, it is not difficult to find class-exclusivist sentiments in activists' statements about the conflict. While Labour activists acknowledged the need for cross-class unity, they still believed that, ultimately, the workers would contribute and suffer most during the war.[53] This class-based view of the war effort led some activists to criticise those sections of the community that, they felt, had not contributed sufficiently. One activist went so far as to support conscription as a way to force the 'middle-class ... fancy sock brigade' to do their fair share of the fighting. Advocacy of conscription was certainly a minority viewpoint in local Labour circles, but this hostility to the middle class still found favour among trades' council delegates. A. H. Cox, for instance, agreed that 'a large body of middle-class young men' who were 'physically capable' had decided not to join the army. 'The working-class', on the other hand, 'had sent a far larger proportion of its young men.'[54]

Throughout the war years, some Labour activists in Northampton began to use more antagonistic terms in their political appeals and written statements.[55] But while statements of this kind were more common than they had been before the war, they were simply not widespread enough to suggest that, by the end of 1918, adversarial images of society had become dominant among Labour activists in Northampton. Indeed, there are a number of examples of activists moderating their views towards employers and the capitalist class during this period. In 1911, James Gribble had favoured 'industrial warfare' and the secession of his trade union from the Labour Party, but by early 1920 he had begun to urge 'the workers' to '*convert* the organisers of industry to see that their greater happiness was bound up with collective ownership'.[56] Furthermore, it is important to remember that resolutions from trade union branches did not necessarily represent the views of the wider membership, especially when one considers the poor attendance rate of trade union meetings.[57] While there may have been a discernible shift towards an antagonistic vision of class relations among some Labour activists during this period, this was far from universal.

As in Bristol, there were also continuities in the way Labour activists conceived of and defined the 'working class'. Despite significant wartime changes in the composition of Northampton's booming boot and shoe industry, activists' restrictive definition of this class largely survived the war years intact.[58] After employers had exhausted the supply of male operatives in trying to meet the wartime demand for army boots, they began to introduce women's labour, with the reluctant agreement of the NUBSO, in traditionally male-only departments.[59] But there is little evidence to suggest that male Labour activists' attitudes to women workers changed as a result of these developments. At a well-attended conference on women's labour in 1916, for example, male trade unionists offered their support to women in their struggle for higher wages and better working conditions, but expressed their opposition in principle to the further employment of women.[60] James Gribble summarised this attitude in the *Socialist Pioneer* in 1916. The advent of women into departments that had traditionally been regarded as male jobs, he argued, had caused 'considerable concern to officials and members of trades unions'. While Gribble believed that employers should pay women the same wage rates as men, he desired the government's assurances that the employment of women was to be a temporary measure only.[61]

Labour activists' attitudes towards foreign workers also remained far from inclusive. As in Bristol, the war encouraged activists in Northampton to clarify their views about nationality, patriotism and race. Some, such as BSP councillor Fred Kirby, interpreted the war in highly nationalistic and even racial terms. During a local controversy involving a German-born tramways manager, Kirby proposed the locking up of all Germans and Austrians because, he argued, they could not be trusted.[62] While Kirby's statements were widely condemned by activists in the Northampton Labour movement, they too justified their support for the war by evoking patriotic themes. The Northampton Trades' Council resolved that Britain had entered the war to defend the 'rights of small nations' against 'Prussian militarism'.[63] The local branch of the BSP agreed with this interpretation of the war and resolved that 'Socialism, Patriotism, and Internationalism are perfectly reconcilable'.[64] These attitudes were not direct products of the wartime period. As I have argued elsewhere, patriotic themes had shaped the class identities of Labour activists in the town since the late nineteenth century.[65] While there was a marked shift in the prevalence of discussions about 'other' categories of worker, there was no concurrent shift in the attitudes of male activists. Their perception of who was, and was not, part of the 'working class' remained largely unchanged throughout the wartime period.

Labourism in wartime Northampton

A similar line of continuity can be drawn between pre-war and wartime articulations of labourist ideology. In Northampton, as in Bristol, Labour activists' wartime demands rested on the key concepts of democracy, constitutionalism, rights, liberty and collectivism. Democracy in particular remained an important concept for local Labour activists. While the question of contesting elections largely diminished in importance during this period, activists still sought to realise their long-held goal of increasing labour representation by demanding representation on various wartime committees. By the end of 1918, trade unionists and socialists sat on the

Citizens' Relief Committee, the Military Tribunal and Naval and Military War Pensions Act committee, which represented a marked rise in the Labour Party's pre-war political influence.[66] As the war drew to a close, Labour activists, now free of their historic commitment to the Liberal Party, also began to demand a greater share of representation in the House of Commons.[67] This desire for parliamentary representation even found favour among a number of important local trade union branches that had previously resisted attempts to stand independent Labour candidates.[68]

Throughout the 1918 election campaign, Labour Party activists in Northampton were also keen to demonstrate their unswerving commitment to the constitutional order.[69] In particular, accusations of Bolshevism during the 1918 election encouraged activists to re-emphasise their loyalty to the English constitution.[70] Walter Halls denied that he was a revolutionary and insisted that it was 'the Coalitionists that were out for chaos'.[71] In any case, accusations that Labour activists wished to overturn the existing order were entirely unfounded. As before the war, they did not consider there to be anything inherently wrong with the 'free and democratic character' of institutions such as the House of Commons.[72] Rather, they criticised the composition of these bodies and argued that the relative lack of working-class representatives on them prevented them from being truly representative. Labour activists in Northampton still sought to improve, rather than subvert, the existing political order.[73]

The concepts of rights and liberty also featured prominently in Labour activists' wartime discourse. For example, Frederick Roberts, a leading member of the ILP and the Northampton Trades' Council at this time, considered conscription 'abhorrent' to 'liberty-loving Englishmen' and 'a serious menace' to the 'freedom and liberty of the Labour movement'.[74] This hostility to the perceived violation of individual and trade union freedoms by the state, however, did not prevent Labour activists from advocating greater state intervention in other areas. Trades' Council delegates favoured a strong government response to rising food prices as a way to protect the working class from extortionate demands.[75] At other times during the war, they urged the government to set coal prices, to control shipping and to impose rent controls.[76] By the time of the 1918 election, the demand for the conscription of wealth had also become a popular demand within local Labour circles.[77]

These collectivist demands were consistent with the national Labour Party's message during the 1918 election. As in Bristol though, this did not represent a significant ideological departure for local Labour activists. In contrast to their socialist allies, those who could best be described as 'labourists' still tended to justify their support for statist solutions in thoroughly pragmatic terms, seeing them as simply effective and, by the end of the war, proven methods of achieving long-held goals.[78] Labourists also only favoured state ownership of *certain* industries and state intervention in *some* spheres of economic activity. There was, for instance, bitter resistance within the local and national NUBSO towards the government's decision to extend unemployment insurance to the boot and shoe trade.[79] This qualified advocacy of collectivist solutions was clearly distinct from that of Northampton-based socialists like William Pitts, who believed that 'the people' should take over the 'whole means of life'.[80] At one election meeting in 1918, Alfred Slinn, a local Labour councillor, offered a perceptive analysis of this somewhat confusing distinction between labourist and socialist ideology. As a socialist, Slinn admitted that he wished to see 'reconstruction upon the basis of a Social Democratic Republic'. He acknowledged, however, that some of those present at the meeting did not want this. Instead, they wanted 'security of employment, better wages, better housing, and food and other commodities at reasonable prices'.[81] This was an accurate description of labourism, an ideology that, despite taking on a more collectivist accent, did not undergo a significant conceptual transformation during the war years.

Conclusion

Although they failed in their attempt to achieve parliamentary representation in 1918, the Labour parties in Bristol and Northampton made steady gains in parliamentary and municipal elections throughout the 1920s.[82] The post-war realignment of progressive politics in these constituencies was the product of both local and national developments, such as divisions within the Liberal Party and the growing legitimisation of the Labour Party, which fall outside the scope of this chapter. This chapter does suggest, however, that the post-war rise of the Labour Party in Bristol and Northampton was not the outcome of a significant change in Labour activists' understandings of class, the social order or ideology during the war years. First, this chapter has argued that continuities within wartime Labour politics were evident in the way Labour activists articulated their understanding of class and class relations. Throughout the war, and as in the pre-war period, activists in these constituencies directed their appeals exclusively towards the working-class section of the community and sought to convince listeners and readers that their organisations were unambiguously class based in both composition and orientation. At the same time, and despite a slight increase in antagonistic sentiments among some activists, their conception of society remained thoroughly non-conflicting in tone during the war years. As before the war, exclusivist attitudes were strong among Labour activists, while antagonistic sentiments were not.

Second, this chapter has suggested that there were continuities in the way male Labour activists defined the working class. Industrial changes brought about by the war forced them to consider the lives and conditions of 'other' workers, especially women, to a greater extent than ever before. Nevertheless, their statements and attitudes during the war years continued to demonstrate the restrictive assumptions that underpin their class identities. Most male activists continued to appeal to women primarily as wives and homemakers rather than as fellow workers, and continued to use highly gendered terms in their political discourse. The war also drew out Labour activists' assumptions about nationality and, at times, race. Pro-war activists in Bristol and Northampton interpreted the war in thoroughly nationalistic terms and claimed that their democratic British instincts had forced them to sympathise with the nations that had been threatened by Prussian militarism. These sentiments had been at the core of labourist identities in these constituencies long before 1914.

Finally, this chapter has argued that in Bristol and Northampton, there were strong ideological continuities between pre-war and wartime labourism. While certain developments during the war changed the political demands of Labour activists, it did not transform the ideological framework on which they were based. Indeed, it was their commitment to the concepts that that had long defined this ideology that shaped their responses to a number of wartime problems. Thus, their desire for representation on wartime committees emanated from their class-based understanding of democracy. Their rejection of extra-parliamentary strategies was based on their continued faith in, and democratic reading of, the English constitution. Their hostility to wartime legislation, such as the DORA and conscription, emerged from the assumption that the constitution granted certain political and industrial rights to all individuals (or, at least, all men). As we have seen, their demands did become more collectivist throughout the war, as demonstrated in their statist electoral programmes of 1918. However, this did not represent the final transformation of labourism into socialism, but simply the next stage in a long-running ideological evolution that had begun in the 1880s.

Notes

1 For examples of revisionist work that emphasises the transformative impact of the First World War, see P. Joyce, *Visions of the People: Industrial England and the Question of Class, 1840–1914* (Cambridge, 1991), p. 8; E. Biagini and A. Reid, 'Introduction', in E. Biagini and A. Reid (eds), *Currents of Radicalism: Popular Radicalism, Organised Labour and Party Politics in Britain, 1850–1914* (Cambridge, 1991), pp. 16–17. More recent studies have not fundamentally challenged this view of the war. For example, see M. Worley, *Labour Inside the Gate: A History of the British Labour Party between the Wars* (London, 2005), pp. 7–8; M. Pugh, *Speak For Britain! A New History of the Labour Party* (London, 2010), p. 100; S. Todd, *The People: The Rise and Fall of the Working*

Class, 1910–1920 (London, 2014), p, 30. There are, however, exceptions. See R. McKibbin, *The Evolution of the Labour Party 1910–1924* (Oxford, 1983), p. 105; D. Tanner, *Political change and the Labour party, 1900–1918* (Cambridge, 1990), pp. 351–3.
2 The single-member constituency of Bristol sent only one Conservative MP to Parliament between 1852 and 1885. The predominantly working-class constituency of Bristol East, created in 1885, continued to elect Liberals consistently until 1923. Conservative candidates were successful on just four occasions in the double-member constituency of Northampton between 1837 and 1918.
3 Joyce, *Visions of the People*, p. 8.
4 B. Drake, *Women in Trade Unions* (London, 1984), pp. 68–9; S. Boston, *Women Workers and the Trade Union Movement* (London, 1980), p. 108; A. Woollacott, *On Her Their Lives Depend: Munitions Workers in the Great War* (London, 1994), p. 17.
5 P. Ward, *Red Flag and the Union Jack: Englishness, Patriotism and the British Left, 1881–1924* (Woodbridge, 1998), pp. 121–6; Pugh, *Speak For Britain!*, p. 12.
6 M. Kidd, 'Popular Political Continuity in Urban England, 1867–1918: The Case Studies of Bristol and Northampton' (PhD dissertation, University of Nottingham, 2016).
7 M. Freeden, *Ideologies and Political Theory: A Conceptual Approach* (Oxford, 1998), pp. 77–84, 438, 444, 447–9, 459.
8 A. Clinton, *The Trade Union Rank and File: Trades Councils in Britain, 1900–40* (Manchester, 1977), p. 64; D. Large and R. Whitfield, *The Bristol Trades Council, 1873–1973* (Bristol, 1973), pp. 16–17.
9 By 1918, the local Dockers' Union had as many members as all the unions of pre-war Bristol combined. Large and Whitfield, *The Bristol Trades Council*, p. 15; R. Whitfield, 'Trade Unionism in Bristol, 1910–1926', in I. Bild (ed.), *Bristol's Other History* (Bristol, 1983), pp. 68–96, 81–3; K. Kelly and M. Richardson, 'The Shaping of the Bristol Labour Movement, 1885–1985', in M. Dresser and P. Ollerenshaw (eds), *The Making of Modern Bristol* (Tiverton, 1996), pp. 210–36, 218; D. Backwith, R. Ball, S. E. Hunt and M. Richardson (eds), *Strikers, Hobblers, Conchies and Reds: A Radical History of Bristol 1880–1939* (Newton Abbott, 2014).
10 *Western Daily Press* (hereafter *WDP*), 12 February 1916; 16 February 1916; 6 May 1916; *Bristol Guardian*, 17 November 1917.
11 Modern Records Centre, Warwick (hereafter MRC), 547/P/1/26, National Union of Operative Boot and Shoe Rivetters and Finishers: Monthly reports (hereafter NUBSO MR), January 1910; *WDP*, 30 December 1918.
12 S. Bryher, *An Account of the Labour and Socialist Movement in Bristol: Part 3* (Bristol, 1931), p. 7; J. Hannam, *Bristol Independent Labour Party: Men, Women and the Opposition to War* (Bristol, 2014).
13 Bristol Records Office, Bristol (hereafter BRO), 32080/TC10/24(b), Bristol ILP General Secretary's Monthly Reports and Press Cuttings (hereafter BILP GS), 6 September 1915; *Bristol Times and Mirror* (hereafter *BT&M*), 28 August 1915; C. Thomas, *Slaughter No Remedy: The Life and Times of Walter Ayles, Bristol Conscientious Objector* (Bristol, 2016).

14 J. Lynch, *A Tale of Three Cities: Comparative Studies in Working-Class Life* (London, 1998), p. 154; British Library of Political and Economic Science, London (hereafter LSE), ILP/5/1916/6, 'Defence before the court-martial' by W. H. Ayles, author's defence speech.
15 Although he had doubts about the war, Bevin 'would have nothing to do with the I.L.P. and the pacifist minority within the Labour party'. A. Bullock, *The Life and Times of Ernest Bevin, Volume One: Trade Union Leader, 1881–1940* (London, 1960), p. 48.
16 *BT&M*, 10 November 1915.
17 Large and Whitfield, *The Bristol Trades Council*, p. 14.
18 BRO, 32080/TC6/2/1, Bristol Labour Party Election Leaflets, T. C. Lewis (hereafter TL), 1918; BRO, 44562/2, Political pamphlet issued by Bristol Central Labour Party for Ernest Bevin's campaign (hereafter EB), 1918.
19 *WDP*, 18 November 1918; 3 December 1918; 4 December 1918; 10 December 1918.
20 *WDP*, 28 November 1918; 2 December 1918; 4 December 1918; 30 December 1918.
21 BRO, 32080/TC10/24(b), BILP GS, 2 April 2015,
22 *WDP*, 13 January 1917; Bullock, *Ernest Bevin*, p. 69.
23 E. Malos, 'Bristol Women in Action, 1839–1919', in Bild, pp. 97–128, 125.
24 For examples, see *WDP*, 4 December 1918; 10 December 1918; 12 December 1918.
25 G. Braybon, *Women Workers in the First World War* (London, 1981), pp. 73–4; S. Kent, *Sex and Suffrage in Britain, 1860–1914* (Princeton, 1987), p. 221; BRO, 44562/2, EB, 1918; *WDP*, 2 December 1918; 4 December 1918, 12 December 1918. For more on the experiences of women in Bristol, see M. Dresser (ed.), *Women and the City: Bristol 1373–2000* (Bristol, 2016); A. Tuckett, *Our Enid: The Life and Work of Enid Stacy, 1868–1903* (Salford, 2016); S. Rowbotham, *Rebel Crossings: New Women, Free Lovers, and Radicals in Britain and the United States* (London, 2016).
26 *WDP*, 8 May 1916; 7 May 1917.
27 Letter 'F. Sheppard' to *WDP*, 11 November 1914.
28 *BT&M*, 10 November 1915.
29 *WDP*, 10 November 1915.
30 *Bristol Observer*, 26 September 1914; *WDP*, 16 February 1916; 8 May 1916.
31 *WDP*, 10 August 1914.
32 BRO, 32080/TC6/2/1, TL, 1918.
33 Bevin at a campaign meeting, *WDP*, 7 December 1918.
34 A local committee of the Provisional Committee of the Workers' and Soldiers' Council was organised in Bristol, but it seems to have faded rapidly. Clinton, *Trade Union Rank and File*, p. 115; *WDP*, 30 July 1917.
35 *WDP*, 14 December 1918; 24 December 1917.
36 *WDP*, 24 December 1917; 2 December 1918; 6 December 1918; 10 December 1918; 14 December 1918, emphasis added.
37 For examples, see MRC, 547/P/1/32, National Union of Operative Boot and Shoe Rivetters and Finishers: Conference reports (hereafter NUBSO CR), 1916.
38 BRO, 44562/2, EB, 1918; BRO, 32080/TC6/2/1, TL, 1918.

39 Large and Whitfield, *The Bristol Trades Council*, p. 14; *WDP*, 7 August 1914; 10 August 1914.
40 BRO, 32080/TC6/2/1, TL, 1918; *WDP*, 25 November 1918; 28 November 1918; 10 December 1918.
41 *WDP*, 15 November 1918.
42 For an example of this view, see J. Tomlinson, 'Labour and the Economy', in D. Tanner, P. Thane and N. Tiratsoo (eds), *Labour's First Century* (Cambridge, 2000), pp. 46–79, 52.
43 Northamptonshire Record Office, Northampton (hereafter NRO), 1977/44/NTC3, Northampton Trades' Council Minute Book 16 July 1913–12 July 1916 (hereafter NTC), 1 October 1914.
44 *Socialist Pioneer* (hereafter *SP*), October 1914; June 1915; December 1915; July 1916. The Northampton BSP joined the pro-war National Socialist Party in 1916.
45 NRO, 1977/44/NTC3, NTC, 17 November 1915.
46 NRO, 1977/44/NTC3, NTC, 27 August 1914; 19 April 1916; *Northampton Mercury* (hereafter *NM*), 17 March 1916; 17 August 1917; NRO, 1977/44/NTC3, NTC, 18 November 1914; 27 October 1915; 10 March 1916; Clinton, *Trade Union Rank and File*, p. 63.
47 NRO, 1977/44/NTC3, NTC, 21 April 1915; *NM*, 28 June 1918.
48 *Northampton Daily Echo* (hereafter *NDE*), 28 June 1916; *NM*, 30 June 1916.
49 *NDE*, 19 November 1918; *Northampton Independent* (hereafter *NI*), 23 November 1918.
50 *NM*, 15 February 1918; *NDE*, 10 December 1918.
51 *NM*, 26 July 1918; NRO, 1977/44/NTC3, NTC, 10 January 1916.
52 Growth was particularly marked in the local NUBSO branches. MRC, 547/P/1/34, NUBSO MR, August 1918.
53 *SP*, January 1916.
54 NRO, 1977/44/NTC3, NTC, 16 June 1915.
55 MRC, 547/P/1/34, NUBSO CR, 1918; Letter 'J. W. Clarke' to *NDE*, 10 December 1918; *NDE*, 14 December 1918.
56 MRC, 547/P/1/27, NUBSO MR, December 1911; *NM*, 9 January 1920, emphasis added.
57 W. Griffin, 'The Northampton Boot and Shoe Industry and its Significance for Social Change in the Borough from 1880 to 1914' (MA Dissertation, University of Cardiff, 1968), p. 165.
58 *NM*, 7 August 1914; *NI*, 12 September 1914; MRC, 547/P/1/30, NUBSO MR, October 1914; NRO, 1977/44/NTC3, NTC, 18 November 1914.
59 MRC, 547/P/1/31, NUBSO MR, September 1915; *NM*, 26 November 1915; 3 March 1916; 30 March 1917; MRC, 547/P/1/32, NUBSO CR, 1916.
60 NRO, 1977/44/NTC3, NTC, 22 March 1916; *NM*, 24 March 1916.
61 *SP*, August 1916.
62 NRO, 1977/44/NTC3, NTC, 1 October 1914. Kirby was subsequently expelled from the BSP branch. *NI*, 24 October 1914; *SP*, September 1914.
63 NRO, 1977/44/NTC3, NTC, 1 October 1914.
64 *SP*, December 1915.
65 Kidd, 'Popular Political Continuity', pp. 62, 124.

66 *NM*, 14 August 1914; 21 August 1914; 28 August 1914; 10 March 1916; 17 March 1916; 7 April 1916; 17 August 1917.
67 BL, 08139.CCC.2, NLRC, 1917; MRC, 547/P/1/34, NUBSO CR, 1918; *NM*, 7 June 1918.
68 BL, 08139.CCC.2, NLRC, 1917.
69 *NM*, 20 July 1917; Clinton, *Trade Union Rank and File*, p. 115.
70 *NM*, 13 December 1918: Coalition Liberal candidate Charles McCurdy claimed that some sections of the Labour party would 'hoist the Bolshevist banner' once in power.
71 *NDE*, 11 December 1918.
72 NRO, 1977/4/NTC3, NTC, 1915.
73 *NDE*, 11 December 1918.
74 NRO, 1977/4/NTC3, NTC, 1915; NRO, 1977/44/NTC3, NTC, 16 June 1915.
75 NRO, 1977/44/NTC3, NTC, 20 January 1915; 24 May 1916; *NM*, 7 August 1914; Clinton, *Trade Union Rank and File*, p. 66.
76 NRO, 1977/44/NTC3, NTC, 17 February 1915.
77 *NM*, 15 February 1918.
78 *NDE*, 25 November 1918.
79 A. Fox, *A History of the National Union of Boot and Shoe Operatives 1874–1957* (Oxford, 1958), p. 381; *NM*, 18 August 1916; 6 October 1916.
80 MRC, 547/P/1/33, NUBSO MR, June 1917; *SP*, January 1917.
81 *NDE*, 6 December 1918.
82 *WDP*, 2 November 1923; 7 December 1923; *NM*, 2 November 1923; 14 December 1923.

5

A stronghold of liberalism? The north-east Lancashire cotton weaving districts and the First World War

Jack Southern

The First World War fundamentally altered the cotton 'weaving belt' areas of Lancashire and was, despite a temporary reprieve in 1919/20, to spell the start of a slow, painful, economic and social decline. The disruption of trade arising from the war ultimately commenced the transformation of an area that prided itself on its independence and ability to 'make' money, to one that by the 1930s many operatives and owners looked to escape. As a reporter from the *Burnley Express* stated in 1930: 'I have heard scores of millowners say, "happen what may, my son isn't going in t'mill" a remarkable attitude in a county and industry where family tradition has always been strong.'[1]

The cotton industry had, up until 1913, experienced an 'Indian summer',[2] and in some towns it was still expanding.[3] There was a steadfast belief in the long-term viability of cotton and in the global importance of cotton towns. Socially, however, a number of issues had developed that had been masked by the positivity emanating from the industry itself. The impact of the short, sharp drop in productivity and disruption caused by the outbreak of war caused these issues to manifest across social relations locally, and confidence to erode. Therefore, the impact of the war in several ways polarised and split apart the communities of the area, challenging the established modes of life.

The focus of this chapter is the impact of the war on the cotton operatives of the 'world's weaving centre' Burnley,[4] with reference to the surrounding districts.[5] This chapter explores how the experience of war fundamentally challenged the local confidence in the cotton industry by primarily looking at the cornerstones of local life: the weaving family unit and trade unionism. Indeed, Burnley was regarded contemporarily to have suffered 'more than any other textile district' from the First World War,[6] and the aim here is to explore the key changes

Table 5.1 World trade in cotton textiles (million sq. yards/ 000 quintals)

	1882–84	1910–13	1926–28	1936–38
UK	4410	6650	3940	1720
Europe	770	1900	2320	1490
USA	150	400	540	250
India	50	90	170	200
Japan	...	200	1390	2510
Other countries	...	260	190	290

Source: Robert Robson, *The British Cotton Industry* (London: Macmillan, 1957), p. 4.

and events the outbreak of war sparked that left a lasting effect on labour.

Little interest has been paid to the combined impact of international war in 1914–18 and the ensuing economic uncertainty upon the cotton weaving towns of north-east Lancashire in a social sense, although the decline of British cotton has been long debated.[7] However, external issues in world markets and internal structural issues together removed the Lancastrian hegemony over cotton. As shown in Table 5.1, the decline of cotton was dramatic, but for much of the interwar period this was seen as temporary. The impact that the process of decline had upon the weaving communities, focused on the export market, therefore demands attention.

The industrial structure of north-east Lancashire was unique. In 1911, for example, the weaving districts employed around three times the amount of females (as a proportion of the population) than the national average.[8] Weaving was also dominated by small manufacturers (rather than a small number of large manufacturers as in other industries), with the belief that the majority of mill owners had worked their way up from the 'shop floor'.[9] It was difficult for a collective identity to develop among the employer classes, and this sense of individual endeavour spread to operatives. The common belief was that 'anyone' could make their fortune in cotton through hard work and luck. This had two main effects. First, it lessened class distinction, and as a result, created more opportunity for what Jeffrey Hill called 'political action'.[10] Second, it encouraged a community-wide engagement in both political and economic life. As such, this was reflected in both the wide-ranging labour movement, and the impetus for the Liberals to respond. In the less urbanised areas, there was a tendency to stay staunchly loyal to the Liberal Party, but within the larger population centres, there was great overlap between the Liberal–Labour ideologies. The reliance upon liberal, laissez-faire ideals meant that the wider area was regarded as a 'stronghold of liberalism', mentally and politically.[11] As Hill again describes, Burnley especially had a 'radical tradition' that remained strong and 'presented a picture of the classic Victorian alliance of small owners and workers against the forces of privilege.'[12] Unlike other northern industrial towns, it remained wedded to this particular Lancashire cotton spirit and epitomised the mentally that was described in 1928 by Ethel Dietrich: 'it has acquired a proud tradition which is shared by employers, investors and operatives who have with their ancestors been born and bred in the industry. Nowhere have the shibboleths of laissez faire clung with such persistence until Lancashire individualism has become a byword.'[13] In the midst of decline this bullish attitude had come to hinder the industry, but, in a practical sense, prior to the war, the collective spirit stood for more than just an individual, and extended to the family and local community units as the basis of local society.

The impact of the war on family structure and the role of women

Weaving dominated the local economy in north-east Lancashire. In Burnley in 1915, out of a population of 106,000 around 40 per cent of male labour, and 76 per cent of female labour, was engaged in the cotton industry.[14] The only other industries of note were coal mining and machine building, both of which were ancillaries to, and reliant upon, the fortunes of cotton. There had been little industrial diversification during the years prior to the First World War. In Nelson and to a lesser extent Colne, progress had been made through the incorporation of 'fancy' or 'fine' cloths, which catered to several markets but, for the majority of the area, the staple good was either 'grey cloth' or medium quality goods, produced for the export market.

Traditionally, operatives tended to live in walking distance from the mill in clusters surrounded by their own extended family.[15] The bonds of family and kinship were also reinforced, and amplified, within the mill environment. Family members were known to work alongside each other, with some sharing the looms. It was also common for multiple generations of families to work in the same mill, while the methods of training weavers entailed an apprenticeship to a family member, or by a 'surrogate'.[16] The familial system was, in theory, mutually beneficial for operative and employer. For the latter, it served as a form of maintaining discipline, and creating a sense of loyalty to the mill. For the operatives it was the basis of the family wage, in that both parents and any children were expected to contribute to a combined income, which individually would be insufficient, but combined meant that the weaving districts were comparatively well paid compared other industrial communities. As well as providing for a higher combined total wage, this system encouraged forms of social security and encouraged savings, further complemented by local institutions such as the Co-operative. Owing to the unique pay structure in Lancashire weaving districts, women were sometimes paid equally or close to men. As Hill argues, this meant that the status of women was not 'structured in inferiority', and gave them a 'sense of importance and self-confidence'.[17] As was shown in a report into family wages in 1909, the averages between six weaving towns and six spinning towns highlighted that although male spinning operatives were paid on the whole nearly double female spinning operatives (31s 8d to 17s 4d) weavers were paid generally closer (28s 1d to 20s 8d) on average.[18] In some towns, such as Nelson, women were paid closer to 30s per week.[19]

Overall, the familial system created a patchwork of dependency, reinforcing community ties.[20] The sense of mutual dependency extended into industrial relations, where the emphasis was on the 'collective good' of the industry. Since the acceptance of the Brooklands Agreement in 1893, the focus of industrial relations was the idea of the 'joint relationship', and of maintaining stability.[21] The familial system also permeated into most aspects of local society, and the self-confidence of women helped create what Michael Savage has called 'a general equality' between men and women at a level not seen outside of the county.[22] Despite the more balanced, family based structure, Carol Morgan has argued that cotton women were not positioned 'nor did they position themselves as equals'.[23] They were, however, involved in decision making, both in the home and workplace. They had roles in trade disputes, local politics and forms of 'soft' authority in respective spheres.[24] The system provided a cultural structure for communities that was stable, established and passed on to future generations.[25]

Women in north-east Lancashire had an active role economically and socially in everyday life. As Susan Pyecroft argues, the role of women nationally, in a general sense, before the war 'reflected the traditional view that women's work was of lesser value and therefore deserved lower pay'.[26] She details a shift for women into more visible public roles and positions through the onset of war, and also from 'hidden' worlds including textile factories. Yet, the societal freedoms enjoyed by cotton operatives were different to those in other parts of the country. One local newspaper report describing the popularity of hockey in 1914 highlights the differences between the young female workers of Burnley and London, and reinforces the dominant local cultural identity:

> The Lancashire lass is not poor as girls go. To say that hockey is cheap would seem a mockery to a London factory hand. A set of London jam or match-factory girls could not hope to play such a game unless they were subsidised by kind ladies. Besides it would make them too hungry. The Lancashire girl can, if she will, organise and run a hockey club without charitable aid.[27]

The established familial system came under attack almost immediately from the outbreak of war. The rivalry that developed between local male weavers and colliers to outdo each other's recruitment figures meant a quick removal of many males from the workplace, and a void socially, culturally and industrially. In addition, a number of men who did not enlist were requisitioned to other roles. For example, by October 1916, 1,350 members of the Colne and District Weavers' Association were serving in either the Army or Navy, 'practically every eligible male weaver'.[28] There thus existed a recalibration of the norm, which although expected under wartime conditions, was exacerbated by perceived external interference of 'outside' bodies.

There grew a belief that those 'outside' of the area did not understand the situation, and if they did, simply did not care. One local survey in 1917 responded to the publication of a Board of Trade report into food prices by arguing that:

> To the wearied and worried housewife, frantically struggling to provide substantial and nutritive meals for her family, the estimate of the Board of Trade ... in the price of food ... had little significance. Such estimates are of value chiefly to those whose business it is to represent human life in figures.[29]

The lack of stable work, as mills stopped working with alarming frequency under declining trading conditions, removed a key element in the established coping mechanisms of the mill community and signaled a shift to external solutions. Women had to adapt to performing a more outwardly authoritative role. For the older married women, there was a shift in emphasis to act as a solo breadwinner. Yet, although relief schemes were undertaken locally, these were generally aimed at men. Added to this, the drop in trade meant that the local union, the Burnley Weavers Association (BWA), could not issue any form of unemployment relief for long periods.[30] The conditions in September 1914 deteriorated to the level where 5th Battalion of the East Lancashire Regiment sent unconsumed rations to distribute to needy families.[31] By late August 1915, around 2,000 families needed relief from the Education Committee's distribution of free meals.[32]

Local initiatives were quickly set up to try and ease the burden. By 1916, the League of Social Service had developed alongside other cross-class organisations to counter the increased cost of living brought on by the war, with some run as a 'municipal enterprise' not for profit, but to feed young fatherless families.[33] A particular focus was the number of 'lonely women' in the town who were offered companionship, entertainment and services, such as letter writing and literacy classes. The most notable group was the little studied Tipperary Room movement, who specifically set out to create a support network for women and gained particular traction among the female industrial populations such as in London, Walsall and Burnley. Set up originally in London in October 1914, as an 'alternative public house',[34] the movement spread to north-east Lancashire with the opening of a room in Padiham in January 1915,[35] and then to Burnley in February of the same year, followed by two further rooms by April.[36]

Despite the speed in which local initiatives mobilised, problems still existed that challenged the community. Burnley suffered from profiteering – with imported white flour, and the unscrupulous methods of acquisition a contentious issue.[37] The milk supply was generally inadequate, but yielded higher profits for farmers than before the war.[38] Accusations were levelled at the local brewers' inflating prices but they in turn blamed the 'fanatical temperance groups' whom they linked to conscientious objection. They sought to portray their industry as a vanguard against internal enemies and issued statements claiming that only their patriotism had stopped them downing tools in the face of agitation and 'insults'.[39]

In more practical terms, even if work had remained stable, the cost of living now far outstripped wages. Solutions were sought through precedent. Yet, the combination of depression and war was a wholly new experience, and where kinship and workplace relationships had previously existed as a coping mechanism, these were now diminished. The severity of the situation, the Burnley Weavers' Association suggested in their May 1917 quarterly report, was that:

> Statesmen usually extricate themselves from similar situations by raising loans, and business men in like circumstances pay the increased prices and pass them on; but the housewife, however astute she may be, is unable to circumvent her difficulties in either of these ways … there is no Solomon among us to tell her by what sorcery she can transform her shrunken weekly income into the necessities of the household from Saturday to Saturday.[40]

There existed a lack of practical strategy to cope with the situation, but the solutions proposed were increasingly women-led and assertive. The Burnley Association for the Care of Friendless Girls, the Girls Friendly Society and the League of Social Service placed emphasis on serving a moral purpose, offering guidance and education to women in need. Many of the organisations had patriotic ideologies. The most famous example in Burnley was twelve-year-old Jennie Jackson, who sold 'comforts' for soldiers dressed as 'Young Kitchener'. The Girls Friendly Society described themselves as an 'Imperial Society',[41] while The Tipperary Room movement was named after the famous song, and naturally through its links to the Soldiers' and Sailors' Association was adorned with Union flags. Patriotism, however, was a complex issue. There had long been a growing peace movement spearheaded by women that from 1917 grew louder in Nelson, and combined with a local ILP campaign to attempt to oust war hero and local MP Captain Albert Smith.[42] The prominence of the peace movement, and the subsequent backlash against it, resulted in 'stormy scenes' that had not been witnessed before.[43] In Burnley, Philip Morrell, a key figure in the Union of Democratic Control (UDC) and outspoken pacifist stood down in 1918 after the local Liberal Association withdrew their support for him.[44]

The increased assertiveness by women is evidenced by the number of lectures and events held that focused on the active role women would play politically after the war. A discussion held by the Padiham Women's Emergency Association in February 1915 perhaps best summarised this shift by arguing that 'The coming generation needed them. This was England's call to Englishwomen.'[45]

The challenges to trade unionism and labour

The anti-war movement was linked to an undercurrent still actively engaged in women's suffrage. Some groups had ceased activities during the war, and indeed softened their ideological position as a sacrifice.[46] Yet in others, such as in Nelson, women campaigners took a more visibly prominent role. The increased female presence in the public arena resulted in successes locally in women's issues such as local facilities for maternity, and women's health more generally. Overall, in Nelson there developed an 'incoherent' mixture of ideologies invested in three broad areas: first, conscription and the treatment of conscientious objectors; second, maternity, infant welfare and women's health; and, third, the peace process.[47]

Despite women's causes gaining more attention, the main political forum was within the trade union. Women comprised the majority of members but they did not hold positions of 'hard' authority. At times, dislocation existed between the female weaving body and the male leadership.[48] Within the mill, tacklers and overlookers were universally men, and again were often recruited through familial patronage, further reinforcing a male dominance over the majority female operative force.[49] Trade union leadership was also overwhelmingly male, and as Alan Fowler has argued, officials were selected on their numerical calculating ability, which through the burden of mill and home roles excluded women.[50] They were, however, comparatively more involved than their female counterparts in the spinning section, and did exert 'soft' authority in other spheres outside of the mill. Owing to the federal nature of cotton trade unionism, the strength of the AWA was reliant on the dominance of local associations. There was thus at times a lack of central control if local issues took precedence. The main rank-and-file could also direct policy and action through sheer size at times, and did so in the period prior to the First World War.[51]

The primary issue that affected all operatives was the protection and advancement of wages. As Joseph L. White has shown, the frequency of strikes in weaving to perceived attacks on wages is very clear.[52] From the turn of the century, concerns grew among the weavers that wages were under attack on two fronts. One was the increasing use of poor quality materials, which due to the fining system in place for poor work reduced wages. Second was the continued existence of non-union workers, which it was believed both undermined the collective strength of the AWA, and allowed said workers to benefit from the efforts of trade unionism without contribution.

A change of leadership for the AWA witnessed an ideological shift leftward around 1910, and increasingly close links to the Labour Party were forged in local districts. This was driven by local associations – especially in Nelson – and from rank and file members. By 1911 unofficial strikes outnumbered official ones by six to one, and in north-east Lancashire were characterised by a new militancy.[53] The result strengthened the membership and created 'a climate akin to a religious revival'.[54] As was argued by AWA Secretary Joseph Cross who was elected in 1906, such enthusiasm was encouraged. He stated that:

> In these days it is absolutely necessary for the workman to take a direct hand in politics and make sure that his wants and needs shall receive full attention and satisfaction at the hands of the legislators.[55]

The AWA attempted to utilise this growing enthusiasm, and support its campaign for wage increases by unionising non-union mills and districts.[56] In 1911, the General Council of the AWA made the decision to financially support local districts in mills with over 85 per cent union membership in refusing to work with non-unionists.[57] The result, after months of agitation, was the threat of lockout from employers. When an agreement could not be reached, the Cotton Spinners and Manufacturers Association (CSMA) carried out their threat in 1912.

The 'great lockout' caused the first real mass dislocation of the workforce since the Lancashire cotton famine of 1861–65, but had two further reaching effects. First, it pitted operative against employer, breaking the notion of effective collective bargaining, in a battle of conditions that the operatives lost. But, second, it pitted operatives (and groups of operatives) against each other, victimising those who wished to remain outside of the union, for example the Catholic Workers Union in Nelson. More importantly it empowered rank and file unionists to act on their own volition in certain areas, and in Colne and Nelson wildcat agitation continued long after the lockout was settled.[58] Therefore, unlike in areas to the south of the weaving district, where, like Burnley, settlement was treated with 'genuine relief and thankfulness',[59] certain pockets of operatives came out of the dispute with a newfound strength and confidence in local collective action. In regard to Nelson, Hill notes that 'there is little doubt that Nelson weavers were in no mood to be dictated to by either employers or union leaders.'[60] White summarises the lockout as part of a wider movement that 'marked a continuation of the workers' propensity to weave a small, dense pattern of strikes fought over local and immediate issues.'[61]

The immediate decline in working conditions and hence wages that the First World War brought therefore created a great deal of pressure upon the AWA to reaffirm its importance. The AWA's main focus was the cost of living and wage increases. Yet following victory in the lockout, the CSMA and local employers were now a more cohesive body. Shortly before the outbreak of war it was decided, with the operatives' input, to operate on 'short time' – closing for four out of sixteen weeks between the February and June 1914 – a decision that left the manufacturers in Manchester 'frankly astonished by the unanimity displayed by the members of the Burnley Manufacturers' Association.'[62] However the newfound unity of the manufacturers contrasted with operatives being exposed to uneven and reduced working hours. The AWA pressured the Board of Trade to utilise the Unemployment Insurance Act 1912, and managed to have emergency grants made.[63] The emphasis rested with the local associations who were financially hamstrung, and in Burnley's case making weekly losses of around £600.[64]

One suggestion to alleviate the distress was that the mills of north-east Lancashire should switch to khaki. However, several issues remained. The machines would be able to weave cotton khaki, but not woollen khaki, and the amount able to do this would only be small (estimated to be 5,000 out of 60,000 looms). Some of the looms in Nelson and Colne, already exchanged and adapted for materials such as sateen, were too light to use. The Yorkshire woollen industry in most cases had the spinning and weaving sectors combined (unlike the areas of specialisation in Lancashire), which would require those in Nelson to acquire the yarn from Yorkshire. There was thus a preference to maintain the separation of cotton and woollen, and merchants were wary of upsetting the status quo.[65] Adaptation needed funds and although some mills did seek to modify their looms, the possibility of damage to the machinery through weaving heavier material created further potential economic outlay. For operatives there was also the psychological element of 'giving up' on cotton.

One possible solution with governmental support was for weavers in depressed areas to migrate to the areas of the West Riding of Yorkshire, where operatives were needed through shortages and nightshift work in khaki weaving.[66] Yet there were no signs of a collective effort. First, the wages for Yorkshire weavers were lower than in Lancashire by around 30 per cent and, second, the lodging houses, taking advantage of the situation, began charging extortionate rates. As the *Burnley Express* argued: 'Burnley weavers who have gone over the border have actually returned home poorer in pocket than when they went, and as they say, they might as well stay at home idle, as they would not be any worse off.'[67] Other attempts to get Burnley weavers to migrate or adapt failed. In November 1915, the mills of Rochdale launched appeals to fill the lack of female operatives, with high wages and 'irreproachable working conditions' to juveniles and older women.[68] A solution that found favour with both the Burnley and Nelson Weavers' Associations was the idea of equipping the army with corduroy uniforms, although this again failed to come to fruition.[69]

The main focus for the AWA was the pursuit of wage increases or a war bonus. From February 1915 as conditions showed tentative signs of improvement, the AWA began to pursue wage advances. For the operatives, there was a joint belief that war bonuses were deserved for their efforts, but more importantly that a wage increase to meet the cost of living was also long overdue.[70] The plea was declined, but as the *Burnley Express* explained there was a local belief that 'no section of the community has been so hard hit as the cotton operatives'.[71] A further application in March for a war bonus on wages was rejected 'owing to the unprofitable and depressed state of business'.[72] The spinning section, threatening to cause another lockout across the industry, managed to achieve their goal of wage advance in July 1915. Their success offered the weaving operatives encouragement, but also caused resentment at being overlooked. The requests were rejected yet again. To add to this setback, the CSMA issued the threat in August 1915 that if depression continued then wages would be reduced.[73]

The AWA were accused of ineffectiveness, and of detachment from the issues affecting everyday operative. In response, they shifted focus to other 'enemies'. In an attempt to finally conquer the presence of non-unionists, they launched strike action in the nearby weaving village of Harle Syke, one of the 'out-districts' that had operated outside of both the AWA and CSMA. As a smaller village, a number of the workers were shareholders in the mills in which they worked and in exchange for stable, regular work with dividends, accepted lower wages. These were due to the 'local disadvantages' of incurring extra transport charges from being more remote. The BWA had maintained a long campaign in Harle Syke over the previous years with mixed results but had reached by their own estimates 60 per cent membership of the operatives working there by August 1915.[74]

In August 1915 a rally was held in Burnley to discuss the efforts of the AWA towards the war bonus, the progress in unionising Harle Syke, and to single out the weavers there as the reason for any bonus being withheld. Leading figures from the AWA openly attacked Harle Syke, and portrayed the operatives there as internal enemies. One speech argued that:

> Harle Syke is the only place that said 'we won't recognise your union'. Either the Harle Syke employer was superhuman in his majesty or the weaver a little below human in his capacity. Either Harle Syke was right and the rest of the county wrong, or Harle Syke was wrong and the rest of the county right ... the weaver who really had British blood in his or her veins would refuse to accept German methods either from German soldiers or English employers ... the policy of terrorism would be no more successful than the policy of non-recognition of the union ... a soldier who ran away would be a coward for life, weavers who didn't strike would be a knobstick for life.[75]

On 18 August a further application for 5 per cent wage advance was rejected. A day later, the AWA handed in 1,200 notices between the eleven companies in Harle Syke. The strike eventually lasted for eight months, but is indicative of the divisions that developed across the local communities of north-east Lancashire. Great emphasis was placed on the financial strength of Harle Syke compared to other districts, and people from across the class spectrum and across north-east Lancashire wrote to the local press to argue the merits and negative aspects of the system that was in place there.

Strikebreaking weavers were assaulted and intimidated, pitched battles were waged with weavers travelling from neighbouring districts to the bus terminus, and as Roland Kippax, a child at the time recalled, the notion of the Harle Syke weavers being traitors was a constant motif. He recalled the placards produced:

> One of these showed a little girl asking her dad 'What did you do in the Great War, Daddy?' The Weavers' Union taking advantage of this, made a copy which said 'What did you do in the Harle Syke strike, Daddy?' And in large capital letters they added KNOBSTICK. These were handed out and pushed through letter boxes of people they knew were working.[76]

For the community of Harle Syke, the strike was an attempt to protect a local working environment that had shielded the village from the harsher aspects of the downturn. The mills divided work across the companies, and through sourcing labour from retired locals and working out shift patterns across extended family members, never totally ceased work. The action was undertaken with direct operative input, and they exercised individualism at odds with the wider collective spirit of the cotton industry. Indeed, at one point when the Harle Syke weavers heard rumours that the local employers had agreed to end the strike with various concessions to the AWA, they launched a counter-strike, downing tools through the indignation at having not been consulted. The *Burnley Express* noted this was 'Gilbertian in its ludicrousness' as now non-unionists were striking against the strike, which, it was argued, was effectively being fought to grant the weavers in Harle Syke higher wages.[77] The collective spirit in Harle Syke delayed any possible solution for several months. The Harle Syke employers were reluctant to guarantee the re-employment of striking operatives – the majority of whom likely came from outside of the village.

The eventual settlement in Harle Syke in March 1916 after thirty weeks was felt to be a compromise, and further damaged the credibility of the BWA and AWA. Operatives did receive a small concession of 5 per cent war bonus in November 1915,[78] but with the threat of reductions dependent on trade. The strike cost around £1,000 per week, with half of the amount being met by the AWA. Although Harle Syke now recognised the AWA, they in turn had their own special status as having 'local disadvantages' recognised, and their desire to pay lower wages accepted.[79] The BWA also launched attacks against other internal 'enemies' in their fight against the cost of living. As has previously been discussed, profiteering locally had become a major issue. The BWA thus publicly attacked the 'unscrupulous profit-makers', and in February 1915, in their quarterly report asked: 'The German who is at war with us we shoot. What shall we do with the British profiteer?'[80]

Despite the blustering rhetoric, the effectiveness of the AWA diminished as the war progressed. The introduction of the Cotton Control Board in 1917 was direct governmental regulation, which significantly altered both orders and working patterns.[81] It also crucially took the emphasis away from the local weaving associations. The decline of influence from the BWA and in turn the AWA, as well as the notable resentment towards employers was perhaps best articulated in a letter to the *Burnley Express* in the midst of the Harle Syke strike. 'A Worker' argued:

> … who is responsible for the Harle Syke strike? The Weavers? No because a large number of them did not want to come out; they were quite satisfied and would rather have a little less money and a bit better work than some of the places in Burnley, where they have to pay extra to get the work done. No it is the Burnley manufacturers who are at the bottom of it all. They do not like to see the Harle Syke people get on, and as for the workers missing out on the war bonus, that is all bluff, because the masters never dreamt of paying one. But it served their purpose to bring Harle Syke in as their excuse … the union have for once been the tool of their masters.[82]

The shift in confidence and the post-war mentality

The post-war recovery and speculative boom created a new confidence in cotton, manifested in 1919–20 through the purchasing of mill shares in the area mostly by absentee speculators, paid for with raised prices to cover debts.[83] Such action was condemned in many circles as the end of 'paternalistic capitalism', and by 1928 it was felt that 'nothing worse could have happened to the industry'.[84] Crucially, it removed the shared sense of ownership and participation from the operatives.

In 1919, employment was still generally unstable.[85] There was consequently little work for returning soldiers, of which Burnley had the third highest number in Lancashire behind Manchester and Liverpool.[86] Yet municipally the investment from speculators created a sense of optimism in some quarters that a form of utopia could be built. Investment in other local industries, such as building and machinery, was undertaken, and profits rose, dividends increased and borrowing and investing were recklessly encouraged. Burnley looked forward to a period of economic prosperity and industrial peace. Redevelopment programmes were proposed to run into the early 1920s,[87] while attempts to rebuild local community came through schemes to unite people. Municipal coal distribution, municipal banks handling cheap loans and municipally owned weaving concerns were all suggested alongside the extension of road building schemes.[88] However, this dawn was a false one in two respects. First, the effects largely failed to be felt by operatives. Second, by 1921 the demand for cotton was all but satisfied: profits fell and interest charges mounted in the face of dropping dividends and investments. The message from employers was of cuts to return to pre-war wage levels, and by 1922, there was a total reduction in list prices of 120 per cent, effectively bringing wages back down to the level of 1914. Altogether operatives suffered wage reductions in 1921, 1922, 1929, 1932 and 1935.[89] Labour MP for Clitheroe Alfred Davis summarised the feeling locally: 'the great forces of wealth and capital were uniting to try and get the workers down to worse conditions of life'.[90]

The AWA never again achieved the stable membership figures it did during the war. In 1914, their membership stood at 197,957, and through the decrease in employment and rising disillusionment, dropped to 169,172 in 1924 and by 1944 had shrunk to 72,556.[91] Operatives were polarised, and in Burnley the National Unemployed Workers Committee Movement became a prominent voice in the early 1930s. In Nelson, the same process of an ideological shift leftwards resulted in the town being regarded as a 'Little Moscow', and at one point there was the very serious possibility of the Nelson Weavers Association forming a breakaway union.[92] In contrast, the Labour Party strengthened its position in north-east Lancashire, and through the elections of Dan Irving in Burnley, Alfred Davis in Clitheroe and Albert Smith in Nelson and Colne together created an enclave in a Lancashire overwhelmingly behind coalition Conservative and Liberal candidates.[93] Labour held both Burnley and Nelson until 1931, when a decade of trade downturn and a series of industrial unrest over attempts to modernise the industry resulted in the 'more looms dispute'.[94] Yet, the shift towards parliamentary democracy over trade unionism and municipal politics meant that Labour suffered 'routs' in the early 1920s that took almost a decade to reverse in both Burnley and Nelson.[95]

Conclusion

The impact of the First World War on the labouring classes of north-east Lancashire was mixed, but it is clear that the war fundamentally altered societal structure. The war years, especially in the case of Burnley, were to be the start of a long, slow and painful decline. Community structure and work patterns were changed, and the cultural norms that had been the basis of local life were seriously challenged. Long lasting rifts were forged and amplified through trying conditions, and although people did band together, dissent did not disappear with the war. The perceived mistreatment that weaving operatives received both internally and externally created a large degree of mistrust. The attempts to rectify this and heal the cotton communities largely failed, and as the industry proceeded into a decade of uncertainty, it became increasingly unstable, economically and socially. Many of these problems pre-date the war, but there is little doubt that the outbreak of conflict accelerated and created new divisions.

Notes

1 *Burnley Express*, 5 July 1930.
2 See Andrew Marrison, 'Indian Summer: 1870–1914', in Mary Rose (ed.), *The Lancashire Cotton Industry: A History Since 1700* (Preston, 1996), pp. 238–95.
3 Burnley Town Guide (Burnley, 1936).
4 Several local and regional newspapers discussed the battle between Burnley and Blackburn for the title of 'world weaving centre', but locally at least, Burnley was considered the leader. See *Manchester Courier and Lancashire General Advertiser*, 25 February 1913.
5 The area includes what was the Metropolitan Borough of Burnley, the Burnley Rural District and the settlements that stretch to Nelson and Colne further north and is collectively referred to as north-east Lancashire throughout this chapter.
6 *Manchester Guardian*, 21 February 1919.
7 For classic arguments see Lars Sandberg, *Lancashire in Decline* (London, 1974) and John Singleton, *Lancashire on the Scrapheap* (Oxford, 1991). For a general overview of other key issues see Mary Rose, *The Lancashire Cotton Industry: A History Since 1700* (Preston, 1996).
8 *Manchester Guardian*, 26 October 1917.
9 W. R. Mitchell's oral interviews with weaving operatives reinforce the importance of the self-made cotton man. See for example *Mill Town Memories* (Yorkshire, 1987).

10 J. Hill, 'Lib-Labism, Socialism and Labour in Burnley, c.1890–1918', *Northern History*, 35:1 (1999), 185–204, 187.
11 See Frank Bealey, 'The Northern Weavers, Independent Labour Representation of Clitheroe, 1902', *The Manchester School* (1957).
12 Hill, 'Lib-Labism', p. 191.
13 Ethel Dietrich, 'The Plight of the Lancashire Cotton Industry', *American Economic Review*, 18:3 (1928), 469–76, 470.
14 *Burnley Express*, 3 April 1915.
15 For a discussion of the importance of family and kinship living patterns, see Michael Anderson, *Family Structure in 19th Century Lancashire* (Cambridge, 1971).
16 See for example Burnley film maker Sam Hanna's experience of going into the mill and being taught by his mother. Sam Hanna, *Better than Chalk and Talk* (London, 1991), online version at http://www.sam-hanna.co.uk/chalk/Contents.htm (accessed 10 August 201), ch. 6.
17 Jeffrey Hill, *Nelson* (Lancaster, 1997), p. 28.
18 *Manchester Guardian*, 26 April 1909.
19 Hill, *Nelson*, p. 27.
20 For the earlier foundations of this process, see Geoff Timmins, *The Last Shift* (Manchester, 1993), pp. 126–48.
21 The various mechanisms for 'machinery' to negotiate disputes were codified in 1908 under 'Joint Rules'. See Edwin Hopwood, *The Lancashire Weavers Story* (Lancashire, 1969), p. 58.
22 Michael Savage, 'Women and work in the Lancashire Cotton Industry', in J. A. Jowitt and Arthur McIvor (eds), *Employers and Labour in the English Textile Industries* (London, 1988), pp. 203–23, 2.
23 Carol E. Morgan, 'Gender Constructions and Gender Relations in Cotton and Chain-making in England', *Women's History Review*, 6:3 (1997), 367–89, 369.
24 Morgan, 'Gender Constructions', p. 381.
25 The tenter system involved a young trainee assisting and learning from an experienced weaver.
26 Susan Pyecroft, 'British Working Women and the First World War', *The Historian*, 56:4 (1994), 699–710, 700.
27 *Burnley Express*, 14 February 1914.
28 *Burnley News*, 14 October 1916.
29 *Burnley News*, 19 May 1917.
30 *Manchester Guardian*, 7 September 1914.
31 *Manchester Guardian*, 7 September 1914.
32 *Burnley Express*, 27 February 1915.
33 *Burnley News*, 22 July 1916.
34 For a discussion of other groups in a wider context, see Laura Mayhall, *The Militant Suffrage Movement* (Oxford, 2003), ch. 7.
35 *Burnley News*, 27 January 1915.
36 *Burnley News*, 24 April 1915.
37 *Burnley Express*, 13 October 1917.
38 *Burnley Express*, 5 December 1917.
39 *Burnley Express*, 22 September 1917.
40 *Burnley News*, 19 May 1917.

41 *Burnley News*, 11 July 1914.
42 Hill, *Nelson*, pp. 69–70.
43 *Burnley Express*, 15 August 1917.
44 *Manchester Guardian*, 30 October 1916.
45 *Burnley Express*, 27 February 1915.
46 See Jill Liddington, *The Life and Times of a Respectable Rebel* (London, 1984).
47 Liddington, *Respectable Rebel*, p. 268, and Hill, *Nelson*, p. 87.
48 Hill, 'Lib-Labism', p. 191.
49 The role of the tackler was a crucial one within the weaving sector. Effectively mechanics, their wages were accumulated through the finished work of a team of weavers. For operatives work could rely on a 'good' tackler, while some tacklers were in-turn accused of 'driving' weavers to increase output. For a discussion of some of the negative aspects associated with the practice of 'driving, see Jutta Schwarzkopf, 'Gendering Exploitation: The Use of Gender in the Campaign Against Driving in Lancashire Weaving Sheds, 1886–1903', *Women's History Review*, 7:4 (1998), pp. 449–74.
50 Alan Fowler, 'Lancashire to Westminster: A Study of Cotton Trade Union Officials and British Labour 1910–39', *Labour History Review*, 64:1 (1999), 1–22, 12.
51 For a detailed discussion of gender in the cotton industry, see Jutta Schwarzkopf, *Unpicking Gender: The Social Construction of Gender in the Lancashire Cotton Weaving Industry 1880–1914* (London, 2003).
52 Joseph L. White, *The Limits of Trade Union Militancy: The Lancashire Textile Workers 1910–1914* (London, 1978), p. 94.
53 Jowitt and McIvor, *Employers and Labour*, p. 213.
54 Bullen, *The Lancashire Weavers Union*, p. 30.
55 Hopwood, *Lancashire Weavers*, p. 79.
56 White, *Militancy*, p. 93.
57 Hopwood, *Lancashire Weavers*, p. 78.
58 Hill, *Nelson*, p. 33.
59 *Burnley Gazette*, 21 January 1912.
60 Hill, *Nelson*, p. 33.
61 White, *Militancy*, quoted in John Benson (ed.), *The Working Class in England, 1875–1914* (London, 2016), p. 80.
62 *Burnley Express*, 12 February 1914.
63 Hopwood, *Lancashire Weavers*, p. 81.
64 *Burnley Express*, 16 January 1914.
65 *Burnley Express*, 18 November 1914.
66 *Manchester Courier*, 16 November 1914.
67 *Burnley Express*, 18 November 1914.
68 *Burnley News*, 24 November 1915.
69 *Wells Journal*, 8 January 1915.
70 *Burnley Express*, 27 February 1915.
71 *Burnley Express*, 27 February 1915.
72 *Manchester Guardian*, 27 March 1915.
73 *Manchester Guardian*, 18 August 1915.
74 *Burnley News*, 21 August 1915.

75 *Burnley Express*, 21 August 1915.
76 *Burnley Express*, 1 August 1978.
77 *Burnley Express*, 13 November 1915.
78 Subsequent bonuses were granted included another 5 per cent and a further 15 per cent, and by 1917, the weavers were in receipt of roughly 35 per cent more than pre-war rates.
79 *Burnley Express*, 22 March 1916.
80 *Burnley Express*, 20 February 1915.
81 The Cotton Control Board was formed as a cross industry association appointed by the Board of Trade in 1917. Among other things, its function was to allocate raw cotton at controlled prices and implement levies on larger companies to be used as unemployment relief. It also controlled wage agreements, and wielded a great deal of control over industry wide negotiations. See Richard Biernacki, *The Fabrication of Labour: Germany and Britain, 1640–1914* (Berkeley, CA, 1997), pp. 495–500. See also, Samuel J. Hurwitz, *State Intervention in Great Britain* (London, 1968), pp. 197–200.
82 *Burnley Express*, 29 October 1915.
83 Peter Firth, *Unemployment and The Weaving Industry In North East Lancashire: 1919–1929* (Self-published, 1994), p. 3.
84 Firth, *Unemployment*, p. 4; *Burnley Express*, 28 January 1928.
85 *Manchester Guardian*, 21 February 1919.
86 *Manchester Guardian*, 3 April 1919.
87 *Burnley News*, 17 December 1919.
88 Walter Bennett, *Burnley* (Burnley, 1948), p. 136.
89 Hopwood, *Lancashire Weavers*, p. 95.
90 *Burnley News*, 15 June 1921.
91 Hopwood, *Lancashire Weavers*, p. 188.
92 See Hill, *Nelson*, pp. 86–106.
93 For example, the two seats in nearby Blackburn were won by the Coalition Liberal and Coalition Conservative candidates and in Accrington the seat was won by the Coalition Conservative candidate.
94 For a technical history of the dispute, see Sue Bowden and David M. Higgins, 'Productivity on the Cheap? The More Looms Experiment and the Lancashire Weaving Industry During the Inter-War Years', *Business History*, 41: 3 (1999), pp. 21–41.
95 Bennett, *Burnley*, p. 137, Hill, *Nelson*, pp. 86–9.

6

Living through war, waging peace: comparing Mary Macarthur and Sylvia Pankhurst

Deborah Thom

The First World War brought full employment and increased opportunities for women workers, a new public role matched by new recognition for political women in public life, especially those who were both socialists and feminists. Two political activists, Sylvia Pankhurst and Mary Macarthur, became more visible in wartime and demonstrate the different ways in which socialism and feminism changed and created change. The contrast between them shows some of the problems of historical naturalism assuming that either socialist or feminist is a unitary category. Three main contrasts emerge by comparing their wartime agitation – the question of the state, the role of independent women's organisation and the idea of what is the legitimate sphere of political action for labouring women.

Mary Macarthur, general secretary of the National Federation of Women Workers (NFWW) established in 1906 to represent women workers in trades where the men's unions excluded women, claimed:

> Of all the changes wrought by the war none has been greater than the change in the status and position of women, yet it is not so much that woman herself has changed as that man's conception of her has changed.[1]

War brought working women new attention, new respect and new material rewards.

Historians have echoed her words, especially looking at left organisations, and the arrival of the franchise.[2] Working women were being examined, photographed and even asked their opinions for the first time. They were represented in new organisations designed to mobilise first an expeditionary army and then the labour force to keep it supplied with shells, bullets and guns as well as aeroplanes, tanks and ships. After war participation came the franchise for women over thirty. To Mrs Fawcett, leader of the NUWSS: 'The war found women serfs and left them free.'[3]

The rhetoric of democracy and freedom being the same thing was characteristic of 1918 enthusiasm and the sense of women having made irreversible strides.

This chapter looks at wartime political organisers representing women in a wider public sphere, creating new power, freedoms and a new visible political presence, asking whether war created new critical socialist feminist politics or whether compromises between the needs of class and gender created organisations that could only flourish in wartime with labour shortage, but not into peace. Ellen Dubois calls this the problem of stretching the hyphen between socialism and feminism and for both these socialists it had to stretch quite far.[4] Mary Macarthur was one leader of working-class women in wartime. Before the war she orchestrated both small strikes and big public campaigns during the so-called great unrest. She was secretary of the NFWW, and she was also actively involved with the general body organising women in trade unions, the Women's Trade Union League.[5] Some papers of both organisations have survived in the TUC's Tuckwell collection.[6] Macarthur ran a paper, the *Woman Worker*, which mixed small stories of local strikes with big public campaigns against the evils of exploitation in workplaces employing women. In this she collaborated with other organisations of the left and of feminism – the ILP's Fabian Women's group, the Women's Industrial Council, the Women's Labour League (WLL) and the Women's Co-operative Guild. But her most visible contribution was through the Anti-Sweating League, challenging the economic and social dangers of women working, often in their homes, for long hours at very low rates of pay, allied with the Liberal *Daily News*. She tracked a child's shirt through all the stages of its manufacture, mostly in homes by outworkers, herself catching typhus on the way.[7] Thus her socialism, which she called Tolstoyan, meaning a belief in mutual aid and manual labour, was associated with antagonism to exploitation and characterised working women as vulnerable in and out of their homes, needing trade unions' protection to prevent them harming themselves and society by accepting low wages and poor conditions out of desperate need.[8] The new 1906 'fair wages' regulations on government work and the 1908 Trade Boards established minimum wages.[9] Her campaigns put her at the head of numerous demonstrations, public meetings and speeches spreading word for both the NFWW and Women's Trade Union League. Probably most famous was the chain-makers strike of 1910, when striking women paraded through the Black Country in the Midlands and then London draped in the chains they made. She was a brilliant, charismatic speaker who found it easy to stand on a soapbox and address all sorts of crowds and saw the advantage of new forms of mass media, especially the popular Pathé newsreels, which showed in cinemas all over the country.[10]

The other notable war activist was Sylvia Pankhurst. She was an artist, passionately committed to the WSPU campaign for the parliamentary vote for women. She, too, was a member of the ILP.[11] She also had an interest in working women, travelling to portray factory workers in 1907.[12] The WSPU she formed with her mother, Emmeline, and sisters, Christabel and Adela, had decided to use illegal methods of political campaigning, eventually including women putting themselves in harm's way, as a dramatisation of their social and political exclusion.[13] They developed techniques of passive resistance in the early days and used arrest to dramatise their cause in court. Sylvia was very much involved in militancy, courting arrest and going on hunger strike when in prison to demand political prisoner status. But she continued also to be involved with Labour activists arguing for adult suffrage. In 1914, she finally left the WSPU and set up her own East London Federation of Suffragettes based in Bow. Both Macarthur and Pankhurst had thus already faced the dilemma of choice over methods of campaigning and relationship to the state and to other reformers. Both had argued for women's participation in state politics nationally and locally, not for an alternative separate domain of female activism or engagement. However, both had succeeded most effectively in developing groups of working-class women activists through organising both in the workplace and the community respectively and putting women's interests first, challenging a simple sexual division of labour.

When war broke out many women activists had to decide how to react. Helena Swanwick wrote: 'War damages everything women most hold dear – their homes and their families.'[14] Suffrage organisations split over the war between those who saw it as manmade and those who saw it as a new opportunity for women to serve. People early on saw the war as historic, a dramatic shift from the past, and begun to record in image and texts instant histories of women. In particular, Women challenged the idea that they were weak trade unionists, socially conservative and opposed to solidarity. Hence many trade union activists had to argue the same sort of case as suffrage activists had been proposing before the war. They had to argue both that women were capable of solidarity and of overcoming sectional, personal interests in support of the greater good, and against naturalistic ideas of gender where men and women followed different, separate and complementary interests. But war encouraged a new definition of both the public sphere and the public interest.

Public commentary focused on men as soldiers and women as mothers and workers. Instant history pushed these concerns further into the public eye. Among the many texts written in the first years of war were some that came out of the organisations representing working women or agitating for reform in their conditions. Clementina Black wrote *Married Women's Work* in 1915. The Fabian women's group's Barbara Drake summed up women's trade unions.[15] But many popular texts celebrated women's work in new places or new jobs as if there had been no working women before, including Jennie Churchill's *Women's War Work*; journalist Hall Caine's

Our Girls Their Work for the War Effort and Gilbert Stone's *Women War Workers*, all 1916, portraying women doing heroic war service and drawing the analogy between women and soldiers both serving their country.

However, for working women's representatives the crucial question initially was women's vulnerability to exploitation in wartime, especially fear of social dislocation caused by unemployment and anxieties about promiscuity. Some suffrage activists founded women police patrols keeping girls out of the arms of soldiers.[16] Mary Macarthur argued against the real suffering created by unemployment, arguing for work not charity. She supported and served on the Queens Work for Women Fund with Queen Mary to set up workrooms for the unemployed to retrain them in useful skills rather than have 'unpaid sister Susie's sewing shirts for soldiers'.[17] Macarthur's socialism had always been about social reform and amelioration. Her Tolstoyism seems to have meant hoping for a return to moral values and more equitable distribution. She was not a revolutionary but a radical. She argued consistently that unions prevented strikes and represented workers – they did not cause agitation but focused it and encouraged negotiation and improved life chances. She also represented all organised women workers. She famously said, 'The working girl has good habits, she is industrious and thrifty'.[18] Here she was arguing against those who believed that the role of unions was ultimately to protect men, by removing women from male jobs. On the contrary, she believed that women benefitted themselves and their society if they worked for wages.

She became, imperceptibly, the person to whom government and the skilled unions representing war workers turned when new policies or institutions were proposed. In 1915, when the government wanted to introduce 'dilution' to allow unskilled or semi-skilled workers to replace skilled ones and thus expand the armament production, no representative of the women was consulted. Skilled men's unions agreed that the Treasury agreement would give women on men's work 'the rate for the district where the job was carried out'. As Sylvia Pankhurst quickly realised, this was not the equal pay celebrated in public. Women on women's work were eventually to be given a protected time rate to ensure that inexperienced workers would not work under exploitative conditions. Macarthur's strategy, uniting all the unions representing women in the Standing Joint Committee of Women's Industrial organisations, was to insist that war work was organised through conciliation and arbitration.[19] She saw state regulation as women's friend. Private manufacture could not, and did not, adequately organise the sudden vast expansion of factory production needed for industrialised warfare on both Fronts. The DORA was designed to extend state control over industry. The Munitions of War Act 1915 extended this principle by controlling the supply and provision of labour as well as essential raw materials. Government moved into controlling shipping and the docks both for troop embarkation and to provide safe shipping for armaments and weaponry, meaning that munitions described a wide variety of tasks.[20] In 1916, government began to build, staff and manage new national factories as it became quite clear that private firms, however controlled, could not keep pace with demand. Macarthur insisted that women participate in all negotiations through the Central Committee on Women's Employment – industrial democracy rather than parliamentary.

For the first time women's labour was in demand and their contributions recognised. Government recognised that trade unionism was essential if this new labour force was to be delivered and managed without discontent. Two major trade unions: the Workers' Union, a mixed, syndicalist general union, and the NFWW set out to organise these women war workers.[21] The NFWW used two main slogans 'Fellowship is life' and 'To fight, to struggle, to right the wrong'. Unionism was seen as moral, based on solidarity and the general interest. Nonetheless, it was also seen as redressing wrongs rather than claiming rights – protective for women and a part of an armoury of protective provisions like factory inspection and welfare provision which also flourished in war time. Their main rivals in organising among war workers, the Workers' Union, focused instead on the concept of 'Unity is strength'. They saw themselves more as a general union for all workers uniting men and women together in joint branches. Both unions' leading figures became thoroughly implicated in new organisations to mobilise industrial production for the first industrialised war. Trade unionists were the most notable contributors to the new relationship of women's unions to unionism in general and to government who needed union support to get the factories working and working faster.

The other major body speaking for labour women, the WLL, by contrast focused on domestic life and working conditions for women rather than women industrial workers. Its general secretary, Marion Phillips, 1881–1932 had been at the London School of Economics and worked with Beatrice Webb on poor law reforms. She was General Secretary, WLL, 1912 and edited *Labour Woman* in 1913, then returned to being secretary 1917–32. Her main interests were women's primary workplaces – their homes. She concentrated on housing, health and motherhood. In general, this body concentrated on influencing Labour Party policy rather than organising independently.[22] But women trade unionists found for the first time that their views were not only being elicited by other trade unionists but by government as well. Trade unions became drawn into the war effort. Labour history has concentrated on the women as part of the story of men. James Hinton's account of the shop stewards who both resisted and supported the wartime government in munitions factories sees the women as objects not as protagonists in industrial struggle.[23] Women's history has seen the trade unionists as creatures of the male unions too.[24] However Macarthur's history demonstrates an extraordinarily successful moment of women's industrial organisation and even, in the way wartime public history was written, a new world of influence.[25] She saw the main moral of wartime as being to demonstrate the value of trade unionism to overcome women's weakness against exploitation by doing it for themselves. She argued in 1916: 'A strike of unorganised workers should always be used to organise a trade union, … if they had been organised in a trade union in all probability the strike would not have happened.'[26]

The NFWW was already involved in spectacular demonstrations about working women and their demands for reform. The 'great unrest' had extended labour organisation in Britain and in Ireland. Disputes around fixed minimum wages for sweated workers and trade boards meant that their use of the mass popular Liberal press was already very visible. Nonetheless, the message of striking chain-makers decked in chains was ambiguous. It showed women of strength forging chains by hand as outworkers. But they were also wage slaves and the slogans on the propaganda for the trade boards to operate a fairer wage structure for the minimum wage involved showed how much less women had been used to earning. The slave metaphor had been popular in suffrage agitation too.[27]

However, agitation for the vote, for union rights and for recognition meant that the use of parades, demonstrations and public space was already well in place before the war. Women's wartime membership of general trade unions grew both absolutely and proportionately and numbers were enormous compared to suffrage organisations or political parties.[28] The success in enrolling many women in unions partly reflects the large numbers of organisers employed to encourage trade unionism, many of them volunteers working for expenses only. The NFWW, in particular, had some 200 while the Workers' Union had 20, but theirs were all paid. The WU recruited on the idea of good fellowship and fun. 'All the handsome boys and all the beautiful girls are joining the Workers' Union.'[29] The NFWW also used its journal to encourage unionism as a social movement, reviving their journal the *Woman Worker* in 1916 specifically for large numbers of women workers. Campaigns started by unionising first, then correcting problems of labour management, especially welfare, which Macarthur saw as a disguised form of exploitation. War workers frequently struck work over questions of organisation, representation and the role of middle management and welfare supervisors. They 'object to being done good to'. As Macarthur put it on equal pay strikes in August 1918, this was not a sex war:

> If women are to win a permanent and honourable place in industry or commerce, they must play the game, they must convince their men colleagues and their employers that they do not intend to be used to degrade standards, upon which their own happiness in the future or what is more important the health and happiness of their children may depend.[30]

Macarthur was neither particularly active nor prominent in suffrage activism herself. However, she did in general insist that whatever reforms were introduced they should include working women. At Labour's 1917 special conference on franchise reform, she moved a motion for full adult suffrage with Robert Smillie, leader of the miners, thus representing the two large groups of people regulated for war production – women factory workers and miners.[31] This was defeated, it was said, to allow some women to get the vote and fear of losing the whole measure by demanding too much. Earlier she had been one of four people consulted by government and representing the Labour interest in setting up the central employment committee on which women were at last included in negotiating the entry of women into production.[32]

Suffrage activists did not intervene directly in the process of organising and mobilising women workers. Macarthur's innovation in wartime was thus to use the central committee on women's employment as the main avenue for negotiation, pay settlement and union recognition throughout the war period.[33] There were five women on this body – Macarthur herself, Margaret Bondfield, both suffragist and unionist, Susan Lawrence also a unionist but mostly known then as a Labour LCC representative, and two titled Ladies – Myddelton and Askwith. Lady Askwith's husband George, 1st Baron Askwith, had met Macarthur as the main arbitrator of the dispute over trade boards in the Black Country, in 1913.[34] Macarthur negotiated with and for war workers when they struck work for equal pay and pensions in 1917 and tried to protect them when the war ended. In the *Woman Worker* she argued consistently for equal pay, protected benefits and representation of women in both party and public bodies.

Although her political language and values were rarely explicit they can mainly be seen in her 1918 election manifesto, standing as MP in Stourbridge. She began:

> I DO not apologise for my sex. It takes a man and a woman to make THE IDEAL HOME and I believe that neither can build THE IDEAL WORLD without the other.

She went on:

> I shall also feel entitled to speak for the WOMAN WHOSE WORK NEVER ENDS – the woman in the home, who faces and solves a multitude of problems every day – the woman who has been too often neglected and forgotten by the politicians, the mothers of the children upon whom THE FUTURE PRIDE AND STRENGTH OF THE NATION DEPENDS.

Here she makes a graphic and simple point arguing against a sexual division of labour and for the recognition of both formal waged work and unwaged domestic labour. Neither sort of work was privileged. It is a classic demonstration of tensions between socialism and feminism – facing the fact that conventional narratives of women's strength lay in identification with home and family but that had traditionally been seen as their weakness too.

Her fourteen points started not with the nation, as in the preamble, but her demanding:

1. 'People's Permanent Peace';
2. Ending conscription;
3. Justice not charity for soldiers and sailors;
4. The speedy return of fighting men;
5. Restoring freedom;
6. A living wage and no unemployment;
7. A man's pay for a man's work;
8. The redemption of pledges;
9. A million new homes;
10. Security of allotment holders;
11. The golden key [by which she meant equal opportunity in education];
12. Fair taxation;
13. Public good not private profit; and
14. The dignity of labour.

She mentioned public health services, temperance based on local regulation of the drink trade, which she called 'trust the people'. It was signed Mary Macarthur but the printed title used her married name Mrs W. C. Anderson.[35] This was quite conventional ILP style – she made every effort to include all local interests in her fourteen-point plan and emphasised her support for serving troops as well as veterans. It is measured and moral in tone. She mentioned 'the people' several times using democracy as principle but not mentioning specific female interests. It is radical but constitutional. She did not discuss the suffrage. She even, boldly, mentioned the controversial wartime attempt to reintroduce the contagious diseases acts through regulation 40d, which had reintroduced compulsory medical inspection of women designated 'common prostitutes' and made an imprisonable offence to have sex with a serving soldier knowing that one was infected.[36] Macarthur's decision to include this as an essential freedom was bold. As Lees Smith pointed out in Parliament, the regulation in fact criminalised soliciting, and neither prevented the transmission of sexually transmitted disease nor protected either women or soldiers. But this was not a popular campaign then or later and those who sought to protect women who did sell sex for money rarely gained much public favour for doing so.[37] Macarthur may have called herself a Tolstoyan but she did in fact have more time for the state than such followers of the simple life professed and she was not averse to using state institutions to support the claims of working women. She had not been in favour of the war as a whole but she had consistently argued for a negotiated peace and women's inclusion in constructing it.[38] She entirely accepted the necessity of political solutions to problems facing organised labour and mostly saw state power as benign provided it was checked by popular accountability.

Christine Colette writes of the WLL that 'The single greatest cause of change in the organisation and activities of the Labour Party and women's groups was war.'[39] Sylvia Pankhurst's wartime career challenges this notion. She remained, compared to Macarthur, much more independent of the contemporary state while echoing the commitment to women and children as her foremost concern. She organised both politically against the government and officials of the day, and, locally, in the community. Winslow points out that this is exactly the same as the dilemma of trade unionists – they can oppose the war altogether or they can attempt to mitigate its consequences – which means collaborating in administering it in a more humane way. She quotes Pankhurst commenting ruefully about her subsidising meals for poor women of the East End of London, 'But I know it is all palliatives; it will not do any good really; I want to change the system; I am going to fight it if it kills me.'[40]

Sylvia Pankhurst found this easier to do with the unions of male workers and had little directly to do with those organising women – apart from her vehement scorn for Macarthur's collaboration with Queen Mary in the Queen's work for women fund.[41] Where she differed from many trade unionists was in her continuing distrust of the Labour Party, emphasising international links to achieve social transformation through revolution. She has historically been seen either as a footnote in the history of international communism, the object of Lenin's scorn in his pamphlet *Left Wing Communism: An Infantile Disorder* or as a footnote to suffrage history, a refugee from her mother and sister and the WSPU. She *has* been seen as substantial in the history of the East End. Her activities in wartime raise the same questions as Macarthur but in the end she answered them in different ways, because she had begun to move out of claims on parliamentary politics and into agitation for revolution. Barbara Winslow argues that she found herself affected by the war in ways that she did not fully understand herself.

> Between 1914 and 1917, the East London Federation of Suffragettes (ELFS) made a shift of which Pankhurst was not fully aware. It changed from a political organisation that mobilised women to fight for political demands themselves to a feminist socialist welfare organisation that attempted to provide the same relief that government should have provided to alleviate the misery caused by the war.[42]

She began organising in 1914 locally around the issues raised by hasty mobilisation to fight with a volunteer army. She recognised the problems unsupported women and children had covering their daily living costs. In some cases they were thrown out of their housing to make way for troops.[43] She later agitated for war widows, unmarried mothers denied separation allowances and begun the claim for 'mothers' pensions' which she was to make against the notion of family endowment put forward by Eleanor Rathbone. The question of who supported people living in poverty was then both a question of practical daily politics and one of long-term demands for restructuring state welfare. She set up her offices in a pub, once the Gunmakers Arms, renamed the Mothers Arms. Lenin's criticism of her in *Left Wing Communism: An Infantile Disorder* alongside German socialists was based on his assertion that revolutionaries should always work for the class rather than the system. He famously said they should support Labour 'as the rope supports the hanged man'.[44] Her journalism, especially in her own newspaper, the *Women's Dreadnought*[45] until the Russian revolution when she renamed it the *Workers' Dreadnought*, increasingly reflected Communist language because she used the language of class. Her columns in a variety of syndicated leftish papers, in contrast, retained a commitment to palliatives – agitating for welfare rights for widows and veterans, for example, with her demand for pensions for both discharged soldiers and for unsupported mothers. Her organisation engaged in practical politics around, quite literally, bread and butter issues. She fed women and children, organised crèches and maternity clinics and challenged the local and well as the national state. All this was aimed at creating revolutionaries as well as protecting local citizens.

However, the practical politics of wartime organising also divided those who opposed the war and wanted to negotiate peace from the majority. The *Woman's Dreadnought* celebrated revolutionary movements elsewhere in Europe, especially the Bolsheviks' rise to power. Pankhurst opposed conscription. She was the first to point out some of the problems created by enthusiastic support for the women's war register to replace men in 1915. She combined community activism in the east End of London with national platforms. Her columns in Labour papers appeared all over the UK. Much of what she did was very popular – she ran a soup kitchen, a crèche and a small factory for women thrown out of work by war. Claude McKay, who became a Communist supporter, partly through contact with Pankhurst in the early 1920s, described her paper as mainly influential as a critique of trade unions more than the Labour Party, 'And in the labour movement she was always jabbing her hat pin into the hides of the smug and slack Labour leaders. Her weekly might have been called the Dread Wasp.'[46] His comment also reflects a limiting misogyny all too characteristic of many sections of the left after the war.

Lenin's criticism of Pankhurst was based upon the same point, that her refusal of conventional parliamentary politics to challenge for power deprived her and others of the platform that electoral politics provided.

Part of the contrast between the two women lay in how they utilised the public sphere. Two photographs of Macarthur (Figure 6.1) and Pankhurst (Figure 6.2) show the differences in performative politics rather clearly. Macarthur was rarely photographed but in the archives of the industrial museum commemorating the pre-war unrest she is seen addressing public meetings using, as public speakers often did, a soap box or orange box to stand up amidst the crowd.

Figure 6.1 Mary Macarthur addressing strikers and supporters in Cradley Heath, 1910.

Figure 6.2 Sylvia Pankhurst outside the headquarters of the ELFS in Old Ford Road, Bow.

By contrast Pankhurst used a podium. She had spent much time before the war agitating for the vote, being arrested and imprisoned. She had to calculate the respective risks of arrest and publicity in public and could not rely on easy police acceptance of her public speaking. However, it was also the case that she saw herself more as a leader than simply a representative. She had rhetorical skill and was adept at rousing a crowd. But she herself described her role as the same as Macarthur's: in the first annual report of the ELFS she wrote on behalf of distressed East Enders in support of dependants' allowances and relief of hunger, 'as a Trade Union or a family solicitor might have done'.[47] But Pankhurst's anti-war activism was not popular, especially when she directly challenged the notion of the war as one made and maintained by popular support. She wrote later how directly campaigns against war affected popular local and national support through a decline in financial support.

She did not just agitate against the method and style of conscription but she agitated against the very idea of any national interest in waging war at all. Though not actually a pacifist, she argued, on democratic and libertarian grounds, that war encouraged tyrannous use of state power and was a gigantic trick perpetrated on the workers. The *Dreadnought* cartoons increasingly used agit-prop depictions of bloated capitalists in spats and top-hats, effectively showing what would later be called the military industrial complex personified in manmade war. She arrayed against these forces images of starving and destitute children, continually making the point that women were primary child carers. Linda Edmondson argues that her ideal of household soviets reflects more William Morris's socialism and idealisation of the Russian commune than the classic European Marxist emphasis on male manual workers.[48] It was European in style but it was the style of anarcho-syndicalists and communitarians rather than Bolshevik workerism. In the 1920s *Dreadnought* she described the organisation of women who worked at home in household soviets: 'In order that mothers and those who are organisers of the family life of the community may be adequately represented, and may take their due part in the management of society.'[49]

The ideal of a new populist politics was undermined, as she found after 8 April demonstration against conscription:

> Always after such incidents, our mother and baby clinics, the day nursery, the restaurants, the factory, all our work for ameliorating distress suffered immediately from loss of donations. A cable repudiating me from Mrs. Pankhurst was published and helped to detach some of the old W.S.P.U. members who still supported us.[50]

Her newspaper became increasingly anti-war. She was an early correspondent with Lenin, celebrating the October revolution in 1917.[51] She spent 1917 agitating against the war and for adult suffrage but in January 1918 she dropped the demands of suffrage from the *Dreadnought* altogether as she increasingly turned against support for the Labour Party and in favour of workers' soviets as the mode of organisation best fitted to transform society. Lenin described her organisation in a footnote: 'The *Workers' Socialist Federation* was a small organisation which emerged from the Women's Suffrage League and consisted mostly of women' and did not comment on the implications.[52] The distinctiveness of a female organisation waging peace was thus lost in a homogenising politics, which lead eventually to a new British Communist Party to whom Labour refused membership.

When Lenin described how he thought revolutionaries should transform British society by using conventional electoral politics – very like Pankhurst's approach, agitating both at home and in the street – he referred only to male spaces of sociability:

> They should go into the public houses, penetrate into unions, societies and chance gatherings of the common people, and speak to the people, not in learned ... language, they should not at all strive to 'get seats' in parliament, but should everywhere try to get people to think, and draw the masses into the struggle, to take the bourgeoisie at its word ... the elections it has appointed, and the appeals it has made to the people; they should try to explain to the people what Bolshevism is.[53]

In 1918, working women were called to factory gate meetings on Armistice Day and told if you have homes to go to, leave your work. Many of them wanted to go. Oral history tells a story of variety. Some women wanted to keep their jobs, others wanted to get equal pensions. Far more had a vision (as did many veterans) of a return to life as it was before the war. The vote had only been awarded to women over thirty to ensure men dominated in the electorate, the majority of war workers were young women. Mary Macarthur saw unionism carry on with 'old faces in new places'. She was quite bitter about the failure of war gains to endure: 'The new world looks uncommonly like the old one rolling along as stupidly and blindly as ever and all it has got from the war is an extra bitterness or two.'[54] She took her organisation into the General Federation of Trade Unions and the General Workers Union.[55] But Sylvia Pankhurst refused to join the new Labour Party uniting workers 'by hand and brain'. She turned increasingly towards the idea of the soviet, supporting a radical new notion of how the state should organise, agitate and educate. Here her community activism was mapped onto an idea of a non-parliamentary participatory form of direct action, which was, as many criticised at the time, utopian about how to mobilise and administer social reform. But it demonstrates the particular history of this activist waging peace in a new international context.

Both women had seen the war give urgency to their causes and increasing public support. But what was their record in public history? Sylvia hardly featured in the popular history of suffrage until quite recently, although she is locally remembered and commemorated in East London. Her 1931 *Suffragette Movement* was republished by Virago in 1976 and this partly encouraged revived interest. Macarthur is remembered in the Black Country for the chain-makers strike but has no blue plaque in London, though Sylvia does – in Chelsea where she lived, rather than Bow, where she worked. However, heritage lottery funding and growth in public and popular history has meant that both these women with reputations partly made in wartime are now remembered and celebrated in new ways of inhabiting public space. Sylvia's anti-war memorial, the stone bomb, by Eric Benfield has been listed and is maintained and supported by locals.[56]

Mary Macarthur is commemorated in the Cradley Heath living history museum but not much in London where she spent most time as a union activist. Smaller amounts of commemorative material reflect that she did not write her own history and biographers wrote after her death. Pankhurst wrote autobiographically in both *The Suffragette Movement: An Intimate Account of Persons and Ideals*, and *The Home Front. A Mirror to life in England during the Great War*, published respectively in 1931 and 1932 by Longmans and Hutchinson. Her doings are recorded through websites as well as books. In 2014, Sarah Jackson and Rosemary Taylor's *East London Suffragettes* celebrated the ELFS in wartime, which demonstrating the range of local activities that Pankhurst initiated and organised. Her toy factory set up workrooms to provide work for women unemployed by war but also produced fair trade artistic objects for poor children, using wood from George Lansbury's wood yard, to replace the German toys that dominated the British toy market. Here local pride gives Pankhurst's career a continuing resonance to place and history which Macarthur's more national impact does not keep in the same way. Barbara Winslow's criticism that Pankhurst should have spent more time with working women seems as anachronistic in its acceptance of a dual power system and gendered domestic labour as Pankhurst's criticising Macarthur for spending too much time with the elite. Both worked across and sometimes at odds with dominant institutions of the day, maintaining a consistent policy of women organising women. Macarthur defended working women and fought for equal pay. Pankhurst did provide welfare for local citizens. Both encouraged a new consciousness of political power but located it in different places. In the end though the main beneficiaries were the Labour Party itself and welfarist policies relating to women. The language of political democracy dominated over syndicalists and revolutionaries alike.[57]

There has been little popular record of anti-war protests of this era nor of the struggles of working women and increasingly that omission makes generations of popular history as taught in schools more and more silent on the subject of opposition and contest to dominant ideas. One of the dominant ideas with which these activists had to contend with was that women had to prove themselves at the same time to government, to male leftists, especially trade unionists, as well as representing the interests of all women and children together. Both used press and public meeting to make a new, temporary public presence for working women. Both explicitly challenged the notion that women's work at home is not political and in this challenge to a sexual division of labour they share far more than divides them, providing a model of reform that was little heeded at the time nor, to Labour's detriment, in the interwar period. Both had changed the system but neither in the way they wanted.

Notes

With thanks to Lucy Bland for generous and patient editing, Lucia Jones and Les Garner for model work on Sylvia Pankhurst, Susan Pennybacker for discussing Claude McKay's comments and to the Cradley Heath museum and Sylvia Pankhurst websites for their wonderful online resource.

1 Quoted by Gail Braybon, *Women Workers and the First World War* (London, 1989), p. 157.
2 Summed up in Gail Braybon, 'Winners or Losers, Women's Symbolic Role in the War story', in Gail Braybon (ed.), *Evidence, Memory and the Great War* (London, 2003), pp. 86–112.
3 M. G. Fawcett, *The Women's Victory – and After* (London, 1920), p. 106, cited in D. Thom, *Nice Girls and Rude Girls: Women Workers in World War* (London, 1998).
4 Ellen Dubois 'Woman Suffrage and the Left: an International Socialist-Feminist Perspective', *New Left Review*, 1:186 (1991), 20–45, 22.
5 C. Hunt, *The National Federation of Women Workers, 1906–1921* (London, 2014); C. Hunt, 'Gertrude Tuckwell and the British Labour Movement, 1891–1921: a Study in Motives and Influences', *Women's History Review*, 22:3 (2013), pp. 478–96.
6 J. Morris, 'The Gertrude Tuckwell Collection', *History Workshop Journal*, 5 (1978), 155–61. Gertrude Tuckwell Papers are in the TUC Library, London Metropolitan University. Sadly, the archive of the NFWW itself did not survive the end of the Union in merger with the General Workers as Dorothy Jones, by then a national organiser for the union, recorded in an interview in 1978.
7 216f in the Tuckwell collection (GT) is on sweating in the shirtmaking trade.
8 M. A. Hamilton, *Mary Macarthur, a Biographical Sketch* (London, 1925); see Thom, *Nice Girls*, chs 3 and 4. There is now an extensive literature on Macarthur as a trade union organiser but there is less on her politics.
9 S. Blackburn, *A Fair Day's Wage for a Fair Day's Work? Sweated Labour and the Origins of Minimum Wage Legislation in Britain* (Aldershot, 2007).
10 D. Thom, '"Free from chains": The Image of Women's Labour in London, 1900–1920', in D. Feldman and G. Stedman Jones (eds), *Metropolis: London. Histories and Representations since 1800* (London, 1989), p. 85–99. The NUT produced an excellent online resource around the chain-makers strike *Women*

Chainmakers: Be Anvil or Hammer, at http://www.teachers.org.uk/files/Chainmakers-A4–24pp.pdf (accessed 24 May 2017), which shows Macarthur's use of newsreel.
11 She designed the WSPU membership card showing working-class women and children.
12 Image of a chain-maker from the London magazine in 1908 reproduced at the excellent Sylvia Pankhurst website, at http://www.sylviapankhurst.com/galleries/women_workers_of_england/pages/2.html (accessed 6 September 2016).
13 Sandra Stanley Holton has summarised this history in her overview 'The Making of Suffrage History', in S. S. Holton and J. Purvis (eds), *Votes for Women* (London, 2002), pp. 13–33. June Purvis has criticised Sylvia's own history of both suffrage and Home Front activism for omissions and self-importance in her article 'The Pankhursts and the Great War', in Alison Fell and Ingrid Sharp (eds), *The Women's Movement in Wartime: International Perspectives, 1914–1919* (Basingstoke, 2007), pp. 141–57.
14 Helena Swanwick, 'The War in Its Effect upon Women', in Marilyn Shevin-Coetzee and Frans Coetzee (eds), *World War I and European Society: A Sourcebook* (Lexington, MA, 1995, 1995), pp. 160–4, 166.
15 Barbara Drake, *Women in Trade Unions* (London, 1920), at https://archive.org/details/cu31924002665507 (accessed 23 May 2017).
16 Louise Jackson, *Women Police: Gender, Welfare and Surveillance in the Twentieth Century* (Manchester, 2006), p. 18, Lucy Bland, *Modern Women on Trial: Sexual Transgression in the Age of the Flapper* (Manchester, 2013), pp. 5–6.
17 Quoting a popular music hall song.
18 *Lancashire Post*, 17 May 1915.
19 Thom, *Nice Girls*, p. 33.
20 The key decision over this was over railway wagons used to transport shells.
21 Richard Hyman, *The Workers Union* (Oxford, 1971).
22 Martin Francis, 'Labour and Gender', in Duncan Tanner, Pat Thane and Nick Tiratsoo (eds), *Labour's First Century* (Cambridge, 2000), pp. 191–220.
23 James Hinton, *The First Shop Stewards' Movement* (London, 1973).
24 Purvis, 'The Pankhursts and the Great War', see footnote 13.
25 Visible in the women's war work collection of documents at the Imperial War Museum from 1917.
26 *Daily Herald*, 23 May 1915, p. 6.
27 Laura Nym Mayhall, *The Militant Suffrage Movement. Citizenship and Resistance in Britain 1860–1930* (Oxford, 2003).
28 Report of the Ministry of Reconstruction, Cd9239, xiv, pp. 94–8 reports Workers' Union and NFWW at about 30,000 each by the end of 1917.
29 See Thom, 'The Bundle of Sticks', in *Nice Girls*, ch. 5. Cathy Hunt also points out the difficulty of finding credible membership records in her excellent history of the NFWW: *The National Federation of Women Workers* (Basingstoke, 2014), p. 14.
30 Transcripts of evidence to the War Cabinet Committee on Women in Industry, 4 October 1918, pp. 10–11, evidence of Mary Macarthur, IWM women's work collection.

31 Jo Vellacott, *Pacifists, Patriots and the Vote: The Erosion of Democratic Suffragism During the First World War* (Basingstoke, 2007), p. 145.
32 Vellacott, *Pacifists, Patriots and the Vote*, p. 24.
33 Gail Braybon, *Women Workers in the First World War* (London, 1981), p. 44.
34 George Askwith, *Industrial Problems and Disputes* (London, 1920).
35 Her manifesto is available online at http://www.unionhistory.info/britainatwork/emuweb/objects/nofdigi/tuc/imagedisplay.php?irn=3000044; http://www.unionhistory.info/britainatwork/emuweb/objects/nofdigi/tuc/imagedisplay.php?irn=3000046; http://www.unionhistory.info/britainatwork/emuweb/objects/nofdigi/tuc/imagedisplay.php?irn=3000045 (accessed 16 July 2016) (capitals in original).
36 HC Debate, 19 June 1918, vol 107 cc444–73; Julia Laite, *Common Prostitutes and Ordinary Citizens: Commercial sex in London, 1885–1960* (Basingstoke, 2011), ch. 7.
37 Sylvia Pankhurst also campaigned against it.
38 M. A. Hamilton, *Mary Macarthur* (London, 1925).
39 Christine Collette, *The Newer Eve: Women, Feminists and the Labour Party* (London, 2009), p. 56.
40 Sylvia Pankhurst's appeal. International Institute of Social history, Amsterdam, Pankhurst papers, 140, p. 32, November 1920, cited in Barbara Winslow, *Sylvia Pankhurst: Sexual Politics and Political Activism* (London, 1996), p. xix.
41 SP papers minutes of the ELFS 1915 report of a delegation to Mary Macarthur.
42 Barbara Winslow, *Sylvia Pankhurst: Sexual Politics and Political Activism* (London, 1996), p. 76.
43 Sylvia Pankhurst, *The Home Front* (London, 1932), pp. 78–82.
44 V. I. Lenin, *Left Wing Communism: An Infantile Disorder*, section on Britain.
45 It is interesting that its original name before publication was the *People's Mate* which seemed to symbolise the notion of women as ancillary to workers with the pun it contains on both friend and marriage partner, but instead she chose the name of the battleships and kept it when she changed to class politics as her primary focus.
46 Claude McKay, *A Long Way from Home* (Rutgers, NJ, 1937), cited in Cultural Studies Lateral Fund online at http://cslateral.org/wp/issue/5–1/claude-mckay-british-left-donlon/ (accessed 23 May 2017). See Winston James, 'A Race Outcast from an Outcast Class: Claude McKay's Experience and Analysis of Britain', in Bill Schwarz (ed.), *West Indian Intellectuals in Britain* (Manchester, 2003) pp. 75–7.
47 ELFS annual report, p. 17 quoted in Katherine Connelly, 'Sylvia Pankhurst, the First World War and the Struggle for Democracy', in *Revue francaise de civilisation Britannique*, XX:1 (2015), at: http://rfcb.revues.org/275; DOI: 10.4000/rfcb.275 (accessed 16 September 2016).
48 This excellent essay situates Pankhurst within several European traditions as well as reflecting on her relationship to her family. Linda Edmondson, 'Sylvia Pankhurst: Suffragist Feminist or Socialist', in Jane Slaughter and Robert Kern (eds), *European Women of the Left* (London, 1981), pp. 76–100.
49 *Workers Dreadnought*, 19 June 1920, p. 1.
50 Pankhurst, *Home Front*, p. 230.

51 There is an extensive literature on Pankhurst including Shirley Harrison, *Sylvia Pankhurst, Citizen of the World* (London, 2009); Kathryn Dodd (ed.), *A Sylvia Pankhurst Reader* (Manchester, 1993); Shirley Harrison, *Sylvia Pankhurst: A Crusading Life 1882–1956* (London 2003); Richard K. Pankhurst, *Sylvia Pankhurst: Artist and Crusader* (London, 1979); Taylor, Rosemary, *In Letters of Gold; the Story of Sylvia Pankhurst and the East London Federation of the Suffragettes in Bow* (London, 1993); Barbara Winslow, *Sylvia Pankhurst: Sexual Politics & Political Activism* (London, 1966).
52 Mark Shipway, 'Anti-Parliamentary Communism: The Movement for Workers' Councils in Britain', at https://libcom.org/library/anti-parliamentary-communism-mark-shipway-1 (accessed 25 May 2017).
53 Lenin, *Left Wing Communism*.
54 *West Sussex Gazette*, 11 December 1919.
55 Gerry Holloway, *Women and Work in Britain since 1840* (London, 2005) p. 177, Hunt, *The National Federation*, ch. 4.
56 Patrick Wright, 'The Stone Bomb', https://www.opendemocracy.net/democracy-protest/article_1131.jsp (accessed 25 May 2017).
57 Ian Bullock, 'Sylvia Pankhurst and the Russian Revolution: The Making of a Left Wing Communist', in Ian Bullock and Richard Pankhurst (eds), *Sylvia Pankhurst from Artist to Anti-Fascist* (Basingstoke, 1992), pp. 121–48.

7

'Industrial unionism for women': Ellen Wilkinson and the unionisation of shop workers, 1915–18

Matt Perry

What did you do during the war Daddy? The question obviously privileges male and military experiences but it also depoliticises. It suggests that radical women occupy a double blind spot in the commemorative reflexes of public discourse. Such figures open up intriguing perspectives on the war, highlighting the complexity of the war experience and its significance to personal trajectories. Ellen Wilkinson who became Minister of Education in the Attlee government and led the Jarrow Crusade provides a case in point. Wilkinson's political journey began in 1908 when she joined the ILP. Alongside her involvement in the labour movement, she also participated in women's and anti-imperialist movements. She was elected as a Labour MP in Middlesbrough in 1924, holding the seat until 1931. She was MP for Jarrow between 1935 and her death in 1947. Until recently, her war has not received in-depth discussion.[1] This chapter connects three aspects of Wilkinson's wartime experiences, shedding new light on her wartime radicalisation and her complex intellectual odyssey. First, it examines her participation in a strike wave among shopworkers. Second, it considers Wilkinson's role as a national (woman) organiser for the AUCE. Finally, it situates her war activity with her intellectual itinerary stressing its formative character.

The AUCE and 'the question of the hour': substituted female labour

Starting work on 30 August 1915, Wilkinson's new post coincided with AUCE reorganisation and consolidation. The AUCE had fractious relations with both the Co-operative Movement and other unions. Indeed, the union believed that the TUC treated it unfairly in adjudications over encroachment with craft unions. This occasioned the AUCE to quit the

TUC in April 1915, reinforcing the union's pugnacity.[2] Whereas the craft unions rejected AUCE encroachment, the AUCE espoused industrial unionism wherein all workers in the co-operative societies should confront the employers in a single union.[3] Sir William Richardson described this moment as the 'birth' of shopworkers' trade unionism. Two national organisers were appointed alongside the new women's organiser post that Wilkinson secured.[4] The union's journal introduced her as a university graduate, the secretary of the Women's War Interests Committee in Manchester and a 'keen suffragist'.[5] Her organising experiences and personal qualities had clearly impressed the union's leadership.

The *Co-operative Employé* carried Wilkinson's organiser's reports.[6] Her early activities acquainted Wilkinson not only with the trade union organiser's hectic routines, but also the specific characteristics of organising women workers. Even at this early stage, she encountered resistance from other unions and male trade unionists. Employers, even within the Co-operative Movement, substituted male workers with cheaper, often young, women with little experience of work or trade unionism. The AUCE's policy of equal pay for equal work led to conflict with other unions, especially craft unions organising within the Co-operative Movement. Unlike some other unions, the AUCE took a progressive stance on women's employment. For instance, it applauded Sylvia Pankhurst's campaigning in the East End of London among women factory workers; she in turn admired the AUCE's stance on equal pay.[7]

War brought a climatic change for trade unionism. With men volunteering for the army in their droves in the early war months and then conscription, a sharp labour shortage occurred and this proved conducive to strengthening the unions. With government and employer encouragement, women found new employment opportunities, resulting in an additional 1.3 million women workers.[8] In the wholesale and retail trade female employment had increased 70 per cent by April 1918, with the total standing at 850,000. By 1918, trade unions had 1.2 million women members, a wartime increase of 160 per cent. Craft unions viewed the replacement of skilled men with the unskilled and women as 'dilution' and had always resisted such intrusions.[9] Dilution was not the same as substitution, as the first entailed the replacement of skilled with less skilled labour, while the latter replaced it on the grounds of equivalent skill. Of course, these two notions overlapped given masculine assumptions about the quality of male work and the introduction of inexperienced women (a point Ellen Wilkinson herself made). Thus, similar objections greeted substitution in the Co-operative Movement and dilution in engineering.

The AUCE's rival, the National Amalgamated Union of Shop Assistants, Warehousemen and Clerks (NAUSAWC, or the 'Shop Assistants' Union'), rejected the notion of equal pay for substituted labour, instead calling for 75 per cent of male wages.[10] There was not even a consensus among

Labour women in favour of equal pay. On 28 July 1917, Wilkinson attended the Standing Joint Committee of Women's Industrial Organisations (SJC, the Labour Party's advisory body on women, formed in 1916) at Central Hall, Westminster, with Mary Macarthur presiding. Wilkinson challenged Marion Phillips, the SJC secretary, for following the commonplace assumption that it took three women to do the work of two men. The AUCE women's organiser recounted her union's successful fight for the principle of equal pay for equal work.[11]

Wilkinson enlivened the substituted female labour (SFL) campaign. In 1915, the general secretary described this 'historical' policy as occupying a 'foremost place' in the AUCE's work and noted that initially it brought 'a veritable storm of indignation … and much vituperation' from the employers.[12] Swiftly becoming an expert on the topic, Wilkinson addressed branch meetings and regional conferences and was included in delegations or in negotiations about this matter. Some societies acceded to the AUCE's demands for equal pay for equivalent work. Others doggedly refused.[13] Wilkinson encountered several chauvinistic justifications for women's low pay. There were, for instance, the claims that women reached their optimum efficiency at the age of 18, implying that junior pay rates were appropriate.[14] The union articulated its position in terms of gender harmony and even as a patriotic duty: equal pay would protect the future pay and conditions of the men serving at the front.

Wilkinson noted that originally the campaign failed to attract women who believed the union would protect the male monopoly in the grocery shops. That changed when they witnessed the unions' – or specifically Wilkinson's – determination.[15] For her, women's entry into the Co-op's grocery shops was 'but one stage of the long and painful march of women to freedom.' Her suffrage days taught her a repertoire of arguments to handle those co-operative societies resistant to change. First, their rationalisations echoed anachronistic bigotry about women's innate incapacities. Wilkinson catalogued male chauvinism's absurd genealogy: whether women had souls, whether women should be paid wages for their work, whether they were fit to look after their own money, whether they could become doctors because they would faint at the sight of blood.[16] For her, trade unionism's future depended on women so the unions needed to embrace equal pay and women's freedom. Although this matched union policy, it was Wilkinson who articulated it with such verve, wit and energy that the AUCE's SFL campaign bore her personal imprint.

Despite the union's formal position, this did not always filter down to the ranks. On several occasions, Wilkinson remarked upon the sparse female attendance at meetings on substitution. For instance, Wilkinson reported that at meetings in Eccles, Oldham and Leeds in early November 1915 the masculine view of substitution as a threat to male wage rates prevailed. In such circumstances, she realised that the union was unlikely to enthuse women.[17] Moreover, it was no straightforward matter to encourage women workers to take industrial action.[18] Barbara Drake noticed that strikes transformed women's attitudes to unions, as collective action made women 'lose their fear'.[19] Wilkinson observed that during the Pendleton dispute, 'women seemed to waver before the fight, [… but] in the thick of it … were among our keenest warriors'.[20] Many women were making 'splendid secretaries', which was the 'most useful war work'. She reflected: 'We women must put silly notions of what we cannot or think we cannot do aside, and seriously tackle the problem of keeping our beloved Union together while the men are away'.[21]

The SFL campaign's success encouraged the union to widen its commitment to women's labour rights. Thus, in 1917, the general secretary anticipated post-war campaigns to secure equal pay for women in formerly male occupations.[22] Wilkinson also identified special women's grievances over inadequate sanitary facilities for women grocery or laundry workers as well as the 'male manager problem', her code for chauvinism, misunderstanding and sexual harassment.[23] Such language demonstrated contemporary difficulties, as Angela Woollacott has observed, in addressing such problems openly.[24] While Wilkinson initially posed this question, eventually the general secretary published a pamphlet on the public health laws to address sanitary conditions in shops.[25]

Wilkinson's industrial unionism for women

If the AUCE's campaign on SFL overlapped with Wilkinson's militant position on labour and women's rights, so too did the AUCE's broader attitude to trade unionism. The 1914 annual delegate meeting (ADM) adopted industrial unionism.[26] When the *Co-operative Employé's* editor introduced Wilkinson, he remarked that she was a 'keen industrial unionist'. This creed framed AUCE's trade union philosophy and organising strategy. Within the leadership it was associated particularly with general secretary Joseph Hallsworth.[27] Industrial unionism had its roots in the new unionism of the 1880s but matured with the transnational current of syndicalist ideas that had spread in Britain during the Great Unrest of 1910–14. Despite the masculine assumptions among these currents, both presented possibilities to redress the heavy male preponderance of the trade union movement.[28]

Syndicalism caused controversy within the trade union movement not least because it rejected craft unionism. As Wilkinson herself observed, right-wing opponents of industrial unionism on trades councils caricatured AUCE encroachment as a threat to even the miners or rail workers' unions. The AUCE did recruit members from the crafts operating within the co-operative societies. Their bitter rivals the Shop Assistants' Union proposed AUCE expulsion from trades councils across the country in spring 1916 with limited success.[29] Voices within the co-operative press supported these calls.

Although the AUCE was not formally part of the Shop Stewards and Workers' Committee Movement, the AUCE leadership sympathised with the Shop Stewards and Workers' Committee Movement's unconventional and militant approach, deemed it to be a model for its own representatives and adopted the terminology of shop stewards.[30] Launched in December 1917 with a demonstration in Manchester, the AUCE's charter encouraged the shop stewards' movement.[31] Underlining this affinity, the union journal lauded the South Wales miners, alluding to the South Wales Miners' Reform Movement and its pamphlet the *Miners' Next Step*. This coincided with an official union discourse of member self-activity and less reliance on union full timers. Likewise, Wilkinson drew on syndicalist language, using the 'fiery cross' metaphor appropriated from James Connolly, 'the hero of my early Socialist days'.[32]

Given her guild socialism, Wilkinson enthusiastically advocated industrial unionism. It clearly attuned with her aspirations for mass recruitment among young, unskilled women workers. While syndicalism had been most influential in male occupations like mining and engineering, in February 1916 Wilkinson proposed in a brilliant piece of intellectual improvisation 'industrial unionism for women', responding to the practical situation during the war of a feminising workforce whose militancy existing understandings of trade union practice failed to recognise. Where traditional trade unionism dismissed these possibilities, her formulation of industrial unionism for women theorised their precariousness and sought a collective organisational answer to their vulnerability. For her, modern industry, with its increasing reliance on women, necessitated such an approach; 'young and floating labour' could only fuse with the permanently employed in a single union based on the 'principle of unity against one form of capital'. Craft unionism in the co-operative movement would therefore condemn the skilled to being replaced and undermined by those it deemed not worthy of a union card. Indeed, the employers preferred 'a hundred competing unions than face one strong one'. The AUCE's successes, Wilkinson argued, vindicated industrial unionism.[33] It had recruited and raised wage rates among the skilled but also the seasonally employed dressmakers and the previously unorganised laundry workers. Thus, while Ellen Wilkinson later prided herself on being a 'practical politician', she was capable of impressive theoretical insight and did not surrender to a blind pragmatism. The yardstick of action in the social movements measured her political thought.

Ambiguities, however, permeated Wilkinson's praxis of industrial unionism. Despite a compelling polemic against the craft unions, she remained silent on encroachment and inter-union disputes that such a strategy might occasion; such tensions clearly had a divisive potential to the employers' advantage. Industrial unionism's ambivalence accommodated the diversity of AUCE opinion, which a stricter understanding of syndicalism would have alienated. The union did not subscribe to the maximum programme of industrial unionism. While the AUCE leadership embraced direct action (within limits), opposed craft unionism, supported union amalgamation, it had greater difficulty with revolution, or full-blown commitment to independent rank-and-file organisation and the rejection of political parties.[34] Ironically, the union had recently opened its political fund for Labour Party candidates. Perhaps most problematic for Wilkinson and the AUCE was the syndicalist critique of the trade union bureaucracy. They circumnavigated this inconsistency via the polemic against craft unionism as though the trade union movement's future simply consisted of the gasps of conservative craft unions and the ascendancy of enlightened industrial unionism.

'Unreasonable guerrilla warfare': the strike wave of December 1915–17

Wilkinson participated in the union's first strike over SFL, which happened in Carlisle between 27 December 1915 and 3 January 1916. It was an impressive success, winning equal pay and vindicating the policy of a single union for co-operative employees. Three months earlier in October, the union submitted wage demands of a 4s advance for adults and 2s for juniors in the context of an eight-year wage freeze for certain grades and the galloping inflation.[35] The Carlisle South-End Co-operative Society management had said that they would discuss wages at the end of December but rejected equal pay because it was employing women on significantly less than the male rate for the job. On 9 December, with the employers refusing talks, the branch sought the national union's permission to take industrial action. On 15 December, Hallsworth visited the district committee in Newcastle and Wilkinson, national organiser Scott and district secretary C. R. Flynn addressed a mass meeting of members in Carlisle. On 16 December, 221 strike notices were served on the management, with more workers indicating their willingness to strike. Female participation was strong under branch chair Miss Harrison's leadership. Eighty new members were recruited, many of them women. When Wilkinson, alongside two AUCE national organisers and Flynn, met with the board on 21 December, the latter asked for more time to consider SFL. Despite circular letters from the management to employees stating that their strike would be illegal, 277 took strike action. A strike committee was elected and meetings held every evening. Picketing was effective, closing all the branches and turning away deliveries. An all-night picket blocked the bakery. Solidarity came from the trades' council and the rail workers' union. Wilkinson addressed a special women's meeting with the local Women's Co-operative Guild to put the strikers' case.[36] On 3 January, a sizeable crowd surrounded the society's quarterly meeting. The following evening the co-operative board called in the union for a settlement that conceded their principal demands: new female employees would be paid the same rate as the men, a pay increase (3s for adults of both sexes and 2s for juniors of both sexes) and no victimisations or legal action against the union. Ironically, despite these advances, Miss Harrison noted at the ADM three months later the union's inconsistency, providing a reduced rate of strike pay to women.[37]

The AUCE registered another early 'hands down' success in the SFL campaign in Coatbridge, Lanarkshire, a coal and iron-making town, 10 miles east of Glasgow. On 12 February strike notices were handed in. The co-operative board's response was to pressure potential strikers and to call their employees to a meeting. Consequently, several members withdrew their intentions to strike. Wilkinson and John Simpson, the Scottish district organiser, persuaded members to meet an hour before the board's meeting with them. At the AUCE meeting, a delegation was designated to demand the union's right to reply. This agreed, the 150 employees marched to the hall, singing 'We'll win the day.'[38] When the employers refused the floor to Simpson, the employees walked out. This unity encouraged those who had wavered to re-sign their strike notices. Careful preparation strengthened the AUCE's hand: the union placarded the town and Wilkinson had won over other trade unionists, gaining support from local miners', railway clerks' and rail workers' officials on the trades council. Confronted with the prospect of a solid strike, after 4 hours' negotiations, the board conceded.[39] In her account of the dispute, Wilkinson observed that the women 'stuck to the cause like limpets.'[40] Although a victory for the union, Wilkinson noted that the women had grievances beyond equal pay. She regretted that she did not have the time to take these up and promised that she would return to deal with them once the pressure of the SFL campaign abated.[41]

Wilkinson apparently made the union more responsive to the new female membership and transcended the officially sanctioned campaign. She believed that women had the capacity to lead union struggles and that this was necessary for any membership drive among new women workers. Wilkinson repeatedly praised women branch officials. Her experience had taught her this. As an organiser for the NUWSS in Manchester, she had conducted campaigns in the region of suffrage movement with the highest proportion of working women. She knew that the labour movement would not adopt more enlightened views regarding women without a battle, having decried the attitude of some in the ILP who foresaw a 'man-made socialism.'[42] Equally, she criticised feminism on several occasions for its neglect of class, going so far as describing Christabel and Emmeline Pankhurst as 'feminine fascists' for abandoning Manchester for Mayfair.[43] Her strategy achieved recognition within the AUCE when, in May 1916, the executive issued a circular encouraging district organising secretaries to make special efforts to find women branch officers. It instructed districts to seek Wilkinson's help to achieve this.

These early battles over SFL drew the Co-operative Movement's ire. The Co-operative Union Ltd's parliamentary secretary H. J. May accused the AUCE of 'unreasonableness', 'extraordinary methods', 'errors of judgement or worse' and 'guerrilla warfare'.[44] Denouncing 'the gang of organisers' (obviously referring to Wilkinson and Simpson) who were 'fleecing' and 'bleeding' the Co-operative Movement, an article in the *Scottish Co-operator* proposed lockouts and the use of the Women's Guild as strikebreakers.[45] By early 1916, Wilkinson could state that the Scottish Co-operative Wholesale Society was in a 'state of panic' over SFL.[46] The *Scottish Co-operator* had hit out that women did not perform equal work and thus should not be accorded equal pay, relying on the self-serving formula that it took three women to do the work of two men.[47] Despite carrying a large majority of the membership combined with successes in recruitment and in industrial disputes, a nagging minority within the AUCE criticised the union's militant stance or its relations with craft unions. One AUCE correspondent to the *Scottish Co-operator* doubted the efficacy of the strikes and the bluff about its 'victories'.[48] Nevertheless, in October 1916, a northern conference of co-operative societies in Newcastle agreed to the principle of equal pay for SFL.[49]

The AUCE's ADM of 1916 was held in Edinburgh on 23 and 24 April. Industrial unionism and SFL held centre stage. On these questions and others, the executive won endorsement from delegates. It was also the first AUCE conference with a woman organiser: 'a most interesting innovation', as the report in the union journal patronisingly remarked, 'adding grace and culture to the permanent staff of the Union, and members of the gentle sex to the Union in gratifying numbers'.[50] The leadership emphasised the union's growth together with its unpopularity and the co-operative management boards and other unions. With membership standing at 51,399, the union had secured 6,355 new members, almost 2,000 higher than the annual average over the previous seven years.[51] On the SFL motion, the delegates were divided. Some recognised the necessity of the executive to make a prompt decision on SFL rather than awaiting consultation with the members. Others were critical. One deemed the executive to have acted unconstitutionally and condemned the idea of equal pay because of the inferiority of women's performance. Another criticised the executive's lack of support for some branches and their inconsistency in negotiations. Despite this dissent, a card vote carried the motion by an overwhelming majority of 31,529 to 1,530. Wilkinson only contributed to the conference against a revision to union insurance regulations that would end the marriage dowry paid to women on leaving service. She argued that this incentive to join the union was necessary given the special employment patterns of young women and the difficulties of recruiting them to the union. These arguments lost out to the demand for equal treatment and the elimination of this special 'bait for women'.[52]

Illustrating growing wartime militancy, 270 unorganised women workers at a Glasgow co-operative underwear factory spontaneously walked out on 11 May over cuts in the piece rate.[53] Those in a nearby shirt factory and a mineral water factory took sympathy action. The strikes of the Clyde Workers' Committee and the mass rent strikes had heightened the atmosphere in Glasgow.[54] The Clyde Workers' Committee became a model for grassroots militancy in other major industrial cities.[55] High rents and poor housing fed into wage demands among AUCE members at Scottish Co-operative Wholesale Society factories. On being notified of the strike, a delegation of Hallsworth, Lumley and Wilkinson approached the Board of Trade on 15 May. The next day, the same three addressed a mass meeting of 500 employees. This passed a motion both empowering the AUCE to negotiate and, if talks were fruitless, to begin the strike procedure. Rejecting the general wage increase, the factory management agreed to the Board of Trade's other terms if the women resumed work. A mass strike meeting unanimously rejected this. Grievances over supervisors' attitudes towards the women also emerged. Ultimately, the parties agreed to arbitration over the piece rates.[56] The union provided a week's strike pay on condition of a return to work. On this basis, the women returned after a dozen days on strike. Wilkinson noted the 'splendid solidarity' of the Glaswegian strikers who, despite considerable hardship, made no mention of breaking ranks until an agreement had been signed. Manifestly impressed, she concluded: 'New trade unionists, they have shown the way to the men.'

In autumn 1916, Wilkinson was involved in a major eleven-week dispute in Plymouth involving both the AUCE's mainly women shop workers as well as dockers. This interrupted the sequence of victories in Wilkinson's organising resumé. Strike notices were posted on 2 September and up to 1,000 workers took part in the strike.[57] Plymouth Co-operative Wholesale Society (CWS) was paying below the national minimum and the dockers and AUCE entered into an agreement to defeat the wage rates. The Shop Assistants' Union (and the bakers) instructed members to cross picket lines, seeing the dispute as part of their campaign against the AUCE.[58] Symptomatic of Wilkinson's involvement, the local Women's Co-operative Guild supported the strike. Wilkinson condemned the 'traitor unions' in her union's periodical. The strikers voted enthusiastically for the settlement reached on 20 November 1916.[59] The long-running dispute's result was at best a draw and the local branch was weakened as a result.[60] The ramifications of the strike were still being felt in early 1917, when it was clear that the employers were not honouring the back-to-work agreement.[61]

From January 1917, Wilkinson began an organising drive in east Scotland. Here the scattered settlements, paternalist traditions, inhospitable winter months and low population density presented particular problems.[62] Grangemouth became the crucial battle. Strike notices were issued on 24 February. Despite management bravado that had promised to defeat any dispute in a local co-op branch, the dispute at Grangemouth was, according to Wilkinson, 'a short, sharp, and wholly successful strike'.[63] She noted that the Falkirk wages board had convinced all local co-operative societies to hold to a 15 per cent maximum, occupational exclusions and denial of AUCE recognition. The settlement at Grangemouth broke the 15 per cent threshold and other local co-operatives followed suit. Grangemouth's five day strike disrupted the town's food supply and the co-operative bakery faced crowds of angry women who blamed the employers. Solidarity from the bakers, tailors and dockers isolated the management and undermined efforts to break the strike. Clearly uplifted by the strike wave, Wilkinson wrote of these 'stirring times in Scotland'. In Grangemouth, the branch held a victory social and dance. To show their deep appreciation for the two campaign organisers the branch presented gifts to Wilkinson and Mr Simpson. Reflecting upon the campaign, the pair noted very satisfactory wages improvements, considerable union recruitment and the election of energetic new branch officials, many of them women. The impact of AUCE successes in Falkirk reached Perth, Lanarkshire, Ayrshire and Glasgow.[64] Further north in Perth and Aberdeen, the co-operative wages board resisted the AUCE. There too, union recruitment – often among young inexperienced staff – accelerated and, even where improvements were not secured, membership remained resilient. In Perth, the union won a 2s a week pay increase.[65]

The AUCE's ADM of 1917 opened on Easter Monday in St George's Hall, Liverpool.[66] Wilkinson spoke to a radical anti-capitalist motion on the 'state disposal of capital and land'. This motion contrasted capital's freedoms with labour's fetters:

> That this meeting, having regard to the fact that all males between eighteen and forty-one years of age cannot sell or dispose of their labour but must use it for the defence of the realm, petition the Government to have all land and capital placed at the disposal of the State, every adult having one vote.

Wilkinson suggested that the compulsion of women workers might follow that of male labour and that influential women hostile to workers' interests were proposing this. Condemning the inadequacy of advances in female wages in the munitions industry, she insisted that all women should get the vote (not simply the proposed over-30 year olds). Furthermore, she complained about the concentration of private wealth during wartime and congratulated the Russian people on their recent revolution, who showed their determination that the wealth of the land should be theirs. Indicating the conference's left-wing atmosphere, the resolution passed unanimously.

Displacement, the AUCE women's department, the laundries

By summer 1917, the SFL's long-term implications became an unavoidable question. Initially, the union's discourse asserted that equal pay for female substitutes guaranteed that wages and conditions would not deteriorate for returning soldiers. The union's position was that the union would both insist that veterans would be reabsorbed and women would not be forced back into the sweated industries.[67] Wilkinson put this case at the Yorkshire district's special conference on 17 June 1917. The union journal noted that this prompted lengthy discussion without indicating its nature. The union organised eighteen conferences on the subject of post-war reconstruction during 1917 and surveyed the membership on the situation.[68]

In October 1917, the union's executive council decided to establish a women's department, putting Wilkinson in charge. The women's department initially had two principal activities: first, to publicise itself to women members; and, second, a national campaign to recruit women laundry workers.[69] A winter campaign of conferences introduced women members to the work of the new women's department. The first meetings occurred in Cardiff, Swansea and Newcastle.[70] At these meetings, Hallsworth emphasised the struggle to improve working women's status. Wilkinson outlined the women's department's objective to 'help and advise women in those matters where their interests were not coincident with men's, and to encourage women to take a greater share in the work of the Union'. The Newcastle conference held on 26 September attracted forty-six female and 140 male branch delegates with forty other women members present as well as observers from the Women's Co-operative Guild and the Newcastle Labour Representation Committee. Further meetings were announced for sixteen other localities.

In the *AUCE Journal*, Wilkinson presented a fuller rationale of her department premised upon her modernist vision of young womanhood:

> The typical Girl of To-day is the well-dressed, capable, independent worker, whose keynote is keenness. She is keen about her work, about her sport, about life. And she is very new. The world that before the war confined her to a few channels, and opposed all her efforts to break through into new work, has thrown open every door, and stands urging

her to undertake responsibilities that would have caused her protecting parents to shudder.[71]

Here Wilkinson was adapting the 'new woman' to her audience of young working-class women. Woollacott found no evidence of such conceptions in the cultural consumption of munitions workers and suggests that such ideas were confined to middle-class women with greater educational and social opportunities.[72] This makes Wilkinson's approach all the more audacious. A wartime revolution, Wilkinson declared, had transformed women's roles. When other unions worried about women as a threat to wages, employment and union prerogatives, Wilkinson argued that women themselves had remained silent. Others – trade union leaders, middle-class and university women – had spoken for them. Wilkinson sought to address their impermanence as well as their desire not to return to the sweated and monotonous work that they had done before the war. Her motif was self-activity: to 'harness the keenness of the modern woman to the great trade union wagon.'[73] Just as the Labour movement needed more women officials, speakers and councillors, so the AUCE needed more women activists. This campaign to enlist the support of women volunteers for the special work of the department secured 120 respondents.[74] The women's department sought to follow up on this success with the 'all-in' movement, seeking to boost female membership and a second wave of activists to achieve this. The women's department also organised a district conference at the Burt Hall, Newcastle over the employers' failure to pay female substitutes war bonuses. One hundred and seven delegates from forty-six branches participated.[75] The department's creation did not eliminate male chauvinism from the union. Wilkinson complained about branch officials' complacent attitude to female recruitment.[76] A lively debate also appeared in the letters' page to the *AUCE Journal* between individual critics of women workers' abilities and those defending women war workers.[77]

This coincided with a wider debate within the trade union movement. In September 1917, Wilkinson attended the SJC conference on reconstruction.[78] The conference drew together the most prominent female labour movement activists. Wilkinson argued for 'equal work for equal pay', despite opposition from Mary Macarthur, of the NFWW and the Women's Trade Union League, and Dr Marion Phillips, WLL secretary. On 19 December 1917, Wilkinson chaired the Organisation of Women in Trade Unions Conference. This conference assessed alternate strategies for organising women workers. Miss Smith-Rose of the Association of Women Post-office Sorters favoured separatist women-only unions like her own. Miss Manican of the Workers' Union advocated mixed branches, observing that women refined the masculine culture of the public house, coarse language and hyperbole. Miss Talbot of the Shop Assistants' Union talked of her union's women's councils: these had educated women members but the union leadership had withdrawn resources fearing the formation of women's branches. Wilkinson relayed the AUCE's precedent of establishing a women's department. Its purpose was to overcome the double trap of separatism and the failure to address women's specific interests when men have greater time and trade union experience.[79] Overall, the consensus of the conference favoured work in mixed branches or unions rather than separatism.

At a conference on women in the unions attended by some hundred or so delegates on 17 October 1918, Wilkinson again advocated equal pay. With greater numbers of women likely to be in industry after the war, equal pay was essential if pay rates were to be defended. To the family wage argument, she ingeniously countered that because working women's work did not stop on returning home, they needed money for help with the housework. Equal remuneration was also necessary to prevent resentment between colleagues and to end the injustice of women being paid less for the same work.[80]

The women's department also sought to unionise the laundry sector. Building on advances in co-operative laundries, this marked a major attempt to break into the private sector. In a sense, the laundry workers held a strategic position between the co-operative and private sectors whereby the AUCE could consolidate both on its expanded female membership and use its collective bargaining successes in one sector to try to raise wages and conditions in the other. Work in this sphere would open wider possibilities in private retail. The organising campaign entailed recruitment drives, conferences and the creation of shop stewards, mainly in Yorkshire and Lancashire. The union made a breakthrough with private laundries in Bradford after a strike threat. As a result of the campaign, by early 1918 the AUCE participated in national collective bargaining with the National Federation of Co-operative Laundries and established a regional agreement with the National Federation of Laundry Associations.[81] By 4 October 1918, Wilkinson could report considerable progress in both branch organisation and pay for laundry workers.[82]

Defeats, peace and Wilkinson's dismissal

In summer 1918, a bitter dispute emerged with Lincoln CWS. In circumstances of AUCE de-recognition and refusal to negotiate over the wage claim, the local AUCE tendered strike notices, gaining support for their case from the Lincoln Trades Council, the National Union of General Workers and the local shop stewards' movement. The local food control committee forced the employers, the Ministry of Labour, and the union into arbitration.[83] The Lincoln dispute marked what was an acerbic low point in the AUCE–Shop Assistants' Union relations. Wilkinson scathingly condemned their wire-pulling.[84] Lincoln connected Wilkinson and the shop stewards' movement who had recently won an illegal local strike.[85] That the Lincoln shop stewards' movement believed any union de-recognition, including that of the AUCE, to be their prerogative mightily impressed Wilkinson.[86] At dinnertime meetings at munitions factories, Wilkinson tapped into the 'ferment' over dilution and was emboldened by the vitality of the shop stewards who were 'not too enamoured with the orthodox trade unionism' (as she put it).[87] An engineering shop stewards committee special meeting offered its full support to Wilkinson and Jagger, whom it had invited specially. For Wilkinson, the atmosphere during their thirty-two meetings in Lincoln 'brought the refreshing memory of the old suffrage campaigns'. These culminated with syndicalist veteran Tom Mann's appearance at a 'huge demonstration' at the Cornhill.[88] Though this was ultimately unsuccessful, the AUCE used the co-operative movement's democratic channels (quarterly meetings, elections and AGM) rather than industrial action.[89] Crucially, the union campaigned to elect sympathetic delegates onto the board at the AGM in August 1918. This strategy floundered, in AUCE's account of events, on the committee's lack of democratic scruples. To an 'incredulous' audience of 1,500, according to Wilkinson, the officers announced a 900 to 570 defeat for the trades council/AUCE slate. This ended the six-month dispute between the AUCE and the Lincoln Co-operative Society.[90] George Harris, the Lincoln CWS secretary, bitterly attacked Wilkinson for falsehood, denying her ballot-rigging charge.[91] In a letter to the *Co-operative News*, the rival shopworkers' union secretary W. H. Neale accused her of trying to bluff the workers. Another correspondent described the AUCE as a 'continual menace to the cooperative movement'.

After defeat in Lincoln, the collapse of the 'big CWS strike' ultimately led to Wilkinson's (temporary) dismissal. Its origins lay with CWS printers in Pelaw and Longsight. Longsight printers were locked out on 30 July. Warrington AUCE printers walked out in sympathy, though other unions sought to cross picket lines. On 26 August the strike re-ignited.[92] At its height, nearly 10,000 AUCE members were on strike.[93] The CWS appealed to the TUC, which called a conference in Derby, at which the AUCE was roundly condemned. On 7 September, the Board of Trade arbitrators, using the DORA, instructed the AUCE to terminate the strike.[94] The dispute's failure led to recriminations, not least, over its £15,000 cost. The executive received complaints about Wilkinson's expenses during the strike and her conduct of apparently issuing strike instructions without the executive's permission.[95] On 19 October the executive summoned Wilkinson to their next meeting. A special delegate meeting in Leeds on 20 October about union amalgamation aired dissatisfaction focused upon permanent union officials and 'alleged delays in action, non-consultation of those vitally concerned, changes in policy'.[96] Long Eaton and Longsight delegates successfully moved a motion for an inquiry. The union's historian believed dissatisfaction stemmed from the strike being extended too far and too fast.[97]

Failing to attend the executive meeting on 3 November, they instructed her to appear before them on the following Sunday.[98] At that meeting, Wilkinson explained herself. Both Wilkinson and the executive were seemingly playing for time, as it was not until their next full meeting that they decided to dismiss Wilkinson. Her notice was to run to 8 February and the executive planned to advertise for a replacement.[99] However, since Wilkinson returned the disputed expenses, the way was cleared for her reinstatement, called for by branches, such as Coatbridge and Gillingham. Her supporters called a special delegate meeting on 2 February, challenging the dismissal because the committee of inquiry had not reported to the ADM.[100] Consequently a special executive meeting on 9 February, the day after her dismissal, reinstated her.[101] While this episode remains rather obscure, it was revealing. Unlike some unions after the war, the woman's organiser post was not in question. Wilkinson antagonised a section of the lay membership, probably for her radicalism and her emphasis on women's recruitment, yet she also mobilised sufficient support to win back her job. Facing institutional discipline, she initially evaded authority, and then acted in a contrite manner rather than quitting on principle. This behaviour recurred in the face of disciplinary threats from both the Labour Party (1934) and the House of Commons (1927). Finally, it shows a left trade union official's difficulties, in the aftermath of a defeat, facing hostility from the membership.

Conclusion

Wilkinson's intellectual development bore hallmarks of her wartime experiences. The AUCE's adoption of industrial unionism with its emphasis upon militant grassroots activity reinforced Wilkinson's commitment to extra-parliamentary politics. With Wilkinson, however, hers was the paradoxical industrial unionism of the left trade union official. As an employee of the union, her fortunes were entangled with its institutional interests and there were limits to the criticisms that she could make of it (and the TUC). Her encounter with syndicalism, industrial unionism and the Shop Stewards and Workers' Committee Movement is significant in that her trade union practices and her heady wartime experiences of struggle radicalised her political engagement. During 1917–20, she shared the journey with many others from industrial unionism or syndicalism to Bolshevism.

Wilkinson's 'industrial unionism for women' ran in parallel with her guild socialism and her feminism. While most of her guild socialist comrades or suffrage sisters came from university activism or elevated social status, she straddled this milieu and the terrain of trade unionism. In effect, she was speaking different languages to different audiences. Her industrial unionism for women was characteristic of mobilising frames connecting multiple social movements and such dynamic composite positions marked her political itinerary. Rather than always forcing these ideas into synthesis, Wilkinson found an overlap; a commitment to women's and worker's self-emancipation through militant action. Wartime experiences set another feature of Wilkinson's politics that resurfaced on many occasions transnationally: her valorisation of humble women in labour, feminist, anti-colonial or anti-fascist contestation. Indeed, for her, women's contribution to these movements was an indispensable index of their authenticity and vitality as a challenge to the status quo.

Notes

1. Betty Vernon, *Ellen Wilkinson* (London, 1982), pp. 46–8; Paula Bartley, *Ellen Wilkinson: from Red Suffragist to Government Minister* (London, 2014), pp. 10–13. With a fuller discussion but emphasizing Wilkinson's mentors rather than her relationship with the strike wave, the shop stewards' movement and industrial unionism, Laura Beers, *Red Ellen: The Life of Ellen Wilkinson, Socialist, Feminist, Internationalist* (London, 2016), pp. 42–9. Matt Perry, *Red Ellen Wilkinson: Her Ideas, Movements and World* (Manchester, 2014).
2. A. Hewitt, *AUCE: Why It Has Withdrawn from the Trades Union Congress* (Manchester, 1915); *Scottish Co-operator*, 13 April 1915; William Richardson, *A Union of Many Trades: The History of USDAW* (Manchester, 1979), pp. 58–64.
3. *Co-operative Employé*, September 1915.
4. *Scottish Co-operator*, 22 January 1915.
5. *Co-operative Employé*, July 1915. *Co-operative Employé*, October 1915.
6. *Co-operative Employé*, October 1916.
7. Interview with Pankhurst, *Co-operative Employé*, September 1915.
8. Irene Osgood Andrews and Margaret A. Hobbs, *Economic Effects of the World War upon Women and Children in Great Britain* (Oxford, 1921).
9. Deborah Thom, *Nice Girls and Rude Girls: Women Workers in World War I* (London, 2000), p. 39.
10. *Scottish Co-operator*, 12 May 1916.
11. NUDAW General Secretary's (GS) reports, Wilkinson's report, 3 August 1917.
12. USDAW archive, AUCE 24th Annual Report 1915, p. 9.
13. *Co-operative Employé*, January 1916.
14. *Co-operative Employé*, December 1915.
15. *Co-operative Employé*, January 1916.
16. *Co-operative Employé*, January 1916.
17. *Co-operative Employé*, December 1915.

18 Angela Woollacott, *On Her Their Lives Depend: Munitions Workers in the Great War* (Berkeley, CA, 1994), pp. 104–5.
19 Barbara Drake, *Women in the Engineering Trades: A Problem, a Solution, and Some Criticisms* (London, 1918), p. 50.
20 *Co-operative Employé*, April 1916. For the terms, *Scottish Co-operator*, 17 March 1916.
21 *Co-operative Employé*, June 1916.
22 USDAW archive, AUCE 26th Annual Report 1917, p. 7.
23 *Co-operative Employé*, October 1915. AUCE Special circular from Wilkinson, 14 January 1918.
24 Woollacott, *On Her Their Lives Depend*, pp. 99, 202.
25 *AUCE Journal*, February 1918.
26 *Scottish Co-operator*, 22 January 1915, 19 March 1915. A motion for industrial unionism at 1915 ADM: 24,572 for and 2,252 against, *Scottish Co-operator*, 16 April 1915.
27 Richardson, *A Union of Many Trades*, p. 59.
28 Francis Shor, 'Gender and Labour/Working Class History in Comparative Perspective: The Syndicalist and Wobbly Experience in the USA, Australia, and New Zealand', *Left History*, 11 (2006), pp. 118–36.
29 *Co-operative Employé*, June 1916. *Scottish Co-operator*, 6 August 1916.
30 *Scottish Co-operator*, January 1918.
31 *Scottish Co-operator*, 22 December 1917.
32 *Time and Tide*, 14 December 1935.
33 *Co-operative Employé*, February 1916.
34 Ralph Darlington, *Syndicalism and the Transition to Communism: an International Comparative Analysis* (Aldershot, 2008), pp. 4–7.
35 *Co-operative Employé*, January 1916.
36 Leek AUCE official and Women's Co-operative Guild activist Harriet Kidd and Margaret Llewelyn Davies (ed.), *Life as We Have Known it, by Cooperative Working Women* (London, 1977), pp. 73–80.
37 Of 20s a day for men and 10s a day for women, *Co-operative Employé*, May 1916.
38 *Co-operative Employé*, March 1916.
39 *Scottish Co-operator*, 25 February 1916.
40 *Co-operative Employé*, March 1916.
41 *Co-operative Employé*, March 1916.
42 *Labour Leader*, 2 July 1914.
43 Ellen Wilkinson, 'Feminine fascism', *Plebs*, May (1933), 110–11.
44 *Co-operative Employé*, March 1916. A. Hewitt, General Secretary 1891–1916, handing over to Hallsworth.
45 *Scottish Co-operator*, 18 March 1916.
46 *Co-operative Employé*, April 1916.
47 *Co-operative Employé*, May 1916. *Scottish Co-operator*, 18 March 1916.
48 A letter from 'a member', *Scottish Co-operator*, 30 June 1916.
49 *Co-operative News*, 14 October 1916.
50 *Co-operative Employé*, May 1916.
51 *Co-operative Employé*, May 1916.
52 *Co-operative Employé*, May 1916.

53 *Co-operative Employé*, June 1916.
54 Joan Smith, 'Labour Tradition in Glasgow and Liverpool', *History Workshop Journal*, 17:1 (1984), 32–56. Joseph Melling, 'Whatever Happened to Red Clydeside? Industrial Conflict and the Politics of Skill in the First World War', *International Review of Social History*, 35 (1990), pp. 3–32.
55 Milton Moses, 'Compulsory Arbitration in Great Britain during the War', *Journal of Political Economy*, 26:9 (1918), 882–900.
56 *Scottish Co-operator*, 26 May 1916.
57 *Co-operative News*, 16 September 1916, 23 September 1916. *The Times*, 23 November 1916.
58 *Labour Leader*, 21 September 1916, 5 October 1916).
59 *Co-operative News*, 25 November 1916, 2 December 1916.
60 Richardson, *A Union of Many Trades*, pp. 71–2.
61 *Co-operative Employé*, January 1917.
62 *Co-operative Employé*, March 1917, February 1917.
63 *Co-operative Employé*, April 1917.
64 *Co-operative Employé*, May 1917.
65 This works struck later that year, CAB 24 26 Report, Ministry of Labour, Labour Situation for the week ending 12 September 1917.
66 *Co-operative Employé*, May 1917.
67 *AUCE Journal*, July 1917.
68 USDAW archive, AUCE 25th Annual Report 1916, p. 1. Hallsworth penned a pamphlet *Labour after the War*. USDAW archive, AUCE 26th Annual Report 1917, p. 10.
69 USDAW archive, AUCE 26th Annual Report 1917, p. 11.
70 *AUCE Journal*, October 1917.
71 *AUCE Journal*, November 1917.
72 Woollacott, *On Her Their Lives Depend*, p. 204.
73 *AUCE Journal*, November 1917.
74 USDAW archive, AUCE 26th Annual Report 1917, p. 11.
75 *AUCE Journal*, December 1917.
76 *AUCE Journal*, January 1918.
77 *AUCE Journal*, December 1917, January 1918).
78 *AUCE Journal*, September 1917. Wilkinson represented AUCE/NUDAW on the SJC 1917–36, NUDAW Industrial General Secretary's reports, 11 October 1936.
79 *AUCE Journal*, January 1918. AUCE GS reports, Wilkinson's report, 31 December 1917.
80 LRD 1 I 03 Joint Committee of Enquiry into Women in the Trade Unions, 17 October 1918.In May 1918 the Fabian Research Department organised another conference over the working of arbitration and the need for more trained women organisers. *AUCE Journal*, June 1918.
81 *AUCE Journal*, January 1918, February 1918, March 1918. AUCE GS reports, 9 January 1918.
82 AUCE General Secretary's reports, Wilkinson's report, 4 October 1918.
83 *Co-operative Employé*, August 1916. *AUCE Journal*, April 1918.
84 *AUCE Journal*, June 1918.
85 Moses, 'Compulsory Arbitration in Great Britain during the War', p. 891.

86 *AUCE Journal*, April 1918.
87 *AUCE Journal*, August 1918.
88 *Lincoln Gazette and Lincolnshire Times*, 17 August 1918.
89 *AUCE Journal*, June 1918.
90 *AUCE Journal*, September 1918.
91 *Co-operative News*, 31 August 1918.
92 *AUCE Journal*, September 1918.
93 *Co-operative News*, 7 September 1918.
94 Trade union department executive (TUDE) meeting minutes, 8 September 1919; *AUCE Journal*, September 1918. *New Dawn*, 7 July 1923.
95 David Reid interview: Amy Mitchell, née Wild.
96 *AUCE Journal*, November 1918.
97 Richardson, *A Union of Many Trades*, p. 84.
98 TUDE minutes, 3 November 1918, *AUCE Journal*, December 1918.
99 TUDE minutes, 15 December 1918, *AUCE Journal*, January 1919. TUDE minutes, 5 January 1919, *AUCE Journal*, February 1919.
100 AUCE notice and resolution, SDM, 2 February 1919.
101 GS Report, Special Meeting, 9 February 1919. Being officially reinstated on 2 March, TUDE minutes, 2 March 1919, *AUCE Journal*, April 1919.

8

The unsung heroines of radical wartime activism: gender, militarism and collective action in the British Women's Corps

Krisztina Robert

On 6 February 1915, the London battalion of the Women's Volunteer Reserve (WVR) marched across the capital in military formation, dressed in the unit's khaki service uniform. Although this was not the first route march of the WVR, it became one of its best publicised of such events. In addition to illustrated press reports, the march also featured in the weekly newsreel shown in cinemas.[1] Press photographs captured the unit marching past Buckingham Palace, accompanied by two policemen walking in step with the column of uniformed women. This image enabled *The Bystander*, a popular magazine, to highlight women's changing political activism. Juxtaposing the picture with a pre-war photograph depicting a riotous suffrage demonstration at the same site broken up by mounted police, the editor contrasted the violent and subversive militancy of the suffragettes with the orderly patriotic militancy represented by the Reserve. Approval for the latter was reinforced by the caption, describing members of the WVR as 'militant servants' of the King[2] (Figure 8.1).

The route march and its press portrayal reveal the political nature of the objectives and strategy of the Women's Corps. Established in September 1914, the movement comprised a series of volunteer units that trained women for auxiliary work, and the government-sponsored Women's Services between 1917 and 1920, whose members released troops for the fighting by replacing them in the support jobs of the armed forces.[3] Route marches were part of the Corps' standard military training. Crucially, however, they were also propaganda exercises designed to attract new recruits, public support and military employment by displaying the Corps' classless, martial femininity and their members' organisation, discipline and training.[4] To gain maximum exposure for such spectacles, publicity for the events was carefully arranged. It is obvious from the published images that photographers were notified in advance in order to secure

The Bystander, February 17, 1915

Tempora Mutantur!
WOMEN BEFORE THE KING'S PALACE THEN AND NOW!

MILITANCY AS IT EXPRESSED ITSELF AT BUCKINGHAM PALACE LAST SUMMER

MILITANCY AS IT EXPRESSED ITSELF AT THE SAME PALACE LAST WEEK
When the Women's Volunteer Reserve marched past the scene of former violence as militant servants of the same King

Figure 8.1 'Tempora Mutantur!', *The Bystander*, 17 February 1915.

ideal shots of the marches and details of the routes and units were sent to newspapers by the Corps' publicists.[5] These tactics were inspired by the pre-war suffrage campaign. Edwardian suffragists had demanded women's enfranchisement by staging quasi-military spectacles to produce live demonstrations of their arguments and by arranging maximum press coverage to circulate these images nationwide.[6] Deploying the same strategy to claim women's right to military war service defined the Corps as a similarly radical political movement. Contemporaries recognised this meaning. Throughout the war, members of the public, the press and military authorities drew frequent parallels between the pre-war suffrage campaign and the Corps, noting continuities in their leadership, objectives and strategies, and engaging in heated debates about the challenge which they posed to existing boundaries of gender and class.[7]

Despite contemporary opinions, historical scholarship has portrayed the actions of the Corps as the opposite of radical activism. In the last four decades, historians of women and gender have overturned previous, celebratory interpretations of the Corps, concluding that the movement reproduced rather than challenged the social order in terms of both gender and class.[8] Scholars have acknowledged that the objectives of the Corps – to recruit women from all classes and organise their work with the armed forces – were potentially radical.[9] They have argued, however, that the militarism of the movement undermined these goals. The military organisation of the units replicated the contemporary class hierarchy and prevented union and feminist agitation, while their martial values, like discipline, stifled protest, promoting obedience to female officers and military authorities.[10] Thus, scholars have claimed, despite resenting their harsh conditions and subordinate status in the armed forces, corps members never seriously resisted these regulations. Content with their mainly traditional female jobs, including 'routine' clerical work and 'nurturing' domestic tasks, women accepted their second-class auxiliary position behind the troops, including no formal recognition and pay in the volunteer units and civilian status, feminised martial symbols and lower pay in the Services.[11] Historians have stressed that such attitudes were encouraged by military authorities and public opinion that refused to recognise corps members as soldiers in order to maintain traditional gender distinctions.[12]

This portrayal of the Corps has been shaped by feminist scholarship's broader conceptualisation of women's radical wartime activism. Defining this concept as organised protest against the militarising state and its agencies, studies have explored the economic and political objectives of such opposition. The former included campaigns for higher wages, fixed rents and equal food distribution, while the latter involved anti-militarist agitation to resist conscription, defy workplace regimentation and bring about a negotiated peace.[13] The radicalism of such actions was signified by female protesters' militant tactics. These ranged from non-violent acts, such as joining unions and attending peace meetings, to more direct action, like strikes, protest marches and street rallies. Accordingly, the heroines of these accounts were munitions workers, union officials and feminist activists. Scholars have praised the concessions obtained by their campaigns, but admitted that such protest failed to alter the structures of women's subordination. Studies attribute this failure to women workers' class divisions. They argue that conflicting class interests fragmented solidarity among female workers, preventing their united gender-based activism.[14] Divergent class interests are also blamed for women's inability to alter the existing gendered division of labour – another radical ambition of female war workers. Scholars conclude that middle-class women claimed new professional posts by advocating traditional discourses of domesticity and motherhood, which enabled authorities and male unions to counter female workers' pursuit of equal job opportunities.[15] Viewed within this framework, self-militarisation and apparent support for social hierarchies and the martial state defined the Women's Corps as the antithesis of radical wartime activism.

The substantial variance between contemporary and scholarly assessments of the Corps suggests that existing conceptualisations define women's wartime agitation too narrowly. Current definitions, I would argue, are still influenced by traditional interpretations of labour history.[16] Concerned primarily with male workers' economic protests, this approach focuses on working men's class solidarity, trade unions and industrial militancy, seeing them as the main source, means and expression of organised radicalism.[17] In the last few decades, however, cultural perspectives have broadened the definition of collective action and its origins. Locating radical agency in multiple identities, like gender, class and ethnicity, these explanations have explored the construction and assertion of political identities, agency and participation articulated through symbolic means of communication.[18] Based on this approach, feminist labour historians have been reinterpreting women workers' pre-war activism as diverse, feminised and pragmatic compared to men's. They have argued that women joined a variety of suffrage, socialist and professional groups and shared a range of educational, militant and 'everyday resistance tactics' in order to contest their triple exclusion from skilled work, male unions and citizenship.[19] First World War studies confirm these patterns of women's activism. Focusing on munitions workers, scholars show how women deployed cultural, benevolent and militant labour tactics within their own support networks and in their relationships with middle-class welfare and union officials. Through these multiple strategies, they improved their working lives, expressed support for the troops and constructed their wartime identity as the makers of weapons directly involved in the waging of war.[20]

This chapter reassesses the political significance of the Women's Corps through these cultural perspectives in order to understand the nature and extent of the movement's radical activism. Therefore, my first aim is to determine the Corps' agenda by exploring its central objective and key strategies. I then examine the political implications and radicalism of this programme and the outcome of its implementation. The discussion focuses on the primary and most controversial goal of the Corps' project: to establish women's military services in Britain by adopting martial organisation and cross-class recruiting policies. In order to evaluate the socially transformative impact of this plan, I analyse the contemporary British meanings of soldiering and measure the Corps' achievements by contrasting its size, roles and status between 1914 and 1920, and by comparing it with other, similar war organisations. I argue that the agenda of the Corps movement, which it had achieved with considerable success, posed a radical challenge to the established social order. By constructing new martial female identities and a new female occupation, auxiliary soldiering, the Corps shifted the existing gendered division of labour, enabled its members to claim citizenship and recast wartime class relations beyond its ranks. Through this analysis, the chapter also aims to contribute to a new conceptual framework of women's wartime political activism. In this respect, it emphasises the necessity of exploring women's cross-class political interaction through a wider range of organisational forms and collective action along with the imperative to identify the multiple, culturally and historically specific meanings of political ideologies, like militarism. It also stresses the need for a more detailed scrutiny of the circumstances in which campaigners develop their objectives and strategies. I demonstrate these points by defining the Corps' military parades as collective action organised by a loose popular movement, whose varied martial structures, symbols and practices enabled its socially diverse membership to pursue their political and professional ambitions through its central agenda.[21] I also analyse the Corps' shifting programme within the fluid military and economic context of wartime Britain to further explain how it accommodated a cross-class membership.

The objectives and strategies of the Women's Corps

The central objective of the Corps – to establish women's military services – developed gradually during the war from the shared ambitions of the female volunteer units and the official Services.[22] Both sections of the movement sought to organise women's non-combatant auxiliary work for the armed forces. The exact definition of this role, however, shifted significantly between 1914 and 1918 due to the changing demands of the war effort. In the first year of the conflict, founders of the movement formed female volunteer units, seeking to participate in home defence in a potential invasion. They hoped to perform combat support duties to release more troops for the fighting and help evacuate civilians from the firing line.²³ This dual purpose was inspired by widespread invasion fears and public desire to increase Britain's military strength.²⁴ From mid-1915, the volunteers had to modify their objectives. As invasion fears receded, public criticism of women's militarism increased, while new opportunities for war work in hospitals and munitions factories depleted the ranks of the volunteers. Simultaneously, however, the army's growing manpower needs created potential openings in military recruitment, catering and transport. Therefore, to justify their martial existence and boost their membership, corps leaders decided to obtain newly available military employment by arranging vocational training for their units, publicising their availability for work and lobbying potential employers.²⁵ From 1917, women's martial job prospects improved progressively. As the military manpower shortage became critical, the authorities decided to release all able-bodied soldiers for combat duty by replacing them in the support jobs of the armed forces with women. This enabled Corps leaders to establish the Women's Services on an official and regular basis.²⁶ Consequently, their ambitions shifted to administering women's mass employment on full-time, paid auxiliary work across Britain and on the Western Front, including the negotiation of terms and conditions and the organisation of recruiting, accommodation, training, uniforms, medical services and the supervision of women's discipline and welfare.²⁷

The primary strategy through which the Corps pursued these objectives was the adoption of military organisation. This was a calculated decision by Corps leaders at key stages of the movement: in 1914 when they created the first volunteer units and in 1917 when they developed the first official Service.²⁸ Military organisation had long been recognised as the instrument of developing discipline. By ensuring compliance with orders, discipline enabled the coordinated functioning of different army units and was thus regarded as the foundation of military efficiency.²⁹ Corps leaders were aware of this, realising that without discipline their units would be unreliable and therefore unacceptable to the authorities, especially near the fighting zone.³⁰ Consequently, all sections of the movement adopted the essentials of martial organisation. This included formalised units and ranks linked in a hierarchical chain of command based on discipline which was instilled through military training, such as drilling and marching, and the adoption of uniforms, insignia and communal activities. However, depending on the type of auxiliary work they hoped to perform, different sections of the Corps adopted different types of militarism. In 1914, the first female units modelled themselves on the Victorian Volunteer Force, whose independent local companies and flat command structure suited the women's plans for helping to defend their communities.³¹ From mid-1915, Corps leaders, who wanted to expand the movement by obtaining paid work for its members, introduced a different organisation. Thus, the Women's Legion (WL) functioned as a private contractor, supplying army camps and garages with specialised workers from its Military Cookery and Motor Transport Sections.[32] Finally, in 1917 the Women's Army Auxiliary Corps (WAAC) initiated a new model, which was copied by the other two Services: the Women's Royal Naval Service (WRNS) and the Women's Royal Air Force (WRAF). Based on the supporting 'tail' units of the army, including the Signals, Medical and Ordnance Corps, whose specialised companies were attached to various fighting units, this structure enabled the mass expansion of women's auxiliary employment with the armed forces.[33]

Introducing cross-class, egalitarian recruiting policies was another strategic decision that Corps leaders made to fill the ranks of their new armies. Expecting opposition to female military units, based on women's alleged incompetence and frailty, initially both the volunteers and the WAAC adopted selective recruiting principles to pre-empt criticism. Thus, when the WVR started recruiting in the autumn of 1914, it appealed for 'qualified motorists, motor-cyclists and aviators' to join the unit.[34] This limited membership to a few hundred middle-class 'sporting and hunting women'.[35] Realising the need to broaden its appeal, the WVR launched a popular movement in December, emphasising that it 'had no class distinctions' and called for women 'from all walks of life' to join.[36] In addition, it introduced instalment plans and appealed for public donations to help poorer 'business and shop girls' to obtain the Reserve's expensive uniform.[37] This move was successful, boosting membership to c.10,000 by mid-1915.[38] However, it was only after Lady Londonderry used her military connections to obtain paid work and free uniforms for her new WL Military Cookery Section that working-class women were able to join the Corps in larger numbers.[39] In 1917, the WAAC also had to tailor its entry criteria to the need for mass recruitment. Seeking to provide workers for a wide range of auxiliary posts, the Service had a cross-class recruiting policy from the start. However, anxious to prove women's fitness for military work, leaders of the Service initially adopted strict medical, nationality and vocational standards for recruits. Women who wore glasses, had a naturalised British parent or did not work for leading employers in their trade were often rejected for foreign service.[40] Struggling to fill their posts, from late 1917 the entry criteria were relaxed and, taking advantage of the increasing closure of munitions factories, the three Services recruited tens of thousands of former munitions workers into their domestic and technical units.[41] In addition, they established 'immobile' sections for older married women who, unable to leave their families, were transported daily to nearby military stations for work.[42]

The dual strategy of the Corps entailed the discursive construction of a series of martial female identities and a new gendered work role. This was dictated by the need to adapt the principles of military organisation and mass recruitment, designed for male combatant troops, to the requirements of female auxiliary units. Chief among these was the question of maintaining discipline and efficiency. Despite their military organisation, due to their exclusively non-combatant role the Corps remained legally civilian, controlling their members through ineffectual fines, fatigue duties and admonition, without the deterrent of physical punishment.[43] Furthermore, although the Corps broadened their recruitment to boost their ranks, the pool of recruits who were both skilled and willing to join up was finite.[44] Corps leaders responded to these problems by developing collective martial female identities, such as the women Volunteers, the WAACs, the Wrens and the WRAFs, and by constructing a new female work role, auxiliary soldiering, defined as skilled, patriotic and prestigious work for modern women.[45] The martial identities were designed to maintain discipline through the bonds of comradeship, honour and pride in the Corps' uniforms, while the prestigious work role was intended to increase competence and professional pride among unskilled recruits and make joining the corps more attractive among skilled women workers.[46] Both the content and the creation of the new gender categories overlapped. Combining military practices with the tactics of suffrage agitation, where many of them had cut their campaigning teeth, Corps leaders constructed the new identities and work role through a range of performative, visual, material and written portrayals.[47] These included public drill practices, cross-town route marches with military or the WVR's own drum-and-fife bands, ceremonial parades with inspections and martial pageants where Corps members enacted their work, like WRAF mechanics building a plane during the Lord Mayor's Show in 1918.[48] In addition, Corps leaders urged women to start vocational training, organised driving, signalling, domestic and clerical courses, and represented the auxiliaries' work, training and parades in publicity campaigns through the positive discourses of modern femininity[49] (Figure 8.2).

The political radicalism of the Corps movement

The Corps' military agenda posed a radical challenge to the prevailing social order. First, the construction of the new female occupation of auxiliary soldiering shifted the existing gendered division of labour. Compared to Continental countries, military service in Victorian Britain became defined as a trade or career, due to voluntary recruitment, a longer service obligation and the ongoing professionalisation of the officer corps.[50] Contemporary recruiting posters, advertising terms, conditions and wages, reflected this. During the same period, military service became demarcated as an exclusively male job. Women, who formerly performed

Figure 8.2 'The W.A.A.C. at the Front: A Woman Chauffeur in a "Tin Hat".'

domestic work for the troops as wives and camp followers, were excluded from the forces through the professionalisation of support services, barrack accommodation and restrictions on soldiers' right to marry.[51] The rationale behind this lay in the separate spheres ideology and the related spatial segregation of gendered work. Defining women as naturally feeble, emotional and frivolous, these norms banned them from military employment and locations, arguing that their incompetence and sexual presence would compromise the forces' efficiency, discipline and morale, while the heavy duties and rough martial environments would undermine their feminine physique and morality.[52] Thus, nursing and philanthropy were the only military roles open to women in the newly formed regular and voluntary nursing corps and war charities.[53] The training and work activities of the Corps overturned this gendered division of military labour. Separating the formerly combined combatant and non-combatant roles of soldiering, the volunteers claimed all support jobs as suitable for women, including waggon and motor driving, care of horses, car mechanics and trench digging which were regarded as men's work even in civilian life.[54] Moreover, the work activities of the WL and the official Services were literally encroaching on male work territory, including army, navy and RAF cookhouses, offices, signal stations, garages, workshops, shipyards and aerodromes, where the auxiliaries replaced most servicemen for frontline duty.[55]

Second, the Corps' martial female identities, work and their portrayals contested the gendered links between military service and citizenship. Since the 1660s, all British troops had been legally servants of the Crown through the monarch, their commander-in-chief, whose shilling they took, uniform they wore and commission they held.[56] In the nineteenth century, this link to the state was extended to the nation. Based on the imperial role of the armed forces, the example of European citizen armies and the 1859 Volunteer Force, which drew previously uninvolved classes into national defence, military service became defined as the training ground of both masculinity and citizenship.[57] This martial concept of citizenship became politicised in the pre-war and wartime years. During the Edwardian suffrage campaign, anti-suffragists argued that since the state ultimately depended on its citizens' ability to defend it, only those who could bear arms qualified for voting. In return, suffragettes represented historical female warriors in their pageants and portrayed themselves as an army fighting state repression.[58] Additionally, in 1917, wartime electoral reform, which enfranchised all servicemen after the introduction of conscription, based citizenship firmly on military participation.[59] In this climate, by portraying themselves as auxiliary soldiers, Corps members laid claim not just to the martial, but to the electoral concept of citizenship too. This was obvious as they observed military etiquette and performed drill and route marches in their khaki, navy and air force blue uniforms. It was also clear from the Corps' visual portrayals, which regularly depicted

Figure 8.3 *The Wrens: Being the Story of their Beginnings & Doings in Various Parts* (London, 1919).

members with symbols of the state and the nation, holding or saluting the Union Jack, the White Ensign and the Saltire or calling British women for patriotic service while embraced by Britannia[60] (Figure 8.3). The Corps' claim to be serving the state was also revealed by its leaders' efforts to associate their units with the Crown. WRNS officers applied for sanction to use the 'Royal' title when christening their Service, while the WAAC adopted the names of female royalty for its camps and rebranded itself as Queen Mary's Army Auxiliary Corps when the Queen became its commandant-in-chief.[61]

Finally, the Corps' recruiting policies contested the rigid class hierarchy of patriotic war service. This did not mean erasing class distinctions among their membership. Based on the different status and wages of occupations, the informal hierarchy of employment sections re-established the class structure in the Services.[62] However, the egalitarian entry criteria levelled opportunities somewhat compared to other agencies organising women's military war work. Both munitions factories and the Voluntary Aid Detachment maintained strict class distinctions, the former providing lady volunteers with better housing, meals and jobs than ordinary workers, while the latter, conversely, offering poorer terms and conditions to its elite volunteers than its paid general service members.[63] In contrast, regardless of class, all other ranks entered the Services through the same admission process, applying through the labour exchanges and sharing lodgings and life with all other recruits in large training depots.[64] This applied equally to Betty Donaldson, a lawyer's daughter, and Ada Gummersall, a domestic servant, who joined the WAAC's driving and household sections.[65] Even after their posting to separate trade sections, all other ranks received the same grade accommodation, rations and amenities. In addition, due to the Services' stress on efficiency, applicants could join the better paid trade sections if they had the required skills, irrespective of class. Thus, Gladys Ottaway, a shop girl who was taught to drive by her manager so that she could replace the enlisted delivery man, was accepted into the WAAC's middle-class driving section after passing the test.[66] Likewise, former domestic servants could join the clerical units once they had completed the WAAC's training course.[67] The Services also offered most of their lower-class recruits their first opportunity for prestigious national roles. Serving with the troops, especially in the war zone, was the highest status war work women could undertake. Praised by politicians, chronicled by the press and portrayed by artists, it was coveted by many middle-class civilians excluded from military war participation by age, health or family circumstances.[68] Thus, by performing martial support jobs, working-class auxiliaries also contested the wartime status of many middle-class civilians.

The radicalism of the Corps' agenda is indicated by persistent wartime criticism that sought to curb its military features and mass recruitment. In 1915, letters to the press protested against the WVR's khaki uniforms and martial training, urging the authorities to ban women's use of khaki and discourage their work near the war zone.[69] Opposition to the Services was less direct, due to their official sanction. However, most military officers initially resisted efforts to replace their male staff with women, while widespread rumours in Britain about the immorality of WAACs hindered recruitment for the Services.[70] All such opposition centred on the Corps' challenge to social hierarchies. Public critics insisted on preserving the gendered division of military service and citizenship, arguing that support duties, such as despatch riding, were 'not ... within women's scope' since they took place 'in the field' and thus could not be separated from soldiers' combatant roles.[71] Critics also claimed that khaki uniforms 'mark men as the servants of their country, the soldiers of their King', 'who are necessarily *men*'.[72] Thus, by 'masquerading in khaki uniforms', women were 'making ... the King's uniform ridiculous', and undermined the status of soldiering and army recruitment.[73] Military opposition also focused on the women's potentially destabilising impact on the forces' masculine qualities. Field-Marshal Haig objected to women's employment in specific jobs, such as postal sorting and storekeeping, claiming that field conditions in France made these roles too complex for women, whose inefficiency would erode soldiers' morale.[74] Other officers refused to share their insignia with the auxiliaries, insisting on different, feminised badges for them.[75] Gendered opposition also reflected class-based criticism.

Sharing popular prejudices about working-class women's uncontrolled sexuality, several army officers expressed concern about the 'likelihood of sex difficulty', disrupting soldiers' discipline in France.[76] Rumours alleging soliciting, high venereal disease and pregnancy rates among the WAACs also targeted working-class women primarily, who comprised the bulk of army auxiliaries and valued their respectability more than other classes.[77]

The professional and political achievements of the Women's Corps

By the end of the war, Corps leaders had achieved their central goal of establishing women's military services. Although critics never accepted this development, 'the Women's Armies', as the press called the Services, had expanded to about 100,000 members by late 1918.[78] The Corps' success derived largely from their adoption of martial organisation, vocational training and professional ethos. After initial resistance, military officers accepted and often welcomed auxiliaries in their commands, employing them on over fifty trades, including highly skilled and confidential duties, such as printing, welding, machining, wireless telegraphy, decoding and intelligence work.[79] In addition to British stations and the supply bases in France, the women also served in the army areas near the fighting zone, in occupied Germany and in Malta.[80] Crucially, many of them worked in mixed workplaces with male co-workers, as numerous staff photographs taken outside offices before disbandment signify[81] (Figure 8.4). Nor did their employment end in 1918. In the aftermath of the Russian revolution, the government was anxious to accelerate soldiers' demobilisation, as protests and mutinies revealed the weakening of discipline after four years of war. Therefore, at official request, the WAAC, the WRAF and the WL served on after the Armistice, releasing troops for discharge.[82] This indicated the authorities' confidence in women's discipline. In return, the armed forces increasingly shared the emblems of their combatant position with the auxiliaries, giving them symbolic military status. This included the granting of brassards and cap badges by army formations to WAAC units attached to them, sanction for WRNS officers' rank insignia similar to their male counterparts' and the authorisation of RAF uniforms and rank badges for the WRAF.[83] This symbolic recognition culminated in the Services' inclusion in the armed forces' Victory March in 1919. For Corps leaders, this gesture was proof of their success along with women's limited enfranchisement, which included auxiliaries who served overseas, even if they were under thirty.[84] Finally, the armed forces' decision to share the profits of the wartime military canteens with the Services enabled the auxiliaries to continue their organised existence after their disbandment as veteran associations, representing the Corps at war

Figure 8.4 Staff photograph of a British army unit on the Western Front, outside an Army Service Corps garage, *c.* 1919.

commemorations and facilitating the re-establishment of the female Services in the Second World War.[85]

The gendered radicalism and egalitarian admission policies of the Services had a further, unanticipated, impact: the class-based radicalisation of the lower ranks of their membership. This was particularly noticeable among working-class women in the domestic and technical sections of the Services. Their recollections indicate that they had adopted their Corps' martial female identities, enjoying outdoor military training, pay parades and bugle calls and developing pride in their cap badges and uniforms which distinguished them from other units.[86] They relished ceremonial parades, such as the march-past during the Queen's Aldershot inspection, and identified closely with the troops, entertaining wounded soldiers and volunteering to share the men's hardships.[87] Simultaneously, however, working-class auxiliaries also developed greater political assertiveness. This stemmed from a sense of achievement about the military importance of their gruelling work and strong bonds of loyalty to their co-workers with whom they shared huts, duties, meals and time off.[88] Empowered by their martial roles and the Corps' egalitarian ethos, they rejected unfair treatment and snobbery from officers and higher-status colleagues by taking a range of independent collective action. This included everyday resistance tactics, like serving unappetising food to snooty colleagues or sharing lewd jokes about officers, and more organised acts of rebellion, such as sneaking back to camp together after curfew, staging a protest march to demand more coal or refusing to work with bullying NCOs.[89] Not infrequently, such action resulted in gaining concessions or even changing regulations. This happened in the WAAC where certain modifications of the regulation uniform became so widespread among the other ranks that staff officers authorised the changes as official in order to restore discipline. Thus new rules sanctioned the wearing of the NCOs' more fashionable cream collars for all other ranks, instead of the unpopular brown ones, along with shorter skirt length on overseas service.[90] These changes reflected the collective assertion of smaller, class-based cultural identities by working- and lower-middle-class women. As one of the rebels explained, 'if enough of you do something, there is nothing that can be done about it. So it was ... esprit de corps, you see, our corps, not theirs!'[91]

Conclusion

This chapter has explored the agenda of the Women's Corps in order to determine the nature and extent of its radicalism as a political movement. The cultural analysis of the Corps' wartime programme demonstrates that both its objectives and strategy represented a fundamental challenge to existing social structures, institutions and relations. By striving to establish women's military services and organise their work with the armed forces, the Corps sought to shift the gendered division of military labour and claim martial and potentially even electoral citizenship for its members. The radicalism of these gendered objectives was further increased by the egalitarian recruiting policies of the Corps. An integral part of the project, without which raising 'the Women's Armies' would have been impossible, they extended the gendered and political benefits of membership in the Corps to women of all classes. Thus, what made the movement truly radical was these closely intertwined gender and class-specific policies at the heart of its project. The radicalism of the Corps' agenda is indicated by its relative distinctiveness regarding the opportunities it provided to its lowest ranks and the strength of public opposition it provoked. Working-class auxiliaries benefited from their war work through prestigious gendered work roles and martial identities, which not only elevated their wartime status, but increased their class-based agency. This enabled them to improve and shape their conditions by taking independent collective action. The malicious rumours that their new status generated illuminate public perceptions of the radicalism of their wartime work. In comparison, as studies have shown, Voluntary Aid Detachment nurses, hospital and munitions workers enjoyed less radical agency or political power at their wartime workplaces, though also facing much less public criticism than the auxiliaries.

The analysis of the Corps' activities also reveals that it was the strategy of adopting military organisation that enabled the movement to achieve its goals. In addition to directly facilitating the Corps' central ambition, military organisation provided the movement with several advantages. As an organisational paradigm, it offered the Corps a variety of associational forms, including the popular volunteer model associated with home defence or the template of the army's specialised support corps supplying combat units with professional services. This variety enabled Corps leaders to adapt their organisation to the changing demands of the military job market. It also allowed them to combine the functions of a political organisation, employment agency and labour union within one movement. Furthermore, martial organisation was less class-specific than either unions or suffrage societies. Therefore, it was more suitable for recruiting a cross-class membership for the movement. Likewise, uniformed parades provided the Corps with a highly versatile form of collective action and means of communication. Training for and performing parades not only developed Corps members' martial qualities, but gave them instant collective identity, mobility and agency. In addition, parades also functioned as the Corps' main channel of publicity, communicating with potential recruits, employers and the public. Similarly to martial organisation, they were easily adaptable to different occasions and messages, and could generate popular support by providing public spectacle and entertainment. Finally, martial organisation facilitated the Corps' agenda because it fitted in with the patriotic and militarised political and institutional culture of wartime Britain. Thus, when exploring wartime collective action, historians should also consider the activism of the Women's Corps which secured both professional and political gains for its membership.

Notes

I would like to thank Lucy Bland, Kelly Boyd, Rohan McWilliam, Clare Midgley, Alison Oram, Katharina Rowold, Andy Simpson and Cornelie Usborne for their comments on this chapter.

1 Letter from W. Adair-Roberts, 29 April 1955, Imperial War Museum (IWM) Documents (Docs), 153; 'Women's Volunteer Force Marches Past Buckingham Palace', *Daily Sketch*, 8 February 1915; 'Tempora Mutantur!', *Bystander*, 17 February 1915; C. Hamilton, 'Legend and Fact', *Liverpool Daily Post*, 28 September 1915.
2 'Tempora Mutantur!', *Bystander*, 17 February 1915.
3 J. Gould, 'The Women's Corps: The Establishment of Women's Military Services in Britain', PhD thesis (London, 1988).
4 Lady F. Balfour, '"Of What Use?"', *Evening Standard*, 15 July 1915.
5 'Women Volunteers Do a Route March', *Daily Mirror*, *Daily News*, *Daily Record*, *Daily Sketch*, all 11 January 1915; K. Robert, '"All That is Best of the Modern

Woman"?: Representations of Female Military Auxiliaries in British Popular Culture, 1914–1919', in J. Meyer (ed.), *British Popular Culture and the First World War* (Leyden, 2008), pp. 97–122.

6 L. Tickner, *Spectacle of Women: Imagery of the Suffrage Campaign, 1907–14* (Chicago, IL, 1988); E. Crawford, *The Women's Suffrage Movement: a Reference Guide, 1866–1928* (London, 1999).

7 S. Grayzel, *Women's Identities at War: Gender, Motherhood, and Politics in Britain and France during the First World War* (Chapel Hill, NC, 1999), pp. 190–225; E. Crosthwait, 'The Girl Behind the Man Behind the Gun: The Position of the Women's Army Auxiliary Corps in World War I', MA thesis (Essex, 1980), pp. 10–12; 'Women's Home Service Corps', *Birkenhead News*, 21 August 1915.

8 Crosthwait, 'The Girl Behind the Man'; J. Gould, 'Women's Military Services in First World War Britain', in M. Higonnet et al. (eds), *Behind the Lines: Gender and the Two World Wars* (New Haven, CT, 1987), pp. 114–25; Grayzel, *Women's Identities*; J. Watson, *Fighting Different Wars: Experience, Memory, and the First World War in Britain* (Cambridge, 2004), pp. 17–58; L. Noakes, *Women in the British Army: War and the Gentle Sex, 1907–1948* (London, 2006), pp. 39–102.

9 Grayzel, *Women's Identities*, pp. 190–2; Noakes, *Women in the British Army*, pp. 53–4, 61–64.

10 Crosthwait, 'The Girl Behind the Man', pp. 9–25, 47–57; Noakes, *Women in the British Army*, pp. 54, 68–9, 87.

11 E. Crosthwait, '"The Girl Behind the Man Behind the Gun": The Women's Army Auxiliary Corps, 1914–18', in L. Davidoff and B. Westover (eds), *Our Work, Our Lives, Our Words* (Totowa, 1986), pp. 161–81.

12 Grayzel, *Women's Identities*; Watson, *Fighting Different Wars*; Noakes, *Women in the British Army*.

13 Grayzel, *Women and the First World War* (London, 2002), pp. 79–97; G. Braybon, *Women Workers in The First World War* (London, 1981); J. Liddington, *The Road to Greenham Common: Feminism and Anti-militarism in Britain Since 1820* (London, 1989), pp. 59–129; S. Ouditt, *Fighting Forces, Writing Women: Identity and Ideology in the First World War* (London, 1994); L. Downs, *Manufacturing Inequality: Gender Division in the French and British Metalworking Industries, 1914–1939* (Ithaca, NY, 1995), pp. 119–85.

14 Braybon, *Women Workers*, p. 80; Watson, *Fighting Different Wars*, pp. 29–41, 94–104.

15 Braybon, *Women Workers*, pp. 112–53; Downs, *Manufacturing Equality*; pp. 147–85; Grayzel, *Women's Identities*, pp. 86–120.

16 K. Navickas, 'What Happened to Class? New Histories of Labour and Collective Action in Britain', *Social History* 36 (2011), 192–204, 6.

17 Navickas, 'What Happened to Class?', pp. 1–4, 6–7.

18 Navickas, 'What Happened to Class?', pp. 3–9, 12–15.

19 K. Hunt, 'Gender and Labour History in the 1990s', *Mitteilungsblatt des Instituts für Soziale Bewegungen*, xxvii (2002), 185–200; K. Cowman and L. Jackson (eds), *Women and Work Culture, Britain c. 1850–1950* (Aldershot: 2005); M. Davis (ed.), *Class and Gender in British Labour History: Renewing the Debate (or Starting it?)* (Pontypool, 2011).

20 A. Woollacott, *On Her Their Lives Depend: Munitions Workers in the Great War* (Berkeley, CA, 1994), pp. 96–112, 136–9, 192–215; D. Thom, *Nice Girls and Rude Girls: Women's Workers in World War I* (London, 1998), pp. 78–121, 144–63.
21 Regarding parades as collective action, see a similar point about the wartime processions organised by Emmeline Pankhurst in N. Gullace, *'The Blood of our Sons': Men, Women, and the Renegotiation of British Citizenship During the Great War* (Basingstoke, 2001), pp. 126–8, 132–3, 159–60.
22 Gould, 'The Women's Corps'.
23 K. Robert, 'Constructions of "Home," "Front," and Women's Military Employment in First-World-War Britain: a Spatial Interpretation', *History and Theory* 52 (2013), 319–43, 333–5.
24 C. Pennell, *A Kingdom United: Popular Responses to the Outbreak of the First World War in Britain and Ireland* (Oxford, 2012), pp. 124–31, 143–56.
25 Robert, 'Constructions of "Home"', pp. 335–42.
26 Gould, 'The Women's Corps', 55–246, 292–339.
27 *In Memoriam May Margaret Stevenson, O.B.E.* (London, 1922), pp. 20–5.
28 'The Women's Volunteer Reserve', *Women's Volunteer Reserve Magazine* 1 (1916), 5; *In Memoriam*, pp. 20–1.
29 J. Solano, *Drill and Field Training* (London, 1915), pp. 1–9.
30 'Women's Volunteer Reserve. Anniversary Meeting', *Tunbridge Wells Advertiser*, May 1915, IWM, SUPP. 38/172; H. Gwynne-Vaughan, *Service with the Army* (London, 1942), pp. 28–30, 44–8.
31 'Women's Volunteer Reserve', Ts. leaflet, n.d. (early April 1915), IWM, Vol. 2/25; H. Cunningham, *The Volunteer Force: a Social and Political History, 1859–1908* (London, 1975), pp. 52–102.
32 J. Cowper, *A Short History of the Queen Mary's Army Auxiliary Corps* (London: 1967), pp. 10–13.
33 E. Spiers, *The Late-Victorian Army, 1868–1902* (Manchester, 1992), pp. 75–84; Gould, 'The Women's Corps', pp. 170–246.
34 'Women's Volunteer Reserve', *The Times*, 20 November 1914.
35 'Women's Help', *Star*, 2 September 1914; Report of the Women's Volunteer Reserve, IWM, Vol. 2/44.
36 'Women in Khaki', *Birmingham Daily Mail*, 17 December 1914; 'Lady Volunteers!', *Hampstead Chronicle*, 21 December 1914.
37 'Women in War', *Evening Standard*, 29 January 1915; 'The Call to Arms', *Morning Post*, 13 February 1915; 'Amazons to the Fore', *Ladies' Pictorial*, 20 February 1915.
38 'Volunteer Notes' *Daily Graphic*, 3 June 1915.
39 Gould, 'The Women's Corps', pp. 45–8.
40 M. Mullins, NAM, 1998–01–83; Gould, 'The Women's Corps', pp. 195–7; A. Bartlett, '"The Day I Remember Best"', *QMAAC Old Comrades Association Gazette*, December (1929), 5–6; L. Parfitt, 'I Was a WAAC', p. 1, NAM, 1998–01–87; K. Bottomley, IWM, Sound, 172.
41 M. Mullins, NAM, 1998–01–83; D. Lamm, 'Emily Goes to War: Explaining the Recruitment to the Women's Army Auxiliary Corps in World War I', in B. Melman (ed.), *Borderlines: Genders and Identities in War and Peace, 1870–1930* (New York, 1998), pp. 376–95; E. Airey, IWM, Docs, 4538.

42 Gould, 'The Women's Corps', pp. 301, 451, 420.
43 Gwynne-Vaughan, *Service with the Army*, pp. 44–8.
44 Gould, 'The Women's Corps', pp. 187–97; V. Laughton Mathews, *Blue Tapestry* (London, 1948), p. 15.
45 E. Barton and M. Cody, *Eve in Khaki: The Story of the Women's Army at Home and Abroad* (London, 1918), pp. 34–41, 164–97; 'The Wrens: Being the Story of their Beginnings & Doings in Various Parts' (London, 1919).
46 Gwynne-Vaughan, *Service with the Army*, pp. 28–30, 46–8; K. Furse, *Hearts and Pomegranates: The Story of Forty-five Years, 1875–1920* (London, 1940), pp. 363–70; Barton and Cody, *Eve in Khaki*, pp. 143–52; *Handbook for the WRAF* (London, 1919), pp. 19–23.
47 Former militant suffragettes included Evelina Haverfield, the founder of the WVR, Vera Laughton Mathews, Principal, WRNS and Margaret Kilroy Kenyon, Area Controller, WAAC. Constitutional suffragists included Mary Chalmers Watson, Helen Gwynne-Vaughan and Alice Low, Chief and Area Controllers of the WAAC.
48 'Members of the Women's Volunteer Reserve on Their Fortnightly Route March', *Daily Graphic*, 12 April 1915; Colonel Reviews the Girls in Khaki', *Sunday Herald*, 16 May 1915; L. Parfitt, 'I Was a WAAC', pp. 16–17, NAM, 1998–01–87; A. Coster, 'Workers on Parade', Getty Images, 3139963.
49 Women Signallers Territorial Corps, Leaflet, IWM, Vol. 7/58; 'Be Prepared!', *Home Service Corps Review*, 10 September 1915, p. 2, IWM, Vol. 6/7; 'The British School of Motoring', *Sporting Times*, 1 April 1916; Cowper, *A Short History*, p. 55; IWM, Photographs, Q 54596; Laughton Mathews, *Blue Tapestry*, p. 17; A. Chauncey, *Women of the Royal Air Force* (London, 1922), pp. 3–19, 27–33; Robert, 'All that is Best of the Modern Woman'.
50 W. Mulligan, 'The Army', in M. Jeffries (ed.), *The Ashgate Research Companion to Imperial Germany*, pp. 383–98, 392; Spiers, *The Late-Victorian Army*, pp. 1–28, 32, 63, 89–151; N. Mansfield, *Soldiers as Workers: Class, Employment, Conflict and the Nineteenth Century Military* (Liverpool, 2016).
51 M. Trustram, *Women of the Regiment: Marriage and the Victorian Army* (Cambridge, 1984), pp. 10–28.
52 Robert, 'Constructions of "Home"', pp. 323–5.
53 A. Summers, *Angels and Citizens: British Women as Military Nurses, 1854–1914* (London, 1988).
54 'Women's Help', *Star*, 2 September 1914; 'Women Volunteer for Trench Digging', *Echo and Evening Chronicle*, 12 April 1915.
55 Robert, 'Constructions of "Home"', pp. 335–41; Cowper, *A Short History*, pp. 11, 23, 27–36; 'The Wrens', pp. 21–42; Chauncey, *Women of the Royal Air Force*, pp. 20–6.
56 J. Childs, 'The Restoration Army, 1660–1702', in D. Chandler and I. Beckett (eds), *The Oxford Illustrated History of the British Army* (Oxford, 1994), pp. 53–4.
57 Summers, *Angels and Citizens*, pp. 101–11; I. Beckett, *Citizen Soldiers and the British Empire, 1837–1902* (Abingdon, 2015).
58 L. Mayhall, *The Militant Suffrage Movement: Citizenship and Resistance in Britain, 1860–1930* (Oxford: 2003), pp. 83–116.
59 Gullace, 'The Blood of our Sons', pp. 169–78.

60 Cover image, *Home Service Corps Review*, 9 January 1917–11 December, 1917, IWM, Vol. 6/29–36; WAAC and WRNS recruiting posters, IWM, Art, PST 4881, 13195; Last two images in recruiting film, 'The Life of a WAAC', IWM, Film, 412; 'The Wrens', p. 5.
61 K. Furse, *Hearts and Pomegranates: The Story of Forty-five Years, 1875–1920* (London, 1940), p. 364; Cowper, *A Short History*, pp. 45, 48–50.
62 C. Wagstaff, IWM, Docs, 4273-P434(R); E. Cooper, IWM, Sound, 3137; 'The Officers' Mess', in G. George, *Eight Months with the Women's Royal Air Force* (London, 1920).
63 Woollacott, *On Her their Lives Depend*, pp. 50–4; Braybon, *Out of the Cage*, pp. 75–77; M. Ingham, *Tracing Your Servicewomen Ancestors* (Barnsley, 2012), pp. 48–58; Watson, *Fighting Different Wars*, p. 275.
64 Gould, 'The Women's Corps', 113–15; 190–203; 206; *In Memoriam*, pp. 21–5; *The Letters of Thomasina Atkins: Private (W.A.A.C.) – On Active Service* (London, 1918), pp. 17–50.
65 R. Leared, IWM, Docs, 13794; A. Gummersall, NAM, 1998-01-64.
66 G. Ottaway, IWM, Sound, 7486.
67 Crosthwait, 'The Girl Behind the Man Behind the Gun', pp. 176–7.
68 L. Ugolini, *Civvies: Middle-Class Men on the English Home Front, 1914–18* (Manchester, 2013), pp. 103–10; Furse, *Hearts and Pomegranates*, pp. 298–301; Bartlett, 'The Day I Remember Best', p. 5.
69 'The King's Uniform', Letters from 'A Woman', 'Another Woman', 'Matron' and M. Rickett, *Morning Post*, 16 July, 19 July, 20 July 1915; 'Women and the War', Letter from V. Markham, *Sheffield Independent*, 30 June 1915.
70 Gwynne-Vaughan, *Service with the Army*, pp. 26, 50–51; Laughton Mathews, *Blue Tapestry*, pp. 14–15; Gould, 'The Women's Corps', pp. 247–91; Watson, *Fighting Different Wars*, p. 168.
71 Letter from W.G.C.L., *Newcastle Chronicle*, 13 April 1915; 'Women and the War', Letter from V. Markham, *Sheffield Independent*, 30 June 1915; Letter from 'A Woman', *Morning Post*, 21 July 1915.
72 'Women in Khaki', *Ladies' Pictorial*, 21 August 1915; 'The King's Uniform', Letter from 'Civilian', *Morning Post*, 26 July 1915, original emphasis.
73 'The King's Uniform', Letter from 'A Woman', 'Another Woman', 'A Man' and 'Civilian', *Morning Post*, 16 July, 19 July, 22 July, 26 July 1915; 'Women in Khaki', *Ladies' Pictorial*, 21 August, 1915.
74 Report by Haig re-alternative suggestions to Lawson's report, 11 March 1917, IWM, Army, 3.4/7.
75 War Office memos on WAAC officers' uniforms, 19 April 1917, TNA, WO32/5252; Gwynne-Vaughan, *Service with the Army*, pp. 16–17.
76 Report by Haig re-alternative suggestions to Lawson's report, 11 March 1917, IWM, Army, 3.4/7; Gwynne-Vaughan, *Service with the Army*, p. 26; A. Woollacott, '"Khaki Fever" and Its Control: Gender, Class, Age and Sexual Morality on the British Homefront in the First World War', *Journal of Contemporary History* 29 (1994), pp. 325–47.
77 C. Masters, *The Respectability of Late Victorian Workers: A Case Study of York, 1867–1914* (Cambridge, 2010), pp. 154–7, 174–5.
78 IWM, SUPP. 32/191, 216. For the most accurate membership numbers provided by the Services' headquarters, see A. Conway, 'Women's War-Work',

Encyclopedia Britannica, 12 (1922), pp. xxxii, 1056–7. For the volunteers, see note 36 above.
79 Gwynne-Vaughan, *Service with the Army*, pp. 35–6; Furse, *Hearts and Pomegranates*, p. 368; Chauncey, *Women of the Royal Air Force*, pp. 20–6.
80 Gwynne-Vaughan, *Service with the Army*, pp. 14 ; Chauncey, *Women of the Royal Air Force*, pp. xiii, 69–94; 'The Wrens', pp. 11–12.
81 IWM, Photographs, Q 5736, Q 95931, Q 5963, Q 5743, Q 8818, Q 19757.
82 Chauncey, *Women of the Royal Air Force*, pp. xii–xiii, 57; Cowper, *A Short History*, pp. 62–8.
83 Cowper, *A Short History of the QMAAC*, p. 35; Furse, *Hearts and Pomegranates*, pp. 364–5; Chauncey, *Women of the Royal Air Force*, p. xii.
84 Chauncey, *Women of the Royal Air Force*, p. 48; Furse, *Hearts and Pomegranates*, pp. 386–90; The Marchioness of Londonderry, *Retrospect* (London, 1938), pp. 134–7; Gullace, 'The Blood of our Sons', p. 177.
85 Gwynne-Vaughan, *Service with the Army*, pp. 73–82; *QMAAC Old Comrades' Association Gazette*; *Wren: the Magazine of the Association of the Wrens*; *WRAF Old Comrades' Association*, IWM, Books, LBY E.J. 1191; LBY E. 5/377; LBY E.J. 5380.
86 O. Castle, IWM, Docs, 9190; O. Taylor, IWM, Docs, 4181; A. Gummersall, NAM, 1998–01–64; A. Kimber, NAM, 1998–01–76; M. Mullins, NAM, 1998–01–83; G. Ottaway, IWM, Sound, 7486; N. Barker, IWM, Sound, 9731; E. Airey, IWM, Docs, 4538.
87 O. Castle, IWM, Docs, 9190; M. Mullins, NAM, 1998–01–83; L. Parfitt, 1998–01–87; M. Holme, NAM, 1998–01–70; F. Parrott, IWM, Sound, 8857.
88 O. Taylor, IWM, Docs, 4181; J. Swann, IWM, Docs, 9373; A Kimber, NAM, 1998–01–76; F. Parrott, IWM, Sound, 8857; Bartlett, 'The Day I Remember Best', pp. 5–6.
89 O. Taylor, IWM, Docs, 4181; M. Hay, *On Waactive Service* (Plymouth, 1932), pp. 116–17.
90 Gwynne-Vaughan, *Service with the Army*, pp. 18–19; Cowper, *A Short History*, pp. 49, 59.
91 R. Ord, IWM, Sound, 44.

9

Charlie Chaplin's war: a British radical in tumultuous times

Richard Carr

Foreshadowing the Beatles, during the First World War the actor, director and film impresario Charlie Chaplin would have been justified to claim that he was 'bigger than Jesus'. This was demonstrably true in Chaplin's homeland of Great Britain where the wartime cinema going audience of up to 20 million people dwarfed the 2 million or so observant souls then taking Anglican Communion.[1] God may not quite have been dead, but people were certainly turning to other, more amusing forms of inspiration during this era of global conflict. As such, just as politicians were wrestling with how far the clamour for democratic reform should be accommodated, a popular class-centric filmmaker like Chaplin was a figure of much discussion in the corridors of power – not least because, his broader implications aside, MPs were often as amused by Chaplin as their constituents. By way of example, in 1915 the Liberal MP Thomas Lough told the House of Commons of a recent trip to the cinema to watch an early comedy: 'what can be more extraordinary than the film [career] of Charlie Chaplin,' he noted presaging many such comments, 'which has turned out to be worth an empire's ransom.'[2] Other politicians, not least the Chancellor of the Exchequer Reginald McKenna, wondered what financial benefits Chaplin's regular and lucrative outputs could bring to the British Treasury.[3] During the war people may have read of the battlefields at home, but they increasingly watched Chaplin on the local cinema screen.

All this is not merely interesting trivia. Charlie Chaplin's Great War has wider significance for two reasons – set out in greater detail in a new biography by the present author, which this article both summarises and extends.[4] First, there was the contentious issue that Chaplin did not fight in a conflict in which hundreds of thousands of his countrymen died, and indeed grew staggeringly wealthy while others toiled at the front. His war therefore intersected with high profile debates about conscription, and the appropriate balance between the power of the state and the preservation of individual liberty in times of national emergency. To paraphrase Peter Mandelson in a rather different context, people were not 'intensely relaxed' about this South London lad growing 'filthy rich' as many of his generation paid the ultimate sacrifice. Chaplin's lack of uniformed service had a set of consequences this chapter will tease out, and served to cement the man as a 'political' figure: a status that would never go away. Through Chaplin we can therefore recapitulate an important set of discussions over life, liberty and the pursuit of happiness.

Second, on a related note, Chaplin's own *weltanschauung* was profoundly shaped by the conflict in ways that demand further elucidation. Chaplin was broadly a left-wing thinker sympathetic to schemes to alleviate the plight of the poor. After all, the Little Tramp was a fundamentally sympathetic character whose escapades involved numerous class based undertones – most frequently the notion that he was 'not good enough' for the women he pursued. Through Chaplin we can therefore explore cross-class dynamics during the conflict, and the evolution of attitudes towards the poor.

The important point is that this evolution was not as linear as we might think. Given his radicalism, one might expect to map Chaplin's views onto those of the Labour Party – gradually moving towards the idea of the 'big state' as the solution for the country's ills. Most famously, in Clause IV of Labour's 1918 constitution the party would commit to secure for the workers 'the common ownership of the means of production, distribution and exchange'. This was taken by some – certainly the party's opponents – to be promising the nationalisation of vast tranches of the British economy. Thus when Chaplin's friend Winston Churchill later described him as someone who would make 'a good Labour Member [of Parliament]', he had Chaplin's economics, as well as his opposition to British rule in India, in mind. The future chairman of that party Harold Laski likewise saw Chaplin as essentially a Labour man, as did many.

Certainly, the war's *general* role in shifting attitudes towards greater state intervention can scarcely be queried. The conflict formed a crucial staging post in W. H. Greenleaf's *Rise of Collectivism*; whereby the hive-mind of British bureaucracy increasingly conceived replicating itself as the decent, progressive thing to do.[5] If the state could expand into previously private spheres through the DORA, and indeed compel people to risk their lives at the front, then it could invest in public services and infrastructure to deliver the much vaunted 'homes fit for heroes to live in' when the guns stopped firing. In large part due to the presence of ex-servicemen within its parliamentary caucus, the war dragged the perennial party of interwar government, the Conservatives, into a grudging – if not uncontested – view that 'something must be done'. And whatever the effects of the 1921 Geddes Axe, it is demonstrably clear that the state *did* do more as a result of the war. From a position where public spending made up around one pound in every six of British GDP in 1914, its lowest interwar equivalent would be comfortably above one pound in four.

So if the war could produce a situation whereby even One Nation Tories could advocate for greater industrial arbitration from the state, why should we care about a radical left-wing filmmaker like Chaplin?[6] The answer, in short, is because that radical did not always conform to the general pattern one might suspect. Chaplin's views on the balance between the state and private sector, the appropriate reach of government into citizen's affairs, and what 'socialism' actually meant were no doubt somewhat idiosyncratic, but also help illuminate the differing conclusions one could reach regarding the meaning of the horror of all the war had wrought. This chapter will therefore reach beyond the years of the war itself in examining the type of questions leftists could wrestle with, and its effects in correcting various *idées fixes*.

War service

But first, the war itself – between 1914 and 1918 more than 5 million British men donned military uniform at one point or another. Against this, Charlie Chaplin was a man of fighting age – twenty-five at the start of the conflict – who did not serve but who nonetheless remained a continual reference point for the British press because of his sheer fame. Having left Britain for America in 1912, Chaplin would read of the war from the salubrious settings of the Los Angeles Athletic Club rather than experience the mud and blood of the trenches first hand. He was, in a sense, the living embodiment of the trend Adam Tooze has recently chronicled – the realignment of the global order from Europe to America.[7]

Crucially, as with America itself, Chaplin's rise to global prominence would go hand in hand with the escalation of the conflict. We can trace this through the media. With sporadic references appearing to 'Chas. Chaplin' appearing in the British local press over the fateful summer of 1914, by the end of that year he was appearing with regularity in such publications. In March 1915, a newspaper catering to the English–Scottish borders praised the local picture house for having 'again shown their ability to cater for the tastes of the Selkirk public by engaging for the Wednesday night a programme entirely of Keystone comedies, in which Charlie Chaplin figures as the chief actor.'[8] By the spring of 1915, to adopt the description of the *Aberdeen Evening Express*, this was clearly a 'well known and popular artiste' across the country.[9]

But the growing 'Chaplinitis' in Britain did not pass without protest, particularly on Fleet Street. During 1915 the Lord Northcliffe owned newspaper *The Times* ran a series of articles entitled 'Notes of a Neutral' which commented on the general atmosphere of wartime Britain. In August 1915, this anonymous columnist reflected on 'the chief popular indoor amusement in England ... the cinematograph theatre'. Out of curiosity, *The Times*' correspondent went to one cinema where they were surprised to see 'not one film shown to give any idea of the work of the British Army or the British Navy'. Instead, 'the whole audience looked forward to the antics of one Charlie Chaplin'. By then Chaplin had become 'the idol of millions of your people'.[10] As we will see, how far such anonymous (and anti-Chaplin) correspondents were the tool of Northcliffe remains an important question.

All this was symptomatic of a general debate as to how far frivolity should be tolerated in times of war. Should the cinema merely be about projecting governmental propaganda, or should the audience receive rather more entertaining fare? What was the overriding purpose of this new technology? Views on such questions could be understandably varied. In December 1915, a letter was published in *The Times* from a wounded soldier furious that no one would take 'the nation in hand'. He noted that 'sometimes a feeling of intense depression would settle on one, and of black despair of England ever facing facts or even words'. He continued, stating that the British 'were indeed depressed at the strikes, at the failure of recruiting in spite, or perhaps because of, the contemptible methods employed, at the demand for war bonuses and unprecedented waste of them ... and, at the general rottenness of taste and feeling in a country which can amuse itself with "Charlie Chaplin" in days like these'.[11] Linking the Tramp with a general feeling of national malaise was certainly not the best review Chaplin could have received, but he had his defenders in the press too. In September 1915, the author Max Pemberton posed the question, 'ought we who remain at home to enjoy ourselves while our soldiers are sacrificing their lives?' He would go on to conclude that since many soldiers and their families 'owe precious hours to Charlie Chaplin' then what was officialdom to 'rob them of his gifts?'[12]

Regardless of where one stood on that question, it was clear that early in the conflict Chaplin had become a political metaphor for the scribes and cartoonists of the press in both Britain and America. In July 1915, the Glaswegian newspaper the *Evening Times* would portray a man with a globe for a face smiling at Charlie while Kaiser Wilhelm II – portrayed with a rat like face – looked on rather upset. The caption read: 'the Crown Prince protests to the world he is being superseded by Charlie Chaplin as the universal laughter-maker'.[13] With industrial strife in the air, two months later *Punch* would run a cartoon of the British wartime Minister of Munitions (and soon to be Prime Minister) David Lloyd George in a derby hat and cane with a man labelled 'Trade Union Congress' laid out at his feet. The caption read: 'The Charlie Chaplin of Politics: The Little Champion (Lloydie George) after bringing certain people (at Bristol) down with a run and giving them a nasty jar, toddles off with a spasmodic raising of the hat to seek other adventures.'[14] Evidently the image of Chaplin could now serve as a catchall for propaganda against the enemy, or as a descriptive means to portray domestic unrest between government and trade unions. This comedian was now part of the political scene, like it or not.

To adapt Stanley Baldwin's famous comment to John Maynard Keynes, the key issue was that Chaplin remained a comedian who was being seen to do very well out of the war.[15] In this regard he was somewhat out of step with his colleagues. As Adrian Gregory has shown, the acting profession as a whole joined in with elements of pro-war jingoism.[16] By the end of 1914, 800 actors had signed up for the British army and theatres had become major recruitment centres for young men to enlist to serve for king and country. Though he later played the doddery Private Godfrey, Arnold Ridley of 1960s sitcom *Dad's Army* was certainly one such heroic example. Joining the Somerset Light Infantry during the First World War, Ridley sustained a series of injuries on the battlefields of the Somme – including taking a bayonet to the groin, shrapnel to the legs and being thumped by a German rifle-butt to the head. Not every performer had such a dramatic war, but the fact that Britain's most famous acting export was passing up the opportunity to do similar did not go unnoticed for long.

The main driver in this process was indeed the aforementioned Lord Northcliffe, owner of the *Daily Mail* and *The Times*. For Northcliffe, unless Britain showed it meant business the French or the Russians might conclude a separate peace with Germany and thus imperil national security. Northcliffe therefore harangued the government through his publications to take various measures to give effect to this. Various high profile consequences followed – the introduction of a National Register for all men aged between fifteen and sixty-five, followed by the October 1915 launch of the Derby scheme for all men of fighting age to attest to their willingness to fight. Conscription itself eventually arrived the following April. Although Northcliffe would fire his main barbs at Chaplin in 1917, it was clear that the issue of his potential service was already 'live' the previous year. Where was the Tramp when so many were joining up?

Intriguingly, *The Economist* weighed in to *support* Chaplin on the issue of conscription in April 1916. Objecting to the British 'policy of commandeering the residue of a population which has already been far more depleted of men than that of Russia', they argued that their anti-conscription position was best illustrated 'by a popular case, the case of Mr Charlie Chaplin'. According to *The Economist*, 'that gentleman is said to be earning £2,500 a week in the United States, yet some Fleet Street luminaries cry out for his recall, to be drilled'. They argued that the financial implications of putting Chaplin to the front simply did not add up: 'if Mr Chaplin, after supplying himself with the necessaries, and perhaps some of the conveniences of life, is remitting £1,000 a week home for investment in the War Loan, he is not only assisting the American exchanges, but he is also paying for some 200 new recruits.' As the *Economist* noted, 'the alternative is to force him into one soldier. [And so] we would ask every public man who has a moment of leisure to reflect upon the case of "Charlie Chaplin," and to reconsider the policy of draining our industries and commerce dry just when their activity and efficiency are most needed.'[17] Here, with some irony given later accusations, the Tramp was being used as an advert for the preservation of free market capitalism.

The facts of Chaplin's non-service are these. The 1916 agreement he signed with the Mutual Film Company explicitly specified that as a British subject 'he shall not leave the United States and run the risk of compulsion in Britain within the life of the contract without the permission of the corporation.'[18] It is difficult to ascertain who demanded this clause – the studio not wanting to lose their cash cow, or Chaplin seeking a way out of the conflict. Certainly from the moment the ink was dry on this contract Chaplin was using it as his formal 'line' to explain why he was not in a uniform. Denying in March 1916 that he was 'hiding behind my player's coat', Chaplin did however note that 'my professional demands do not permit my presence in the Mother Country.'[19] This was a questionable defence – if actors such as Buster Keaton and Adolphe Menjou could join the American Army during the war then it was not beyond the realm of possibility for Chaplin to seek similar service, whatever his global fame.

Indeed, on 5 June 1917 Charlie Chaplin finally appeared to bow to pressure and formally registered for the American military draft in Los Angeles. On 22 June, Northcliffe's *Weekly Dispatch* haughtily claimed that 'nobody would want [Chaplin] to join up if the army doctors pronounced him unfit, but until he has undergone medical examination he is under the suspicion of regarding himself as specially privileged to escape the common responsibilities of human citizenship.'[20] Here we encounter something of a grey area. In short, Chaplin very possibly was unfit to fight. A history of asthma, chronic nervousness and a malnourished childhood may well have stood him in poor stead to serve the allied effort in the trenches. He also would probably not have made a great soldier. As his studio aide Harry Crocker later stated, 'Charlie was a pacifist. He not only realised the fatality of war, but the futility of his attempting anything which smacked of action.'[21] At the same time, many of those who *did* fight would no doubt have claimed similar.

In any event, Chaplin does seem to have evaded serving in the American army through underhand means. Assumed to be at least 5 feet 5 inches tall, he had somehow dropped an inch by the time of his army physical. At an alleged 5 feet 4 and 129 pounds, Chaplin was deemed to be too small to don an American military uniform – a stance accepted by the

British. Alf Reeves, Chaplin's manager, later further exaggerated when claiming that 'No one could expect Charlie to join up as he only weighs 8st, and no army doctor would accept him.'[22] With the British minimum height requirements at 5'4' from October 1914 (lowered to 5'2' from July 1915) even the fiction surrounding his height did not actually preclude his service in the British Army, but London did not pursue the matter. In December 1917, Chaplin claimed he was 'ready and willing to answer my country's call to serve in any branch of military service', but the call never came, and he was not about to force proceedings.[23]

Charlie's defence at not serving was twofold – he was entertaining the troops (and their loved ones) through his on-screen performances, and these performances were generating a revenue stream that greatly aided the Allied war effort. In March 1916, he remarked in an open-letter to the British people that 'If, in my modest sort of way, in occasional bits of cheery nonsense as "Charlie Chaplin" of the films, I can instil a moment of brief relief from the brunt of the fray, this is my contribution to the men at the front'. Although Chaplin was no jingoist, in an age of global conflict he was careful to add the flowery proclamation that the war had demonstrated that 'the days of Wellington and Nelson were not lived in vain, for the spirit that underlies present England is no less strong in courage and in absolute fearlessness'.[24] Entertaining these warriors was thus his input to defeating the Kaiser.

Contrary to Edmund Blackadder's cynicism in *Blackadder Goes Forth*, the troops do seem to have enjoyed Charlie's work.[25] In November 1916, a gathering of 400 hundred wounded soldiers from across the Allied nations was held in the ballroom of the Savoy Hotel, London. Before an afternoon of tea, food and smoking, there was held 'an exhibition of cinematograph films, with Charlie Chaplin as the *pièce de resistance*'.[26] Moreover, the Imperial War Museum in London retains images of a tank named 'Charlie Chaplin' (lost on 9 April 1917 during the First Battle of the Scarpe), of several soldiers dressed in Little Tramp costumes when off duty, and of a Charlie Chaplin scarecrow built in tribute by Tommies to guard a road.[27] American sources also defended Chaplin's comedic value for the frontline too. In August 1917 the *Portland Oak Journal* noted that:

> there is one argument ... which will strike one as absurdly illogical. It suggests that Charlie might amuse the troops in billets if his condition did not warrant him going into the trenches, [but] in billets Charlie would be able to amuse a select few of his comrades at any one time. At the present time he is, on the film, affording entertainment to millions, not least among them being the boys in khaki and blue.[28]

Through his comedies Chaplin could claim to 'be' at the front, even if this was only through the cinema reel.

In any case, alongside his entertainment value (a question of individual taste) there was secondly the more concrete issue of money. Mirroring *The Economist*'s defence of his actions in 1916, Chaplin noted a year later that 'I have invested a quarter of a million dollars (£50,000) in the war activities of America and England, contributing to both loans. I registered for the draft [in America], and have not asked for exemption. Had I been drawn I would have gone to the front like any patriotic citizen.'[29] It is impossible to disprove this theory but, for many, the implication was clear: Chaplin was buying his way out of service.

To sugar this pill he began to work the conflict into his films. The September 1918 release of *The Bond* – a naked piece of propaganda for the American Government's Liberty Loan drive – was his first effort in this regard. This essentially plot-less short walked viewers through the three successive 'bonds' of friendship, love and marriage, before turning to 'the most important: THE LIBERTY BOND'. The film was not much to speak of, but the fact that Chaplin had produced it for free and donated proceeds to the war effort again bought him some space with officialdom. It also coincided with the bond drive of which he was a significant part. Touring America with Douglas Fairbanks, Mary Pickford and other stars, Chaplin spoke to crowds reaching 100,000 people – persuading them to lend up to US$17 million a time (over US$300 million in 2017 dollars) to the US government. It also had significance in his own political development. As film scholar Steven J. Ross notes, 'the war bond tour gave Chaplin his first insight into the political uses of stardom. He discovered that people were more interested in hearing what he … had to say than any congressmen, senator or even President.'[30]

In October 1918, Chaplin released the more famous comedy *Shoulder Arms* – predominantly set in the trenches of France. After the successful release of his film *A Dog's Life*, Chaplin was 'worried about getting an idea for my second picture [for his new employers First National]. Then the thought came to me: why not a comedy about the war?' Friends warned Chaplin off the project, with Cecil B. De Mille telling him that 'it's dangerous at this time to make fun of the war'. Still, 'dangerous or not, the idea excited' Chaplin. Planned as a five-reeler taking in the Tramp's home life before the war, his service during it, and a celebratory banquet at the end, Charlie eventually 'thought it better to keep Charlot a nondescript with no background and to discover him already in the army'. Initially dissatisfied with the film, it was only when Douglas Fairbanks saw the film and laughed hysterically that Charlie was persuaded to go ahead with its release. 'Sweet Douglas,' recalled Charlie in the 1960s, 'he was my greatest audience.'[31]

For all its clowning, *Shoulder Arms* was clearly a pro-war film. It included some nice slapstick gags: Charlie applying a gasmask to mask the smell emanating from some Limburger cheese, the Tramp finding it difficult to learn the straight legged march of the American army with his natural inclination to bow his feet, and the remark, when asked how he singlehandedly captured thirteen German shoulders, that he 'surrounded them'. But beneath the comedy, the Tramp is essentially a patriotic soldier who serves bravely for a noble cause. Trench life was not idealised – the Tramp is shown sleeping in a trench full of water and as scared to go over the top – but the overall effect is of a decent man doing his bit. Even the end, when Charlie captures the Kaiser only for it to be revealed that the film has been a dream all along, reinforces the righteousness of allied participation in the conflict. *Shoulder Arms* suggests that it *should* be the dream of all Americans to do this (and by extension, all citizens of the Entente), and that getting the pretty girl and the acclaim from previously sceptical soldiers as a result of serving in the war was a potential reward. Perhaps because Chaplin towed this line the *Coventry Evening Telegraph* saw it as his 'cleverest and funniest film', while the *Burnley News* found Chaplin as 'frolicsome as ever'.[32]

By continuing to produce his comedic films Chaplin ensured he would survive the war – no small concern in a conflict that saw one in eight British soldiers killed. But his lack of service was not an issue that went away anytime soon. During Chaplin's 1921 visit to London to promote his film *The Kid* he received letters containing a white feather – the symbol of wartime cowardice. Other correspondents went further and affixed 'an ironic German cross for his war effort'. Even if one British soldier would send Chaplin four of the medals he had won on the battlefield because 'you have never been properly recognised', the recipient of this generosity would now be a worried man.[33] When the young journalist Alistair Cooke mentioned the song 'Oh, the Moon Shines Bright on Charlie Chaplin' to the actor in the early 1930s, Chaplin noted that its lyrics 'scared the hell out of me'. Given the song referenced Chaplin's desire to go to any lengths to get out of serving – '[Charlie]'s going barmy to join the army, but his old baggy trousers they'll need mending before they send him to the Dardanelles' – this was scarcely surprising. The song was symptomatic, Cooke believed, of 'the insensate jingoism of wartime Britain', which had been stoked by 'the holy indignation of comfortable editorial writers against any famous Englishman abroad who had not dashed home to join Our Boys Out There in Flanders Field'.[34] Maybe so, but Chaplin had taken a decision, and that decision had consequences. As Chaplin's politics drifted to the left the consequences became more apparent. Indeed, as the American right and the House Un-American Activities Committee attempted to label Chaplin a Communist in the 1940s and 1950s his perceived lack of patriotism during the First World War served to support that theory. As the Republican Senator Harry Cain would put it in 1949, 'Chaplin has sat out in luxurious comfort in two wars in which his native Britain and his hospitable United States were involved, in the defense of those freedoms which he perverts so glibly.'[35] He had failed the ultimate test of manhood.

Chaplin's political views

The war had other, less direct but nonetheless crucial political developments for him. Aside from his global fame Chaplin remains an interesting source for analysis because he combined generally being regarded as 'left-wing' with a concurrent mistrust of the concept increasingly associated with it: big government. In a sense, this was perfectly understandable. But to interrogate this evolution we must briefly outline Chaplin's background, and the war's effect upon it.

Born in South London in April 1889 (the same week as a man he would later parody, Adolf Hitler), the alcoholism of an absentee father and the mental instability of an only sporadically present mother meant Chaplin's childhood was undeniably grim. His early encounters with 'the state' as a concrete entity were therefore uniformly negative even before the war lent them a new emphasis. Chaplin did not enjoy the little schooling he received and was beaten by one teacher to the point of almost passing out for supposedly starting a fire in the toilets at the Hanwell School for Orphans and Destitute Children. He saw the workhouse somewhat briefly (thirty-two days) as an inmate, but had a more sustained experience of its horrors through the plight of a mother who was also committed to various South London Asylums whose conditions varied until Chaplin gained the wealth to pay for more comfortable arrangements. Notions of late Victorian reform, even the much trumpeted work of the London County Council, were always rather abstract to the young Charlie. Theories of socialism and communism meant little next to the realities of subjugation and the cane.

In a less direct but still formative experience, Chaplin did not buy into the state sponsored jingoism of his youth either. When the Salisbury government tried to sell the British public on the virtues of the conflict it was conducting against the Boers, the young Chaplin despised this 'Epoch of whiskers: bewhiskered kings, statesmen, soldiers and sailors, Krugers, Salisburys, Kitcheners, Kaisers and cricketers – incredible years of pomp and absurdity, of extreme wealth and poverty, of inane political bigotry of both cartoon and press.'[36] Playing at war with his friends, he later recalled that 'I never wanted to play the part of a British general, upright and stiffly military, who received the surrender: I asked for the role of ... the defeated Boer leader, because his harrowed face and bent figure gave more ample scope for characterisation.'[37] Whether in terms of education, public health or defence policy, Chaplin had little faith in the power of political elites. His ambivalence towards the concept of war, and his unwillingness to actually fight in one, could be traced from an early age.

Chaplin's pre-war years were not just about what he did experience, however, but what he missed out on. Out of school before his teenage years and employed thereafter in theatres and music halls, the famous reforms of the 1906 Liberal government held little benefit for Chaplin. He was too old for free-school meals (or the earlier provisions of the Conservative enacted Education Act 1902) to have any effect, and was likewise too young (as was his mother) to receive an old age pension. Even National Insurance was of no use to someone who's career saw him gain regular bookings by the 1910s. He did not vote in either of the 1910 general elections and thus, as a result of relocating to America from 1912, would never vote in any such national contest on either side of the Atlantic. This was a world famous figure, undoubtedly sympathetic to the plight of the poor he would depict in his films, who had not been imbued with the usual social-democratic sympathies of many of his contemporaries. When George Lansbury later described him as a 'socialist' this was always only half-true at best. Socialists believe in the power of the collective to change the world for the better: Chaplin certainly vacillated on this point, perhaps because he had not directly 'felt' it.

To risk his life for such a state, as we have seen, was beyond the pale. Instead Chaplin used the First World War for something rather different: to make staggering amounts of money. Having previously earned £10 (~US$50) a week working in the theatres for Fred Karno, Chaplin's film contracts successively brought him US$150 each week from December 1913 at Keystone, US$1,250 from November 1914 at Essanay, US$10,000 from February 1916 at Mutual, and over US$20,000 in his June 1917 'million dollar a year' contract at First National. Just counting the returns from his movie studio contracts, his wage had increased 137-fold in under four years in the USA. During the war Chaplin therefore acted like the consummate capitalist and intelligent market actor, selling his wares to the highest bidder. As His Majesty's Treasury cottoned on to the explosion in Chaplin's (and other film stars') popularity, they imposed 1d/8d per foot levies on the positives/negatives of all films imported into Britain. A two thousand feet film such as Chaplin's *The Immigrant* would therefore generate around £66 of ad valorem tax for each negative bought into Britain. Given there were five thousand British cinemas in operation and Chaplin released twenty films from the introduction of the so-called McKenna Duties on imported luxuries in September 1915 to the end of the war, the economics of keeping Chaplin out of uniform and in the studio were again obvious.

Both Chaplin's capitalism and his early political thoughts are worth teasing out partly because of the consistently pro-Communist views opponents in America would later attempt to pin on him. Despite his wealth by the early 1920s Chaplin was being watched by the FBI as a person of suspiciously pro-Soviet sympathies, and in later years the House Un-American Activities chaired by Congressmen Martin Dies and then J. Parnell Thomas would publicly query the motives behind his lack of American citizenship. Some of this was indeed overdone, and much can indirectly be laid at the door of Communist newspaper the *Daily Worker*. In 1944 that publication described Chaplin as 'a long friend of the Soviet Union since 1917'. During the visa problems that would eventually lead to Chaplin's exile from America for allegedly violating the terms of the McCarran Act in 1952, it noted that 'a year or so after 1917 Chaplin joined the ranks of artists and professionals who upheld the world-shaking Russian revolution'.[38] Later right-wing opponents leapt onto these idle boasts, noting that 'the *Daily Worker*, official organ of the Communist Party, has reviewed the life and activities of Chaplin in the most glowing terms'.[39] There was smoke but not always fire here. Some loose lips would go on to sink the ship of Chaplin's American career.

Yet such accusations were not total hokum. During the First World War and its immediate aftermath Chaplin undoubtedly surrounded himself with left wing thinkers such as the American pamphleteer Max Eastman (of the revolutionary publication *The Masses*) – who called himself the 'only Socialist agitator who opposed the world war and supported the Russian revolution and yet managed to stay out of jail'.[40] The film icon pointedly admired Eastman's 'restraint' and after Chaplin had seen Eastman deliver a lecture entitled 'Hands Off Russia' in March 1919 he invited him to his film studios to discuss life and politics. Indeed, soon after the war was over studio hand Jim Tully recalled that 'the radicals came for [Chaplin's] attention and pity. He was worried constantly for the poor in Russia, when that unhappy country was mentioned. [*Ten Days That Shook the World* author] John Reed's name came in the conversation, and then Max Eastman's.'[41] Chaplin later described himself as 'intellectually a fellow-traveller' of such types. Chaplin was also in touch with the author Upton Sinclair – later to run for the Governorship of California in 1934 on a programme to create 'a new state income tax, increased inheritance levies, and other taxes on wealth' – during this period. In August 1918, Sinclair wrote to Chaplin to thank him for their first meeting: 'when I came to meet you, it was with no intention of butting in on your affairs, except as a Socialist always butts in everywhere – to make the other fellow into a Socialist!'[42] The war had cemented Chaplin as someone with left-wing sympathies.

Indeed, the polymath Rob Wagner (alternatively a script writer, Socialist Party organiser, and high school wrestling coach) would be employed by Chaplin not only for the official task of answering fan mail from 1915, but to informally help shape the actor's political views. Recalling their early days, Chaplin wrote that 'I bought books on sociology and I began to realise that there were many unseen forces at work in our social system. It was not that I was for socialism. What I was against, as Rob Wagner pointed out, was the abuses of capitalism.' Chaplin continued: 'Socialism casts grey aura over everything, I would argue, and that if we did not work for profit there would be no incentive. Rob would counter my ignorance with the fact that 'the Post Offices system throughout the world was not run for profit but for service'.[43] Some of this obviously hit home. In 1921 Chaplin himself commented on recent British policy in this regard: 'it was one of the greatest mistakes the Government could make to restore the railroads to private ownership. The postal department is run by the government and I see no reason why the railroads should not be [too].'[44]

In the Chaplinesque view of the world, the war had shown that certain industries should remain the preserve of the collective and not private industry. Yet, perhaps paradoxically, Chaplin feared public sector encroachment on individual liberty as much as the vicissitudes of the free market. In 1921, Chaplin told Thomas Burke that while 'many people have called me a socialist my radical views have been much misunderstood. I am not a Socialist, nor am I looking for a new order of things'. Distancing himself from socialism in practice was arguably utterly self-serving – Chaplin was an inveterate tax avoider and thus did not want 'Uncle Sam' to get its hands on his money. But it also reflected both his youth and the strong aversion he had towards conscription during the First World War. There was an element of hypocrisy to his world view, but it was not just that. Chaplin respected the achievements of business, believed in making money and thought that government could not do the heavy lifting of improving the conditions of the workers on its own. Where capitalism could prove productive and not predatory then he was quite prepared to back it.

The hero in this vision was a man he would later mock mercilessly in his 1936 film *Modern Times*: Henry Ford. In 1914, Ford had made the announcement that he would voluntarily shorten the working day for those in his automobile factories from nine to eight hours, and, even more dramatically, introduce a new wage scale that doubled the minimum daily wage for his workers from US$2.34 to US$5. In 1919, this became US$6 and then by 1929 US$7. This move was precisely the type of capitalism the early Chaplin so admired. 'For a long time,' Chaplin pronounced, 'capital has held sway and declared that the present order is the only one. But Henry Ford's methods rather disprove that, don't they?' Ford's new wage scale had 'made profitable sharing absolutely practicable' and he was justly 'getting all the business of the country because he is fair'. The only question was how to increase minimum wages across the board: 'Henry Ford has proved the practical result of paying the workers well and keeping them happy.'[45] When Chaplin toured Ford's Detroit factory in 1923 he did so as a starry-eyed admirer, with Ford's mixture of opposition to warfare and pioneering leadership of his particular industry mirroring

Chaplin's own experience. Both had successfully managed to walk the line between personal antipathy to the conflict and the practical realities of not being seen as overtly against it, too.

Ford was the exemplar of a supposedly new capitalism, but clearly not all capitalists could or would convert to the idea of paying higher wages overnight. So what to do in the interim? Here Charlie Chaplin was an enthusiastic convert to the movement known as Social Credit – propagated by the English engineer Major Clifford Hugh (C. H.) Douglas, formerly of the Royal Aircraft Establishment (RAE). The origins of this philosophy were also primarily located in the First World War, although Douglas acknowledged his own debt to previous theories of under consumption propagated by thinkers such as J. A. Hobson. Working at the RAE, Douglas observed that the cost of producing most goods was greater than the various salaries, wages and dividends paid out to the workers and management who made them and this, he argued, would produce periodic moments of economic destabilisation as demand collapsed. For his part, Chaplin was certainly reading Douglas as early as his European tour of 1921, and would eventually back his schemes for the government to print money to be given as a direct transfer payment to low-paid workers: the so-called 'National Dividend.'[46] By 1931, in the wake of the Wall Street Crash, Chaplin would begin to demand that governments 'reduce the hours of labor, print more money, and control prices.'[47] As the world became more radical, so did he.

Conclusion

The war then imbued within Chaplin something of a contradictory *weltanschauung*. On the one hand, the first thirty years of his life provided much practical evidence that 'the state' was a bad thing. The workhouse for him and the battlefield for others both illustrated the dangers of government. Donning a military uniform, holding a passport or paying taxes were three aspects of the modern state Chaplin found to varying degree odious. Equally, as someone who had pulled himself up by the force of his own abilities through the private sector, he always retained a belief in the power of capitalism. The market had its flaws, but if it had allowed *him* to rise to the top it could not be all bad.

Yet Chaplin was also someone who, at least in the abstract, thought the Russian Revolution was a positive development for humanity. As his biographer Theodore Huff later noted, 'having seen poverty in his own childhood, Chaplin was naturally interested in any plans for social betterment ... he was drawn to any doctrine which seemed to promise or vaguely connote freedom.'[48] In 1917, it was not so clear that this was Russian Communism, but as Jonathan Davis points out in Chapter 11, it was not so clear that it was not, either. In the late 1920s and early 1930s the search for a 'solution' to the problems the First World War even led Chaplin to brief flirtations with pro-Fascist sympathy – something unexpected for a man who would go on to make the Hitler baiting film *The Great Dictator*. The unconventional and loose monetary policy expressed by Social Credit was perhaps something of an interventionist half way house. The war had suggested good men could do positive things with the state. The trick, as ever, was working out who to empower. If interwar political elites could barely figure such issues out, maybe we should not judge Chaplin too harshly.

Notes

1 A. H. Halsey, *Trends in British Society Since 1900: A Guide to the Changing Social Structure of Britain* (London, 1972), p. 30.
2 House of Commons Parliamentary Debates [thereafter HC Deb], 13 October 1915, vol 74, c. 1306.
3 HC Deb, 21 September 1915, vol 74, c. 361.
4 Richard Carr, *Charlie Chaplin: A Political Biography from Victorian Britain to Modern America* (Basingstoke, 2017), elements of pp. 55–83. With permission from Taylor & Francis.
5 W. H. Greenleaf, *The British Political Tradition, Vol 1: The Rise of Collectivism* (London, 1983).
6 On the minimum wage question, Harold Macmillan, *The Middle Way* (Basingstoke, 1938).
7 Adam Tooze, *The Deluge: The Great War and the Remaking of Global Order, 1916–1931* (London, 2015).
8 *Southern Reporter*, 18 March 1915.
9 *Aberdeen Evening Express*, 30 March 1915.
10 *The Times*, 28 August 1915.
11 *The Times*, 6 December 1915.
12 Via Carr, *Charlie Chaplin*, p. 77.
13 *Evening Times*, 8 July 1915.
14 *Punch*, 25 September 1915.
15 Cited in varying ways, including as 'a lot of hard-faced men who look as if they have done very well out of the war'.
16 Adrian Gregory, *The Last Great War* (Cambridge, 2008), pp. 72–3.
17 *The Economist*, 29 April 1916.
18 As per the *Cornishman*, 30 March 1916.
19 *Liverpool Echo*, 29 March 1916.
20 Suzanne W. Collins, *Calling All Stars Emerging Political Authority and Cultural Policy in the Propaganda Campaign of World War 1*, PhD thesis (New York University, 2008), pp. 303–4.
21 Harry Crocker, 'Charlie Chaplin: Man and Mime', Margaret Herrick Library, Los Angeles, California, Harry Crocker Papers, VII-11
22 Reported in *Aberdeen Evening Express*, 17 April 1918.

23 *New York Sun*, 7 December 1917.
24 Printed (amongst others) in *Liverpool Echo*, 29 March 1916.
25 In the BBC sitcom the eponymous Blackadder, played by Rowan Atkinson, remarks that 'I find [Chaplin's] films about as funny as getting an arrow through the neck, and then finding there's a gas bill tied to it!'
26 *The Times*, 22 November 1916.
27 See e.g. Q3237, Q5524 and Q8904 within the Ministry of Information First World War Official Collection, Imperial War Museum, London.
28 *Portland Oak Journal*, 5 August 1917.
29 *New York Sun*, 7 December 1917.
30 Steven J. Ross, *Hollywood Left and Right: How the Movie Stars Shaped American Politics* (Oxford, 2011), p. 20.
31 Charlie Chaplin, *My Autobiography* (London, 1964), pp. 218–19.
32 *Coventry Evening Telegraph*, 28 December 1918; *Burnley News*, 7 December 1918.
33 Crocker, 'Man and Mime', VIII-4.
34 Crocker, 'Man and Mime', VIII-4.
35 A speech clipped by supportive voices in the press e.g. Hoover Institution, Stanford University, California, USA [HOOV], Elizabeth Churchill Brown Papers [ECB] Box 18 Folder 13.
36 Chaplin, *My Autobiography*, p. 54.
37 Crocker, 'Man and Mime', 1–23.
38 'Fact Sheet Containing Pertinent Material Pertaining to the Communist Affiliations and Activities of Charlie Chaplin,' Hoover Institution, Stanford University, California [HOOV], George Sokolsky Papers, Box 241 File 3.
39 Clipping of 1949 Senator Cain Speech, HOOV, Elizabeth Churchill Brown Papers, Box 18 Folder 13.
40 Theodore Huff, *Charlie Chaplin* (London, 1952), p. 260.
41 'The King of Laughter' manuscript, Charles E. Young Research Library, UCLA, Los Angeles, California, Jim Tully Papers, Box 82 file 250, f.1.
42 Sinclair to Chaplin, 18 August 1918, Lilly Library, Bloomington, Indiana, Upton Sinclair Papers, Box 2.
43 Scribbled note, undated 1950s, Cineteca di Bologna, Bologna, Italy, Charlie Chaplin Archive.
44 Undated newspaper clipping 'The Serious Opinions of Charlie Chaplin', 1921, Municipal Archives, Montreux, Switzerland, Charlie Chaplin Scrapbook 12.
45 Undated newspaper clipping 'The Serious Opinions of Charlie Chaplin', 1921, Chaplin Scrapbook 12.
46 Charlie Chaplin, *My Trip Abroad* (London, 1921) p. 147.
47 Carr, *Charlie Chaplin*, p. 160.
48 Huff, *Charlie Chaplin*, p. 260.

10

Irish Labour and the 'Co-operative Commonwealth' in the era of the First World War

Marc Mulholland

This chapter takes a long-run view of attitudes to socialism in Ireland before, during and immediately following the First World War. In doing so, it highlights the specificity of the Irish form of socialism in the idea of the 'Co-operative Commonwealth'. To begin with, then, we should note that from its origins in the mid-1820s until the 1870s, socialism as it developed in Europe was overwhelmingly an anti-statist ideology. It envisaged future society as based upon co-operative enterprises possessed by the workers. Among the pioneer socialists, Robert Owen, William Thompson, Charles Fourier, Étienne Cabet and Louis Blanc were all believers in autonomous co-operatives disassociated from the state, even if, as in the case of Blanc, they anticipated the state playing an initially 'tutelary' role in helping workers to establish their own producer co-operatives.[1] In fact, it is easier to count those socialists in the pioneering generation who favoured the state operating the means of production. Constantin Pecqueur, a relatively obscure theorist even in his own time, is the only one who stands out.[2]

These first-generation socialists were seeking to reverse the tendency towards proletarianisation and wage-slavery. Most workers attracted to socialism were artisans used to operating in workshops, which they could easily imagine operating without owner-appointed managers. In so far as the International Workingman Association of the 1860s and early 1870s took a position on the future of society, it inclined towards a co-operative vision. Nonetheless, from about 1870 the socialist ideal of the future moved markedly in a statist direction. 'Collectivism' became the dominant ideology, which imagined future socialist society as large-scale industry organised at state or municipal level. This was theorised both by orthodox Marxists, such as Karl Kautsky, and Fabian reformists in Britain. The domination of statist 'collectivism' was most striking in countries where large-scale industry most considerably displaced the artisan workshop.

In Ireland, however, land ownership remained the key question. Here the peasant sense of psychological possession in the land they worked was undeniable, even if they lacked legal ownership. Peasant agitation against landlordism, peaking in the Land War of 1879 to 1882, but recurrent thereafter, so suppressed rent levels that landlords accepted as a deliverance the Wyndham Land Act 1903, which encouraged them to sell their land to the tenant farmers. A peasant proprietorship came into existence. The leading Marxist theoretician of the Second International of working-class parties, the aforementioned Karl Kautsky, wondered whether the extinguishing of Irish landlordism could provide a model for the transition from capitalism to socialism. Just as Irish rents had been squeezed until Irish landlords gave up the ghost, so might the profits of the capitalists be cut back by worker militancy until they sold up their private property in the means of production to the socialist commonwealth.[3]

The establishment of peasant proprietary, however, had not solved all problems for Irish farmers. They struggled with debts owed to local merchants: the notorious 'gombeen men'. In 1889, Horace Plunkett established a co-operative creamery – the Irish term for dairy – jointly owned by farmers. This initiative spread, and in 1894 he formed the Irish Agricultural Organisation Society (IAOS) to promote co-operatives. Plunkett hoped for a moral revitalisation of Irish society, and his programme was summed up as 'better farming; better business; better living'.[4] By 1910, there were nearly 900 co-operative societies organised by the IAOS, with a membership of nearly 100,000 and an annual turnover of more than £250,000.[5] This was by no means a clearly anti-capitalist initiative, and radical co-operators, unmindful of the precarious position of small Irish farmers, were inclined to see it as 'very like the combinations made by other private traders to exact higher prices at the consumers' expense'.[6]

Irish 'syndicalism'

Nonetheless when, from about 1905, the second wave of anti-statist socialism took off internationally – a phase that was to last for about twenty years – Ireland had an established co-operative tradition. While the first wave of co-operativism had been based upon the artisan workshop ideal, the second wave was more closely connected to the de-skilling of labour and in particular the upsurge of trade union militancy. Unskilled or semi-skilled workers, moving from trade to trade, were replacing the detail worker. This meant a reduction in strategic bargaining power on the part of workers. Success in strikes required a strategy that employed both numbers and shock. There spontaneously developed the wildcat strike, sympathy strikes, local general strikes and 'blacking' of recalcitrant employers. This syndicalist tendency was particularly powerful in the Mediterranean countries, where anarchism had long retained purchase, but also in the USA and in the UK.

There was scant evidence that this relatively unskilled workforce had any more confidence in its ability to manage production than the previous generation of trade unionists. They were not analogous to the artisans, confident in their ability to run the workshop, who had characterised the labour movement of the first three-quarters or so of the nineteenth century. However, the growth of a managerial and technical component of the wage-earning class raised the prospect of co-operative production units based upon an alliance between unskilled and semi-skilled workers, on one hand, and 'experts', on the other. The theorist of syndicalism, George Sorel, imagined a future of sacralised labour uniting the manual worker and the engineer.[7]

Ireland was an early and persistent centre of syndicalist militancy. Here it was closely associated with the socialist trade union organiser James Larkin, to the extent that syndicalism in Ireland was known as 'Larkinism'. Instead of set piece battles preceded by long negotiations, Larkin would call workers out at short notice, and then escalate the dispute by encouraging sympathy strikes. To overcome the employer advantage, sabotage and intimidation were regular tactics. In the 1907 Belfast strike, Larkin, for the National Union of Dock Labourers, organised dockers and carters against the steamship companies. The business elites of the city complained to the government that:

> horses have been stopped and unyoked, bags containing grain, flour, and feeding stuffs have been cut ... Vans have been overturned, precipitated into the river, or set on fire in the streets. Drivers of bread carts have been prevented making delivery, and their vans have been looted. ... [All] authority seems to be paralysed. Bands of lawless persons assume control of the streets under the guise of strikers.[8]

The army was deployed on streets and there was even a police strike. This was the industrial dispute as social warfare.

As the sympathy strike involved the 'blacking' of employers formally outside the issue in dispute, it upset orderly industrial relations and was frowned upon by the British trade unions. Nonetheless, in 1911 syndicalism came to Britain, with epicentres in south Wales, Liverpool and Scotland. In this context, Larkin's new union, the Irish Transport and General Workers Union (ITGWU), active from early 1909, grew considerably in extent. It reached a cataclysmic culmination with the famous 1913 lockout. In this struggle over the right of workers to join the ITGWU as a syndicalist union, some 25,000 workers struck or were locked out by a combine of employers led by William Martin Murphy.

Maybe 100,000 individuals were directly involved. Again, workers attempted to strengthen their position through non-lethal violence. As a song of the period put it, to the tune of 'Memory of the Dead', a well-known nationalist ballad:

> They dared to fling a manly brick,
> They wrecked the blackleg tram.
> They dared give Harvey Duff a kick,
> They didn't give a damn.
> They lie in jail and can't get bail,
> Who fought their corner thus;
> But you men, with sticks, men,
> Must make the peelers cuss.[9]

Again, it must be stressed that workers in this phase of syndicalism were not motivated by a strong desire to manage by themselves their places of work. In so far as these workers had a sense of psychological possession, it seemed to be focused on their union and the working-class districts in which they lived rather than the means of production by which they laboured.[10]

The 'Co-operative Commonwealth'

During the lockout struggle, Larkin often promoted the idea of the 'Co-operative Commonwealth'.[11] This was a quite well-established synonym for socialism, but in syndicalist circles, and in Ireland, it was increasingly adopted as a designation differentiated from 'state socialism' (or 'collectivism'). Larkin admitted that the Co-operative Commonwealth was still 'a long way ahead in Ireland,' but it was the ultimate aim.[12] Part of the appeal of the slogan for Larkin was its filiation with versions of Catholic social teaching, particularly that of the Jesuit priest and Chair of Political Economy at the National University, Father Thomas Finlay.[13] Finlay was a long-standing supporter of the Co-operative Movement in Ireland. As the *Freeman's Journal* pointed out, however, his vision was rather different from that of Larkin:

> Father Finlay seems to contemplate the continuance of that distinction between the capitalist and the worker ... In fact, in that respect, the so-called co-operative movement in Ireland is not being a cooperative movement at all. Its purpose has been organisation of small capitalists for combined cheaper and better production ... But the original aim of cooperation was Mr Larkin's aim, to solve the Labour problem by organising industries in which the workers should be the proprietors. The old co-operators method was thrift; Mr Larkin's is the general and the sympathetic strike directed to the ultimate capture of the means of production.[14]

Plunkett, the protestant leader of the IAOS, took pains to distinguish his own ideal of the Co-operative Commonwealth from that of the socialists. In particular, he rejected any notion of class struggle.[15]

Nonetheless, the editor of the IAOS journal, George William Russell (also known as AE) in a searing letter to the press, tied the 1913 lockout struggle into the flow of Irish history since the Land War:

> The landlords of industry will have disappeared from Ireland when the battle begun this year is ended. Democratic control of industry will replace the autocracy which exists today. We are working for the cooperative commonwealth.[16]

It seems that the Co-operative Commonwealth slogan was appealing to Irish workers in a way that state socialist collectivism was not. Larkin's opponents in the lockout struggle certainly believed that the use of the Co-operative Commonwealth slogan was an inspiration to the workers.[17]

Larkin was no theorist, and in so far as the Irish socialist version of the Co-operative Commonwealth was developed analytically, this fell to James Connolly, the Irish Marxist and activist. Connolly compared contemporary wage-worker militancy to the Irish Land War of 1879 to 1881. As he observed, many of the techniques of mass mobilisation and intimidation of scabs were used in both struggles. But there was a significant difference between the old peasant-based Land League and in the new wage-earner based ITGWU. As Connolly intimated:

> The strength and power of the political agitation of the Land League lay in the fact that its representatives were the servants and mouthpieces of a class who were already organised and holding the means of production with a revolutionary intent. They were not asking government to give them possession, they were already in defiant possession and demanding that such possession be legalised.[18]

The power of the Land League had been in its members' possession of the agricultural means of production. Landlords were to be removed as unnecessary excrescences. There was no such clear correlation between the peasant family holding tight to their farm and the wage-worker employed in the capitalist enterprise. As Connolly said in 1915: 'workers [are] in control of nothing but their labour power.'[19] Nonetheless, Connolly did see a certain parallel. The Land League demonstrated, 'what could be done by the working class of any independent nation should it resolve to make its ... economic struggles in factory, workshop and mine the generating force of its political passions and programs.'[20] Connolly hoped that militant trade unionism would in effect challenge for control of the means of production, generating a revolutionary consciousness of possession, as expressed by the militant trade union, on the part of the proletariat.

As the economic control of the bourgeoisie preceded their political control, Connolly thought, so too would proletarian economic possession of the means of production precede their political power.[21] Through industrial militancy, workers would effectively take possession of their workplaces, and then move on to formally expropriate the capitalists. But Connolly admitted that workers were not likely to develop a sense of possessiveness in any particular workplace. 'A stationary engineer works today at the construction of a new building, three months from now he is in a shipyard, six months from now he is at the mouth of a coal mine.'[22] So this meant that the 'One Big Union' of industrial unionism, subsuming all craft and sectional demarcations, was the appropriate vehicle. Industrial unionism was the means by which working-class possession of their means of production would be established:

> In the light of this principle of industrial unionism every fresh shop or factory organised under its banner is a fort wrenched from the control of the capitalist class and manned with the soldiers of the revolution to be held by them for the workers.[23]

Connolly, therefore, hoped that the workers' sense of property in the means of production would develop in the course of class struggle itself.[24]

During the lockout, Larkin undertook a 'Fiery Cross' campaign across Britain campaigning for solidarity strikes. He received an enthusiastic response from mass meetings organised by the *Daily Herald* Leagues, which were keen to 'popularise militant industrial unionism as a weapon for the assertion of working class power'.[25] W. P. Ryan, the *Herald*'s Irish correspondent, looked forward to the unionisation of agricultural workers and the development of 'an aggregation of co-operative commonwealths', both rural and urban, in Ireland.[26]

Connolly and Larkin primarily blamed the British trade unions for the failure of Dublin workers to win the lockout struggle. They had argued strenuously for sympathy strikes in Britain, but British trade union leaders limited themselves to admittedly generous financial and food aid. Nonetheless, the Irish Labour leaders were also painfully aware that the Irish working class lacked the kind of disciplined organisation that would make the Co-operative Commonwealth an imminent possibility. After the defeat of the Transport Union, therefore, a priority was raising the self-discipline of the workers. The formation of the Irish Citizen Army was a means to this end. Jack White, its commandant, wrote in the *Daily Herald* on 18 December 1913 that:

> The supreme object of labour in the present day I take to be, emancipation from wage slavery and organisation into co-operative industries owned and managed by the workers; and the first step towards its realisation is a high state of discipline and organisation on the part of the workers,

the habit of acting in concert, and the emergence from their own ranks of natural leaders. Drill is nothing but the science of natural combination and, especially in the case of unskilled workers, whose standard of education is not high, it is the best, and perhaps the only foundation on which to build the capacity for mental combination in an industry or other enterprise. A military or semi-military organisation, with its accompaniment of order, punctuality, and willing obedience, is the best possible basis for industrial organisation.[27]

One aim of the Irish Citizen Army, therefore, was to produce a disciplined working-class consciousness of common control over the means of production.

There was, already, a minority of wage-workers considered ripe for co-operative enterprise. In February 1914, Larkin in conjunction with George Russell, Jack White, Countess Markiewicz and the Dublin Labour councillor Richard O'Carroll, launched a 'New Campaign' to turn the Irish Transport Union into a production co-operative 'as a competitor with the bosses'. In the first instance, this meant an attempt to organise an Irish Builders Co-operative Society, organising those skilled building workers still blacklisted after the lockout.[28] Builders were typically a combination of tradesmen – bricklayers, masons, hod-carriers, scaffolders – and labourers. Once contracted to a job they largely organised themselves. As such, they had long veered between a conservative craft-sectionalism and a radical enthusiasm for co-operative labour cutting out the capitalist contractor, two expressions of the same class and occupational consciousness.[29] It is not surprising, therefore, that builders were in the vanguard of industrial co-operative ambitions. Larkin's departure to America in 1914 and the outbreak of the war, however, put paid to the Builders' Guild scheme in Ireland.

Ideological ferment during the First World War

James Connolly was certainly demoralised by the collapse of the Second International at the outbreak of world war in 1914. In reaction, he moved closer to nationalist separatists. It seems likely a common enthusiasm for the 1840s agrarian radical, James Fintan Lalor, who Connolly somewhat inaccurately read as a proto-socialist, brought him closer to the Republican separatist Padraig Pearse.[30] Lalor had wished to see formal property in land vested not in the Crown but in the sovereign people and then allocated to those farmers working the land. This had parallels with the Plunket–Finlay–Russell vision of a Co-operative Commonwealth, in which the community would own productive property, but the workers would possess and organise it. But so far as Sean O'Casey was concerned, Connolly fell in the rebellion not as a martyr for Irish socialism but for the Irish nationalism into which he had subsumed his cause.[31]

In the same year, George Russell published his book *National Being*. Russell wished to see the agricultural co-operatives link up with industrial co-operatives of the urban working class. Clearly, however, Russell expected farmers to remain in the lead. Wage earners lacked those resources of independence necessary for the early introduction of co-operative production. Russell wrote of:

> [T]he proletarian in our cities who was insecure in the labour by which he lives. ... [His] ... absolute dependence upon the autocrats of industry for a livelihood is the greatest evil of any, for it puts a spiritual curse on him and makes him in effect a slave. ... [In contrast,] our farmers are already free. The problem with them is not now concerned with freedom, but how they may be brought into a solidarity with each other and the nation. To make our proletarians free and masters of their own energies, in unison with each other and the national being, is the most pressing labour ... before us.[32]

In his view, therefore, proletarians were less amenable to the Co-operative Commonwealth than farmers. Russell nonetheless proposed that workers, through their trade unions, should first establish co-operative stores, then co-operative factories to supply these stores and the farmers. State law should limit shareholders to receiving no more than a fixed dividend of about 5 per cent in any industry while vesting actual control of industry in the worker shareholders.

Russell's book had a significant influence on Irish workers, according to Daryl Figgis, the Sinn Féin propagandist. His promotion of the 'Co-operative Commonwealth' was appealing. As Figgis wrote, 'few words were more frequently heard in the ranks of the workers: it took a higher rank in their thoughts than even the question of increased wages'.[33] Irish workers, he fondly hoped, were moving beyond narrow 'wagery'.

This notion of 'wagery' derived most influentially from an Irish man long active in the British socialist movement. S. G. Hobson was born in 1870 the small Quaker village of Bessbrook in Ulster. The family moved to England where he was schooled, but Hobson always remained intensely proud of his Irish antecedents. As a young man he was an active supporter of Parnell in Irish nationalist circles in Britain, but he became deeply involved in Fabian socialism from 1891. Hobson was elected to the Fabian executive in 1900, where he represented the left wing. Despite his absorption in British affairs he maintained Irish connections and was friends with Roger Casement and cousin of the republican organiser, Bulmer Hobson.[34] He became associated with the *New Age*, a literary journal edited by Alfred Richard Orage, which had links with George Russell and other Irish writers. In its pages, Arthur Joseph Penty called for a revival of medieval guilds.[35]

Hobson was influenced by the upsurge of industrial unionism and syndicalism and attempted to incorporate its ethics into socialist doctrine.

His cogitations arrived as a book, *National Guilds*, in 1914. As Max Beer wrote: '[t]he book must be regarded as one of the most important documents of the labour unrest which dominated British home affairs in the years 1908 to 1913.'[36] Hobson condemned wage-earning, or 'wagery', as a condition in which the workers labour-power was treated as nothing but a commodity. He argued for trade unions to pursue a 'plan of campaign' – a term taken from Irish land agitation – involving industrial militancy to win an effective monopoly by trade unions over the labour supply. This would lead to such a squeeze on profits that capitalists would agree to being bought out by the state, which in turn would lease production to worker guilds.[37] 'Wagery' would be replaced by workers in control of their own means of production.

Hobson made little of his Irish background in making his case, but another writer for the *New Age*, in reviewing James Connolly's *Labour in Irish History* in 1914, suggested that Ireland might have a particular role to play in the emergence of Guild Socialism:

> Ireland is, in many ways, more favourably situated than any other country for the solution of the economic muddle of our time; she produced in William Thompson a predecessor of Karl Marx: she experimented with remarkable success Owen's cooperative communism; now she practically has the land in her own hand, and the power of self-government. What would she do to make English political economy obsolete in Ireland?[38]

This was written in the expectation of Home Rule coming to Ireland. But the outbreak of the war changed all these calculations.

Laurence Byrne, who worked for the agricultural co-operative organisation and championed the Co-operative Commonwealth in the wage-labour movement, saw new opportunities for industrial co-operation arising out of wartime mobilisation. Those organisations improvised by the belligerent governments for war production could be taken over by the groups of workers involved after peace.[39] But, writing under the name Andrew E. Malone, in June 1918, he bemoaned the lack of concrete progress in Ireland:

> Irish workers are evidently not very keenly interested. If they were, they would now be building up an industrial cooperative movement at least as strong as their trade union movement. That is not being done. Outside Belfast the industrial cooperative movement barely lives. Dublin with its 25,000 trade Unionists should have a cooperative organisation second to none in the world, yet cooperation in Dublin just exists. It is the same in Cork, Waterford, in Limerick, in Derry; in fact it is the same in all our towns.[40]

There was no industrial co-operative movement analogous to the rural co-operatives, whereas, Irish Labour was flexing its muscle.

From about 1917, the Irish Labour movement recovered strongly from the lockout defeat and the disorganisation of wartime mobilisation. In particular the ITGWU grew rapidly. In 1914 there were 110,000 workers in unions affiliated with the 'Irish Trade Union Congress and Labour Party'. By 1920 this had risen to 250,000, with 130,000 in the ITGWU alone. Peak congress membership was reached with 300,000 in affiliated unions in 1923.[41] Intimately connected to this explosion of membership was a rapid escalation in strike activity in pursuit of higher wages ('wagery' was certainly not passé). William O'Brien, a former comrade of Connolly and a leading figure in the Irish Trade Union Congress and Labour Party, applauded this strike militancy in 1918, but pointed out its limitations:

> To attempt to level up wages is a fatuous policy – a mere temporary expedient ... The only real and genuine remedy is to be found in the control of industry in the interest of the community by the working-class ... it is the only proposal which can ultimately satisfy the conditions of the new social order which we all desire shall supersede the present system of wage slavery, under which the worker is a mere piece of goods, a commodity, dehumanised and degraded, in the hell of labour's chattel market.[42]

At a meeting in Armagh, Robert Getgood, district organiser of the Workers' Union, insisted that there would be no peace in the industrial world until all workers were united in one body, whereby they could control of the means by which they earned their living. Felix Hughes, of the Postal Clerks' Association, which in Britain was in the vanguard of the movement towards industrial democracy, advocated a Co-operative Commonwealth.[43] J. J. Hughes, assistant-secretary of the ITGWU, insisted that the genuine Christian must reject the degrading and brutalising competitive system in favour of the Co-operative Commonwealth.[44]

Labour during the War of Independence

The largest single category of strikers comprised agricultural labourers. Almost 19 per cent of all strikers between 1914 and 1921 were building workers.[45] As we have seen, this was the trade best adapted to co-operative guild organisation. Between 1921 and 1924 a worker owned Dublin Building Trades Guild operated, winning contracts to build 129 houses. The aim, an Irish labour leader said, was to show 'that the workers were capable of building houses cheaper and better than they could be built by the capitalists of Dublin or any other city'.[46]

As Trades Councils renamed themselves Workers' Councils, and local general strikes saw workers' committees assume temporary powers of governance, the press began to speak of 'soviets in Ireland'. The Irish

Unionist Alliance, representing Southern Irish unionists, sent a deputation to Westminster in May 1919 to draw:

> attention to the present very serious condition of things in Ireland ... A large section of Irish labour had been captured by the International Bolshevist movement and was being organised by the Irish Transport and General Workers' Union. The literature now being issued by the leaders of the movement was of an extreme revolutionary character ... Already Soviet Councils had been established in town and country, and the Irish Co-Operative Commonwealth, modelled on Russian lines, already controlled over a 1000 cooperative societies in Ireland.[47]

Most of these co-operatives, of course, were agricultural and 'non-political' rather than socialist. A speaker at the 1919 annual general meeting of the IAOS 'referred to the extraordinary hold the co-operative movement had on the country at the moment. Probably never in the history of the country had there been such a tremendous burst of enthusiasm for anything of a non-political character as there was at present for cooperation.'[48] There was certainly a hint of millenarian audacity about the co-operative movement. Horace Plunkett told the audience that 'there is reason to believe that the dream of a Co-operative Commonwealth – one in which the workers will increasingly become capitalists through co-operative ownership – may find its first realisation in this country.'[49] His optimism was understandable. Co-operative societies in rural Ireland reached a peak membership of 157,766 in 1920.[50] Father Finlay was insistent that this did not mean class war socialism:

> Their ambition – and they proclaimed it loudly – was to see one day in Ireland the Cooperative Commonwealth. But that they did not mean that they were socialists or communists – far from it. No man was less a socialist than the Irish farmer. The programme of the communist was the community of property, and what Irish farmer would subscribe to a program of a party which began by depriving them of the proprietorship of his own holding?[51]

But the insistent anti-socialist rhetoric of the mainstream co-operative movement was itself indicative. It had to come to terms with post-war class radicalisation.

In January 1919, the Catholic Rev. P. Cahalane MA gave a lecture on 'Labour and Social Policy'. 'New forces and new movements are unchained by all great wars', he began, 'and we may safely say that the force let loose by the war now ended, the one that is emerging with ever increasing energy into public life, is that of organised labour.' He distinguished between Bolshevism, collectivism and Catholic socialism. The Bolshevik dictatorship of the working classes was socially untenable, but he did welcome the growth of co-operative societies in Russia, of which there were about

50,000 in existence. Collectivism was the Labour policy evolved by the labour movement in various countries in the decades before the war before the war. 'There is nothing repugnant in the socialisation of industry by the state, provided, of course, there is legitimate compensation. But the policy of giving the control of industry to the state, whether capitalist or labour, is questionable and open to serious objections.' State socialism implied strict discipline and loss of political liberty. In rural Ireland the question could hardly arise. 'Catholic socialism', in contrast, favoured the universal extension of private ownership to workers of all kinds on the lines of peasant proprietorship. It placed religion and family property in the forefront of and condemned the dictatorship of any one class. Cahalane concluded:

> If only the national question were settled once and for all, we could all devote our full attention to social matters. But in the meantime there is no reason why workers should not organise and form cooperative societies for production and distribution. This is the Sinn Féin economic policy, and there is a big future before it. It is the national democratic way for putting property into the hands of all workers.[52]

This form of Catholic socialism appealed to the legacy of James Connolly. The Rev. Dr Coffey, Professor at Maynooth College, insisted that James Connolly did not favour state socialism, but 'group ownership' such as had characterised the old Gaelic system. This could be updated as 'an industrial guild system'.[53]

The Irish Trade Union Congress and Labour Party adopted the Co-operative Commonwealth as its goal at a meeting specifically convoked on first and 2 November 1918. This was not just a synonym for state socialism, as Thomas Johnson pointed out in opposing a 'collectivist' amendment:

> ... one might liken it [the amendment] to what would be aimed at in a Collectivist State, rather than in a Workers' Republic, and that it was rather inspired by the ideas and ideals of Sidney Webb and Arthur Henderson as against James Connolly and George Russell. He would ask the Congress to subscribe to James Connolly and George Russell rather than Sidney Webb and Arthur Henderson.[54]

The next month, however, Labour declined to contest the general election, leaving the field open for Sinn Féin in southern Ireland. It had proved impossible to agree a position on national self-determination that would not lead to an irrevocable split with unionist workers in Ulster. As the Labour leader Thomas Johnston explained, 'if the North had made up its mind to run candidates on the programme of the Irish Labour Party ... the executive's decision would have been a very different one'.[55] Irish Labour did not feel it could present its programme without agreeing a united front on the national question.

In most of Ireland, Labour became more or less an adjunct to Sinn Féin, which presented itself as a national liberation movement rather than a political party as such. Irish Labour convinced itself, as it said in an open letter to the British Labour Party in 1921, that radical co-operative reconstruction would have to await British disengagement.[56] Crown forces, less self-denying, targeted such co-operatives as existed. British 'reprisals' in the summer of 1920 destroyed about one hundred co-operatives – creameries, mills and bacon factories.[57]

Irish Labour was not in the vanguard of the Irish War of Independence. Instead, it approached at a tangent. It is notable that the main contribution of labour to the independence struggle involved strikes against militarism: the anti-conscription general strike of April 1918, the city-wide general strike against martial law in Limerick in April 1919, the general strike in support of political prisoners in April 1920, the national rail industrial action against Crown forces munitions transport from May to December 1920. These all helped the IRA (Irish Republican Army), one way or another, but they were directed first against the militarisation of society. The well-supported April 1922 labour strike in protest at the militarism of both sides in the civil war – the government and anti-treaty IRA – was consistent with the actions that had preceded.

Trade union militancy was not limited to nationalist Ireland. The 1919 engineering strike in Belfast was of international significance. Notably, something approaching a worker sense of ownership in the means of production existed here. The worker cadre in Belfast possessed 'scarce skills ... difficult if not impossible to replace'.[58] This reinforced a psychological sense among wage-earners of possession in the work practices and organisation of their industries, reinforced by a pride in protestant economic achievement that included even unskilled workers.[59] Workers were no cats-paws of Unionist employers. They felt a genuine sense of dual ownership in the industrial might of Ulster. The Belfast strike was of such scale and sweep, with the strike committee taking over quasi-governmental functions, that it was identified, along with the localised general strikes in Winnipeg and Seattle, as the most striking example of proletarian power displayed in relatively stable liberal democracies in the revolutionary year of 1919. The American industrial syndicalist thinker, Frank Tannenbaum, pointed to its significance:

> In Belfast the streets were cleaned, mail delivered, hospitals cared for, milk delivered, garbage taken away by permission of the central organisation of the workers. ... The strike committee was forced into making political decisions ... What is this but evidence of the fact that power shifts from the political grouping to the industrial as the workers organise?[60]

The protestant proletarian sense of psychological possession over the means by which they worked soon turned to the exclusion and persecution of Catholics disloyalists. 'Industrial democracy' took a sectarian form, with a shipyard workers meeting in July 1920 'respectfully' suggesting to employers that in hiring 'first consideration be given to loyal ex-servicemen and Protestant Unionists'.[61] There were large-scale expulsions of Catholics by their fellow workers from engineering works in 1920. The complexity of marine industrial production, and its extremes fluctuations in employment blending into post-war chronic depression, militated against any sense of exclusive worker possession of the means by which they lived.

In the meantime, Labour's standing down in the electoral contest of 1918 had 'created a very friendly feeling between us and Sinn Féin', as William O'Brien put it.[62] Though Labour had no representation in the newly elected Irish parliament and government (which of course was not recognised by Britain), Irish Labour was asked to submit a draft of Dáil Éireann's 'Democratic Programme'. A key paragraph, however, was removed by Sinn Féin from the final version. This had been the most explicit on the Labour ideal of the Co-operative Commonwealth:

> It shall be the purpose of the Government to encourage organisation of the people into trade unions and cooperative societies with a view to the control and administration of the industries by the workers engaged in the industries.[63]

Though this paragraph was rejected, Sinn Féin by no means bluntly rejected the Co-operative Commonwealth. Before the First World War, the Protestant Republican Ernest Blyth had been particularly interested in radical interpretations of the Co-operative Commonwealth.[64] At 'Labour Day' in Bray, before a large demonstration, Seán Etchingham, a veteran of the 1916 rising in Wexford, called for unity between wage-workers and farmers: 'It would be the beginning of the Co-operative Commonwealth to have the farmer and the labourer working on co-operative lines.'[65] Etchingham helped establish a fisheries co-operative, with financing from the Dáil's National Bank.[66]

Laurence Ginnell before the war had been a politician in the ranks of the Home Rule movement, but after 1916 he switched to Sinn Féin. Ginnell in 1894 had published a book on the pre-conquest legal system of Ireland. This scholarly volume had circulated in socialist circles in Scotland, where it presumably influenced James Connolly. Ginnell had described a medieval Ireland that lacked absolute private property in the means of production. 'At no time did the land belong either to the state in the broad sense or to the individual absolutely. Each clan was a distinct organism in itself, and the land was its property.'[67] For Ginnell, this old Brehon system pointed to a particularly Irish social system for the future:

> We intend our Republic to be a cooperative commonwealth as much as possible. That will be in strict harmony with the old Brehon system ... [We] look to a future Ireland where most of the branches of business

will be carried on by a cooperative system. By that we hope to escape from the difficulties of countries in modern times with labour problems. We intend that the workers shall be to some extent owners of the institutions in which they work, and that their prosperity shall increase with the prosperity of the institution, participating in its prosperity and participating in its direction. Some of the workers are very intelligent men.[68]

Professor Eoin MacNeill, Minister for Industries in the underground government of the Republic, when lecturing on the industrial programme of Sinn Féin, rejected class conflict but stated that 'the economic aim of Ireland should be a co-operative commonwealth'.[69] Aodh de Blacam, the semi-detached publicist for Sinn Féin, actively researched socialist co-operative ideas, including guild socialism. He thought that the class situation of farmers lent itself more to co-operative living than did the consciousness of urban wage earners. 'It is true that men of one craft like to gather together when a technical problem is up for decision,' he conceded, 'but when work is over their associations cut right across occupational lines … Thus the rural commune harmonises with social idealism, expresses the true communal spirit, as the Guild-owned factory in the city can never do.'[70] De Blacam overlooked the narrow individualism of rural life, but he also cut to a real problem here. The wage-worker, as Marx had observed, felt a sense of ownership in his or her labour power much more than in his or her place of work.[71] This placed a substantial barrier to the formation of proletarian production co-operatives within the interstices of capitalist society. Co-operativism in Ireland always remained much more a rural and farming than an urban and manufacturing ethos.

Reaction

There clearly existed a vibrant if internally fissured idealism of the Co-operative Commonwealth in these tempestuous years. But it was not to last. A leading British guild socialist of the post-war period, Margaret Cole, admitted that the national guilds in Great Britain, as 'an immediately practical proposal' could not survive the post-war slump of 1921 and the precipitous decline of trade union militancy that followed.[72] The same went double for Ireland. The Irish Labour Party's programme of 1921 declined to present any proposals 'respecting the claim for extension of the sphere of workers' control over the industries in which they are concerned'.[73] In the Civil War of 1922–23, ideas of social reconstruction rapidly fell back, to be replaced by rancorous disputation over the 1921 Anglo-Irish Treaty and a conservative consolidation of the existing economic fabric. In practice, as Mary Daly points out, the parlous condition of the new state required it to defer to Irish banks, which in turn took their orders from the British Treasury. There was a marked continuity in administrative elite personnel from the years of British rule in both the private and public sectors. This as Daly puts it, 'reflects the absence of a social revolution and the lack of alternative expertise.'[74] Normal capitalist development, rather than experiments in the Co-operative Commonwealth, was the path of least resistance in newly independent Ireland.

A Catholic intellectual, writing in favour of the Co-operative Commonwealth in 1923, realised that 'the first years of Irish-government will be the critical ones in the life of the nation' because 'in a few years vested interests may become so established economically … that radical reform will be impossible.'[75] In fact, the moment of opportunity had already passed. By 1924, disillusionment with 'vision' had set in. 'It were time we stopped talking nonsense about a Co-operative Commonwealth, whichever sort of thing that may be, and building up industries on cooperative principles', wrote a columnist in the *Southern Star*. 'Such talk has been going on for a quarter of century, and it has brought practically no results, excepting a few failures.'[76]

In Ireland, as in Britain and internationally, socialist co-operativism receded as the movement disintegrated into a bewildering array of tendencies from the communist left to the fascist right. In Ireland, the anti-treaty radical-nationalist Fianna Fáil party proved most adept at incorporating the small farmer, working class, petty bourgeois and déclassé into a broad alliance that paid a diffuse lip-service to distributed property while in practice prioritising bourgeois accumulation.[77] The Catholic Church, reinforced by the encyclical *Quadragesimo Anno* (1931), reconfigured its toleration of 'Catholic socialism' in favour of virulently anti-socialist corporativism, and Irish Labour in the south was ideologically hemmed in.[78] In fact, objective forces were as strong as these subjective constraints. The First World War crystallised a configuration of industrial capitalism around massive plants that offered little scope for worker management. The capitalism of the 'massified worker' produced either conformity or statist collectivism. The only viable alternatives seemed to be private-property capitalist hierarchy or statist managerialist hierarchy (Ireland quite nimbly combined the two with its innovative 'semi-state industries' in the interwar period).[79] Until the decline of the 'massified' industrial proletariat from the 1960s, the socialist ideal of associated producers would remain locked in a statist mould.

Notes

1 M. Louis Blanc, *Organisation du travail* (Paris, 1839, 1847), p. 20.
2 According to J. P. Mayer, Pecqueur conceived the centralized state as '*propriétaire, entrepreneur* and *capitaliste* alike'. *Political thought in France from Sieyès to Sorel* (London, 1943), pp. 46–8.

3 Karl Kautsky, *On the Morrow of the Social Revolution* (London, 1909), p. 6.
4 F. Hall and W. P. Watkins, *Co-operation: A Survey of the History, Principles and Organisation of the Co-operative Movement in Great Britain and Ireland* (Manchester, 1937), pp. 186–91.
5 Ernest Barker, *Ireland in the Last Fifty Years* (Oxford, 1919), p. 72.
6 G. D. H. Cole, *A Century of Co-operation* (London, n.d. [1944]), p. 251.
7 G. D. H. Cole, *The Second International* (Vol. III of *A History of Socialist Thought*) (London, 1956), part II, pp. 816–17.
8 'Memorial to the Government', *Belfast Weekly News*, 8 August 1907.
9 Patrick Galvin, *Irish Songs of Resistance* (New York, 1972), p. 54.
10 The strike was most solid in areas such as the working liberties and Kilmainham area. In the August riots, workers battled to defend their homes in the Corporation Buildings and Inchicore from police incursion. Scabs were often attacked by 'roughs' as they travelled near or through working-class residential areas, rather than on the picket line. Pádraig Yeates, *Lockout: Dublin 1913* (Dublin, 2001), pp. 17, 75, 176.
11 Keith Harding, 'The "Co-operative Commonwealth": Ireland, Larkin and the *Daily Herald*', in Stephen Yeo (ed.), *New Views of Co-operation* (London, 1988), pp. 88–107, 96.
12 *Evening Herald*, Saturday, 4 October 1913, p. 2.
13 'Mr Larkin's Utopia', *Evening Herald*, 17 December 1913.
14 'The IAOS', *Freemans Journal*, 11 December 1913.
15 'Ugly Past', *Evening Herald*, 10 December 1913.
16 Pádraig Yeates, *Lockout: Dublin 1913* (Dublin, 2001), pp. 346–7.
17 'Dublin Housing Problem', *Irish Independent*, 5 November 1913.
18 James Connolly, 'Michael Davitt' [1908], in Owen Dudley Edwards and Bernard Ransom (eds), *James Connolly: Selected Political Writings* (London, 1973), pp. 209–14, 214.
19 James Connolly, Speech to Dublin trades Council [1915], in Aindrias Ó Cathasaigh (ed.), *The Lost Writings of James Connolly* (London, 1997), pp. 168–71, 170.
20 Connolly, 'Michael Davitt', p. 212.
21 James Connolly, 'Future of Labour' [1908], in Edwards and Ransom, *James Connolly: Selected Political Writings*, pp. 275–85, 283.
22 Connolly, 'Industrialism and the Trade unions' [1910], in James Connolly, *Selected Works*, 2 vols (Dublin, 1987), vol. II, p. 261.
23 Connolly, 'Socialism Made Easy' [1908], excerpted in Peter Berresford Ellis, *James Connolly: Selected Writings* (London, 1973, 1997), pp. 149–53, p. 153.
24 The eccentric political unionist and cultural nationalist, Standish O'Grady, in contrast urged workers to up sticks and move to the countryside, there to establish labour communes: 'Get the land, get the machineries, aim not at money, but at the co-operative creation and generous diffusion of wealth', *Irish Worker*, 9 November 1912; Standish James O'Grady, *To the Leaders of Our Working People*, ed. Edward A. Hagan (Dublin, 2002), p. 39.
25 Bob Holton, *British Syndicalism, 1900–1914* (London, 1976), pp. 193–4.
26 W. P. Ryan, *The Labour Revolt and Larkinism* (London, 1913), p. 9.
27 *Daily Herald*, 18 December 1913.

28 Murray Fraser, *John Bull's Other Homes: State Housing and British Policy in Ireland, 1883–1922* (Liverpool, 1996), pp. 129–31.
29 Catriona Clear, *Social Change and Everyday Life in Ireland, 1850–1922* (Manchester, 2007), p. 29; R. W. Postgate, *The Builders History* (London, 1923), p. xv.
30 Thomas P. O'Neill, 'James Fintan Lalor', in J. W. Boyle (ed.), *Leaders and Workers* (Cork, 1967), pp. 37–45, 45.
31 P. O Cathasaigh (Sean O'Casey), *The Story of the Irish Citizen Army* (London, 1919, 1980), pp. 52, 64.
32 AE, *The National Being: Some Thoughts on an Irish Polity* (New York, 1916, 1937), p. 32.
33 Darrell Figgis, *AE (George W. Russell): A Study of a Man and a Nation* (New York, 1916), pp. 92–3.
34 S. G. Hobson, *Pilgrim to the Left: Memoirs of a Modern Revolutionist* (London, 1938), p. 994.
35 Frank Matthews, 'The Ladder of Becoming: A. R. Orage, A. J. Penty and the Origins of Guild Socialism in England', in David E. Martin and David Rubinstein (eds), *Ideology and the Labour Movement* (London, 1979), pp. 147–66.
36 Max Beer, *A Short History of British Socialism*, 2 vols (London, 1919, 1940), vol. II, p. 365.
37 S. G. Hobson, *National Guilds: An Inquiry into the Wage System and the Way Out* (London, 1914, 1919), pp. 100–4.
38 A. E. R., 'Views and Reviews', *The New Age*, 14:25 (1914), p. 789.
39 Andrew E. Malone, 'Irish Labour in War Time', *Studies: An Irish Quarterly Review* June (1918), 319–27.
40 Andrew E. Malone, 'Irish Labour in War Time', June 1918, p. 327.
41 Arthur Mitchell, *Labour in Irish Politics, 1890–1930* (Dublin, 1974), p. 137.
42 *Report of the Irish Labour Party and Trades Union Congress*, August 1918, p. 18.
43 'Trade Union Aims', *Freemans Journal*, 25 October 1919, p. 6. Carter L. Goodrich, *The Frontier of Control: A Study in British Workshop Politics* (London, 1920, 1975), pp. 246–8.
44 'Amazing Doctrines Preached at the Town Hall', *Connacht Tribune*, 13 December 1919.
45 Emmet O'Connor, *Syndicalism in Ireland* (Cork, 1988), pp. 26, 29.
46 Murray Fraser, *John Bull's Other Homes: State Housing and British Policy in Ireland, 1883–1922* (Liverpool, 1996), p. 236.
47 'Soviets in Ireland', *The Times*, 30 May 1919.
48 'Women's work', *Freemans Journal*, 11 April 1919.
49 'The Future of the IAOS', *Irish Independent*, 12 December 1919.
50 Patrick Mary Doyle, 'Reframing the "Irish Question": the role of the Irish co-operative movement in the formation of Irish nationalism, 1900–22', *Irish Studies Review*, 22:2 (2014), 267–84, 237.
51 'Moyculien store', *Connacht Tribune*, 25 September 1920.
52 'Literary and Debating Guild', *Irish Examiner*, 31 January 1919.
53 'Evils of Capitalist System', *Freemans Journal*, 19 January 1920.
54 P. Joy, 'Ireland a Co-operative Commonwealth (Continued)', *The Irish Monthly*, April (1923), 78–84, p. 204.

55 Arthur Mitchell, *Labour in Irish Politics, 1890–1930* (Dublin, 1974), p. 100.
56 'From Irish Labour to British Labour', *Freemans Journal*, 18 January 1921.
57 Dorothy Macardle, *The Irish Republic* (London, 1937, 1968), pp. 347–8.
58 John Lynch, 'The Belfast Shipyards and the Industrial Working Class', in Francis Devine, Fintan Lane and Niamh Puirséil (eds), *Essays in Irish Labour History* (Dublin, 2008), pp. 135–56, 137.
59 James Winder Good, *Ulster and Ireland* (Dublin and Cork, 1919), p. 281.
60 Frank Tannenbaum, *The Labor Movement: Its Conservative Functions and Social Consequences* (New York, 1921), p. 133.
61 Henry Patterson, *Class Conflict and Sectarianism* (Belfast, 1980), p. 136.
62 Conor Kostick, *Revolution in Ireland; Popular Militancy 1917 to 1923* (London, 1996), p. 147.
63 Quoted in Pat Walsh, *Irish Republicanism and Socialism: The Politics of the Republican Movement, 1905 to 1994* (Belfast, 1994), p. 19.
64 Michael Laffan, *The Resurrection of Ireland: The Sinn Fein Party, 1916–1923* (Cambridge, 1999), p. 255. Pádraig Yeates, *Lockout: Dublin 1913* (Dublin, 2001), pp. 357–9.
65 'Labour day', *Wicklow News-Letter*, 3 May 1919.
66 Arthur Mitchell, *Revolutionary Government in Ireland: Dáil Éireann, 1919–22* (Dublin, 1995), p. 91.
67 Laurence Ginnell, *The Brehon Laws: A Legal Handbook* (London, 1894), p. 9.
68 American Commission on Conditions in Ireland, *Evidence on Conditions in Ireland* (Washington, 1921), p. 484.
69 'Economic Warfare', *Kildare Observer*, 19 April 1919; 'Irish Commonwealth', *Irish Independent*, 14 April 1919. See also 'Ireland's Future', **Limerick Leader, 22 September 1920.**
70 A. de Blacam, *What Sinn Fein Stands For* (London, 1921), pp. 180–1.
71 Karl Marx, *Capital* [1867] (New York, 1906), pp. 258–9.
72 Margaret Cole, *Growing Up into Revolution* (London, 1949), p. 101.
73 'The Country in Danger!', in William O'Brien (ed.), *Forth the Banners Go* (Dublin, 1969), appendix H, p. 304.
74 Mary E. Daly, *Industrial Development and Irish National Identity, 1922–1939* (New York, 1992), pp. 14–15.
75 P. Joy, 'Ireland a Co-operative Commonwealth (Continued)', *The Irish Monthly*, April (1923), p. 205.
76 'Co-operation', *Southern Star*, 3 May 1924.
77 Richard Dunphy, 'Fianna Fáil and the Working Class, 1926–38', in Fintan Lane and Donal Ó Drisceoil (eds), *Politics and the Irish Working Class, 1830–1945* (Basingstoke, 2005), pp. 246–61, 246.
78 Niamh Puirséil, *The Irish Labour Party, 1922–73* (Dublin, 2007), pp. 60–1.
79 Oliver MacDonagh, *Ireland* (Englewood Cliffs, NJ, 1968), pp. 122–4.

11

Russia's war and revolutions as seen by Morgan Philips Price and Arthur Henderson

Jonathan Davis

At the start of the First World War, the liberal journalist Morgan Philips Price and the new leader of the Labour Party in Britain, Arthur Henderson, supported their government's conflict against the Central Powers. Price greeted the news cautiously and offered a reserved backing to the Liberal politicians who took the country to war; Henderson moved quickly from an anti-war stance to one of unqualified backing for the Triple Entente. Over the next four years these two pre-war liberals shifted politically to the left, and the common factor in their political transformation was Russia, a country which both men spent time in during the revolutionary period. Both men were guided by their Russian experiences and two very different viewpoints emerged.

The downfall of Tsarism and the rise of Lenin's Bolsheviks had a significant impact both in and out of Russia, and European socialism could not be the same again. The split between reformers and revolutionaries dictated the development of post-war socialism and the socialist internationals. This was also one of the issues that influenced how Labour's relationship with revolutionary Russia and the Soviet Union developed. The long-term themes that characterised Labour–Soviet relations, including a shared interest in socialist ideology, personal relations and the changes in the international situation, began in this period as Price and Henderson considered them carefully while in Russia. What they saw there shaped their views of Russia's politics and politicians, and this then helped to shape Labour's attitude towards the revolutions, the USSR and its socialism. This was the start of Labour's interest in what Kevin Morgan calls the diverse 'roads to Russia' which were 'followed at different times by planners, co-operators and revolutionary elitists'. And he notes that some, like A. A. Purcell – the subject of his final book in his three-volume assessment of Bolshevism and the British left – introduced a 'fourth such road ... by which the active trade unionist and trade union official might come to see in Soviet Russia the attempted realisation of a shared aspiration to the good society.'[1] At the same time of course, the USSR was also seen as an anti-democratic dictatorship that denied its citizens the very freedoms that Labour was fighting for at home.[2] Soviet Russia attracted a great amount of interest in the Labour Party and this was fuelled in the first instance by what Price and Henderson saw during their time in this revolutionary country.

This chapter will assess what these two witnesses to Russia's war and revolutions found while in Russia in 1916 and 1917. It will argue that their time in the country helped to change their liberal views, and as both were, in their own way, important opinion formers where British socialism was concerned, it is important to see how Russia influenced their ideas. Morgan Philips Price became a Bolshevik sympathiser and, in the face of anti-Soviet assaults by British politicians and the press, a defender of the revolution that brought Lenin's party to power. Arthur Henderson did not go that far, but his view of how the international labour movement should approach the war during and after the February revolution was profoundly influenced by his official visit there. After he left David Lloyd George's government, he helped to write Labour's new constitution in 1918. This included the radical socialist Clause IV, which called for the securing of the full fruits of workers' labour and the common ownership of the means of production.

Price and Henderson shared a political outlook before the First World War and their respective journeys to Russia. Neither man could be described as a socialist before 1914, as they were both more on the liberal left, although it is true that the distinction between 'socialist' and 'left-liberal' can be hazy. Price's daughter, Tania Rose, said that he 'described himself as more or less a socialist in home affairs and a Whig where foreign policy was concerned'.[3] He was a journalist for the liberal newspaper, the *Manchester Guardian*, as well as a former parliamentary candidate for the Liberal Party. He had spent time in Russia before 1914, first visiting in 1908 on family business and then returning in 1910. The country was not an unknown quantity for him – he knew it and its language well.

Despite his anti-war feelings, Price supported the British government in 1914. However, he soon joined with the newly formed anti-war UDC, where he found a home alongside other likeminded protesters, including his cousin Charles Trevelyan and former Labour leader Ramsay MacDonald. Price's travels took him across Russia during the war and revolutionary period, as he accepted an offer from the *Manchester Guardian*'s editor C. P. Scott to be the paper's special correspondent in Russia. He spent time in Petrograd, Moscow, the Caucasus and the Volga region, and he wrote many stories about the changing countryside in light of the peasants' activities.⁴ Price focused on the consequences the war had for Russia and its people, and according to Jonathan Smele his despatches 'reflected his unswerving opposition to the war and his increasingly radical outlook'.⁵ Ultimately, Price became a Bolshevik sympathiser because of what he saw in Russia.

A note of caution should be added here, which is that the more radical he became, the less impartial he became. As his criticism of how the Allies treated the Russians grew, so too did his desire to paint an ever more rosy picture of early Bolshevik rule. Smele notes that his reports were 'undeniably partial', that Price admitted later that he was 'abandoning objectivity', and that what he wrote 'somewhat exaggerated the situation in Moscow'.⁶ Indeed, Price made his views of the radicalism in Russia quite clear in the opening of his book *My Reminiscences of the Russian Revolution*, where he quoted the eighteenth-century Whig politician Charles James Fox, who said of the French Revolution, 'How much is it, by far the greatest and the best thing that has ever happened in the history of the world.' Price then dedicated the book to 'those leaders and to the rank and file of British Labour who by speech, pen and action have defended the Soviet Republic of Russia against the onslaughts of the international bondholders'.⁷ Although he later came to regret his pro-Bolshevism he initially made 'no apology for defending the Russian Revolution and the party with which it will be forever associated'⁸ and he defended his reports as 'a healthy antidote to the kind of rubbish that was being circulated throughout the world' about the Soviet regime.⁹

Arthur Henderson came to learn about Russia from a different starting point. He had been a Liberal Party agent, uncomfortable with the fact that he had to oppose a Liberal candidate when he first won a parliamentary election for the Labour Party in 1906. J. M. Winter notes that Henderson's early political views were 'indistinguishable from non-conformist Liberalism' and, before the war, 'his work in the Labour Party was almost always at odds with its socialist section. His cautiousness and conservative attitude as chairman of the Parliamentary Labour Party in 1908–10 and as party secretary from 1911 on were repeatedly and severely criticised by the socialists of the Independent Labour party'.¹⁰ He was made secretary of the British section of the Second International after Labour affiliated to it and in 1914 he became leader of the Labour Party, taking over after Ramsay MacDonald resigned as chairman in protest against the war.

Henderson initially voted for Britain to take a neutral stance over the war, and he moved a resolution at the anti-war rally in London's Trafalgar Square, which sought 'to unite the workers of the nations concerned in the efforts to prevent their Governments from entering upon war'.¹¹ Once war came, he supported it because of a mixture of patriotism and belief that an innocent Belgium should be protected. He genuinely hoped that this war would lead to a more stable and effective European democracy and acknowledged the important part that Russia had to play in this process after the February revolution.

He joined Lloyd George's War Cabinet and in 1917 went to Russia on official governmental business. This was not somewhere he had been before, and in contrast to Price, he did not speak Russian and knew little about Russian affairs. The purpose of his Russian visit was to gauge the political mood of the country's socialist leaders and to encourage them to continue with their war efforts. But, like Price, Henderson's views on political matters were altered by his time here, and upon his return he left his position in the War Cabinet because of differences of opinion over certain issues including the Stockholm Conference of international socialists.

Price in pre-revolutionary Russia

Morgan Philips Price travelled widely in Russia. This gave him a less metropolitan view of events than Arthur Henderson, who only stayed in Petrograd and Moscow. In the Caucasus, Price pursued the 'truth of the situation'.[12] Having seen 'Central Russia and the Western theatre of war during 1914 and part of 1915', he decided to go to the East and visit the Caucasus again.[13] His journeys over the Caucasus front and his 'long sojourns in Tiflis [Tbilisi] during these months', enabled him 'to see what was going on in Asiatic Russia'. He noted that the gulf between the rulers and the ruled was widening every day, and the only question was, 'When would the crash come?'[14] His experiences shaped his understanding of unfolding events and he became increasingly aware that the country was staggering through the war towards revolution.

Price claimed that the war was being fought by Russia not as a war for freedom but rather as 'a diversion to keep the Russian people occupied at home, so that they should forget their internal troubles'.[15] There were two wars being fought here – the 'external war against the armies of the Central Powers and Turkey, and the internal war against her own suffering people'.[16] It is this type of reporting that makes it easy to see why Price became a convert – albeit quite short-lived – to revolutionary socialism and Lenin's Bolsheviks. He witnessed the religious persecution of the Ruthenes in Galicia, saw how Jews suffered pogroms in the rear of the armies in Poland, and wrote that the 'massacres of the Moslems on the Asiatic front was no less criminal, if less extensive, than the Turkish massacre of the Armenians'.[17]

Price's reports demonstrated clearly the deepening sense of crisis and the differences of opinion over the war that existed between the political parties. In March 1916, he wrote to his cousin C. P. Trevelyan from Tiflis explaining that the reactionary right was expected to pursue the war aggressively. He suggested that the centre-right liberals in the Kadet Party were the most keen to continue the war to the end. The Kadets and other 'kindred parties' were 'bitter haters of everything German in the country ... They dislike Germany's economic hold over Russia and want to see Russia develop independently of outside influence ... These Progressives, or Russian Liberals ... are ... on foreign questions most chauvinistic of any party in Russia ... They are the modern representatives of the old Slavophile school ...'[18]

On the left, Price astutely equated the Russian Social Democrats with the German and British socialists who split into opposing groups at the start of the war. He thought that about half of them, together with the socialist revolutionaries, were for the war 'because they think that Russia is threatened with German militarism. They seem to be like the English Trade Unionists. The other half, like the ILP in England, have been uncompromisingly against the war from the first, and are now.'[19] As the war continued, this split became even more relevant as an anti-imperialist war mood grew among Russia's exploited masses.

Price highlighted the many factors that contributed to the radicalisation of the Russian people. The economic crisis and the crumbling economy had devastating effects, with the cost of living rising 'by 75 per cent' while 'wages in industrial centres increase only very slightly and the income of the peasants not at all ... the whole burden is falling on the poor and they are beginning to get pretty restive.'[20] Russians from the middle and lower classes and intelligentsia felt the same as the economic pressures were becoming ever more serious. And all knew that the real cause of their suffering and their dire economic situation was the continuing war. On his visits to the frontlines Price spoke with many 'common soldiers' whose first question was 'When is this war going to end?' They told him that they wanted to go home as they had had enough, a statement which was said to him 'not ten or a hundred times but I should think a thousand times these last three months.'[21] This war had also driven millions of peasants into the army 'to be mutilated on the fronts or die of disease in the rear.'[22]

By 1917, the food crisis and the war combined to bring the revolutionary movement to a head. Price suggested that mankind would 'endure much, but when their stomachs are empty, they begin to demand the reason why. It is not difficult to trace a connection between the decrease in the food supplies of Russia during the war, and the increase of the revolutionary spirit.'[23] The most 'potent cause' of this spirit was the 'suffering through shortage of food in the towns and the large industrial centres during the winter of 1916–17.'[24] United through privation, the 'wage-earning proletariat' was 'politically the best organised section' of society, while the peasants 'of whom the youngest and best were in the army became for the first time in history a united revolutionary army. These two forces, the organised proletariat and the peasant army, between them guaranteed the success of the Revolution.'[25]

While in the Ukrainian city of Khar'kov (then part of the Tsarist Empire), Price wrote on the consequences of the erroneous distribution of resources. Russia was 'more or less faced with famine. The reckless commandeering of livestock during the first twelve months of the war, by which large quantities of cattle were often driven together without sufficient fodder or attendance, resulted in much fruitless destruction and waste.' The slaughtering of 'high-class breeding cattle' and 'last year's precipitate retreat' led to 'the destruction and loss of large stores behind the army lines. The consequence is that at the present moment meat in Russia proper, apart from rising fourfold in price, is practically unobtainable.'[26]

At the end of 1916, Price wrote from Tiflis about the political and economic crisis emanating from the overall food issues, and his reports were published by F. W. Hirst in the Liberal paper *Common Sense*. Sensing that the mood had become even more radical, Price said that it should 'not be forgotten that the causes of the economic crisis ... have deep roots and these cannot be removed simply by a change in the political orientation of the Government or by Constitutional reforms.'[27] And he was proved correct. Just over one month after his words were published, Russia had exploded into revolution. At the start of February, Price declared that there were 'remarkable events' in Petrograd where the 'air was full of weird and uncanny rumours. All one can do is to sit tight and wait till something happens, and before the year is over I expect something is pretty sure to take place, more or less exciting.'[28]

1917: the first Russian revolution

Price described the first revolution of 1917 as coming 'like a thief in the night' and asked how often its possibilities had been discussed in Russia 'during the last two and a half years that followed the outbreak of the Great War!'[29] Wild rumours had been circulating in the 'distant provinces' where he had been located, and he sent back many stories from the Caucasus detailing the uprising before he moved up to Moscow to learn how the 'Metropolises of Russian culture had responded to the great event.'[30]

The complexity of the situation was expertly described by him when he wrote about the revolution in Moscow. Telegrams 'indicated food riots in the capital; revolts among sailors of the Baltic Fleet. News was held back; rumours circulated, the atmosphere was electric; the bureaucracy nervous. Only when it was certain that the capital was in the hands of a workers' council and that the soldiers of the garrison had joined, did the satraps of Tsarism in Moscow lay down their authority.'[31] The Moscow crowds, Price observed, 'consisted broadly of two elements' – a 'well-dressed section of middle-class people, students, officers, advocates, doctors' and 'common soldiers, workmen, small handcraftsmen, who could be detected at once by their weather-worn, collarless shirts'.[32]

Overhearing their conversations, Price said that they drifted 'on to one main topic, which was evidently engaging the attention of all: bread and peace'.

> The question of how to get food and how to stop the war was pushing itself to the surface, worrying the public mind, demanding an answer. No one liked to talk openly about it, because everyone had for so long been drilled into silence. But everyone knew that a fifteen-million army was eating up the material resources of Russia … that the railways were no longer equal to the transport burden, that the cereals formerly exported to Western Europe were now more than absorbed by the army … that the workmen of several big towns had been several days without bread, while the Grand Dukes and profiteers had large stores in their houses.[33]

Price reported on the feelings of 'well dressed' Muscovites at Strastnaya Square and the Pushkin monument, who were 'standing around a couple of soldiers just back on leave from the front'. Some did not want to end the war simply because there was not enough bread, while others feared that the 'Germans will come here, and that will be the end of the Revolution'. A soldier suggested that perhaps they would not come if they explained that they would leave them alone; someone else demanded the liberation of 'our brother Slavs in Galicia from the Austrian yoke, and the Poles from the Germans'. According to Price, this 'well-dressed' person had, 'judging from his looks … been for four years "arm chair patriotic"'. An officer spoke up and reported that he had been wounded several times and said 'something about Constantinople and the need of a commercial outlet through the Dardanelles. The two soldiers did not seem to think that that affected them very much, and began to talk about army rations, which had been reduced. Prussian militarism was far off; only things near and practical seemed to affect them.'[34]

In Russia's capital city, the workers, soldiers and sailors reconvened the workers' council (*soviet*), which they had formed during the 1905 revolution. The Petrograd Soviet, which shared power with the more liberal Provisional Government, attracted independent socialists and those affiliated to a party. In its early days, the Marxist Mensheviks and the agrarian Socialist Revolutionary Party were the most popular, and Lenin's Bolsheviks formed only a small group. And regarding Price's earlier division of pro- and anti-war socialists mentioned above, we can note a mood broadly equivalent to the ILP evident in the Soviet. Many delegates called for a peace based on 'no annexations and no indemnities' while others argued that if the conflict was to continue, it should be to defend the revolutionary gains that had been made and the country from German attacks. This became known as 'revolutionary defencism'.

From here on, an important theme in Price's writing was the rise of Lenin's Bolsheviks throughout the year. He recorded how the revolution spread across the country and how it contributed to the Bolsheviks' ranks. The party began the period with around 25,000 members but had somewhere between 250,000 and 300,000 by the time it took power in October. Price was of the opinion that soldiers in the garrison towns began to follow Lenin because they had faith in him to stop a war that they knew had little to do with them, and workers turned towards him as they believed the end of the war would bring food. While this reflected the revolutionary slogan of 'Bread, Land, Peace' it did not suggest that Russians were turning to Lenin because of a total commitment to Marxism. Recalling a meeting at which Lenin spoke, Price said that his name had been on people's lips 'for many weeks past'. Price described him as a 'short man with a round head, small pig-like eyes, and close-cropped hair' whose words 'poured from his mouth, overwhelming all in a flood of oratory. One sat spellbound at his command of language and the passion of his denunciation.' He did also note that 'when it was all over one felt inclined to scratch one's head and ask what it was all about'.[35]

This increasingly radical mood led a concerned British government to send Arthur Henderson to Russia to ascertain what this meant for its war effort. Henderson had already sent a telegram to Russia's workers urging them not to pull out of the war, believing that they should impress upon their followers that 'any remission of effort means disaster to the comrades in the trenches'.[36] This pro-war stance was not supported by all British socialists though. The anti-war ILP member Bruce Glasier sent an alternative message to the Russian people, rejecting Henderson's call to continue fighting. Glasier hoped that their Russian comrades would 'not believe that this message, with its stinted sympathy and pro-war obsessions, represents the extent of the sympathy and interests of the British Socialist and Labour Movement in the great revolutionary uprise of the Russian democracy'.[37]

Whatever the feelings about the war – and this was still a primary concern – there was a very excited mood in the wider labour movement about the February Revolution. Large meetings were held which brought socialists together in London's Albert Hall and in Leeds which welcomed the news and sent fraternal greetings and congratulatory messages.[38] This was the Labour background to Henderson's journey to Petrograd and the reports from both Henderson and Price kept British socialists well informed about the consequences of the February revolution, the end of Tsarism and the inclusion of socialists in the Russian government.

For the British government, however, there were other concerns, most importantly the effect the war would have on Russian actions. On 11 May, the War Cabinet discussed a telegram from Petrograd from the British Consul at Odessa, and there was dismay at the 'deplorable lack of discipline in the Russian army stationed in the vicinity, and the very poor prospects of any offensive on the part of the Russian forces'.[39] There was also great discussion in the War Cabinet as to whether Henderson should replace Sir George Buchanan as ambassador. Buchanan's 'great services' to his country were recognised. His 'telegraphic appreciations of the situation' were 'nearly always proved right' and he played a 'very courageous part in circumstances of exceptional difficulty'. But now Henderson's colleagues 'generally agreed with the views placed before them by Lord Robert Cecil that, in existing conditions, he is no longer the ideal British representative in Petrograd'. Buchanan was seen as being too close to the old regime and the Cabinet feared that this 'may diminish the confidence in him of the present Russian Administration'.[40]

It was accepted that the British representative in Petrograd 'should be a person calculated to exercise a powerful influence on the democratic elements which now predominate in Russia to pursue the war with energy'. Henderson was therefore invited 'to make a personal sacrifice and to go to Petrograd on a similar footing to that of M. Albert Thomas'.[41] He was an interesting choice of representative as he had had no 'exposure to foreign negotiations'[42] and accounts of his experience of foreign affairs suggest that he was largely uninterested in them until the start of the war.[43]

According to F. M. Levanthal, Lloyd George chose Henderson either because he wanted to get him 'out of his hair' or because 'he believed a prominent British trade unionist would make a more suitable envoy to the socialist government than a more traditional diplomat like Buchanan who had long been associated with the Tsarist regime'.[44] J. M. Winter and Chris Wrigley assume that the second option was the real reason, and it is easy to see why: in revolutionary Russia, a pro-war Labour figure with no ties to Tsarism was in a better position to take the Allies' message to the radical Petrograd Soviet. The acting consul-general in Moscow, Robert Bruce Lockhart, agreed that replacing Buchanan with Henderson was the British government's desired outcome, but noted that once Henderson arrived in Russia, he realised that 'no good purpose would be served by the removal of a man who understood Russia far better than he did'.[45] According to Michael Hughes, Henderson 'quickly acknowledged that the traditional institutions of "Old Diplomacy" could not be so easily circumvented as he had once believed'.[46]

The other issue that determined Henderson's trip to Petrograd was the socialist conference in Stockholm that some left wingers wanted and that others argued forcefully against. The dual role he played as a British politician thus came to cause him some difficulty as he had to negotiate with his Cabinet colleagues and the labour movement over Stockholm. Lloyd George was not in favour of any such conference where belligerent socialists would fraternise with Allied socialists. Sections of the labour movement denounced the gathering to such an extent that the leader of the National Sailors' and Firemen's Union, Havelock Wilson, informed his members that they would not be working on any ship that sailed to Stockholm or Petrograd until the German government 'make restitution to the relatives of Allied and neutral seamen who have been murdered when endeavouring to escape from their sinking ships that were torpedoed by German submarines'.[47] Wilson need not have worried at this point, as the Labour Cabinet member was also against such a conference.

Arthur Henderson left for Petrograd on 23 May and reached Russia on 1 June. Apart from a brief stay in Moscow, his six weeks were spent in Petrograd, a city he did not like due to the chaos and lack of order.[48] He met with a number of leading figures including the head of the Provisional Government, Prince Georgiy L'vov, and the man who would soon succeed him, Aleksandr Kerenskiy. Kerenskiy's 'courage and capacity' impressed Henderson a great deal, although he was concerned that he was 'paralysed by a sentimental attachment to revolutionary ideas' which he was 'not quite strong enough to overcome'.[49] The journalist Harold Williams, 'whose knowledge of Russia is recognised as being exceptionally extensive and intimate', placed himself at Henderson's disposal, summarised the main newspapers for him and 'usually spent part of the day giving me information as to the latest events and movements of public opinion'.[50]

Henderson's report to the War Cabinet covered many issues including labour concerns and material efficiency. But it was the political situation, especially the growth of the revolutionary left and the war, which concerned him most. He spoke about both when he addressed the Petrograd Soviet and the Moscow Soldiers' Council as he tried to shore up support for the moderate government and for the war. In Moscow, he told delegates that he was 'anxious to see freedom' in all of the warring countries, that Britain would continue to 'defend her own freedom' and that in the post-war era both sides would need each other. Consequently, 'we must fight together'.[51]

Henderson realised that the government had an uncertain future. The unwillingness of employers to accept any form of state control concerned him as in Britain this had been 'essential for the successful prosecution of the war'. There was a lack of a 'steadying' influence 'akin to our Trade Unions' to moderate the 'outrageous' demands of the 'undisciplined' workers.[52] And the rising tide of extremism and the growth of the Bolsheviks worried him at a time when the 'Dualism of Government and Sovyet [sic]' coincided with the 'disintegration of the Russian State fabric'. This had been caused by a revolution following 'a long period of inept administration' and the two 'react on each other'. The government consisted 'broadly of Socialists who derive their mandate from the Sovyets [sic] and Liberals who derive theirs from the late Duma. On the whole the Liberals ... have the greater share of capacity, or at any rate experience, but they have no clear constituency to stand upon.'[53] Henderson found it difficult to explain how this situation worked in practice as it was far removed from the type of politics he was used to. In his mind, the government as a whole 'and the Liberal Ministers in particular are in practice responsible to no one; the Socialists are responsible to the Sovyet [sic]'.

> Day by day and night after night Skobeleff, Chernoff, Pieshekhanoff, Kerenski, Tsereteli had to justify themselves to a body which had no legal standing, was not representative of the nation, but which enjoyed unlimited moral authority over the populace of the capital. In June the All-Russia Congress of Sovyets began its sittings and the Socialist Ministers appeared before it to give an account of themselves and their policy, and to ask for help in carrying on the business of the State. When Kronstadt revolted the Government sent orders and the Sovyet sent delegates. Representatives of the Sovyet visit the armies to persuade the troops to obedience; they enforce with appeals and arguments the representations of the Government to Finland and the Ukraine. So far they have never used force, and the Government dare not, but in Petrograd their word is law.[54]

Like Price, Henderson concluded that the 'working classes may be divided into Socialists of the more moderate type, usually described in Russia as Menshevikis [sic] and Maximalists (extremists), generally known as Bolshevikis [sic]'. He had opportunities to ascertain the Moderates' views, but his 'knowledge of the views and tendencies of the Maximalists is mainly a matter of deduction from their published utterances and articles in their own Press.'[55] In his Appendix (B) he went into more detail about all of the main Russian parties, including the Kadets who were 'Radicals' with a 'broad social programme' and 'brilliant leaders' and who were 'Strongly pro-war and pro-Ally'. The Socialist Revolutionary Party was 'popular and very active' but was 'displaying a tendency to split into two factions mainly on the question of the war'. The pro-war section 'follows Kerenski', the 'extremist faction which plays fast and loose with the war question ... echoes the cries of the extremist Socialist Democrats'. And the *Trudoviki*, the moderate socialist 'Labour Group', of which Kerenskiy had been a member, was 'colourless' and would 'probably disappear.'[56]

Henderson noted that the Social Democrats (the Marxists) 'include a number of warring factions, some of them more bitterly at feud with each other than with the so-called bourgeois parties. The question of the war has made the grouping still more complicated. The main dividing line is between the Bolcheviki [sic] and Mensheviki [sic]'. The Bolsheviks were 'extremists' who demanded 'the immediate realisation of the maximum social democratic programme' while the 'Mensheviki [sic] are as Socialists evolutionary, and aim for the present only at the Socialist minimum. But factions and factions are now in a fluid state.'[57]

He noted that:

> Bolsheviki [sic] is now the synonym for the noisiest and most extreme wing of the Socialists. They are certainly the most active party. They opposed participation in the Coalition Government and now violently attack the Socialist Ministers. Recklessly anti-war, pro-German, and anti-Ally. The followers of Lenin are even more extreme, but the two tendencies shade off into each other imperceptibly. German agents and reactionaries work under the Bolshevik flag.

In the Petrograd Soviet, 'the Bolsheviki are numerically in a minority, but are influential through their energy'. The 'Mensheviki are split into two factions, internationalist pacificists [sic] and advocates of a war of defence. The Internationalists lean towards the Bolsheviki. Plechanov [sic], the leader and theoretician of the Mensheviks, is unpopular with Socialists owing to his ardent advocacy of the war, and his group stands rather apart from the rest.'[58]

Party politics aside, Russia's involvement in the war remained a constant concern and Henderson sought to maintain a Russian presence. He acknowledged that the new government had a difficult balancing act to maintain, advocating on the one hand the country's military defence and on the other a peaceful end to the war with no annexations or indemnities. Assessing the problems of the war after February, Henderson found similar things to Price but drew different conclusions. Whereas Price saw the anti-war mood in a positive light, while also being concerned for the Russian people, Henderson noted that there was 'much in Russia to-day which must fill a patriotic Russian with indignation and shame'. There were 'soldiers at the front debating whether they shall fight, soldiers in barracks debating whether they shall go to the front or allow the guns to go ... villages on the Volga levying toll on passing steamers ... the police disbanded ... workpeople stopping essential industries, and peasants concealing the food on which the life of the nation depends.' He concluded that these 'were not the hopes of the revolution'.[59]

Henderson was worried about Russia's anti-war mood and the Provisional Government's future. Put simply, the 'political stability of Russia' depended 'on the continued existence of the Provisional Government'.[60] He was certain that it was better to have a moderate and liberal Russia – albeit a weakened one – fighting with the Allies rather than a Russia led by the Bolsheviks. Therefore, there was 'nothing, short of compromising a material interest of our own or our Allies, that we ought not to do to sustain the credit of the Provisional Government'. However, it was 'not easy to help Russia because her chief trial to-day is anarchy, which no amount of foreign sympathy advice will mitigate or restrain'. Henderson identified the main problem as being the deep suspicion of England, which meant that:

> ... the most tactful offers of help may be distorted by extremists into demands for control, and used as counts in the agitation against the Government and the Allies. On the other hand, any appearance of coldness or neglect is at once seized upon by Bolsheviki to prove that Russia is being betrayed by her Allies, and by Nationalists to prove that the Allies have discovered that they are being betrayed by Russia.[61]

Henderson discussed the proposed Stockholm conference with the Menshevik leader of the Petrograd Soviet, Irakli Tsereteli. Henderson's views on this conference began to change here as Tsereteli 'showed little interest in a proposed Allied Socialist Conference in London' because his real interest was to have the Stockholm conference 'before the meeting of the Allied governments, in order to take some of the edge off the differences that separate the belligerents. This is in line with the whole policy of his group, which is to bring pressure from within to bear upon all governments the direction of a general renunciation of imperialist aims.'[62]

Henderson's views on the war and the Stockholm conference were altered by his time in Russia. Though he continued to believe that the new post-revolutionary governments – both the Provisional and the Soviet – should not take the country out of the war, he grew concerned with the post-war situation and the development of European democracy. His pamphlet in 1917, 'A World Safe for Democracy', made it clear that the Russian contribution was necessary for more than just allied victory. Though some allies may have judged the February revolution by its 'immediate effect upon Russian military strength', he argued that the important thing was that they did so 'from the point of view of its lasting and profound influence on the development of world democracy'.[63] And though some may have cared little about whether Russia was a democracy or an autocracy, viewing the revolution only through the 'prism of the country's immediate contribution to the war', the new Russia needed to be safeguarded, as a 'democracy at war, if convinced of the righteousness of the cause for which it was fighting, would be a more reliable and longer-staying partner'.[64]

Henderson concluded that in the interest of any future Anglo-Russian friendship and a peaceful world, 'we are bound to stand by [Russia] faithfully and generously till the end' although 'we should be wiser, if the war is to last beyond the coming autumn, not to reckon on her being able to give us sustained and effective support'.[65] Henderson assumed that the Russians would fight on, at least in the short term. They no longer had 'a national idol to fight for' and had 'not yet replaced it by a national ideal'. This helped some to realise that 'they must go on fighting while they can'.[66]

After he returned from Russia and left his Cabinet post,[67] Henderson discussed Russian matters with Lockhart who noted that his views on the situation 'were not very different from my own'. His mind had been changed regarding Stockholm and he was now 'entirely in favour of establishing contact with the Bolsheviks'.[68] Russia had encouraged Henderson to move with the new, more radical, times.

Price and Bolshevik power

From the summer onwards, Price's reports increasingly focused on the rise of the Bolsheviks. More garrison towns were turning towards Lenin's party in elections to local soviets, though this was not so much a political conversion to Marxism as the Bolsheviks were now the only ones untainted by support for the war. Recalling his journey through the provinces before October, Price noticed that 'every local Soviet had been captured by them'.[69] And the worsening material conditions and the deepening political crisis ultimately led to the end of Kerenskiy's government with the Bolshevik seizure of power in late October. Price claims that the government fell because it had no supporters. The 'bourgeois parties and the generals at the Staff disliked it because it would not establish a military democracy. The revolutionary democracy lost faith in it because after eight months it had neither given land to the peasants nor established State control of industries nor advanced the cause of the Russian peace programme.'[70]

The new political situation excited the former Liberal candidate. Price wrote that 'we are living under the iron heel of the proletariat. The navy is magnificently revolutionary and so is the army at the front. The workmen in the factories also are armed to the teeth. It is a splendid thing to be able to use the armed forces of the country against the landlords and the capitalists. That is what armaments are for!'[71]

However, in his reports after the Bolshevik revolution, Price combined his support for the new order with a quest for the truth, even if that highlighted problems with the new system. Towards the end of 1917, he reported from provincial Russia where the 'pinched faces and ragged clothes' of the peasants coming into Kazan from places such as Vladimir and Kostroma to buy flour 'told eloquently of the state to which the war has reduced these forest dwellers of North Russia'.[72] Having been removed from the boat he was on by 'revolutionary soldiers' who commandeered the second-class compartment, he settled down for the night with a group that included women from nearby towns returning from market, mechanics from cotton factories further up the Volga, a Tartar fisherman and 'an officer, the only member of the "intelligentsia" present'. They were all 'comrades in misfortune' and Price listened to their conversation as he tried, and failed, to sleep on this cold night.[73]

The discussions all concerned food. It was the 'essence of politics' that loomed 'larger even than the question of war and peace, for in international politics the stomach seems to be a more influential factor than the brain'. In a dramatic statement, Price declared that last year 'food, or rather the absence of it, made the Revolution; this year it seems to be on the verge of destroying it'.[74] He highlights the divisions that people felt existed in their day-to-day lives, as one peasant from Vladimir told the group that they were lucky 'down here in the south' as they were living 'in paradise … with your flour at 30 kopecks a pound and your eggs at 15 kopecks each. You come up north, my boys, and you'll find no honey there'.[75]

One of the mechanics claimed that there was plenty of corn but that it was being hidden in the villages as 'the speculators have got hold of it'. He said that it would be 'no good until they are searched and made to give it up'. A southern peasant woman said that they had just enough food for themselves but there was great concern that work and food could simply dry up in the forthcoming year. With no machines, horses or men, and with no food in the *ambar* (the public village granary) the woman said that 'we, too, shall see the kingdom of hunger'.[76]

Bolshevism may have succeeded politically in Petrograd, but socioeconomic problems remained throughout the country. Price commented that the traditional 'widespread and deep-seated' suspicion of governments still prevailed in the early Bolshevik era, and this contributed to the struggle that developed between the 'Bolshevik disciplinarians and intellectual Anarchist elements, supported by the small village proprietors and the food speculators, who gathered round the old Socialist Revolutionary Party'. He was uncritical of the fact that the proletarian dictatorship 'came gradually to rest upon a minority of the population' as this minority was 'the most intelligent, conscious and disciplined section' of the population.[77]

As the Soviet idea spread, Price said that this 'titanic work' was as yet only watched 'with sympathetic interest by the Western proletariat' but it was rousing a passionate longing 'in the hearts of those who live away from Moscow and to the south and east of the country'. He believed that the revolution would spread to areas of the world where 'native peoples were kept trapped and oppressed' and that the Bolshevik example would 'not pass unheeded' for those living 'under feudal agrarian castes backed by the navies, armies and finance of Western European capitalism'.[78]

Conclusion

One of the main differences between the Russian experiences of Morgan Philips Price and Arthur Henderson was the way that the events influenced them. Price's ideas were very much guided by his worry for Russia and its people, especially the poorer sections of society. His views were shaped by his own politics as well as his journalistic instincts that drove him to find 'the truth'. Arthur Henderson was guided by his official status as the British government's representative in Petrograd, his time in the War Cabinet, and his own left-liberal views. His primary concern was the ongoing war and how events in Petrograd and beyond would influence Russia's role in the conflict.

Both men had their politics changed by what they saw in Russia. Price moved away from his traditional liberalism towards revolutionary socialism. He became more sympathetic to Bolshevism and a staunch defender of the October Revolution. His reports combined a genuine concern for the Russian people with a profound interest in revolutionary ideas as a solution to the problems created by imperialism and militarism. Henderson's Russian experiences did not turn him so far leftwards, but his time in Petrograd and his discussions with leading moderate socialists helped him to understand revolutionary socialism and its consequences a little more. And it was this understanding that led him to redraft the Labour Party's constitution in 1918. It may be that, where Labour was concerned, the most immediate legacy of the Bolshevik Revolution was the adoption of the socialist Clause IV and an acceptance that Labour was a socialist party.[79] What this meant was, naturally, open to interpretation. Just as socialism in revolutionary Russia was influenced by liberal progressive, moderate and Marxist socialists, so too was Labour's ideology. And it was this that made Russia such a captivating country for Labour's supporters – it could be all things to all Labour people.

What was happening in Russia – especially from 1917 onwards – had a significant impact on Labour's politics and ideas.[80] And the reports of Price and Henderson on aspects of Russia's development contributed much to Labour's own understanding of different forms of socialism, and this was crucial at a time when its political identity was being defined by the consequences of the First World War and the Russian revolutions.

Notes

1 Kevin Morgan, *Bolshevism, Syndicalism and the General Strike: The Lost Internationalist World of A. A. Purcell* (London, 2013), p. 12. Also see his *Bolshevism and the British Left Part One: Labour Legends and Moscow Gold* (London, 2006) and *The Webbs and Soviet Communism* (London, 2006).
2 As well as Morgan's works on Labour's interaction with revolutionary Russia and the USSR, see Jonathan Davis, 'Left out in the Cold: British Labour Witnesses the Russian Revolution', *Revolutionary Russia*, 18:1 (2005), 71–87; Jonathan Davis, 'An Outsider Looks in: Walter Citrine's First Visit to the Soviet Union, 1925' *Revolutionary Russia*, 26:2 (2013), 147–63; Andrew Williams, *Labour and Russia: The Attitude of the Labour Party to the USSR 1924–1934* (Manchester, 1989).
3 Tania Rose (ed.), *Dispatches from the Revolution* (London, 1997), p. 4.

4 See for example Price's reports from Samara, 'Through the Russian Provinces: The Peasants and Their Land Programmes', *Manchester Guardian*, 4 December 1917 and 'Through the Russian Provinces: How the Peasants Are Taking Over the Land', *Manchester Guardian*, 5 December 1917.
5 Jonathan D. Smele, '"What the Papers Didn't Say": Unpublished Despatches from Russia by M. Philips Price, May 1918 to January 1919', *Revolutionary Russia*, 8:2 (1995), 129–65, 130.
6 Smele, '"What the Papers Didn't Say"', p. 131.
7 Morgan Philips Price, *My Reminiscences of the Russian Revolution* (London, 1921), n.p., preface.
8 Price, *My Reminiscences*, p. 7.
9 Smele, '"What the Papers Didn't Say"', p. 131.
10 Jay M. Winter, 'Arthur Henderson, the Russian Revolution and the Reconstruction of the Labour Party', *Historical Journal*, 15 (1972), 753–73, 754.
11 F. M. Leventhal, *Arthur Henderson* (Manchester, 1989), p. 50.
12 Morgan Philips Price, *War and Revolution in Asiatic Russia* (London, 1918), p. 271.
13 Morgan Philips Price, *My Three Revolutions* (London, 1969), p. 37.
14 Price, *War and Revolution*, p. 271. Also see Price, 'The Russian Campaign in Asia', *Manchester Guardian*, 24 February 1916.
15 Price, *War and Revolution*, p. 270.
16 Price, *War and Revolution*, p. 270.
17 Price, *War and Revolution*, p. 270.
18 Price, 'Memorandum to C. P. Trevelyan', Tiflis, 30 March 1916, in Rose, *Dispatches*, pp. 18–19.
19 Price, 'Memorandum to C. P. Trevelyan', p. 19.
20 Price, 'Memorandum to C. P. Trevelyan', p. 19.
21 Price, 'Memorandum to C. P. Trevelyan', p. 19.
22 Price, *War and Revolution*, p. 271.
23 Price, *War and Revolution*, p. 272.
24 Price, *War and Revolution*, p. 274.
25 Price, *War and Revolution*, p. 274.
26 Price, 'Memorandum to F. W. Hirst' Kharkov, 30 November 1916, in Rose, *Dispatches*, p. 22.
27 Price, 'Memorandum to F. W. Hirst' Tiflis, 9 December 1916, in Rose, *Dispatches*, p. 24.
28 Letter to Anna Maria Philips, 1 February 1917, in Rose, *Dispatches*, p. 27.
29 Price, *Reminiscences*, p. 11.
30 Price, *Reminiscences*, p. 11. For a description of the upheaval in the Caucasus, see Price 'How the Revolution Came to the Caucasus', *Manchester Guardian*, 27 April 1917.
31 Price, *Reminiscences*, p. 12.
32 Price, *Reminiscences*, pp. 12–13.
33 Price, *Reminiscences*.
34 Price, *Reminiscences*, pp. 13–14.
35 *Manchester Guardian*, 17 July 1917.
36 *Labour Leader*, 22 March 1917.
37 *Labour Leader*, 22 March 1917.

38 For more on these meetings, see Ian Bullock, *Romancing the Revolution: The Myth of Soviet Democracy and the British Left* (Edmonton, 2011), ch. 2; Jonathan Davis, 'A New Socialist Influence: British Labour and Revolutionary Russia, 1917–1918', *Scottish Labour History*, 48 (2013), pp. 158–79.
39 National Archives (from here NA) War Cabinet 136, 11 May 1917.
40 NA, CAB 23/2, War Cabinet 144, 23 May 1917.
41 NA, CAB 23/2, War Cabinet 144, 23 May 1917. Thomas was a French socialist Minister of Munitions who was sent to Petrograd as a special ambassador in order to encourage the Russians not to pull out of the war.
42 Leventhal, *Arthur Henderson*, p. 64.
43 Henry Ralph Winkler, *British Labour Seeks a Foreign Policy* (New Brunswick, 2005), p. 29.
44 Leventhal, *Arthur Henderson*, p. 64. Winter, 'Arthur Henderson' p. 759; Chris Wrigley, *Arthur Henderson* (Cardiff, 1990), p. 114.
45 R. H. Bruce Lockhart, *Memoirs of a British Agent* (London, 1935), p. 187.
46 Michael Hughes, *Inside the Enigma: British Officials in Russia, 1900–1939* (London, 1997), p. 98.
47 Reuters Correspondent, 'Seamen's Message to Russia', *Manchester Guardian*, 7 June 1917. For a full discussion on Stockholm, see David Kirby, 'International Socialism and the Question of Peace: The Stockholm Conference of 1917', *The Historical Journal*, 25:3 (1982) pp. 709–16.
48 Hughes, *Enigma*, p. 99.
49 NA, CAB 24/4, Arthur Henderson, 'British Mission to Russia June and July 1917', 16 July 1917, p. 9.
50 NA, CAB 24/4, Arthur Henderson, 'British Mission to Russia', p. 1.
51 Reuters, 'Mr Henderson addresses Moscow Council', *Observer*, 1 July 1917.
52 Cited in Leventhal, *Arthur Henderson*, p. 65.
53 NA, CAB 24/4, Arthur Henderson, 'British Mission', p. 6.
54 NA, CAB 24/4, Arthur Henderson, 'British Mission', pp. 6–7.
55 NA, CAB 24/4, Arthur Henderson, 'British Mission', p. 1.
56 NA, CAB 24/4, Arthur Henderson, 'British Mission', pp. 11–12.
57 NA, CAB 24/4, Arthur Henderson, 'British Mission', p. 15.
58 NA, CAB 24/4, Arthur Henderson, 'British Mission', p. 15.
59 NA, CAB 24/4, Arthur Henderson, 'British Mission', p. 9.
60 NA, CAB 24/4, Arthur Henderson, 'British Mission', p. 10.
61 NA, CAB 24/4, Arthur Henderson, 'British Mission', p. 10.
62 NA, CAB 24/4, Arthur Henderson, 'British Mission', p. 12.
63 A. Henderson, 'A World Safe for Democracy', in F. Bealey (ed.), *The Social and Political Thought of the British Labour Party* (London, 1970), pp. 86–7, 87.
64 Henderson, 'A World Safe for Democracy', p. 87.
65 NA, CAB 24/4, Arthur Henderson, 'British Mission', p. 12.
66 NA, CAB 24/4, Arthur Henderson, 'British Mission', p. 12.
67 For details, see NA, CAB 23/3, War Cabinet, 212, 11 August 1917.
68 Lockhart, *Memoirs*, p. 198.
69 Morgan Philips Price, 'Bolshevik Ascendency: Causes of Kerensky's Downfall', *Manchester Guardian*, 20 November 1917.
70 Price, 'Bolshevik Ascendency'.

71 Price, 'Letter to C. Lee Williams', Petrograd, 30 November 1917, in Rose, *Dispatches*, p. 103.
72 'The Voice of the Russian People on the Revolution', *Manchester Guardian*, 7 December 1917.
73 'The Voice of the Russian People'.
74 'The Voice of the Russian People'.
75 'The Voice of the Russian People'.
76 'The Voice of the Russian People'.
77 Price, *Reminiscences*, p. 379.
78 Price, *Reminiscences*, p. 388.
79 For further discussion on Clause Four, see Davis, 'A New Socialist Influence', pp. 170–2.
80 For more on the Soviet influence on Labour's ideology, see Jonathan Davis, 'Labour's Political Thought: The Soviet Influence in the Interwar Years', in Paul Corthorn and Jonathan Davis (eds), *The British Labour Party and the Wider World* (London, 2008), pp. 64–85.

12

The Stanford connection: David Starr Jordan, eugenics and the Anglo-American anti-war movement

Gavin Baird and Bradley W. Hart

As Europe descended into the abyss of war in the late summer of 1914, one of the world's best-known peace advocates was visiting the genteel surroundings of Cambridge University. Shocked by the rapid escalation of violence and realising that his life's mission of preventing young men from being sent to die on the battlefield had failed, this high-profile academic bemoaned that the mere 'incident' of Franz Ferdinand's assassination had allowed 'appeals to greed, patriotism, and revenge' to capture the European imagination and prevented a diplomatic solution from being reached.[1] As the war unfolded over the coming weeks, this American, like thousands of others, found himself trapped in London due to restrictions on travel.

Despite the extensive political connections he enjoyed in Britain, this peacemonger by his own admission knew little about British politics. What he did know was that Britain's Labour and Liberal politicians – with the notable exception of David Lloyd George – seemed to be more closely aligned to his views on the conflict than their Conservative counterparts and that these links should be cultivated. Over the next four years of war he would therefore utilise these connections in an effort to convince his fellow Americans that their country should act as an impartial arbiter to bring the war to an early end, while at the same time avoiding direct military involvement that would involve sending their own young men to die in European trenches. As such, pacifism could be a truly transnational Anglo-American phenomenon as much as it was embedded in the politics of each country.

The reason somewhat marginal figures on the British left were able to exact such influence in the USA was in large part because of the prominence of the man who found himself stranded in London during the early months of the war. He was David Starr Jordan, the chancellor of

Stanford University and an internationally renowned authority on matters of war and peace. Since the Spanish-American War of the late nineteenth century Jordan had turned from academic pursuits to increasingly virulent anti-war rhetoric. The nearer global war came, the more vital such activity would appear. Indeed, in 1914 he had only recently completed a European tour that included an extended visit to the Balkans, positioning him as an authority on the unfolding conflict (in his own mind, at least). Moreover, as this chapter makes clear, Jordan enjoyed extensive connections on the British left, becoming a close confidant of Norman Angell and gaining introductions to other members of the Labour and Liberal left as a result. He was also close friends with future US President Herbert Hoover, a Stanford graduate who would go on to arrange relief for nearly 200,000 Americans who found themselves stranded in London at the start of the war and, later, millions of Europeans facing starvation at the end of the conflict.

Crucially for the purposes of this volume, Jordan utilised his extensive contacts on the British left to advance his arguments against American military intervention in the conflict until it eventually came in 1917. Over the course of the conflict, he maintained correspondence with key anti-war voices in the Labour Party, particularly those associated with the UDC. While the UDC, formed in 1914 to oppose the influence of the military in the British government, harnessed the support of politicians such as Ramsay MacDonald and Frederick Pethick-Lawrence, along with commentators such as H. N. Brailsford, it was Jordan and similar voices that helped spread their gospel over the Atlantic. Several UDC-supporting figures would travel to the USA to speak out against the conflict, including at the intervention of Jordan, thus interjecting their views into the American political discourse. These voices were eventually drowned out by the drumbeat of war, but it is instructive that Jordan believed their contributions were significant enough to entice them to undertake the potentially-treacherous journey to California in the midst of the war and risk the potential consequences of speaking out against the conflict.

This chapter considers the relationship between Jordan and the Labour anti-war left during the First World War while at the same time considering the impact this relationship had on American politics. In doing so, it helps contextualise other articles within the present volume – for the debates outlined elsewhere in these pages had consequences outside the British Isles. Though academics such as David S. Patterson have begun to explore the connections outlined in what follows, more work could be done to illuminate this important story.[2] Although national circumstances could differ, opponents to intervention in the First World War were often united in tactics, rhetoric and, indeed, personnel. The fact that the First World War began, as Adam Tooze has recently illustrated, the start of American global dominance (eclipsing, in part, the British) lends this story a further important backdrop.³ Further, Jordan's interest in using the principles of the eugenics movement to justify his anti-war stances lends new evidence to the arguments advanced by David Redvaldsen about the appeal of biological determinist ideas to the political left.⁴ Jordan not only provides an intriguing example of how anti-war activism could spring from a variety of intellectual sources but also demonstrates how the eugenics movement itself was increasingly influenced by a range of emerging ideas in the early twentieth century.

To tease out this story, in the first section Jordan's early career and time as the president of Stanford University will be examined to establish his significance as an international expert on matters of war and peace, as well as outline his early brushes with controversy. In the second section, Jordan's relationship with Labour and Liberal politicians will be considered, and in the third section the arguments of his 1915 book *War and the Breed*, which argued for pacifism on a eugenic and biological basis, will be recapitulated. In short, while Jordan is today a generally forgotten figure beyond the confines of Stanford University, in his own time he was one of the world's most famous intellectuals and his relationship with both American and British political figures is therefore worth examining. Fundamentally, this was a well-connected man whispering in some influential ears.

The rise of David Starr Jordan

To understand David Starr Jordan's war we must first analyse his background. Certainly, his academic career was marked by exceptional success from the beginning. He began collegiate life as a botany student at Cornell University in New York state in 1869 and quickly became known for his work ethic and intellectual curiosity. His work was so highly thought of that he became 'an instructor his junior year' and graduated in four years with a master's degree in place of the traditional BA because the faculty purportedly felt that his work deserved a higher degree than that received by his classmates.⁵ Jordan then entered academia and became a professor of natural science at Lombard University in Galesburg, Illinois. After several moves (and further professorships in both biology and subsequently natural history), he rose to become president of Indiana University in 1885.

At the time of Jordan's appointment, Indiana University was one of the least progressive and most poorly-equipped universities in the state. Most of the university's students were in the 'preparatory department,' which served as a high school for the city of Bloomington. Nearby religious universities persuaded state legislators to withdraw funding from the 'godless institution' while many citizens saw the state university as an 'expensive luxury' that could easily be discarded.⁶ Jordan was subsequently able to change the nature and reputation of the university by enticing alumni to donate, giving undergraduates more course flexibility and disbanding the preparatory department entirely. These executive decisions led to the university doubling in size and attracting faculty that enjoyed the academic atmosphere of Jordan's institution. While Jordan enjoyed remarkable professional success as president of Indiana University, his time there was marred by personal loss. In 1885, he suffered the death of his wife, and a year later his youngest daughter. He remarried in 1888 but shortly thereafter lost his father. These personal losses, coupled with his simultaneous administrative successes, would colour Jordan's future academic career and his international anti-war advocacy.

In March 1891, railroad magnate and progressive Republican politician Leland Stanford (California's first Republican governor in the 1860s and later US Senator for the state) and his wife Jane paid Jordan a visit to Bloomington, Indiana. They had come to offer Jordan the presidency of Leland Stanford Jr. University, a new institution that would open its doors later that year. Stanford University, as it would become widely known, was effectively the Stanfords' living memorial to their son (who had died at just fifteen of typhoid) and the recipient of a sizable portion of their wealth. Enticed by the promise of academic openness and the reasonable expectation of a generous endowment, Jordan accepted the position and moved to the sleepy enclave of Palo Alto, California.

The new institution was bedevilled by both financial and intellectual difficulties. The former saw Jordan having to be adroit in raising funds but it was arguably the latter that posed greater difficulty. This became evident in 1893 when Jordan hired Edward A. Ross as a professor of economic theory and finance. Jordan held Ross in the highest personal regard, describing him as 'one of the ablest, most virile and clear classroom lecturers' that he had ever seen.[7] But with this academic fervour came a political and economic outspokenness that made Ross notorious in Republican political circles. Once at Stanford, he furthered his ardent reputation by speaking to audiences about his political views. Following a series of articles in which Ross echoed the views of Democratic presidential candidate William Jennings Bryan by advocating the free coinage of silver, Jane Stanford claimed that the professor was 'erratic and unsound'.[8] She met with Jordan and demanded that he resign if he continued to defy the university's stated policy of political and confessional neutrality.

In order to appease Stanford while keeping Ross on faculty, Jordan advised that he step down from his position as a professor of economic theory and finance and accept an appointment as a professor of sociology. Ross accepted the compromise, and from August 1897 to the end of the century he kept a low political profile.[9] In May 1900 this changed when he put himself in the spotlight again by delivering a high profile anti-immigration speech in San Francisco. Addressing this working-class audience with a heavy-handed condemnation of unrestricted immigration from Asia, he impoliticly declared that 'it would be better for us to turn our guns on every vessel bringing Japanese to our shores rather than to permit them to land'.[10] When Stanford read the quote in the *San Francisco Call* the next day she was furious and demanded again that he be dismissed from the university. This placed Jordan in another predicament as, on the one hand, firing Ross would be a clear violation of his academic freedom. On the other hand, his refusal to dismiss Ross would undoubtedly anger Stanford and potentially put the university's livelihood in jeopardy. Academia and politics had intersected, and not for the last time in Jordan's life.

After some back and forth, Ross eventually tendered his resignation, causing a temporary storm in the press. But the Ross affair held wider significance for two reasons. First, it illustrated the intellectual climate that Jordan had cultivated in his years as Stanford's leader. Rather than encouraging its academics to take a leading role in public debates relevant to the day – the gold standard/silver standard debate was the most significant issue of the 1896 election – Jane Stanford continued to insist on the university's apolitical orientation, even when it meant muzzling a professor whose public utterances reflected nothing more radical than a view held by much of the country. Jordan would later tread carefully in his own political activities even after Jane Stanford's death, frequently cloaking his views in the guise of pure academic inquiry rather than political opinion, as he would with his later anti-war advocacy.

Second, the Ross affair illustrated a less-than-appealing aspect of Jordan's personality that would increasingly assert itself in his later years. This was his personal arrogance, coupled with his insistence that his views were always correct. Just as he had concluded that his only mistake in the Ross affair had been to not act quickly enough (stating he should have fired him 'when [Ross] first became troublesome'), he would later insist that his views towards war were motivated only by personal benevolence and the objective lessons of science. His early intellectual curiosity had to some degree been superseded by the arrogance of certainty: henceforth, he would tend to believe he was right, and the only necessary inquiry was to muster the best evidence to prove the correctness of his views.

To his credit, Jordan was prepared to travel to broaden his mind during this early period. His academic profile gave him a platform that saw invitations for him to explore the globe, including, most notably, a visit to Berlin. Importantly, such knowledge would inform his later advocacy. When debating the merits of whether Britain could have stayed out of the war in 1914, he would go on to write that '[Foreign Secretary] Grey's failure seemed to me to rest not in intrigue – of which he has been more or less unjustly accused – but in lack of knowledge concerning the temper of continental Europe.'[11] Jordan would not lack such experience, as we will see.

Perhaps understandably given his ability to court controversy, in 1913 Stanford University's board of trustees, now led by alumnus and future US President Herbert Hoover, appointed Jordan to the newly-created position of chancellor. This role was created in order for Jordan to continue to have an influence on university affairs but less executive power. Jordan accepted the position and was replaced as president by John Caspar Banner, a professor of geology and fifteen-year vice president of the university. The next several years brought about drastic changes to the university, many of which Jordan fought against fervently. By way of example, mandatory military training during the First World War, the creation of a structured general education programme and the requirement of students to pay tuition were all causes that Jordan opposed, but to no avail. He had other battles to fight.

A global peacemonger

Jordan's anti-war advocacy began during his presidency of Stanford and extended well beyond its end. Although as a university president he had voiced more of a concern with student safety than global security, things began to change with the outbreak of the Spanish–American War. As the conflict began to escalate in late April 1898, Jordan conversed with a group of faculty members who expressed their concerns about the American war effort and the McKinley administration's intentions. Several professors expressed a belief that the war was being pursued for the profit of American companies.[12] Jordan found this argument so convincing that he became an anti-war advocate nearly on the spot, and would publically express his newfound beliefs only days later.

On 2 May 1898, Jordan was slated to give an open lecture on the importance of higher education. One day prior to the event, Commodore George Dewey led the USA to a decisive victory over the Spanish in the Battle of Manila Bay. After receiving news of the battle, Jordan changed the subject of his lecture to focus on the war.[13] The next day he abruptly announced to the audience that he would be speaking on the war effort, which led to a resounding round of applause. The speech that followed was an impassioned jeremiad on the future of the American military. In it, Jordan proclaimed that the USA was at a turning point as a global force and that it could either maintain its legacy of promoting friendships and emphasising domestic progress or choose a path of empire and pay the monetary and costs of militarism and democratic destruction. Knowing that the USA was likely to secure a victory, he called for the USA to pull out of Cuba and the Philippines after the Spanish were defeated in order to demonstrate that the war was fought for mercy rather than conquest.[14] The Stanford chancellor concluded his lecture by warning the audience of the USA's potential to become an imperialist power resembling Britain, which he argued was a state that was occupied in 'imposing her rules upon sullen peoples' and making everyone suffer as a result.[15] Jordan's 2 May lecture proved to be an emphatic break from his previous quiescence on current affairs, and he became known increasingly for his anti-war efforts following the Spanish–American War.

From 1898 to 1914, Jordan became increasingly involved with a wide variety of foundations and organisations designed to promote world peace and anti-colonialism. In 1898 he became a founding member of the Anti-Imperialist League, which was led by a board that included the likes of former president Grover Cleveland. The league attempted to assert its influence in domestic politics by meeting with noted statesmen including William Jennings Bryan in an effort to convince him to focus his efforts on ending imperialism rather than advocating free silver. Jordan's anti-war activism gained truly international recognition once he became the chief director of the World Peace Foundation in 1909.[16] As its head he presented a series of lectures about the views of Benjamin Franklin and the biological costs of war. He gave sixty pro-peace lectures in Japan and five in Korea in an effort to further the East Asian peace effort in 1911. Between the Spanish–American War and the Great War in Europe, Jordan became the world's best-known peace advocate and used this platform to further both his anti-war and eugenicist views.

In this new role as an international expert and speaker on the consequences of war, Jordan embarked on an extended tour of Europe in the months before the outbreak of war. Traveling across the continent, Jordan visited a range of local dignitaries and 'investigated' local conditions that might lead to future conflict. He took a particular interest in the Balkans, which had been the scene of ethnic unrest for years and would soon become the tinderbox that sparked the First World War. Many of his travels were undertaken with British writer and anti-war advocate Norman Angell, who invited him in 1914 to speak to a summer school of 'younger English pacifists' in Buckinghamshire. There Jordan delivered an address concerning his views on the Balkan situation (briefly meeting G. K. Chesterton in the process, who he described as 'an adroit and versatile maker of paradoxes ... hating the Prussians in order to admire them and at times admiring them in order to hate them') before embarking on a visit to Ireland.[17]

As mentioned, Jordan and his wife were visiting Cambridge when the first European declarations of war were made. As he recalled in his memoirs, Jordan believed that the war had been primarily brought about by German arrogance and aggression, coupled with the inability of European governments to restrain their own worst impulses. 'That the ministries of Germany and Great Britain alike hoped to avoid war may well be believed,' he argued. 'Yet the final decision lay not with diplomatists or people, but with a weak egotist [the Kaiser] vacillating between rashness and cowardice, obsessed by love of military display.'[18] After Britain's entry into the conflict, the ship on which the Jordans had booked return passage home was pressed into government service and as a result they were unable to return to the USA until September. Over the course of his forced residence in London, Jordan joined the National Liberal Club ('as a means of studying the Public Opinion of the Nation') and further cultivated his network of British contacts.[19]

Perhaps he took comfort in such elite level conversations because the reaction of the British masses had proven more troublesome to him. Indeed, Jordan was demonstrably shocked by the shift in opinion he had observed in Britain in the early weeks of the war. As he later recalled, 'general public opinion in England had long been resolutely set against war … but with the invasion of Belgium feeling changed, overnight as it were.'[20] Two days before the British declaration of war the Liberal trade unionist John Burns had resigned from the cabinet in protest, claiming he would 'take no part in any war, for any purpose.'[21] Burns and Jordan would continue to talk about how the horrors of mass bloodshed could be avoided in the early weeks of the war, but with no practical consequence.

Given Jordan's long-standing peace advocacy and scepticism towards colonialism, his contacts in London tended to come from the Labour and Liberal sides of the political spectrum. He remained close with Angell and was evidently present when he told a gathering of pacifists at Salisbury House that the outbreak of war meant 'we were not successful – we were merely right.'[22] Jordan's connection with Angell gave him access to a wide spectrum of the anti-war left as well. During a visit to Cambridge, Jordan stopped at the home of left-wing author Henry Noel Brailsford, who he found to be 'personally a very interesting man' who possessed 'an unrivaled acquaintance with the world politics of Europe, on which he is one of the most voluminous as well as most consistent and accurate writers.'[23] Introduced to Labour Party leader and future Prime Minister Ramsay MacDonald, Jordan felt him to be 'a man of keen mind, broad education, and thorough understanding of political affairs' who was also 'an uncompromising foe of war and its adjunct, secret diplomacy, the seamy side of which he has rigorously unveiled.'[24] Certainly MacDonald's opposition to the war against the voices of many in his party rendered the link a fruitful one, but Jordan was most impressed with Ethel Snowden, the wife of future Chancellor of the Exchequer Philip Snowden, who he described in his memoirs as 'one of the most eloquent and attractive women in the range of my acquaintance' (in contrast, her rather more dour husband was not mentioned on his own in Jordan's memoirs at all).[25]

At the same time, Jordan admitted that he possessed almost no knowledge of the Conservative Party and seems to have had almost no contact with Tory politicians. The one partial exception was an encounter with future Conservative Prime Minister Winston Churchill, who was then going through his phase as a Liberal. Jordan's view of the future PM was withering: Churchill was, he wrote, 'a brilliant, irresponsible boy, speaking on each side of most questions with equal cheerfulness, and as administrator reckless in his waste of men and money'. With rumours circulating that Churchill might shortly return to the Conservative Party, Jordan reported one 'indignant Conservative' told him that 'no one can "rat" twice!', perhaps deliberately echoing Churchill's famously similar assessment of the situation (he would indeed return to the Conservative Party in 1924).[26] Jordan was also unimpressed with Churchill's views on the unfolding conflict, claiming that 'when the war was young and relatively popular, Winston Churchill was reported to claim it as his war'.[27] The horrors of Gallipoli would only give extra weight to such concerns.

Finally returning to the USA in September, Jordan embarked on a speaking tour of the country and gave more than seventy speeches 'in opposition to war and the war system' while simultaneously publishing articles opposing American involvement in the conflict.[28] The war had been caused, he told muckraking journalist Ida Tarbell, by 'the infamous philosophy of Pan-Germanism'. 'The Great War would never have come about, Kaiser or no Kaiser, if we had not to deal with a great nation gone wild with an obsession. While the Imperialism of England is rapidly dying away, that of Germany has taken a most acute form,' he told her.[29] In late 1914, Jordan was present in San Francisco at a meeting of the American Peace Society, which passed a resolution calling for neutral American mediation between the Allies and Central Powers. Given his international reputation, Jordan was nominated to present the resolution directly to President Wilson. On 12 November, he was welcomed to the White House along with fellow peace activist Louis Lochner, prepared, in the words of one historian, to speak to the president 'as one former college president to another'. While the president listened to the two men's arguments, he made no commitment to the idea of the USA calling for peace talks between the belligerents. The president's worry was that the allies might resent American intervention in the conflict and, even worse, American proposals might simply be outvoted in a multi-national conference setting. While Jordan was optimistic that the president could be convinced to embrace the peace movement's position, his intervention had in fact had little effect.[30]

As the war dragged on, however, Jordan began to re-evaluate his view of the conflict's origins. Instead of primarily blaming the Kaiser and German aggression for the outbreak of war, he now began to cast opprobrium on the British. In 1917, he denounced:

> the influence of Northcliffe, Curzon, Milner and Carson, the Prussians of England ... It is this Prussian group of England with which the Tories of America are so eager to ally themselves, today. For the world struggle is not between British and Germans, between armies and armies. It is between privilege on the one hand, money aristocracy, the conscious 'highbrows' in universities and churches, the democracy of the world. Woe to our Republic if we ally ourselves with the wrong side. And the wrong side is the one to looks to Victory without Peace, to glory or to money, to war for war's sake, whatever the gloss of superstition or patriotism that may be thrown over it.[31]

Even David Lloyd George, whom Jordan had found to be 'warm-hearted' and 'eloquent' though lacking 'both principle and foresight' back in 1913, increasingly became a target for his ire. Convinced that Lloyd George's Coalition Cabinet was packed with 'reactionaries' intent on continuing the war for their own interests, Jordan claimed that 'in every government by coalition the more violent members tend to overrule the others. They are like spoiled children demanding to be appeased. And while the German ministry has purged itself of its ultra-Tory elements, the like have entered and dominated the once liberal ministry of Great Britain.'[32] Even with Labour's Arthur Henderson in the Cabinet from 1915, this had a ring of truth. Indeed, the notion that the British would need a positive platform in order to keep men fighting was one that would only increase as the war dragged on, eventually culminating in Lloyd George's January 1918 publication of the country's 'war aims.'

In any case, Jordan's increasing scepticism towards the British government and the British interpretation of the conflict carried real consequences. Jordan was, after all, associated with a major university and one of America's most prominent peace activists. His arguments against the British were soon bolstered by the anti-war contacts he had cultivated in London during the early days of the war. In 1915, he invited Ethel Snowden to California to deliver a series of speeches 'against the theory and practice of war', including one at Stanford, and he later extended an invitation to women's rights campaigner Emmeline Pethick-Lawrence, the wife of future Labour MP and anti-war activist Frederick Pethick-Lawrence.[33] Both women made a series of public appearances that were evidently well received. Anti-war Labour politicians – and their wives – were therefore a key aspect of Jordan's campaign to bring the war to a peaceful end and prevent American intervention in the conflict. As the belligerent nations showed no sign of ceasing hostilities, however, Jordan realised that preventing American intervention would require more than lectures and speaking tours. He soon embarked on a publishing project that would become perhaps his most notorious work.

War and eugenics

In 1915, David Starr Jordan fully transitioned from being a university chancellor who made occasional anti-war lectures to a published author who combined his interest in human biology with his passion for peace. As the First World War entered into its most violent chapters, Jordan published *War and the Breed*, a lengthy book examining the effect of warfare on human biology, specifically the prospect of evolutionary degradation within the human race. No doubt remembering the apparent lesson of the Ross affair, Jordan attempted to use his academic standing and acknowledged expertise as a biologist to present arguments that he believed could not be easily discounted by critics or lead to the accusation that he was vacillating in his views. *War and the Breed* was intended to be an unassailable scientific account of how warfare was simply bad for humanity.

Jordan found intellectual inspiration for his arguments in the international eugenics movement, factions of which had previously argued that warfare generally had positive effects on human biology by killing off large numbers of 'the weak'. This had become a controversial view since the outbreak of war, however, not least because it very much appeared that many of Britain's 'best' from Eton, Oxford and Cambridge were dying on the battlefield in astonishing and disproportionate numbers. The mainstream of Britain's eugenics movement would eventually abandon the idea that warfare was biologically beneficial, but only after the war's costs had become clear.[34] Jordan had long been associated with international eugenics in both the USA and Britain, speaking before interested groups in both countries and lending his scientific reputation to the furtherance of eugenic causes. In 1913, he had been invited to speak before a gathering of the Eugenics Society in London on the soon-to-be-apropos topic of 'War and manhood', but found the audience to be 'ultraconservative' and inclined to think that war was 'a national blessing, however trying to individual men'. Jordan's subsequent speech denouncing this very idea evidently came to an awkward end when the eugenicist who had been given the task of officially thanking Jordan for his address told the audience that 'the address did not prove to be what he had expected' and complimented Jordan's 'range of information' and 'volubility' rather than the contents of the speech.[35]

Jordan's contention that warfare was actually unhelpful to human biological progress ('dysgenic', to use the parlance of the period) was the basis of *War and the Breed*. Jordan opened the work by stating its purpose, which was to study the war system and demonstrate its effect on the human race and racial development. According to Jordan, the war would inevitably leave every nation exhausted and humiliated as millions wondered why this effort was pursued with such blind ignorance. As a result, the human race would become 'less courageous, less wise, and feebler in the body and spirit than they were before this terrible and senseless sacrifice'.[36] He then drew from Darwinian evolutionary theory to argue that war removes the best and brightest people from their societies, leaving the later repopulation effort up to those who were unfit for battle or too cowardly to serve. The resulting generation would thus be substantially weaker than its predecessor, and this phenomenon would only intensify as the ferocity of military action increased.

Before we consider this argument, it should be noted that Jordan's views would not necessarily have alienated him from the British left. A cursory glance at supporters for the wider eugenics movement in the first half of the twentieth century shows it included not only scientists like Francis Galton, but also names latterly associated with the 'progressive' wing of British politics: Beatrice and Sidney Webb, John Maynard Keynes, Harold Laski – as well as publications such as the *Manchester Guardian* and the *New Statesman*. Pro-eugenics arguments *could* alienate those associated with the Catholic Church or the merely sceptical, but there was no guarantee of this. The increased left-wing veneration for the planned society could often incorporate, rather than exclude, a pseudo-scientific approach to population policy.

In this case, Jordan justified his hypothesis using the field of study that he knew best: organic evolution. He defined evolution as a study of the orderly changes that take place between generations, stating that evolution is like a river 'throwing off races and species as it flows' through the process of natural selection.[37] According to Jordan, there were four factors that led to evolution: variation, heredity, selection and segregation. What Jordan feared most was that the war effort would lead to a 'reversal of selection' in which the organisms that are best fitted to survive are destroyed while inferior types are the only ones remaining that are able to reproduce the species. In other words, war could have only dysgenic consequences; there was no chance of the species experiencing biological improvement. As with many eugenicists of the period, there was an element of racism in all this. While Jordan argued that equality of opportunity and impartiality under the law should always be maintained, he stated that 'there will always be differences of attainment' between races based purely on their biological differences.[38] In his mind, the highest potential had been reached by the 'blonde races' of Europe. This made the First World War even more tragic since it was primarily Europeans who were being killed. The conflict could therefore become an evolutionary disaster for all humankind.[39]

Jordan then turned his sights to militarism and war selection in Western Europe in order to demonstrate the damaging setbacks that the 'blonde, blue eyed' European societies were supposedly experiencing. Using one belligerent power as a case study, he proclaimed that 'Europe had no finer stock than that of France, and no modern people has suffered from the ravages of war and glory.'[40] Despite the costly blunders of imperial France in previous decades, Jordan argued that a 'good stock' allows for racial recuperation, which he argued had happened to the French people over the twenty years before the war. This refortification of the good stock had been the result of peace, coupled with economic and industrial advancement. At the same time, however, he argued that France was still biologically recovering from the many conscriptions and the large-scale bloodshed of the Napoleonic era.

Jordan then turned to the question of whether human nature can in fact change to prevent wars from breaking out in the first place. Here he argued that 'human instincts change very slowly, and by the long process of selection and adaptation.'[41] At the same time, Jordan noted that human customs are formed rapidly through the influence of association. Going further, Jordan stated that if a nation makes peace a custom that the instincts of its population will eventually change in favour of pacifism. Once one country adopts this firm stance in opposition to war, he argued, other states will follow, and widespread conflict would become a thing of the past. 'When men come to see nakedly what their wicked institutions mean, they will no longer live and die to maintain them', he wrote.[42]

Jordan concluded *War and the Breed* by issuing grim predictions for the First World War. The conflict would only end, he argued, when its combatants had reached a potent combination of exhaustion, starvation, sorrow, mourning and, ultimately, bankruptcy. There would be no sweeping victory for any power. Since neither Germany nor the Allies had made any significant strides in the war, there could be no sense of real victory at the war's end and all sides would find themselves defeated. This was the problem with modern militarism, he went on, because it led to an 'eagerness to find something for over-grown armies and navies to do', and the resulting evolutionary damage to the human race would continue until a profound societal shift took place.[43] He confessed himself baffled by the fact that 'a few resolute men, reckless of consequences, brought on the Great War'. Yet he still professed to find solace in the fact that a few equally resolute men could potentially make war impossible in the future.[44]

War and the Breed was a remarkable statement of anti-war principles presented from a fundamentally eugenic perspective. In some ways Jordan was ahead of his time and correctly anticipated the view that the mainstream of the eugenics movement would take towards warfare after 1918. However, the intrinsic racism of his argument, though not unusual for the time, is troubling. Though Jordan was a consistent opponent of colonialism, his argument against it here was essentially based on the idea that superior European states were 'wasting' their best men colonising far-away, inferior peoples, just as they were wasting valuable "stock" in the First World War. Perhaps this was mere political expedience, and Jordan believed his arguments would be better received if he argued against both imperialism and war from a set of intrinsically racist premises that might be convincing to both hardened right-wing colonialists and pacifists. On the other hand, the fact that the bulk of his argument was based in the idea that the First World War was a civil conflict between supposedly-racially-superior Aryans was clearly a major flaw in his logic. This was an error in judgement that would carry major consequences for Jordan's later reputation.

Keeping America out of the war

War and the Breed was notable not only for the vehemence of Jordan's arguments and the fact that it was fundamentally based in racism, but also for the widespread exposure it gained. Jordan sent copies to a wide range of contacts on both sides of the Atlantic, many of whom found it to be a general expression of their own sentiments. Frederick Pethick-Lawrence, for instance, told Jordan that he found himself 'so fully in sympathy with the work you are doing. There are so few people who really understand that one feels a peculiar bond of union with those who do.'[45] American journalist Will Irwin later praised the book as one of the most memorable pacifist works from the period, and the only that 'came out of Armageddon unshaken'.[46] It would quickly make Jordan a host of enemies as well.

As the war dragged on, Jordan became increasingly worried that his own country might join in the conflict. This concern was a long-standing aspect of his relationship with the British left. In August 1914, Fabian Society thinker and co-founder of the London School of Economics, Graham Wallas, wrote to Jordan expressing the view that:

> the fate of civilisation in the present crisis may depend chiefly upon the action of the United States. The war must come to an end some day, but the patient efforts of a neutral and disinterested Power may make the difference between one year and ten years of fighting and starving. That Power can only be America; for she alone among the Great Powers is really disinterested.[47]

Given that Wallas was effectively endorsing the notion of America acting as an independent arbiter for peace, Jordan told Wallas that his letter was 'admirable' and would be passed along to the White House.

Two years later, however, the prospect of American involvement had taken on more militant implications, and Jordan's tone changed accordingly. In 1916, he told Wallas that 'I believe it is the duty of the United States to keep out of the war, because it is futile as well as ruinous, a "brawl in the dark" leading to no end which can be forecast. A declaration of war, unavoidable at times, is a confession of impotence, throwing aside all reliable on law or right.' Echoing his growing concern that Britain was being led into the conflict by men with their own militarist agendas, 'no body of men in the world', he told Wallas, 'interests me more than those who are struggling to make Great Britain a real democracy and on whom the awful nightmare of Pan[-]germanism has descended.'[48]

Jordan's changing interpretation of the First World War was therefore deeply coloured by his interactions with the anti-war British left. He now believed that the conflict had been created fundamentally by the actions of the German Kaiser but also by anti-democratic reactionaries in Britain. As the bloodshed dragged on with no end in sight and no major effort made to reach a peaceful conclusion, Jordan increasingly adopted this latter view. His denunciations of 'Pan-Germanism' in the British Cabinet were a clear indication that he increasingly blamed the British government for the continuance of the war, even if he still held the Kaiser mostly responsible.

Jordan's worst nightmare eventually came true when the USA entered the First World War in 1917. The arrival of the American military on the Western Front gave the beleaguered Allies the boost they needed to begin beating back the exhausted German army and establishing the conditions that would eventually lead to German surrender the following year. Jordan himself was in Washington DC on the day Congress passed the declaration of war against the Central Powers. He departed immediately for the West Coast, sending a cable to the San Francisco *Bulletin* that read 'We are now in the war; the only way out is forward.'[49] Over the coming months, Jordan would make great efforts to demonstrate his patriotism and (newfound) support for the war effort. This was undoubtedly genuine to some degree, but it also reflected how the American political climate had changed since he had invited anti-war British speakers to Stanford in 1915. Failing to support the war effort publicly not only exposed pacifists to potential mob violence and vigilantism but was also effectively illegal under the Wilson administration's anti-sedition legislation. For many anti-war activists, this meant having to directly denounce their past views and actions.

Despite his protestations that he was now doing all he could to support the war effort, Jordan quickly fell under suspicion. In 1918, he was investigated by naval intelligence after it received reports that he was distributing copies of a pamphlet entitled 'Eugenics and War', which it deemed to be 'seditious in character'. Subsequent investigation revealed that Jordan's 'representatives' at Stanford were willing to send free copies of the pamphlet through the mail to anyone who asked. The fact that the pamphlet had been published before the US declaration of war had, in the opinion of the investigator, 'no bearing on the more important fact that it is now sixteen months after our entrance into the war, being sent through the mails by its author'. Naval intelligence recommended Jordan's prosecution under the Espionage Act for his activities and sent a full report to the new president of Stanford University, R. L. Wilbur. No action was seemingly taken, but the investigation itself was a major blow to Jordan, who vehemently denied that any of his activities were seditious or designed to harm the American war effort.[50] 'From time to time during the course of 1917 and 1918, I underwent annoyances from superheated or superserviceable heresy-hunters, but hundreds of other men suffered more grievously than I,' Jordan recalled in his memoirs. 'Abroad the struggle for democracy also counted its victims; hysterical intolerance is a natural product of war.'[51]

As the war drew to a close and the peacemaking process began, Jordan was among those who voiced scepticism about the Treaty of Versailles. Laying much of the blame on Lloyd George for undermining Wilson's noble intentions at the Paris Peace Conference, Jordan believed that the peace had been immediately squandered:

> The Great War was in its essence a neighborhood quarrel in which those who suffered most were the least to blame, and from the consequences of which none may escape. The supreme error of the Paris Conference lay, it seems to me, in the long delay between armistice and Conference peace. It should have been possible, as indeed it was virtually necessary, to build at once a *modus vivendi* for Europe's restoration, leaving all relatively minor matters of indemnity, reparation, boundaries, and self-determination – even the League of Nations – to be settled in due season and in cooler blood by councils and commissions.[52]

His opinion on Wilson himself, however, was surprisingly positive, all things considered: 'Wilson's failures and successes I interpret as springing alike from a noble ambition to make his administration stand out in high relief on the records of history ... his lofty expressions of American idealism will give him ultimately a higher place than his admirers now claim for him.'[53] In Jordan's eyes the blame for the faults of the treaty therefore lay with the cynical French and the British, not the American president. Reiterating his view that the conflict had been an intrinsically European rather than American undertaking, in 1926, he told former (and future) Labour PM Ramsay MacDonald that 'It is true that we did not throw away everything as Europe did, for we did not regard it as our war.'[54]

Conclusion

After years of failing health, David Starr Jordan died in 1931. He is today remembered almost exclusively as Stanford University's first president, and in this role he had an undeniably significant impact. While many changes were made to university policies following his resignation, Jordan's overall academic philosophy lived on. Jordan is generally viewed as a university president who amassed a considerable amount of power but seldom used it directly. He chose to influence others by wit and logic rather than force and was able to successfully navigate the university through trying times. Although he was not always well thought of by his subordinates or the public, his place in Stanford's history is cemented and over the years he has become seen as a 'figure of heroic proportions'.[55]

Jordan's reputation beyond Stanford is more controversial, however. The Ross affair was his first major foray into the world of politics outside the academy, and he seemingly took the lessons of the episode to heart. Ironically, his own political views would eventually put him on the radar of another Stanford president. After 1898, Jordan increasingly turned from the life of an academic to the realm of political activism, traveling incessantly and spreading the pacifist message. As would become evident in 1915, however, this message was intrinsically muddled with the logic of racist eugenics, severely damaging the weight of his arguments and accomplishments in this field. While Jordan's views on warfare were actually more humane and progressive than most of the pre-1914 international eugenics movement, the racism present in his writings ensured that his legacy in this area and others would be tarnished. Some of Jordan's conclusions were admirable and ahead of their time – warfare does not make states biologically stronger, colonialism corrupts both the coloniser and the colonised, as George Orwell would compellingly argue in a later era – but the logic that led him to these conclusions was fundamentally unsound.

Throughout his career, Britain played a key role in Jordan's eugenics and anti-war activism. Norman Angell (a former resident of San Francisco) was perhaps his greatest influence, advising him on where to travel in Europe and giving him introductions to key figures on the left. Anti-war women including Ethel Snowden played a key role in his early anti-war advocacy in the USA, giving credence to the argument that not everyone in Britain (or any belligerent power) was in favour of the war. At the same time, Jordan was frustrated by the failure of these anti-war voices to reach a negotiated end to the conflict, as reflected by his increasing pessimism about the prospects for British democracy and anger at Lloyd George.

Jordan closed his memoirs by reflecting on the impact he made in the course of his career on thousands of students and faculty members at Stanford University: 'It is comforting to feel that one's labors have borne ample fruit in other lives, as well as in his own!' he wrote.[56] As in academia, Jordan believed his intentions in the anti-war movement to be pure and borne from humanitarian considerations alone. It is easy to conclude that his post-academic career was ultimately a failure. After all, he failed to convince President Woodrow Wilson to mediate an end to the First World War, failed to prevent American entry into the conflict, and ultimately failed to prevent the groundwork being lain for the Second World War at the peace table of Versailles and afterward.

Nonetheless, Jordan's legacy extends beyond these points. As a major anti-war leader, he gave voice to what millions of Americans believed about the conflict and at the same time granted an important platform to Britain's anti-war voices as well. While ultimately these efforts failed to achieve his objectives, they significantly impacted the course of American politics in a critical period, for better or worse. Jordan's legacy remains clouded for good reasons, but his arguments deserve wider consideration within the historical context and prejudices of their time. Given that Jordan's significance extended far beyond the Stanford quadrangle in his own time and after, his story is one worth examining to understand the international politics of war and peace at a critical moment in history. At the very least, we should move beyond a comprehension of the various peace movements in purely national terms.

Notes

1. David Starr Jordan, *The Days of a Man: Being Memories of a Naturalist, Teacher, and Minor Prophet of Democracy* (New York, 1922), p. 634.
2. David S. Patterson, *The Search for Negotiated Peace: Women's Activism and Citizen Diplomacy in World War 1* (London, 2008), passim.
3. Adam Tooze, *The Deluge: The Great War and the Remaking of Global Order, 1916–1931* (London, 2015).
4. David Redvaldsen, 'The Eugenics Society's Outreach to the Labour Movement in Britain, 1907–1945', *Labour History Review*, 78:3, pp. 301–29.
5. Edward McNall Burns, *David Starr Jordan: A Prophet of Freedom* (Stanford, 1953), p. 3.
6. Burns, *Prophet of Freedom*, p. 4.
7. Burns, *Prophet of Freedom*, p. 14.
8. Burns, *Prophet of Freedom*, p. 15.
9. Meanwhile, the election of 1896 ended in a rout of Bryan and the free silver lobby by the pro-gold standard Republican William McKinley.
10. Burns, *Prophet of Freedom*, pp. 15–16.
11. Starr Jordan, *The Days of A Man*, p. 645.
12. Burns, *Prophet of Freedom*, p. 22.
13. Burns, *Prophet of Freedom*, p. 23.
14. Burns, *Prophet of Freedom*
15. Burns, *Prophet of Freedom*.
16. Burns, *Prophet of Freedom*, p. 25.
17. Starr Jordan, *The Days of a Man*, pp. 617–18.
18. Starr Jordan, *The Days of a Man*, p. 636.

19 'Report of David Starr Jordan, October 5, 1915', World Peace Foundation Correspondence, David Starr Jordan Papers, Hoover Institution.
20 Starr Jordan, *The Days of A Man*, p. 638.
21 Starr Jordan, *The Days of A Man*, p. 639.
22 Starr Jordan, *The Days of A Man*, p. 639.
23 Starr Jordan, *The Days of A Man*, p. 476.
24 Starr Jordan, *The Days of A Man*, p. 477.
25 Starr Jordan, *The Days of A Man*, p. 478.
26 Starr Jordan, *The Days of A Man*, p. 482.
27 Starr Jordan, *The Days of A Man*, p. 635.
28 'Report of David Starr Jordan, October 5, 1915', World Peace Foundation Correspondence, David Starr Jordan Papers, Hoover Institution.
29 Letter from Jordan to Ida Tarbell, October 12, 1914 (Tarbell, Ida Correspondence, David Starr Jordan Papers, Hoover Institution)
30 Barbara Kraft, *The Peace Ship: Henry Ford's Pacifist Adventure in the First World War* (New York, 1978), p. 30.
31 'Report of an Address at Ford Hall Boston, 1917' (untitled speech on American Entry, Folder 12, Box 56, David Starr Jordan Papers, Hoover Institution).
32 Untitled speech on Great Britain, Box 56, Folder 17, David Starr Jordan Papers, Hoover Institution.
33 Starr Jordan, *The Days of a Man*, p. 478.
34 See Richard Carr and Bradley W. Hart, 'Old Etonians, Great War Demographics and the Interpretations of British Eugenics, c.1914–1939', *First World War Studies*, 3:2 (2012), 217–39.
35 Starr Jordan, *The Days of a Man*, pp. 460–1.
36 David Starr Jordan, *War and the Breed: The Relation of War to the Downfall of Nations* (Stanford, 1915), 1.
37 Starr Jordan, *War and the Breed*, p. 3.
38 Starr Jordan, *War and the Breed*, p. 33.
39 Starr Jordan, *War and the Breed*.
40 Starr Jordan, *War and the Breed*, p. 150.
41 Starr Jordan, *War and the Breed*, p. 200.
42 Starr Jordan, *War and the Breed*, p. 214.
43 Starr Jordan, *War and the Breed*, p. 237.
44 Starr Jordan, *War and the Breed*, p. 220.
45 Letter from Frederick Pethick-Lawrence to Jordan, 7 March 1915 (Pethick-Lawrence, Frederick Correspondence, 1915–1919, David Starr Jordan Papers, Hoover Institution).
46 Starr Jordan, *The Days of a Man*, p. 639.
47 Letter from Wallas to Jordan, 18 August 1914 and Jordan's subsequent reply (1/55, Graham Wallas Papers, London School of Economics and Political Science Library Special Collections).
48 Letter from Jordan to Wallas, 24 April 1916 (1/55, Graham Wallas Papers, London School of Economics and Political Science Library Special Collections).
49 Record of Activities of David Starr Jordan since April 1917 (Box 84, Folder 23, David Starr Jordan Papers, Hoover Institution).
50 Letter from Wm. C. Van Antwerp, Naval Intelligence, to F. W. Henshaw, 25 August 1918 (Box 84, Folder 24, David Starr Jordan Papers, Hoover Institution).

51 Starr Jordan, *The Days of a Man*, p. 751.
52 Starr Jordan, *The Days of a Man*, p. 759.
53 Starr Jordan, *The Days of a Man*, pp. 759–60.
54 Letter from Jordan to MacDonald, 11 November 1926 (Box 72, Folder 17, David Starr Jordan Papers, Hoover Institution), original emphasis.
55 Burns, *Prophet of Freedom* p. 22.
56 Starr Jordan, *The Days of a Man*, p. 779.

13

The problem of war aims and the Treaty of Versailles

John Callaghan

Why did Britain go to war in 1914? The answer that generated popular approval concerned the defence of Belgian neutrality, defiled by German invasion in the execution of the Schlieffen Plan. Less appealing, and therefore less invoked for public consumption, but broadly consistent with this promoted justification, was Britain's long-standing interest in maintaining a balance of power on the continent, which a German victory would not only disrupt, according to Foreign Office officials, but replace with a 'political dictatorship' inimical to political freedom.[1] Yet only six days before the British declaration of war, on 30 July, the chairman of the Liberal Foreign Affairs Group, Arthur Ponsonby, informed Prime Minister Asquith that 'nine tenths of the [Liberal] party' supported neutrality. Asquith privately came to a similar estimate, as did the *Manchester Guardian*.[2]

These calculations proved to be very wide of the mark. Only four members of the government privately resigned in protest when the decision for war was taken and two of them recanted before the decision became public. Dissenters later complained of having been kept in the dark during the July crisis, of secret diplomacy and secret entanglements, much as foreign policy critics had complained, intermittently, for years past. As the individuals who favoured intervention went to work – Grey, his Foreign Office advisers, Eyre Crowe and Arthur Nicolson, Winston Churchill, much of the Conservative Party leadership – supported by newspapers such as *The Times* and the *Spectator* – the dissenters were counselled to hold their peace as delicate negotiations to avoid war proceeded. Norman Angell launched the British Neutrality League on 28 July and Graham Wallas set up the British Neutrality Committee on 31 July but the mass of Radicals in Parliament remained silent and by the time these groups met it was already too late to affect decision making. In any case, many observers thought there was little to worry about; as late as

3 August the press reported that no British Expeditionary Force would be sent to the continent and any involvement in the war would be a limited naval commitment (though the Tory press was already demanding much more and there was a sense in some quarters that the war might prove popular).

A crisis meeting of the International Socialist Bureau (ISB) of the Second International convened in Brussels on 29 July, with Keir Hardie and Bruce Glasier in attendance for the British. Here the delegates resolved to organise demonstrations against a possible war but could conceive of no other actions. When Angelica Balabanova reminded the other leaders of the Vaillant–Keir Hardie resolution (at Copenhagen in 1910) to stop war by general strike she elicited only surprise and lack of interest.[3] The ILP's *Labour Leader* and the *Daily Herald* supported demonstrations against war on 30 and 31 July, respectively. Fifteen to twenty thousand people assembled to protest against war in Trafalgar Square on Sunday 2 August. The main speakers included Hardie and Arthur Henderson, supported by prominent trade unionists like Bob Smillie and Ben Tillet. Secret alliances and pacts that could lead to war without the pretence of broader consultation were denounced. The Cabinet doubters were informed by similar worries – they could see that Britain's involvement was inevitable given the naval commitments to France that Grey insisted upon. On 3 August, Grey addressed the House of Commons warning that neutrality would have numerous 'perilous consequences' for Britain's vital interests and that Belgian independence had to be the 'governing factor' in determining Britain's stance; failure to defend it and the whole of Western Europe would succumb to a single dominant power. With the Conservative Party and the Irish Parliamentary Party supporting Grey, it was Ramsay MacDonald who first questioned the Foreign Secretary's rhetoric in the Commons, pointing to the massive disproportion between intervention for the defence of Belgium and the prospect of 'a whole European war' which would change the continental map.[4] Twenty-two Radical MPs followed MacDonald in resolving for neutrality immediately after the two-hour Commons debate was brought to a close. Neutralists dominated the adjournment debate that followed that evening, but it did not matter. Overnight Asquith persuaded two of the Cabinet rebels to change their minds. Grey and Asquith composed an ultimatum to Germany on the morning of 4 August and war was declared by the king that night. In explaining to the House why Britain had gone to war, two days later, Asquith focused solely on the question of Belgian neutrality.

On 5 August Labour's Executive blamed the outcome on secret diplomacy but the parliamentary group voted for war credits hours later and the War Emergency Workers' Committee was set up to monitor economic and social problems that the war might create. The leadership resolved that 'under the circumstances it was impossible for this country to remain neutral'. MacDonald resigned as party chairman and Henderson took his position. Those Radical MPs who remained convinced that the war was an avoidable disaster took a similar view to Labour's Executive, voting for war credits so that Britain might prevail in the conflict, yet maintaining their criticism of Grey. A Labour circular issued on 7 August attributed the conflict to balance of power politics and secret diplomacy, as the Radicals had argued in the House. Grey was blamed for committing Britain to France without consulting Parliament or informing the public. In the second week of August MacDonald helped to set up the UDC, which continued to question Britain's role in the war along these lines. However, Labour's Executive moved just as rapidly towards practical measures of support for the war effort. By the end of August it was promoting enlistment to the armed forces and had agreed a political truce for the duration, following the TUC's decision to support an industrial truce. Though the ILP opposed the war, on both pacifist and socialist grounds, it lost members and it was soon clear that the labour movement was solidly behind the war effort, as were most Radical MPs, most Irish MPs and most feminists. Even the UDC – and doubting figures such as Hardie and MacDonald – agreed that the war had to be fought to a finish now that it had started.

Expectations and aims

Some of Grey's critics foresaw that the war would be 'catastrophic'. They had good reason. France, Germany and Russia had all massively increased their armies in 1913.[5] Josiah Wedgwood predicted it would also cause revolution when he criticised the foreign secretary's 'jingo' speech in the Commons on the evening of 3 August. The *Manchester Guardian* drew attention to Grey's attempt to minimise the 'appalling catastrophe' of war the next day and on 6 August Kitchener, the newly appointed war secretary, told the Cabinet that it would have to 'put armies of millions in the field' and expect the war to last years.[6] This was at a time when many people expected little more than naval engagements and a resolution of the entire crisis by the end of the year. Yet within a month of the commencement of fighting casualties had reached around 300,000 on the Western Front, though there was no indication of this in the British press.[7] On 15 October, *The British Labour Party and the War* explained that Germany had caused the war and that Britain fought for democracy against German militarism, as well as in defence of Belgian neutrality. Labour's annual conference, planned for January 1915, was cancelled.[8] By the end of the year Britain alone had sustained 90,000 casualties.[9] Enthusiasm for the war nevertheless remained high and prominent figures from the Labour movement were drawn into war work, serving on a variety of ad hoc state committees, tribunals and commissions.

The purpose for many was to 'see it through' but loftier, more ambitious, even spiritual targets were also set. Speaking in Dublin in September 1914 Asquith said the purpose of the war was 'the substitution of force ... a real European partnership, based on the recognition of equal right, and established and enforced by common rule'. David Lloyd George, speaking in London on 19 September, told a mass meeting at the Queen's Hall that he envied young people who now had the opportunity of sacrifice in the 'great war for the emancipation of Europe from the thraldom of a military caste'. They had been 'living in a sheltered valley for generations' but fate had raised them to a level where they could see the things that really matter 'the great peaks we had forgotten, of Honour, Duty, Patriotism ... the great pinnacle of Sacrifice pointing like a rugged finger to Heaven'. Asquith and Grey were both brought to tears by the peroration, relieved that the great Radical had spoken so emphatically in support of their decisions.[10] Similar nonsense was spoken and written in Germany and France and, as Marc Ferro points out, it elicited similar sentiments of 'mass exuberance, mysticism, patriotic frenzy, appeals to the judgement of history, to divine mercy'.[11] All parties to the war claimed that they were fighting for civilisation – even Germany, whose army engaged in atrocities and cultural vandalism in Belgium in August 1914. Regime change in Berlin was already being spoken of, together with an international settlement that would reduce the risks of future wars, if not abolish them altogether.

The inter-Allied conference of socialist and labour parties, meeting on 14 February 1915, despite the patriotic sentiment that it represented, was not content to confine its arguments to those of mainstream opinion. It referred to 'the profound general causes of the European conflict, itself a monstrous product of the antagonisms which tear asunder capitalist society and of the policy of Colonial dependencies and aggressive Imperialism ... in which every Government has its share of responsibility'. A victory for German militarism would destroy democracy and liberty in Europe, it claimed, but there could be no justification for 'the economic crushing of Germany' when the war was over. The governments of Germany and Austria were at fault but not the people of those countries. The socialists of the Allied countries, the conference asserted, 'demand that Belgium shall be liberated ... that throughout all Europe, from Alsace-Lorraine to the Balkans, those populations that have been annexed by force shall receive the right to freely dispose of themselves'. The resolution then stressed that the delegates were 'inflexibly resolved to fight until victory'. However, these delegates would also oppose any attempt to transform an essentially defensive war into a war of conquest. In so doing they sought a justification for supporting the war compatible with their record of criticism of secret diplomacy, militarism and imperialism, and their support for democracy and even 'the peaceful Federation of the United States of Europe and the world'.[12]

In effect Labour argued that Germany's bad behaviour outweighed 'the contributory negligence of British foreign policy in consequence of its imperialism, irrationalism, secret diplomacy, arms trading, and capitalism'.[13] H. G. Wells came to the assistance of proponents of this argument when he coined the phrase 'war that will end war' – a catchphrase that became popular by the end of 1914.[14] The defeat of Germany would be the defeat of German militarism and the making of a lasting peace. Thus one could support the war effort while calling for new principles and institutions that would make war much more unlikely in the future. Before the end of August 1914 G. Lowes Dickinson, a Cambridge academic and Liberal, was already drafting a plan for a future League of Nations with this end in view. But open opposition to the war was confined to persecuted minorities, like the 16,500 officially recorded conscientious objectors. Fear may have been a factor in keeping the numbers so small. For all the rhetoric denouncing 'Prussianism' Britain itself became much more intolerant, authoritarian and centralised as the conflict unfolded and people thought to be opposed to the war – like MacDonald and Bertrand Russell – were made to pay for their dissent. Repression alone, however, does not explain the small scale of open opposition.

Even pre-war peace societies such as the Quakers, the Peace Society, the National Peace Council and the International Arbitration League were thrown into confusion and division when the war began, while most of the churches enthusiastically rallied to its support.[15] The need to moralise the conflict seems to have been met. British intervention was widely seen as fully justified. The 2.7 million volunteers to the armed forces of the first twenty-four months of the conflict were the most visible and important expression of this belief. More people opposed compulsory military service than the war itself, as did the TUC, in September 1915, and the Labour conference of January 1916. But the Military Service Act, which came into force in March 1916, was careful to exempt Ireland, where opposition was widespread, and provoked none of the resignations from the coalition government that Labour had threatened. It was left to the tiny No-Conscription Fellowship – led by ILP and Liberal dissidents like Fenner Brockway, Clifford Allen and Bertrand Russell – to campaign against the Act. The organisation claimed 15,000 members by the summer of 1916 but was probably exaggerating.[16] The vast majority of Labour and trade union people accepted that efficient prosecution of the war made conscription necessary. Opponents knew that they were isolated and likely to face harassment and imprisonment if their opposition became active. The ILP found its membership falling after it opposed the war in a statement of 13 August 1914. Within the BSP it took until 1916 before its pro-war leaders, like H. M. Hyndman and Robert Blatchford, were forced to resign from the organisation. Membership, never very high, shrank during the war. Other centres of opposition were even smaller.

The UDC, Angell and Brailsford

Among those who took a critical stance, the UDC was the most important hub of sustained thinking about the causes of the war and how it should end. It brought together neutralists, advocates of a League of Nations (or some sort of international authority), isolationists and others who believed that the war was unnecessary and would solve nothing. Most were Liberals, many would join the Labour Party when the war ended.[17] The UDC could not develop a 'party line' on the war, given the differences within its membership, but it started with guiding principles. Many of its arguments came to the surface within the Labour Party when the events of 1917, especially the revolution in Russia, encouraged proponents of a new statement of war aims. Labour leaders, such as MacDonald and Henderson, subscribed to the guiding principles of the UDC, namely that there should be no territorial adjustments because of the war without the consent of the people affected by them; that parliamentary sanction should be required before Britain entered any arrangement, undertaking or treaty; that British foreign policy should not be guided by balance of power principles but should aim for the establishment of a Concert of the Powers and international council, operating in public view for the arbitration of international disputes, together with an international court capable of interpretation and enforcement; finally, that any peace settlement should aim for drastic reduction of armaments by consent of all the belligerents and nationalisation of their arms industries and regulation of their arms exports. In May 1916, a fifth principle was adopted at J. A. Hobson's prompting, intended to eliminate economic warfare by the promotion of 'free commercial intercourse among all nations by expanding the principle of the Open Door'. Protectionism and autarky led to war, according to this old liberal argument, free trade generated interdependence, prosperity and co-operation.

Norman Angell had developed the thesis that war would be rendered futile by virtue of growing economic interdependence in his 1909 pamphlet, 'Europe's Optical Illusion', subsequently known as 'The Great Illusion'. When war broke out he argued that popular opinion in Britain had been mobilised for the elimination of 'the evil doctrine of Nietzcheanism and brute force', as represented by the German state, in the hope that Europe could be made forever free from war and militarism. The war, on this reading, was not so much against another nation as against an 'evil spirit'.[18] This was a favourite trope of the politicians and press in Britain. Pro-war propagandists, such as Wells and Professor Gilbert Murray, equated victory for the Entente with the defeat of both militarism and autocracy (even in Russia). Angell, a neutralist in August 1914, wanted an Allied victory once the war began, but stressed that crushing Germany would not achieve the desired results, it would simply 'expose us to a renewal [of war] at no distant date [and] fasten the shackles of militarism more firmly than ever upon the long-suffering peoples of Europe.'[19] Before the year was out he felt the need to argue against those in officialdom who wanted Germany partitioned or wiped off the map. Already there was talk of returning Alsace-Lorraine to France, of the creation of a new Poland at Germany's expense, of the transfer of German colonies to other hands, of the destruction of her fleet, the dethronement of the Kaiser and the dismemberment of Austria. Against all this Angell cautioned that without Germany's consent no peace could endure. States have powers of recuperation; the national spirit can be provoked by vengeful defeat and no balance of power could survive under such circumstances. For 'Prussianism' to be defeated, as political rhetoric insisted it must, it had to be recognised as a state of mind affecting all the Great Powers. To free ourselves from it, Angell insisted, we must promote mutual co-operation and display 'a frank recognition that nations do form a society', which can be regulated.

Lowes Dickinson put the point more forcefully for American readers in December 1914. If the war had been caused by militarism, secret diplomacy and intrigue, peace depended on an extension of democracy to international relations. Foreign policy would have to come under democratic scrutiny, the self-determination of nations would have to become a cardinal principle and armaments would have to be subject to national and international controls. Nations would have to submit their disputes to arbitration and conciliation by a 'League of Europe'.[20] Thinking along these lines was inspired above all by the perception that war could be avoided. The way the First World Great had come about was at the root of this thinking. Though profound long-term causes of war – imperialism and capitalism – were often mentioned, the short-term unfolding of the July crisis from a dispute in the Balkans to a general European war by dint of alliances and the decisions of tiny elites was what critical analysis fixed upon. So when the Fabian Society, for example, set up an International Agreements Committee in January 1915, to investigate methods for maintaining peace, it generated a conference in May of that year, and two articles that appeared in the *New Statesman* in July, which focused on 'Suggestions for the Prevention of War'. Leonard Woolf, at the centre of this endeavour, published *International Government* in 1916, which put a Fabian construction on the liberal argument that commerce drove global integration forward by forcing states to adopt global rules and regulations. Woolf showed that the process was already underway and could be taken further by identifying issues on which states would submit to arbitration and conciliation by an International Court and an International Council over-representing the Great Powers and able to apply sanctions leading up to military force.[21]

Dissident opinion was divided and dynamic on many matters. H. N. Brailsford repeated many of Angell's views in his account of *The Origins of the Great War* but his focus on the war as the postponed sequel to the Balkan War of 1912, explained it as a 'co-operative crime' of Germany and Russia, essentially concerned with the domination of Eastern Europe and utterly remote from any British interest. Both Britain and France, on this view, had been dragged into it by the 'mechanical fatality' of their alliance with the 'unscrupulous and incalculable Empire' of Tsarist Russia. Both should negotiate for peace, Brailsford argued in the winter of 1914, before they were dragged into a prolonged fight to determine who would dominate in the East.[22] Bertrand Russell initially took a similar view to Brailsford. But when he looked to the war in the East, in November 1914, his loathing of Tsarist Russia and his admiration for German culture got the better of him. In a UDC pamphlet he openly accepted the argument that Germany in the East was defending civilisation against the backward Slavs.[23] While the war in the East had what he called a certain 'ethnic inevitability', the war in the West was the result of alliances built in response to 1870 and the 'folly' of Germany's naval programme. Russell soon dropped these pro-German sentiments. But he actively campaigned against the war, later as a prominent member of the No Conscription Fellowship (NCF). He published his most detailed study of British foreign policy in December 1915 in reply to officially sponsored propaganda written by Professor Gilbert Murray. Russell now accepted that Germany bore the greatest responsibility for the outbreak of the war, and its subsequent conduct, but held fast to the conviction that the 'maxims' of British foreign policy had led to Britain's unnecessary involvement. He maintained that Britain's foreign policy since 1904 had strengthened the war party in Germany, weakened the friends of peace and supported France and Russia 'in enterprises which were inherently indefensible'.

As the war dragged on, Russell repeatedly warned of its dangers to European civilisation. Only pride, fear and hatred prolonged the conflict. In July 1916, he wrote leaflets for the NCF in which he referred to Germany having 'repeatedly offered terms of peace'.[24] At the end of the year he argued that Bethmann-Hollweg's peace note, delivered to the American embassy on 12 December 1916, signalled that Germany was receptive to peace overtures. At the same time, he warned against the sort of peace that the advocates of 'total victory' would bring about – a peace based on fear and humiliation. This was what the new coalition government formed by Lloyd George promised. Russell wrote an open letter to President Woodrow Wilson, as these steps were taken in December 1916, in the belief that the USA could put a stop to the unnecessary slaughter.[25] But he was sceptical about ideas for a League of Nations and in January 1917 argued that such a body could easily become a new Holy Alliance dedicated to maintenance of the international status quo.[26]

One thing these dissenters were agreed upon was the death of the Liberal Party and the better prospect of the Labour Party championing an enlightened foreign policy. UDC arguments reiterated many of the criticisms of foreign policy that had been common currency among Labour and Radical MPs since the beginning of the Boer War. But Labour was seen as the rising force that could make alternative approaches to foreign policy a reality, especially after the Liberal Party split between supporters of Asquith and Lloyd George in 1916. Labour's practical support for the war effort did not automatically contradict such hopes. Even UDC members regarded a British defeat in the war as unthinkable. Many Labour men – like Henderson – supported the war effort but did not endorse the foreign policies that had led to it and believed wars could be avoided if the right people and policies were put in place. French and British socialists meeting on 14 February 1915 in London made that clear, as did the Labour and trade union conferences of 1916 and 1917.[27] Labour's co-operation in the war effort, moreover, was believed to give it a stake in the construction of a just peace. A just peace would mean meeting the claims of workers in Britain and asserting the values of the Labour movement in the international arena. Before the end of 1915 it was clear that President Woodrow Wilson and the USA might play a role in strengthening that case.[28] Even the Cabinet considered some sort of international peacekeeping body in the summer of 1915. Wilson, as Philip Snowden pointed out to Labour supporters around the same time, publicly aligned himself with the arguments of the UDC.[29] In the presidential campaign of 1916 he transformed this more radical case into a national agenda, while Britain seemingly moved in the opposite direction under Lloyd George.

While Wilson argued for a 'peace without victory' his supporters in the USA thought they had seen the first signs of hope in Britain when the Labour Party conference unanimously voted for a 'an international League to enforce the maintenance of peace' in January 1917.[30] Wilson's 'Peace without Victory' speech had been delivered the day before the conference began on 22 January and the delegates stood cheering when it was read to them. In France the socialist party gave Wilson's address a similar reception, though both parties remained committed to military victory. Small groups of socialists – without French or British participation – had met at Zimmerwald (5–8 September 1915) and Kienthal (April 1916) demanding a 'peace without annexations or indemnities'. The Russian Revolution and the overthrow of Nicholas II on 15 March made such demands urgent problems for the Allies. The Provisional Government formed immediately after the Tsar's abdication contained liberals from the Duma, but the Petrograd Soviet was led by Zimmerwaldists committed to a negotiated peace and some of these entered a coalition Provisional Government formed on 5 May.[31] Initially these events did not threaten a separate peace in the East. On the contrary, the Allies and the Provisional Government expected a more efficient prosecution of the war now that the Tsar was gone. Even so a 'peace without annexations or indemnities' was not what the Allied governments had been planning for.

Secret treaties

Lewis Harcourt, Secretary of State for the Colonies under Asquith, drew up a secret memorandum as early as March 1915, called 'The Spoils', in which he outlined the imperial gains in Africa, Asia, the Middle East and the Pacific that Britain could expect to make out of the war.[32] Most of Germany's colonies had fallen into British hands by February 1916 and arrangements were made with France, Japan and the Dominions to make these losses permanent. Secret deals were also made with Italy and Tsarist Russia involving major territorial transfers and plans were laid for the dismemberment of the Ottoman Empire in the Middle East. Publicly, however, the talk was of restoring Belgium, perhaps destroying Germany as a naval power and punishing it for breaking international law, while somehow turning it into a democracy.[33] When the USA entered the war in April 1917, President Wilson was informed of the secret treaties and lost no time reiterating his demand for 'peace without victory'. But American entry into the war reinforced the case of those who wanted an Allied military victory over Germany by making it more realistic, as did their initial reading of the revolution in Russia. Many of those of who wanted a negotiated peace recognised the problem. But Wilson's rhetoric combined with that of the Provisional Government in Petrograd also strengthened the prospect of a just and lasting peace. Labour was at any rate now prepared to consider a proposal of the Dutch and Scandinavian socialist parties that a conference of the social democrats of the belligerent countries should be held on neutral ground (Stockholm) to formulate peace terms – to the extent that it decided in May to send a delegation to confer with the Russian socialists.[34] In the event the delegation was refused permission to depart by the Sailor's and Fireman Union when it attempted to board ship at Aberdeen. Lloyd George meanwhile instructed Henderson to visit Russia in response to demands from the Provisional Government for urgent discussion of war aims and associated Allied fears that Russia would negotiate a separate peace. In Petrograd Henderson discovered strong support for the proposed conference in Stockholm and returned convinced of the need for negotiations before the Eastern front collapsed completely. Labour's Executive came out in favour of the Stockholm conference upon his return and an emergency conference, convened to discuss the proposal on 10 August, supported it by a large majority – the first time the unions had wavered about the 'fight to a finish' line. Henderson was forced to resign from the Cabinet on this issue (to be replaced by Labour MP George Barnes) and both the British and French governments scuppered the proposed international conference by refusing to grant passports.

The episode is significant chiefly as evidence of new thinking among the war's Labour supporters. More evidence was supplied by a successful TUC resolution in September demanding a voice for the working class at any future peace conference. Labour's Executive used this prompt to declare the need for a statement about war aims to be ratified by an inter-Allied conference of socialist parties as the first step in uniting the left of all the belligerent countries.[35] But before this was taken any further the Bolsheviks seized power in Russia. On 22 November Leon Trotsky published the secret treaties entered into by the Allied powers, exposing what he denounced as secret capitalist diplomacy and imperialist robbery.[36] By the middle of December the *Manchester Guardian* began publishing the details and continued to do so into 1918. They were greeted in left-wing circles with 'shame and anger' but also as weapons to support the cause of Woodrow Wilson.[37] They also permitted the Bolsheviks to strike a noble pose, since among the deals they repudiated were those that would have annexed the Straits and Constantinople to Russia and given it 'full liberty of action' in northern Iran.[38]

The Bolshevik disclosures had revealed, according to the secretary of the ISB, that the governments of the Allies were 'in opposition to the traditions of our Movement ... in denial of the moral conceptions which underlie our Movement'. These governments had not responded with any enthusiasm to Wilson's agenda. But Labour's *Memorandum of War Aims* – approved by a special conference of the TUC and Labour Party on 28 December 1917 – echoed Wilson by claiming that the 'fundamental purpose of the British Labour Movement in supporting the continuance of the struggle is that the world may henceforth be made safe for democracy'. To achieve this, it went on to list all of the demands associated with the UDC – including a League of Nations, open diplomacy and the self-determination of nations. Denouncing imperialism in general the *Memorandum* wanted the administration of dependent peoples by a commission of the League of Nations in places like the Middle East and envisaged a vast neutral state composed of all tropical African territories south of the Sahara and north of the Zambezi.[39]

In January, Lloyd George made a speech to the British Trade Union League at Caxton Hall that appeared to embrace Wilsonism, persuading Henderson that the prime minister stood closer to Labour than ever before.⁴⁰ Three days later Wilson unveiled his Fourteen Points. Labour now demanded a joint statement on war aims from the USA and British governments and called for an international conference of socialist parties to consider the *Memorandum*, adding that the social democrats in the Central Powers should state their own war aims and demand that their governments do the same. In February, an inter-allied conference of socialist parties took place and the *Memorandum* was expanded, though not significantly altered. In March, the rapacious Treaty of Brest-Litovsk was concluded and the fact that only the Independent Social Democratic Party voted against it in the Reichstag did not augur well for Labour's initiative. In fact Vandervelde and Huysmans, on behalf of the ISB, told the SPD majority that the Treaty of Brest-Litovsk stood in complete disregard of the democratic peace that the inter-Allied conference had just endorsed.

The ISB began to collect responses to the *Memorandum* from the social democrats in the belligerent countries. While the Austrian social democrats accepted the proposed League of Nations, the principle of no annexations and indemnities, and the right of self-determination, it cast doubt on the idea that democracy could emerge victorious from the defeat of either side in the struggle. A negotiated peace was needed and the right of self-determination must be extended to all colonies. The *Berliner Tageblatt* rejected one-sided indemnities altogether and the SPD theoretical journal *Die Neue Zeit* wondered why the idea of international control over colonies should be limited to tropical Africa and not extended, say, to Ireland. Was this not a cover for the extension of 'English world hegemony' it wondered? The social democrats of Germany and Austria certainly did not see how democratic regimes could emerge from their military defeat.⁴¹ Heinrich Cunow, editor of *Die Neue Zeit*, reacted to Labour's proposals for the democratic control of foreign policy by observing that such general principles already had the support of the SPD majority, Bethmann-Hollweg and Pope Benedict XV, among many others. Such talk was cheap. Labour wanted the self-determination of nations but did not mention Ireland, Egypt, India, the former Boer States, Cyprus or Malta in its *Memorandum*.⁴² Even the socialists of the neutral countries had sympathy for this argument while the Marxist Independent Social Democratic Party went much further, stating that a durable peace required the socialists in every country to fight their own governments and prepare for socialism. This was as far as the discussion went. Interest in a negotiated peace in any case declined with the German spring offensive of 1918 and the Allied riposte that began in August. Germany's defeat soon followed. Social Democrats entered the government at the beginning of October under politically volatile circumstances and by 12 October Germany accepted Wilson's demand for the evacuation of occupied territory. Soon the threat of social revolution in Germany became apparent.

The general election and the peace conference

In the December 1918 general election all prominent ILP candidates and UDC figures who stood as Labour candidates were defeated. The UDC now had 650,000 members but the fifty-nine Labour MPs who formed the official opposition were almost all former trade union officials sponsored by unions. Labour's election manifesto had referred to 'the present world catastrophe', which it took as evidence of 'the culmination and collapse of a distinctive industrial civilisation ... the workers will not seek to reconstruct'. The Paris Peace Conference opened on 18 January and in February the pre-war Second International took the first step to reconstruct itself at Berne. The Berne conference objected to most aspects of the peace settlement unfolding and conveyed its opposition to Clemenceau through a delegation, which included Henderson and MacDonald. MacDonald was one of the first in Britain to denounce the proposed League of Nations as a sham.[43] It would be dominated by the victorious powers and represent states not peoples. By June 1919, however, Labour's annual conference accepted that the League's deficiencies might be remedied[44] and there was already evidence of popular enthusiasm for the League in, for example, the growth of the League of Nations Union, formed in 1918 only days before the armistice. But Morel, Hobson and other UDC figures who had joined the Labour Party saw only a Carthaginian peace in the decisions taken in Paris. The Berne conference agreed with them but made clear, as Labour had done in the *Memorandum*, that the sort of League it wanted – representing peoples not governments and able to enforce its decisions in collective action – depended on the prior triumph of socialism and democracy in the participating countries.[45] Nevertheless the victorious powers stood accused of malicious intent to punish Germany, establishing a new balance of power and laying the foundations for economic damage in Europe for years to come. The National Executive Committee concluded that the peace treaty 'was defective not so much because of this or that detail of wrong done, but fundamentally, in that it accepts, and indeed is based on, the very political principles or premises which were the ultimate cause of this war.'[46] Yet when the Treaty came before Parliament the Labour group approved it and subjected it to only mild criticisms.

No doubt some Labour members had travelled a long way in four years from the belief that the war was a justified defence of Belgian neutrality to the realisation that it had been a catastrophe with identifiable causes susceptible to rational intervention. But others had always taken both views – that though the war must be fought to victory, it could have been avoided and many of its causes were forces and practices that Labour opposed on principle. By 1918, more people doubted that any great issue of principle could be identified to justify the carnage, but at least Wilson had invested the conflict with a noble meaning and goal. Labour's immediate rejection of almost everything connected with the peace settlement reflected the immense disappointment of those who had taken the 'peace without victory' slogan seriously. But root and branch rejection of the Treaty of Versailles never had popular support and it took only another few years for Labour's leaders to adjust to the facts. By 1922, all were convinced that Britain had to make use of the existing League.

The numerous contradictions and inconsistencies in Labour's thinking only became apparent with the passage of time. The *Memorandum of War Aims* not only wanted the world made safe for democracy, the peace it sought was said to depend on the spread of democracy to 'all countries' coupled with the frank abandonment of 'every form of imperialism'. These preconditions were not likely to be realised soon. Yet Labour also wanted, 'forthwith', a League of Nations, the suppression of secret diplomacy and the control of foreign policy by popularly elected legislatures. It envisaged progress towards the abolition of conscription and profit-making armaments firms, as well as arms controls. Critics of the *Memorandum* observed that Labour did not envisage a British withdrawal from Empire or even propose consistent opposition to its imminent expansion. Did the party understand that such a global enterprise had to be policed, that the scale of defence needs was therefore also global and that the risks of future military conflict were correspondingly greater? Labour was committed to the trusteeship conception of empire and advocated international supervision of peoples deemed unable to govern themselves. In that sense the League of Nations' mandates – associated with Jan Smuts – was an idea that can be traced to the work of Labour intellectuals as they pondered the future of the former German colonies. In practice the goal of trusteeship was often conflated with the prevailing condition of the Crown Colonies and British colonial policies at any particular time. Critics of the imperial reality existed but were few in number and mostly ignored. Complacency about the benevolence of the British Empire was deeply ingrained in the British political culture and the Labour Party fully shared the view that it was already an example of the trusteeship idea in action. The vast central African state, which Labour envisaged between the Sahara and the Zambezi under international supervision, was meant to deal with the German colonies only. Philip Snowden perceived a nationalist rather than internationalist mentality in this thinking.[47] But he was a rare (and short-lived) doubter. The more common condition was to give very little thought to the Empire at all. Certainly it seems unlikely that many Labour people had really thought much about the implications of Empire for any future Labour government. Yet through this portal Labour would accept foreign and defence policies which it officially abhorred in 1919.

The war's immediate aftermath was admittedly an emotional time of exceptional events when Labour was only just emerging as a functioning political party. The desire for a more professional image and performance in Parliament under MacDonald's leadership after 1922 would make its own contribution to the process of 'growing up'. The marginalisation of the party' s principal foreign policy thinkers – Morel, Woolf, Brailsford, Hobson and the like – was an inevitable part of the process, as was the elimination of any rhetoric concerning the peace treaty that implied the sort of class analysis favoured by the Bolsheviks. In reality the national sentiment that had been encouraged and drawn upon for purposes of fighting the war could not be conjured away. From 1921, Labour's foreign policy interests turned to the question of economic stability, economic growth and employment. Growing trade with Germany and Russia was proposed to address these issues. Linked to these interests was a growth in opposition to their continued punishment by economic or military means.[48] In substance Labour's policy was not much different to Lloyd George's. However, resistance to the growing pragmatism of the Parliamentary Labour Party was kept alive by the anger and cynicism generated by the constant drip of decisions and events which came after the main peace settlement, such as British support for Poland during the Polish–Soviet conflict over Ukrainian territory (1919–21), the Anglo-Irish War (1919–21), the danger of war with Turkey (1922) and the crisis of reparations payments which led to French military occupation of the Ruhr in 1923. Across the Empire resistance to British rule was such that the Foreign Secretary, Lord Curzon, privately declared in 1919 that 'every place is a storm-centre'.[49] Some other people had taken Wilson's rhetoric seriously, though neither Wilson nor British Labour paid much attention to them.[50]

Notes

1. Zara S. Steiner and Keith Neilson, *Britain and the Origins of the First World War* (London, 2003), p. 236, 242.
2. Douglas Newton, *The Darkest Days: The Truth Behind Britain's Rush to War, 1914* (London, 2014), p. 20.
3. Marc Ferro, *The Great War, 1914–1918* (London, 1973), p. 38.
4. See D. Marquand, *Ramsay MacDonald* (London, 1977), pp. 167–8.
5. Steiner and Neilson, *Britain and the Origins of the First World War*, p. 230.
6. Newton, *The Darkest Days*, pp. 246, 262, 280.
7. Adam Hochschild, *To End All Wars: How The First World War Divided Britain* (London, 2011), p. 103.
8. The British Labour Party and the War (pamphlet, Labour Party: London, October 1914), passim.
9. Hochschild, *To End All Wars*, p. 126.
10. John Grigg, *Lloyd George: From Peace to War, 1912–16* (London, 1985), pp. 161–7.
11. Ferro, *The Great War*, p. 122.

War aims and the Treaty of Versailles   255

12 'Declaration of the inter-allied conference of the socialist and labour parties', 14 February 1915, LSI 3/5/1i, Labour archive, People's History Museum (PHM), Manchester.
13 M. Ceadel, *Semi-Detached Idealists: The British Peace Movements and International Relations, 1854–1945* (Oxford, 2000), pp. 188–9.
14 H. G. Wells, *The War That Will End War* (London, 1914).
15 Ceadel, *Semi-Detached*, p. 198.
16 M. Ceadel, *Pacifism in Britain, 1914–45: The Defining of a Faith* (Oxford, 1980).
17 They included C. P. Trevelyan, Norman Angell, E. D. Morel, Arthur Ponsonby, J. A. Hobson, H. N. Brailsford, G. Lowes Dickinson, and Bertrand Russell.
18 N. Angell, *Shall This War End German Militarism?* (London, 1914), p. 1.
19 Angell, *Shall This War End*, p. 3.
20 G. Lowes Dickinson, 'The War and the Way Out', *Atlantic Monthly*, 114:December (1914), 820–37.
21 L. Woolf, *International Government: Two Reports Prepared for the Fabian Research Department* (London, 1916), pp. 10–11, 90–1, 216–30.
22 H. N. Brailsford, *The Origins of the Great War* (London, 1914), pp. 3, 13, 15, 17–18.
23 B. Russell, 'War, The Offspring of Fear', in Andrew G. Bone and Michael D. Stevenson (eds), *The Collected Papers of Bertrand Russell*, vol. 21 (London, 2008), pp. 37–47.
24 Russell, 'What Are We Fighting For?', in Bone and Stevenson, *Collected Papers of Bertrand Russell*, vol. 21, p. 419.
25 Russell, 'Letter to President Wilson', in Richard A. Rempel et al. (eds), *The Collected Papers of Bertrand Russell*, vol. 14 (London, 1995), pp. 21–4.
26 Russell, 'Two Ideals of Pacifism', in Rempel et al., *The Collected Papers of Bertrand Russell*, vol. 14, pp. 28–31.
27 *Labour Party Annual Conference Report 1916 (LPACR)* (London, 1916), pp. 6–7.
28 T. J. Knock, *To End All Wars: Woodrow Wilson and the Quest For a New World Order* (Princeton, NJ, 1992), pp. 36–7, 57.
29 Knock, *To End All Wars*, p. 78; M. Swartz, *The Union of Democratic Control in British Politics in the First World War* (London, 1971), p. 131.
30 *Labour Party Annual Conference Report*, January 1917, p. 24.
31 F. King, 'Dilemmas of a Democratic Peace: World War One, the Zimmerwald Manifesto and the Russian Revolution', *Socialist History*, 48 (2015), 8–33.
32 Newton, *The Darkest Days*, p. 305.
33 See D. Stevenson, *The First World War and International Politics* (Oxford, 1988), pp. 106–39.
34 H. Meynell, ' The Stockholm Conference in 1917', *International Review of Social History*, 5 (1960), 1–25, 202–25.
35 G. D. H. Cole, *History of Socialist Thought*, vol. 4, part 1 (London, 1961), p. 58.
36 L. Trotsky, 'Statement by Trotsky on the Publication of the Secret Treaties', 22 November 1917, at https://www.marxists.org/history/ussr/government/foreign-relations/1917/November/22.htm (accessed 27 June 2016).
37 *Daily News and Leader*, 13 April 1918; *Herald*, 20 April 1918.

38 F. Seymour Cocks, *The Secret Treaties and Understandings: Text of the Available Documents* (London, 1918), pp. 15–25.
39 Labour Party, *The Memorandum of War Aims* (London, 1919), pp. 8–10.
40 J. Grigg, *Lloyd George: War Leader 1916–18* (London, 2003), pp. 380–3.
41 'Statements of national parties to the inter-allied war aims memorandum', n.d., LSI 1/21, PHM, Manchester.
42 'The War Aims Memorandum of the Allied Socialists and the Projected League of Nations', LSI 1/14, a document which reproduces the gist of Cunow's article in *Die Neue Zeit*, 'The Projected International Conference at Berne' published in number 10, 7 June 1918, PHM Manchester.
43 *Labour Leader*, 20 February 1919.
44 *LPACR*, 1919, pp. 139–42.
45 'The League of Nations', resolution of the Berne Conference of the Labour and Socialist International, LSI 4, Labour History Archive, PHM, Manchester
46 Arthur Henderson, *The Peace Terms, a manifesto of Labour's NEC* (London, 1919), p. 3.
47 H. Winkler, 'British Labour and the Origins of the Idea of Colonial Trusteeship, 1914–19', *The Historian*, 13:Spring (1951), 154–72, 157, 162.
48 *Unemployment: The Peace and the Indemnity* (London, 1921), p. 5. This originated as a paper by Brailsford for the advisory committee on international questions.
49 D. Gilmour, *Curzon* (London, 1994), p. 512.
50 I rely here on Erez Manela, *The Wilsonian Moment: Self-determination and the International Origins of Anticolonial Nationalism* (Oxford, 2007), p. 21.

Index

'Labour Party', 'trade union' and 'unionism' are so ubiquitous throughout this work that they are not indicated here.

Amalgamated Union of Co-operative Employees (AUCE) 11, 126–41
Amalgamated Weavers Association (AWA) 9, 97–103
Angell, Norman 221, 226, 227, 236, 240, 245, 246, 247
Asquith, Herbert 1, 42, 63, 240, 241, 243
Astor, Nancy 8, 67
Attlee, Clement 11, 126
Australia 62
Austria-Hungary 29, 38, 40, 83, 207, 243, 246, 251
Ayles, Walter 76–7

Bacon, Alice 4
Baldwin, Stanley 4
Barnes, George 43, 45, 47, 49, 250
Bethmann-Hollweg, Theobald 247, 251
Bevin, Ernest 43, 50, 51, 79
Blatchford, Robert 7, 17–31, 245
Bolsheviks 35, 43, 75, 117, 119, 192, 201–4, 207–16, 250, 254
Bonar Law, Andrew 2, 42, 54, 58
Bondfield, Margaret 60, 114
British Socialist Party 23, 47, 80, 83, 244
Burns, John 36, 227

Cambridge University 220, 226, 227, 230, 244

Castle, Barbara 4
Cecil, Robert 59, 64, 65, 209
Chaplin, Charlie 12, 166–80
Churchill, Winston 5, 43, 110, 167, 228, 240
Clarion movement 17, 25
Clause IV 2, 13, 167, 202, 216
Clynes, J.R. 48–50
Communist Party of Great Britain (CFGB) 10, 11, 43, 45, 51, 120
Connolly, James 130, 186–95
conscription 3, 10, 22, 27, 28, 46, 75, 82, 84, 97, 115, 117, 119, 147, 154, 166, 170, 178, 194, 232, 244, 253
Conservative Party 2, 3, 4, 38, 42, 44, 46, 47, 50, 58, 60, 67, 103, 107, 100, 131, 167, 176, 220, 228, 240, 241
cotton industry 9, 10, 90–104, 214
Curzon, Lord 43, 229, 254

Defence of the Realm Act (DORA) 75, 79, 86, 111, 139, 167
dilution 11, 45, 111, 127, 139

Fabian Society, the 1, 13, 109, 110, 143, 182, 189, 233, 246
Fawcett, Millicent 5, 6, 108
feminism 3, 4, 6, 16, 108, 109, 115, 133

257

Fourth Reform Act (1918) 6, 56, 57–9, 64, 66–8
France 5, 7, 20, 29, 36–41, 51, 65, 156, 173, 197, 232, 241–3, 246–9

Germany 5, 20–5, 29, 30, 35–8, 40, 44, 50, 51, 157, 170, 205, 227–8, 232, 241–52
Glasier, Bruce 22, 26, 27, 208, 241
Grey, Edward 13, 21, 224, 240–3

Haig, Douglas 156
Hardie, Keir 17–19, 26–30, 36–8, 241–2
Harle Syke 100–2
Henderson, Arthur 13, 37, 38, 42, 43, 44, 47–53, 193, 201–16, 229, 241–2, 245, 248–52
Hodge, John 37, 46–9, 52
Home Rule debate 190, 195
Hoover, Herbert 221, 225
Hyndman, Henry 17–31, 245

Independent Labour Party (ILP) 5, 17–19, 22, 25–7, 29–30, 36–8, 44, 46–8, 60, 76–80, 81, 84, 96, 109, 115, 126, 132, 203, 205, 207–8, 241
Indiana University 222–3
Ireland 2, 7, 12, 13, 14, 42, 113, 182–97, 226, 244, 251, 254
Irish Labour Party 13, 182–97
Irish Trade Union Congress 191, 193
Irish Transport and General Workers Union (ITGWU) 184, 188, 192
Italy 38, 65, 249

Japan 30, 92, 224, 226, 249
Jarvis, Dan 2, 5
Jaures, Jean 36
Jordan, David Starr 13, 220–37
Jowett, Fred 36, 37, 44, 48

Kautsky, Karl 20, 182, 183
Kerensky, Alexander 43, 210, 211, 214
Keynes, John Maynard 170, 231
Kitchener, Lord 96, 175, 242

Lansbury, George 121, 176
Larkin, James 184–8
Lee, Jennie 8, 65

Lenin, Vladimir 116, 117, 119, 120, 201, 202, 204, 207, 209, 212, 214
Liberal Party 1–4, 8, 35, 45, 48, 50, 51, 58, 60, 65, 73, 75, 76, 80, 81, 84, 85, 92, 103, 166, 176, 201–3, 214, 220, 221, 222, 228, 240, 244, 248
Lloyd George, David 1, 3, 13, 28, 36, 37, 42, 43–5, 48, 49, 52, 58, 81, 202, 204, 209–10, 220, 229, 235, 238, 243, 248–50, 254
London County Council (LCC) 48, 61, 175
London School of Economics (LSE) 58, 112, 233

Macarthur, Mary 10, 60, 108–22, 137
MacDonald, Ramsay 8, 13, 17, 18, 26, 27, 36, 37, 38, 42–4, 48, 202, 203, 221, 227, 241, 242, 244, 245, 252, 254
Markievicz, Constance 8, 66, 188
McKenna, Reginald 166, 176
Mensheviks, the 221, 225, 226, 227
Military Service Act (1916) 79, 244
Munitions of War Act (1915) 45, 112
munitions workers 6, 10, 11, 37, 39, 41, 43, 45, 112, 135, 137, 139, 148, 150, 151, 155, 159

National Federation of Women Workers (NFWW) 10, 108–21, 137
Northcliffe, Lord 168–71, 229

Pankhurst, Christabel 10, 133
Pankhurst, Emmeline 10, 133
Pankhurst, Sylvia 5, 10, 11, 108–22
Parliament (Qualification of Women) Act (1918) 8, 56–68
Phillips Price, Morgan 13, 201–16

Quakers, the 61, 189, 244

Reichstag, the 36, 251
Roberts, George 28, 46, 49
Russell, Bertrand 244, 247
Russell, George William 186, 188, 189, 193

Russian Revolutions (1917) 3, 10, 11, 13, 79, 117, 119, 136, 157, 177, 179, 192, 201–16

Samuel, Herbert 8, 57, 58, 60–6
Second International 17, 26, 29, 35, 36, 43, 51, 183, 188, 203, 241, 252
Sinn Féin 8, 13, 60, 66, 189, 193–6
Snowden, Ethel 13, 60, 227, 229, 236
Snowden, Philip 13, 28, 34, 36, 37, 38, 248, 253
Social Democratic Party (SDP) 17, 19, 21, 22, 23, 225
Sozialdemokratische Partei Deutschlands (SPD) 22, 23, 35, 36, 44, 50, 251
Stanford University 13, 220–36
Steel-Maitland, Arthur 38, 42

Trade Union Congress (the TUC) 37, 41, 45, 46, 48, 50, 54, 126–7, 139, 140, 169, 191, 193, 244, 250

Union of Democratic Control (UDC) 13, 97, 202, 221, 242, 245, 247, 248, 250, 252

United States of America 3, 13, 14, 15, 35, 40, 41, 49, 168, 169, 170, 171, 172, 174, 176, 177, 188, 194, 220–37, 246, 247, 249

wages 39, 41, 49, 50, 83, 85, 94, 96, 98, 99, 100, 102, 103, 106, 109, 111, 113, 128, 131, 135–8, 147, 152, 155, 178, 179, 189, 191
Wallas, Graham 13, 233, 234, 240
Webb, Beatrice 112, 231
Webb, Sidney 44, 193
Wilkinson, Ellen 5, 10–11, 126–41
Wilson, Woodrow 228, 234–7, 247–54
Women's Army Auxiliary Corp (WAAC) 12, 151–9
Women's Labour League (WLL) 3, 109, 112, 116, 137
Women's Royal Air Force (WRAF) 12, 151, 152, 157
Women's Royal Naval Service (WRNS) 12, 151, 155, 157
Women's Social and Political Union (WSPU) 5, 10, 109–10, 116, 123
Women's Volunteer Reserve (WVR) 11, 12, 145, 152, 156
Woolf, Leonard 246, 254

EU authorised representative for GPSR:
Easy Access System Europe, Mustamäe tee 50,
10621 Tallinn, Estonia
gpsr.requests@easproject.com